The Calling, Rebellion, and Punishment of Jonah,
and Other Sermons
by Henry Smith

The Calling, Rebellion, and Punishment of Jonah, and Other Sermons
By Henry Smith

Edited by C. Matthew McMahon and Therese B. McMahon

Changes made to this edition do not affect the overall language of the document, nor do they change the writer's intention. Spelling, grammar, and formatting changes have been made, and modernized wording is used in specific cases to help today's reader more fully grasp the intention of the author.

Published by Puritan Publications
A Ministry of A Puritan's Mind
4101 Coral Tree Circle #214
Coconut Creek, FL 33073
www.puritanpublications.com
www.apuritansmind.com
www.puritanshop.com

First Electronic Edition, 2012
First Paperback Edition, 2012
Manufactured in the United States of America

eISBN: 978-1-937466-69-5
ISBN: 978-1-937466-70-1

CONTENTS

Contents

INTRODUCTION

Henry Smith, who is apostrophized in Piers *Penniless'*
Supplication (1592) as *Silver-tongued Smith*, was a celebrated
preacher in Elizabethan London at St. Clement Danes. On
leaving Queens' College, Cambridge, he continued his studies
with Richard Greenham, rector of Dry Drayton,
Cambridgeshire, who imbued him with Puritan principles as
he did other leading men of the time. In 1575 he also entered
Lincoln College, Oxford, graduating in 1579.

Though as the eldest son and heir of Erasmus Smith of
Somerby and Husbands Bosworth, Leicestershire, he was heir-
apparent to a large patrimony, he prepared to enter the
Ministry of the Church, but, owing to conscientious scruples
on the matter of subscription, he determined not to undertake
a pastoral charge, but to content himself with a Lectureship.
Strype, in his Life of Bishop Aylmer, speaks of Smith as "an
eloquent and witty man who in 1587 became Reader or
Lecturer at St. Clement Danes, at the desire of many of the
parishioners, and by the favor of the Lord Treasurer who dwelt
in the same parish and yielded contribution to him."

Thomas Fuller also, in *A Life of Henry Smith* which he
prefixed to the first *Collected Edition* of his works, said of him:
"He was commonly called the Silver-tongued preacher, and
that was but one metal below St. Chrysostom himself. His
Church was so crowded with auditors that persons of good
quality brought their own pews with them, I mean their legs,
to stand thereon in the alleys. Their ears did so attend to his
lips, their hearts to their ears, that he held the rudder of their
affections in his hands, so that he could steer them whither he
was pleased." Wood, too, tells us that Smith was "esteemed
the miracle and wonder of his age, for his prodigious memory
and for his fluent, eloquent and practical way of preaching."
(*Athenae Oxon.* i. p. 603). And in our own time Marsden, in his
History of the Puritans, has described Smith's Sermons as "noble
examples of English prose and pulpit eloquence, and as being
free in an astonishing degree from the besetting vices of his
age—vulgarity and quaintness and affected learning."

Owing to ill-health he resigned his Lectureship about the end of 1590, and retired to Husbands Bosworth, where he died the following summer, and was buried July 4th, 1591, although some (like Brooks) place his death at 1600.

His *Collected Sermons* passed through the following editions:—1592, 1593, 1594, 1595, 1599, 1604, 1607, 1609, 1612, 1613, 1614, 1617, 1618, 1619, 1620, 1621, 1622, 1631 and 1632. Now also added is this current version of 2012.

J.B.
and
C.M.M.

THE CALLING OF JONAH

"The word of the Lord came to Jonah the son of Amittai, saying, "Arise, go to Nineveh, that great city, and cry against it; for their wickedness has come up before Me.""—Jonah 1:1-2

You have heard the sweet song of old father Simeon, like the pleasant song of a sweet bird before her death, setting forth the joy of the righteous that embrace Christ Jesus. Before Christ Jesus vouchsafed to come to us, we would not come to Him, but in all our doings we wrought our condemnation, and through the innumerable heaps of our iniquities labored to drive Him without all hope of mercy from us. So we continued like flies, which flutter about the candle, until they have consumed themselves. When we had done as much as in us lay to drive Him away from us, *then He saved us*, and recompensed good for evil to us: so that if God had loved us no more than we loved ourselves, we might have perished in our sins, and our blood should have been on our own heads. If Christ is the light of the Gentiles, let us embrace Him, and everyone walk as becomes the children of light. But many shut their eyes against it, lest they should see; and not only do many smother their own light, but the sun says to the moon, *Shine not*; and the moon says to the stars, *Do not be bright*: and many have smothered their light so long, that the damp has put out the candle. And so they labor to bring the darkness of Egypt on Goshen; so that their eyes have forgotten to see. So many go out of the way, because they would not look on the candle; and the devil gives to everyone that which he wishes, so it may be for his hurt. But who can but pity, that with the same manna which comes from heaven, and feeds many to life everlasting, so many are poisoned, and find it is nothing but the savor of eternal death? The Jews had no cause to envy our Light, for He gave them glory: He was poor, and yet He gave them riches: He was counted base, and yet He made them honorable: He was condemned, and yet He made them beloved. They were full of darkness, and He brought them light; but they condemned His light, and so procured their own condemnation. And therefore now it has come to pass that they have become vagabonds on the earth, and the most condemned of all other nations, and in every people have a dwelling, ever since they prophesied evil to themselves, saying, His blood be on us and our children, goodness has put on the face of bashfulness among them.

If you embrace Christ as Simeon did, then Christ is your glory; but if your glory consists in beauty which fades, in gay clothing which wears, in wealth which wastes, or in gold that rusts, then Christ is not your glory.

We have gone long with an old man, and now we have lost him; but we are loathe to part with him, he is such a good companion; nevertheless we hope to find him again in Jonah. We have gone but slowly with him, as with an old man that is not very swift of foot; but now we must run with Jonah as with a post, lest Nineveh be destroyed.

The Prophecy of Jonah. I do not need to show the authority of Prophets; but concerning their sorts and differences, there are three sorts of Prophets. The first were such as called on the name of the Lord in prayer for the people, and received an answer from the Lord in the people's behalf; of which sort was Samuel. These were called *Seers*, (1 Sam. 9:9). A second sort of Prophets were such as God raised to expound the Law, and declare the will of God to the people, when the priest and such as should do so were slack in their callings, of which sort was Isaiah, Jeremiah, Ezekiel, Daniel, Hosea, Joel, Amos, Obadiah, and the rest of the holy Prophets. A third sort were such as have been since Christ, working such like effects; of which sort was the Prophet Agabus, of whom mention is made in Acts 11:28.

Now in the second sort of these was Jonah, whom God sent to declare His will to the people; to whom also the Lord did reveal the subversions of kingdoms, the overthrow of tribes, the captivity of nations, the calamities that were to come to the sons of men for iniquity and rebellion against God.

As all wise men were not born at once, nor lived

9

together; so these Holy Prophets have not been at once, but were raised up by the Lord God, some here, some there, according to His pleasure, and as He saw the people stand in need of them by reason of the corruption of the times. And furthermore, the Lord has not at any time revealed to one of these all things that might be revealed, but as much as was sufficient for them, everyone in their time and place. Neither has any of them told as much of the will of God as might be declared, nor fully expounded His laws; but the Patriarchs left some to the Prophets, and the Prophets left some to the Apostles; but they have left none for us, but they have all set open the whole will of God to us; and every Prophet now brings only gold, myrrh, and frankincense, like the wise men that came to see our Lord.

There are three things that moved me to take this story in hand above all others: first, because you know the story, and therefore can the better conceive of the matter, as I go forward with it: secondly, because it is brief, and does contain a great deal in a little: thirdly, because it is most agreeable for the time and state of this sinful age in which we live, and therefore most convenient for us. It is manifest that Jonah lived in a very troublesome time, namely, in the time of Jeroboam the son of Joash, king of Israel, a wicked king, though not he that is called the Jeroboam that made Israel to sin: for of this second Jeroboam, in whose time he prophesied, it is written, "He departed mot from all the sins of Jeroboam who made Israel to sin," (2 Kings 14:24); which commends the Holiness of Jonah, in that he, in the midst of their corruption wherewith all the people were overthrown, he was uncorrupted and unspotted, and called to be a Prophet among the people of God. For he had prophesied in Israel before He was sent to Nineveh, as the Word also tells us, (2 Kings 14:25). This lays open and magnifies the great love of God, in that He sent a Prophet to admonish this ungodly people, when as He should have sent a thunderbolt to terrify them, or rather utterly to destroy them; so that there mercy stopped before judgment.

His name was *Jonah*, which signifies a *dove*; which

admonishes us, that as we labor to be as wise as serpents, so we should also desire that we might be as simple as doves. His father's name was Amittai, which signifies *truth*. I wish that truth were every preacher's father.

There are two special things contained in this history. The first, the great mercy of God showed to three sorts of men; the Ninevites, Jonah, and the mariners. In respect of the Ninevites, that He sent a prophet to Nineveh, a city of the Gentiles, which were strangers from the covenant, from the promise, and strangers from the commonwealth of Israel, and converted them by his preaching, and so God spared them now.

In regard of Jonah, that being, for his disobedience in flying to Tarshish when he was sent to Nineveh; thrown into the sea, God prepared a great fish to swallow him, and in his belly, even in the bottom of the sea, where there was no hope of life for him, preserved him, and after three days delivered him from there safe; and then did not cast him off, but continued him in his calling, and worked powerfully by him, both in the ship, converting the idolatrous mariners, and in Nineveh, humbling the king and the whole city. And, lastly, when he had most unworthily doubly murmured and justified himself against God, He contented Himself with a gentle and mild reproof of him.

In consideration of the mariners, that having been idolaters all their lives, and now in danger, giving the honor of God to their own fancies, God yet converts them, so that they called on Him, and sacrificed and made vows to the true God; and by His mighty power having the wind and seas calmed, were then and forever saved.

The second thing is Jonah's fall and rising again. His fall, first sinning, both flying from God, and murmuring, and in that justifying of himself. Secondly, sustaining his punishment, manifold and long fears, casting into the sea, and continuing in the belly of the great fish three days, and afterward his reproof and conviction. His rising, first, repenting in the ship, in the belly of the great fish, and being cast out of it. Then also

11

faithfully discharging his duty, crying against Nineveh courageously.

We have seen Jonah afar off; if we would, we might see him nearer. "He that receives a prophet in the name of a prophet] shall receive a prophet's reward," (Matt. 10:41). Therefore let us prepare our ears to hear and receive the Word of God preached by the ministers; and let us think that Jonah has come again to our houses to preach: and whether it is forty days, or forty weeks, or forty years, they that live like Sodom shall be punished like Sodom. But as our Savior says to His disciples, "Pray you that your flight is not in the winter, nor on the Sabbath day," (Matt. 24:20); so say I to you, Pray that the Lord's coming is not on the week-days, for if He comes then, how shall He find you? Therefore I pray you learn at least now and give good ear, that you may hear sufficient for all the week.

The word of the Lord came to Jonah the son of Amittai, saying, "Arise, and go to Nineveh," etc. Here I observe, that Jonah did not go before he was sent; for going to preach to Gentiles, it was needful that he should have a special calling and commission from the Lord Himself; for it was unmeet to "take the children's bread and cast it to dogs," (Matt. 15:26), unless he had a special commandment from God so to do. None ought to take on them the function of preaching in the Church, unless they have their warrant or authority from God as Aaron had, (Heb. 5:4). And although they do not have their authority in that form and manner as Jonah had his, namely, as it were by word of mouth even from God Himself, *Arise, and go to Nineveh,* yet they must have their warrant from Him, or else their calling is *unlawful*. But now here is another authority crept into the Church, that makes so many idols, which have eyes and do not see, tongues and do not speak, ears and hear not; and that is this, when one stalls up another into Moses' chair, not having Moses' rod, nor Moses' spirit. But this gall will not hold spurring. Further I observe, that as the Word of the Lord came to Jonah, so the word of the Pope came to his priests, Jesuits, and seminaries, but so and in such sort many times, that they are drawn to Tyburn, while masses are said for them at Rome.

12

The Word of the Lord came to Jonah, etc. That which came to him was not always with him: but so it was, that when the Word of the Lord came to any of the Prophets, then they were well furnished with ability to teach, to preach, to reprove, or to command, whomsoever the Lord would have so handled. As by example, Nathan the Prophet bid David the king that he should build a temple, (2 Sam. 7:3; 1 Chron. 17:2), and a little after he came and bid him that he should not build it: where we see, that when he bid him build it, then the Spirit of the Lord came not to him, to bid him so to do. And therefore the Spirit of God came to him the very same night, and bid him that he should go to David, and bid him that he should not build it. For this is evident, that as God Himself is constant, so His Spirit and His Word are constant, and therefore never says and unsays one thing.

Again, the Prophet Elisha said that the Shunammite's soul was vexed, but the Lord had hid it from him, (2 Kings 4:27), and had not as then declared the same to him: which does make us aware that the same Word whereby the Lord has and does reveal marvelous things to the Prophets was not now on him, neither is always on any Prophet; but according to the will of God it comes to them, to reveal to them what He would have them to do, and *when it pleases Him.*

Also Daniel said that the Lord did not reveal the king's dream to him for any wisdom that he had more than any living, (Dan. 2:30), but only for the king's sake, and for the poor people of God's sake. And so you must think of us that are the ministers of the Gospel that the Lord does not reveal His will to us for any wisdom or worthiness that is in us more than other men, but for your sakes, and that we might reveal it to you. Therefore hear us even for this cause, because the Lord has revealed to us these things for your sakes and good.

From the calling we come to the charge, *Arise, and go to Nineveh, that great city, etc.* God comes and finds us all asleep, then He presses us to arise; for they are not fit to convert others which are not yet converted themselves; according to that saying of Christ to Peter, "When you are converted, strengthen your brethren," (Luke 22:32), teaching them by your *experience*. Now-a-days men take on them to reprove others for committing such things as themselves have practiced, and do practise without amendment, notwithstanding their diligence in teaching others their duty: they can teach all the doctrine of Christ saving three syllables, that is, *Follow Me*. Therefore these are like some tailors, which are busy in decking and trimming up others, but go both bare and beggarly themselves. Yet they will not let us pluck out the beam that is in their eyes, until we have plucked out the mote which is in our own eyes.

Go to Nineveh. Nineveh was the greatest and most ancient city in the land of Assyria, and the name of it signified Beautiful; which name was rather given for the greatness and beauty of it, than the name of Asshur, which was the builder and first founder of it, as we read in the book of Genesis, (Gen. 10:11). It had a fair name, but foul deeds, like this city.

Go to Nineveh, etc. God would not suffer any people to be untaught; therefore He has written this name in great letters, easy to be read of all. "The heavens declare the glory of God, and the firmament sheweth His handy work. There is no speech nor language where their voice is not heard. Their line is gone out through all the earth, and their words into the ends of the world," (Psa. 19:1, 3, 4). In them is manifest, for all, what may be known of God: for His eternal power and Godhead are seen by the creation of the world, (Rom. 1:20). But especially He teaches some by His Word also: therefore He sent to the old world Noah, Lot to Sodom, Moses to Israel, and here Jonah to Nineveh. But when Paul with Silas and Timothy had gone throughout Phrygia and the region of Galatia, they were forbidden of the Holy Spirit to preach the Word in Asia. After they were come to Mysia, they essayed to go into Bithynia; but the Spirit suffered them not, (Acts 16:6, 7).

Go to Nineveh. The Jews would not hear the Word of God by Jonah, and therefore the Lord sent him to Nineveh. They that grieve the Spirit quench the Spirit. Then Jonah the

Prophet goes from Samaria to Nineveh. The Word was in Samaria, it went then to Nineveh. The Gospel was at Ephesus, it has come into England, it is gone out of the city; but it may depart from England again. "Wherefore let him that thinks he stands take heed lest he fall," (1 Cor. 10:12).

But the Prophet goes from Samaria to Nineveh. That was, first, to shake off the dust of his feet, to witness against them their obstinacy and hardness of heart. Secondly, to let them see that the wicked Gentiles were more righteous than they, in that they repented at the voice of one Prophet, yes, and that with *one sermon*; whereas they refused and resisted all the holy and worthy Prophets that God sent to them. Thirdly, it may be, to signify, that the Jews, for their contempt and negligence, should be rejected, and the Gentiles should be received into the favor of God, that they might be a holy and sanctified people to the Lord in their trouble.

That great city. Nineveh had fifteen hundred towers in it, as some write, and a hundred and twenty thousand little children, (as it is noted in the end of this story, Jonah 4:1); therefore it may well be called a great city; but the greater it was, the more ungodly it was: for as one man takes sickness of another, so one man is infected by the wicked words and evil example of another, and so taught to sin the more, until the measure of sin be full.

And cry against it, etc. First God bids him arise, and shake off all impediments, and then go and call them to the battle. Now He bids them cry out against them, and so terrify them. Every Prophet is a crier, as appears where the Lord bids Isaiah to lift up his voice like a trumpet, (Isa. 57:1). Every Prophet must both be plain and bold; and this many times makes the poor servants of God to speak their minds as plain and bold as if they sat in judgment. John was a voice, (Luke 3:4); a voice would not serve, he was the voice of a crier: and yet he could not make all the crooked straight, nor the rough plain, (Isa. 40:4). And because all the preachers of the Gospel should cry, that is, preach zealously, in the Acts 2 it is written, the Holy Spirit came down in fire and tongues. But this fire is quenched, and the tongues are tied up, so that they that should cry are stark dumb. But though they cannot speak, they can see if a great benefice fall, though it is a hundred miles off; and Pharaoh had more care of his sheep than we have of our souls. If preachers were not dumb, and their hearers deaf, they needed not to cry one to another; but such is the dumbness of preachers, and the deafness of all sorts of hearers, that there is great slowness of followers, so that there is but little good done, and but a few fruits gathered. If you were not deaf, we do not need to cry; but because you are dull of hearing, therefore we cry with mouth, with heart, with hand, with foot, and with all the powers of our bodies, to you: and yet how little do you regard it! But are not you commanded to hear, as well as we to cry? Yes, the cock crows when men are asleep; Yes, the cock crows, and yet Peter still denies his Master, (Matt. 26:74). Before you cry to the Lord, hear what the Word cries to you; and let not your works cry for vengeance while your tongues cry for mercy. When men hear the preacher speak against pride, hypocrisy, covetousness, or against any other sin, then they look one on another, as though it belonged not to them: but who can say, I have made my heart clean, (Prov. 20:9).

And cry against it. Our sins buffet God on every side, as the Jews buffeted Christ, first on the right side, then on the left side, and never leave, until they have provoked Him to cry against us. When God *cries*, then we should *weep*, considering why He cries; for there is nothing that can provoke the Lord to cry but sin, and that He ever cries against. Do what you will, and say what you will, and the Lord will not be offended with you, unless you sin; but if you commit sin, He is just, and therefore will not leave, until He has by crying slain either you, or sin that reigns in you: for as an angry man ever pursues that which he hates, until he has destroyed it; so the Lord crosses and follows us with His judgments, until He has slain that which most deadly He hates,—sin.

And cry against it, etc. Reproof is the most necessary office; yet it is least regarded, yes, it is most abhorred. Now we think, if one reproves us, he hates us. But the Lord says. "Thou shall not hate your brother in your heart; you shall in any wise rebuke your neighbor, and not suffer sin on him," (Lev. 19:17); noting thereby that if we flatter any in their sin, or see them sin, and not reprove them for it, it is a manifest sign that we do it of hatred, how great love and good-will soever we pretend toward them; seeing the matter tends to the hurt of their souls, and the offence of God. Yes, if a preacher reproves sin, he is thought to do it of hatred, or of some particular grudge; and to be too busy, too bitter, too sharp, too rough; and therefore they say, *He should preach God's love and mercy, for he is a preacher of the Gospel; he tells us of, and threatens us with, the law, and so throws us down too low, some to despair.* As though we preached the law only or chiefly, and not the Gospel also continually to them that loath and strive against their sins, though they sin grievously. Others, as though they were galled, will say, *Let him keep his text;* or they will say, *He is beside his book;* as though no text in Scripture reproved sin. And so of all doctrines the doctrine of reproof and reprehension of sin is *most condemned,* and *least esteemed.* But let a preacher preach dark mysteries, or profane speeches, or unprofitable fables, or frivolous questions, or curious inventions, or odd conceits, or brain-sick dreams, and any of these will be more welcome to them than reprehension, which is most profitable and most necessary of all. Balaam's ass never spoke but once, and then he reproved, (Num. 22:28). Then if Balaam's ass reproved Balaam, how much more ought Balaam to reprove asses, or such as will be no otherwise than beasts in their behavior! But persuade yourselves, (beloved), which is most true, though we speak as if we were angry with you, and threaten as if we would hurt you, and cry against you as if we hated you, yet we love you in the dearest blood we have; and therefore, though with persecution we preach the law, to lead you to the Gospel, we preach judgment, that you may find mercy; we preach hell, to bring you to heaven; whatsoever and howsoever we preach, we do all to fill your hearts with joy in believing, and, having made you fruitful in all good works, present you without spot, no, glorious also, as a virgin most beautiful, to the Lord of all grace and glory, Christ Jesus.

Here we have heard of Jonah called, and charged to cry; but what should he cry? Indeed it is not expressed in this place. But what then? Why then, the Papists may say, that he was charged to cry against them for neglecting their traditions. Assuredly they may with as great truth, and as much probability, as they do gather out of divers places of the New Testament, that they ought to be observed, (John 16:12; 21:25; Acts 1:3; 2 Tim. 1:13). But Jonah has not left it doubtful what he was to cry; for in the third chapter, verse 2, the charge is repeated, and so expressed, *Preach to it the preaching that I bid you.* He was then to cry what God had commanded him. Oh that none would cry but what God has commanded! But what did God command him to cry? Even that which he afterward cried: *Yet forty days, and Nineveh shall be overthrown.* Overthrown? Yes, ancient Nineveh, fair Nineveh, proud Nineveh must be *destroyed.* No man sits so high but destruction sits above him, and will fall on all that persist in their defection. Justice would have come against them before it cried against them; but God the most gracious would have them cried against, that they might cry out woe and alas for their sins, so preventing deserved and threatened vengeance: for they hearing the cry of God, cried out themselves, and that in great humbling to God; so God heard their cries, and took pity on them.

Isaiah was commanded to cry, and he cried, All flesh is grass, and all the goodliness of it is as the flower of the field: the grass withers, the flower fades; because the Spirit of the Lord blows on it: Surely the people are grass, (Isa. 40:6-7). John was commanded in the spirit of Elijah to cry, and he cried, "Prepare you the way of the Lord, make His paths straight," (Matt. 3:3). And Jonah was commanded to cry, and he cried, "Yet forty days, and Nineveh shall be overthrown." And all the preachers of the Gospel are commanded to cry aloud, "Spare not, lift up their voice like a trumpet, and show God's people their transgression, and the house of Jacob their sins," (Isa. 58:1). And then also, if they thereby are truly humbled, to proclaim to them, *their iniquity is pardoned*; for they have received of the Lord's hand doubled for all their sins, (Isa. 40:2). It is required of the disposers of God's secrets, that they are found faithful, (1 Cor. 4:1-2). And woe it is to them that love the pleasures of sin more than the glory of God!

For their wickedness has come up before Me. We have heard the charge itself given; it was heavy news, that a most beautiful city, a most rich city, a most populous city, and a most ancient city, must be overturned, and that within forty days! What is the cause? *Their wickedness has come up before Me.* As if he had said, Nineveh has followed her lusts, and forgotten the law, to satisfy her desires; she has notoriously despised her sovereign, defied all well-meaning, all good dealing; and this is known to the just Judge, and at His bar she is arraigned, and her accusers stand crying at the bar of justice: therefore she may no longer be forborne, execution of justice has to be done. Let her therefore prepare for death; and that she may, Cry against her, *Yet forty days, and Nineveh shall be overthrown*; *for their wickedness has come up before Me.* When God sends cries to a people, it is a most manifest sign that their wickedness has come up before Him, which causes Him to exclaim, to cry out against them. And then if they will not repent, while God's cries continue crying among them, the Lord of hosts will rise up in arms against them.

Their wickedness. Will you see the Ninevites in a scroll, that with you, the daughters of Nineveh, may see that wealth and wickedness were brought together, prosperity and security kissed each other? "Nineveh," (says Nahum) "was like a pool of waters, most populous, and full of all store," (Nah. 2:8-9); which to increase, it was wholly full of lying, deceit, and fraud, full of robbery, oppression, and all violence, a bloody city: whereby it increased in wealth, and flourished in honor and glory; and therefore, as Zephaniah has it, was a rejoicing, a rioting city, sat securely, and proudly condemned others, saying, "I am, there is none beside me," (Zeph. 2:15). Moreover it was the mistress of witchcrafts, (Nah. 3:4), a most idolatrous

19

city: Yes, they sold people through her whoredoms, and nations through her witchcrafts, and made others idolatrous like herself, (2 Kings 16:10).

Their wickedness has come up before Me. Sin mounts up on high, like the tempter, which led Christ to the top of the pinnacle, to behold all the pleasures of the world at once: and then, because we have fallen down before the god of this world, and tempted the God of heaven, whether He is just or not, therefore wrath speaks out of the fire, Now you have taken your pleasure, you must also take your punishment. A most heavy and grievous thing it is if you knew what you are doing here, and what your sins are doing at the bar of God's just judgment for even now before you came here you were serving the *devil in sin*; but now it is too late to speak of it. And where are they now? Flesh and blood could not stay them, nature could not stay them, pleasures could not stay them, riches could not stay them, nor they could not stay themselves, but they are ascended up before the face of the eternal God, to stand at His bar, and cry for vengeance to fall on us, for committing such heinous sins against the Majesty of God. An arrow is swift, the sun is swifter, but sin is swiftest of all; for in a moment it is committed on earth, it comes before God in heaven, and is condemned to hell. Though Nimrod could not climb to heaven, his sins flew up to heaven; and though we stay below, our sins ascend high, like the tower of Nimrod; but they fling us down to confusion, and we become Babel: for when we sin, we are as the shell-fish, which the eagle takes, and flies into the air with, and then lets it fall on the rocks, and so dashes it in pieces, and then devours it: for the wrath of God takes us up on high, and throws us down low on the rocks of shame, and contempt, and terror of conscience: and so having crushed us, and bruised our very bones, consumes us with double death, the grave devouring us, hell swallowing us.

Has come up before Me. To them which ask how our sins ascend and fly up before God, I answer, God here speaks to us after the manner of men, who cannot see a thing afore it is brought to them, even where they are, and before them: so that hereby is signified, God had seen their wickedness. We fast as before Him, we pray as before Him, we give alms as before Him, and we do every good thing as before Him; because we do it freely, and as it were not caring who looks on us: but we sin as behind Him; because we hide and cloak our sins, and commit them in secret, loathe that men should spy them out; our conscience in such actions accusing us, and instantly telling us we are about doing that which we cannot justify. And we suppose that we sin behind Him, because we sin here below; saying with ourselves in the consideration of our blinded hearts, as Eliphaz accused Job to have said, "Is not God in the height of heaven? and behold the height of the stars, how high they are! And you say, How should God know? can He judge through the dark cloud? Thick clouds are a covering to Him, that He sees not, and He walks in the circuit of heaven," (Job 22:12-14). But then chiefly we imagine that God does not behold us when man cannot see us; as if God could not know when man cannot spy. But let us not deceive ourselves, for God sees not as man sees. Man can see but only outward things committed in action; but God sees, and knows, and searches the secrets of the heart, yes, the most secret thoughts and imaginations of it. Again, man can but see one thing at once; he cannot turn his right eye one way, and left eye another; he cannot see before him and behind him with one look; but God sees all things at all times. Though we sin as closely as we can for fear of hatred, or shame of the world, or for any other respect; yet God says, *Your sin has come up before Me.* For though we cover it, and hide it, and color it, yes, and, as it were, bury it as much as lies in us, yet all is open to Him. Therefore He says, *Your sin has come up before Me.* For when we speak evil, He is all ears to hear us; and when we do evil, He is all eyes to behold it. Therefore, O foolish man! do not think that God does not see that which man does not see; for when He looks up, He cries all below also; and when He looks down, He cries all above also. If He should not, much wickedness should lie in darkness unregarded, and men should not be terrified from sin, but rather by the example of others allured to sin freely, secretly:

for Ananias might have gained by his craft, if God had not seen his heart, which men did not see; but God saw his distrustful and dissembling and corrupt heart; therefore he lost his goods, and his life too, (Acts 5:5). If God had not seen that which men do not see, Gehazi might have gained a bribe for his labor, when he ran after Naaman the Syrian, and told him a lie for his profit, (2 Kings 5:22). But God seeing his fetches, which men did not see, turned his bribe to leprosy, and so made him a leper for his labor. A fearful example for such as take bribes; yet many care not what bribes they take, so men see it not. The man that said, Be merry, my soul, and take your pleasure for many years, (Luke 12:19), might have done it, had not God seen him. But He spied him falling to godless security, and threatened him that night to bereave him of his soul. Do not forget it, you that abound in wealth, whose cup runs over. If God had not seen Achan take up the piece of gold, he had kept it to himself for his labor, and no man should have known where he had it, (Josh. 7:1). But God seeing it, (though closely done), rewarded him with shame in the sight of *all* Israel. O Lord, what is man that you so watch him! Achan would never have stolen if he had known that God saw him. Gehazi would have never taken a bribe if he had thought that God beheld his doings. Will you steal, the owner of a shop looking on you? Will you speak treason in the king's hearing? Neither should we lie, nor swear, nor steal, nor hurt, nor be profane at any time, if we considered that the Lord sees us, and remembers that He watches us. If we would do this, sin might go a begging for want of service. Therefore if you would mark but this part of my sermon,—*that God sees all*, you would refrain from those things secretly that are to the offence of God, which you for fear or shame will not do before men; and you would say, even when your hand is at it, *I will not do it, because the Lord sees me*. But as when we sin, though in secret, He is all eyes to see us; and when He cries it requisite to make some example, to teach all, that when man cannot nor will not discover us, He will show that He saw us, then He is all at hand to punish and plague us, and in the end to root us out from all our pleasures;

so when we repent, He is all mercy and love; and when we amend our lives, and leave all our wicked ways, to walk before Him ever after in holiness, then He is all truth and righteousness, to forgive us all our former wicked life, and to wash us from all our uncleanness. Now therefore repent of all the evil that you have done, lament truly, run and speedily move as fast as ever you can to the throne of grace; prove whether your repentance will not as boldly stand before God, and as powerfully cry for pardon, as your sins speedily came up before God, and vehemently cried for punishment. No doubt the angel that cried, "Babylon the great is fallen, is fallen," (Rev. 18:2), though he cried mightily with a strong voice, cried not so audibly as you shall hear the Spirit of Truth crying and assuring you, *Your sins are forgiven you*; *The God of glory loves you*; *Sin shall no longer reign in you*, (Rom. 6:14); *No evil shall hurt you*, (Psa. 91:10); *No good thing shall be wanting to you*, (Psa. 34:10); *All things shall work together to the best for you*, (Rom. 8:28). Will you anymore? He shall ever dwell with you, in whose presence is fullness of joy, and at whose right hand there are "pleasures forevermore," (Psa. 16:11). Repent therefore, but repent *truly*, loath all sin, grieve that you have committed any, fly away from every sin, yes, whatsoever occasions of it, and all "appearance of evil," (1 Thes. 5:22); but "love the truth" also, (2 Thes. 2:10), and follow all holiness, and, as much as you have in you, and "have peace with all men," (Heb. 12:14); and the God of peace will increase your peace in Christ Jesus. All which even this point that we speak of, *viz.*, whatsoever we do God sees us, most sufficiently assures us of all this. For this so often is repeated in Scripture, (Rev. 2:2, 9, 13, 19; 3:1, 8, 15), *I know your works*, is spoken as to rouse the dead Sardians, (3:11), and to heat the lukewarm Laodiceans, (3:15), so to commend the faith, hope, love, patience, *etc.*, of the other Churches, and so to establish and set them forward in that, knowing He is just, and a rewarder of them that diligently seek Him, (Heb. 11:6).

Their wickedness has come up before Me. Sin once committed casts no doubts of coming presently before God; but the thoughts of the heart of the carnal man, thinking of the way to heaven, are the faint spies that went to the land of Canaan, which say that journey is farther than you are able to go all your life, the way is like a thicket, and the door like a needle's eye; therefore it is impossible for you to come here. But when you send faith, hope, and love, (those messengers of peace and truth), they will bring you word, saying, Your ruffs must be ruffled, and your fardingales crushed, pride must be put off and other sins; and none shall be kept out of heaven, but such as love the world better than heaven, or such as will take their sins with them; for they are unbeseeming the fashion of that country: so that ere we come thither we must leave them, like the shadow when we go in at the door, and we must shake hands with them, and bid them farewell.

THE REBELLION OF JONAH

"But Jonah rose up to flee to Tarshish from the presence of the Lord, and went down to Joppa; and he found a ship going to Tarshish: so he paid the fare of it, and went down into it, to go with them to Tarshish from the presence of the Lord."—Jonah 1:3

The charge given to Jonah has here been spoken of. Now it follows to be showed how it was by Jonah discharged. First, Jonah rebelliously neglected it; then, being chastised, and so repenting, he faithfully discharged it. First, therefore, let us consider his rebellion, and afterward we shall see his correction.

But Jonah rose up to flee to Tarshish from the presence of the Lord. We cannot stand to speak of Tarshish, nor what it is to fly from God, but this shall be our meditation: Jonah the Prophet was commanded to go to Nineveh, and there to cry out against sin, to preach against pride and all kinds of ungodliness, thereby to reclaim them, and stir them up, in laying open their sin, and the punishment that hanged over them, that they might speedily repent, and so turn away from them the wrath of God thereby deserved. How beautiful should have been the feet of him that should have brought so powerful a message as should have wrought such a happy effect! How blessed should Nineveh have been, when the Lord had vouchsafed them so great mercy! But still one fly mars the whole box of ointment, (Eccl. 10:1). As soon as he was commanded to go there, Satan stood in the gap, and enticed him to go to Tarshish; for he thought, that if he could let Jonah from going to Nineveh, then, first of all, he should put a singular Prophet out of God's favor, and bring on him some judgment, not only inward, as torment of conscience, decay of gifts, or the like, but visible also, whereby the people to whom he had preached might think he was some false prophet; as they are ever ready to condemn for hated of God whom they see grievously afflicted. And so, secondly, the people should be

25

hardened in their sins, and obstinately condemn ever after him, his like and their preaching too: and, thirdly, the goodliest, the most populous, and the wealthiest city in Assyria should be destroyed, the good with the wicked, the young with the old, one with another, all should unrepentant die in their sins, and so the very angels in heaven should mourn. So that he thought he should by stopping Jonah every way gain well by his labor. Therefore he comes to Jonah, he flatters him, he tempts him: so he begins with him: It is good that men *look before they leap*; *haste makes waste*; words are not always to be taken as they properly signify; one thing is often spoken, and another meant: but do you think God means *you* should go to Nineveh? Why? does He regard idolaters, and His professed enemies, so that, to have them admonished of their ruin, He will bring shame on His own people? For the very going of a Prophet from Israel to preach to Nineveh must needs proclaim that there is more hope of most sinful Gentiles than of natural Israelites. And how could you seem so to think of your own nation, your own brethren, your own blood, the chosen of God? Or if you do, shall you not thereby procure their utter hatred forever, and make them to detest both your person and your preaching, whatsoever you have here now, or hereafter shall teach them? What? for your faithful prophesying here among God's people, will God, do you think, recompense you,—you whom He has made reverend, and to be honored of kings and princes of Israel, recompense, I say, you with shame and contempt among heathens, yes, with a cruel death, or with a more miserable life? For what other success may be hoped for at the Ninevites hands of such a message by you? For you know they have all Jews in contempt; therefore, when you shall come among them, and tell them not these few words only, and in this form which God has spoken them in, (for if you so do, who will not count you rather a madman, than God's Prophet?) but at large, that there is One all-seeing, most just, almighty, and ever-living God, and no more; and so all their gods are no gods, but *idols*; and that they above all others have given His glory to stocks and stones, worshipping them for gods, alluring and enforcing others likewise to dishonor Him; that they have abused His blessings most unthankfully, most ungodly, to all excess, and are most proud condemners of their betters, and most notorious drunkards, gluttons, fornicators, adulterers, thieves, oppressors, witches, murderers, and the like; and therefore have so provoked Him that is most merciful and patient, that He will, without all pity, destroy man, woman, young and old, high and low, among them, yes, their very city also, and all that is in that, whereby they have been so wicked, and that within forty days. When, I say, you, being a Jew, shall tell them this, so in despite revile, (for so they will take it), so utterly condemn them and their gods, will not the best of them mock and despise you? Will not the rest gnash their teeth at you, and be ready to tear you in pieces, put you to exquisite torments, condemn you to some horrible death, or continue you in intolerable pains in a most bitter life? *No question.* Think not therefore that your good God, your most kind and tender Father, will recompense your faithfulness with sending you so far to sustain such misery; it were impiety to think He willed it; it is blasphemy, terrible blasphemy, to think He commands it. For it is to condemn Him of unkindness, for you have showed fervent love; of untruth, for He has promised it should go well with the just; of injustice, for godliness should have the reward due only to wickedness. Yes, He should seem contrary to Himself, to charge you cruelly to murder yourself, which has commanded all to kill none, if He should will you to provoke that bloody city so. But the very thing itself also argues, God meant nothing less than to commit you to such danger, or that you should do to the proud Ninevites such a message. For to what end should you so cry against that city? To make them fly, and so to free them from destruction? How should you then not be found a false prophet, and God a liar? What then? To bring to repentance, and then to spare them? How should not God so again be found untrue, and you His lying messenger? What then? To convert them, and so to destroy them? What justice is that? And how contrary is this to His promise to Solomon! (2 Sam. 7:14-15). Therefore it is manifest God meant not you should go and cry so against Nineveh; but signified that you were as good, for any good may be done here, to exclaim so like a frantic man against Nineveh, as to preach in Samaria any longer now. Men here are so hardened that they condemn all: some people are so cloyed, that they loath all: the best little esteem *all* that is preached: of none is the Word accounted precious, of none reverently heard. And therefore you should for a time, to make the Word precious, and to sharpen men's affections towards it, give over preaching here, and, where you will, refresh yourself a while. Now here you may not be idle: at Tarshish you may be quiet; you may at Tarshish, that famous city, among the strangers of many countries, hear many strange things, much delight you in the variety of their manners, in the abundance of all things with great pleasure live. No time so fit as this to see the world. At Joppa you have a ship waiting there. Do not make a small account of this "kindness of God," defraud not yourself of the "granted good."

So Satan is ever crossing, tempting, enticing us, when we are or should be addressing ourselves to do the will of our God, So was Moses, Jeremiah, Ezekiel, Nehemiah, Christ Himself tempted, being about most notable works. What did our Savior say to Peter? "Satan has desired to have you, that he may sift you as wheat," (Luke 22:31). Who are these whose peril Satan so earnestly desires? Even Peters, and James, and Johns. No marvel, for Christ Himself, though acknowledged the Son of God, was most fiercely assaulted of the tempter forty days, and then indeed was left, but *it was only for a season*, (Luke 4:13). Therefore never dream of a truce with Satan, whosoever you be, whatsoever you are about to do: for the enemy, the envious foe, the tempter, the false accuser, goes about continually, "seeking whom he may devour," (1 Pet. 5:8). Now his manner of tempting is, first and most usually with flattering, but yet very often with most terrible threatening. For whatsoever we do or feel comes from one of the three spirits, the spirit of *Satan*, the Spirit of *God*, or *our* spirit. Now our own spirit of itself is always occupied about worldly things, seeking delight by pleasures, not disquieted by threats. The Spirit of God is gentle, loving, and meek, not forcing, not threatening. Therefore Christ says, "If any will follow Me, let him deny himself and take up his cross daily," (Luke 9:23). And mark His spirit. He does not say, *You shall follow Me, and, You shall deny yourselves, and take up your cross*; but, *If any will follow Me, let him deny himself, and take up his cross*; Let him. The same is to be seen in the Canticles, where He says, "Open to Me, My sister, My love, My dove, My undefiled; for My head is filled with dew and My locks with the drops of the night," (Song of Songs 5:2). For when she opened not to Him, making most unmeet excuses, though He bad most lovingly prayed, and lively urged her to open, and she most unkindly, most unworthily had denied; yet he went His way mildly, without any threats. But the spirit of Satan takes another course: for when by lying and deceit he cannot allure to sin, he threatens most fearfully with grief, or loss of goods; solitariness, and want of pleasure; and sometime by his ministers, imps of his own likeness, he threatens death and deadly torments, whatsoever they may inflict on any. Christ says, "If any will follow Me;" *If you will*: but he says, *I will make you follow me, and do as I bid you*; else you shall have fire and wood, scalding lead and burning pitch: if you will not follow me, you shall, whether you want to or not. We will make you do as we command, says his eldest son Antichrist, usurping authority over nations, and inflicting torments on the saints. His order of tempting is, first, to make us doubt of the Word of God; whether such or such doctrine is true, such and such an action be commanded, such and such a promise, such and such a threatening, is certain. Then, secondly, he falls to flat denying of it: This doctrine, these promises, these threatenings are false; this thing is not commanded, this action is not commended. And then he comes in with his contradiction, contrary assertions, and countermands: for there is no commandment of God, but the devil commands the contrary, and he is ever gainsaying that which God says. For our God says to Adam, "If you eat of the forbidden fruit, you shall surely die," (Gen. 3:3): the devil came, and he told them, first, It is not certain you shall die; then, You shall not die; then, thirdly, "You shall be as gods, knowing good from evil," (Gen. 3:4, 5). God says, "Submit yourselves one to another in brotherly love," (1 Pet. 5:5). The devil says, first, You do not need to abase yourselves so much; secondly, You should not yield to others; then, thirdly, Advance yourselves, and condemn others. God says, "Love your neighbor as yourself," (Matt. 22:39): the devil says, first, Love little and outwardly; then, Love none but yourself; then, inwardly, Hate your enemies, envy your betters, disdain your equals, despise your inferiors. God says, "Labor for that food that perishes not," (John 6:27): the devil says, first, *Care not much for it*; then, secondly, *Condemn it*; then, thirdly, *Stir not an inch for it*. God says, "Forsake the world," (Rom. 12:2): the devil says, first, *Do not neglect the world*; then, *Love the world*; then, thirdly, *Give over yourselves to the world*: above all, *Follow the world with all the lusts of it*.

Now the means whereby the devil tempts are arguments fetched, some from the mind and reason of man, or from the customs of the world; some from the Holy Scriptures, either corrupted, or wrong applied; now in consideration of the persons, then in regard of the thing itself, *etc.* In respect of the persons to whom he should preach, and himself, Jonah is here tempted, and in this way reasons with himself: *I have long preached to the Jews, which are the chosen people of God; and seeing they will not hear me, it is in vain to preach to these Gentiles, which never heard of God or godliness, and therefore will esteem my words the less.* So Jonah loathes to lose his labor; and puts in a doubt where he needs not, because he considered not the great power of God in men's hearts. The Ninevites are heathen people, and therefore (says Jonah) *why should I venture myself among them? For seeing my own countrymen kick against my words, and cannot abide to hear the word which comes from the Lord to reprove sin; then how much more shall I be despised by these, and persecuted to death!* So flesh and blood stands staggering when it should do any good, misdoubting troubles, jealous of his own case; but when it goes about to do any mischief, it never considered the danger, it does not weigh the following woe. Yet doing good, it is uncertain whether all will not according to, or even above, our hope succeed; it is more likely we should be kept safe: but doing evil, mischief most certainly is procured not danger only, but loss of the best things commonly, peace of conscience or spiritual graces, of some blessings always; or at least not receipt of those things which much would rejoice us. For sure this was a sore temptation, to bid a man (being in reasonable good estate touching his body and life) that he should go and preach to a savage heathen people, that never heard of preaching, and that this doctrine, that there is but one only true God, (Deut. 6:4), to them who will serve a thousand, and cannot abide the contrary to be spoken. If a preacher were commanded to go and preach at Rome's gates against Antichrist's jurisdiction, and the idolatry that is so inordinately used in that synagogue of uncleanness; seeing that it is a matter for which they torment and kill all that preach it sincerely, I fear it would hardly come to pass at all, that this preacher would go from a reasonable quiet estate touching his body, to venture his life among such cruel tyrants: I fear he would rather content himself with his present case, than commit himself to so likely misery.

If I go to preach to these infidels, saying, "Yet forty days, and Nineveh shall be overthrown," then (says Jonah) *it may be they will repent, and God will have mercy on them*; so I shall be counted a false prophet for my labor. And so we regard our credit more than the glory of God in the obedience of His will: and rather than we would receive any reproach by our doings in the sight of the world, we rather choose to enter into no great action touching the glory of God, and the good of the Church.

In respect of the Israelites and himself he is this way tempted: *If I leave mine own people, and preach to the Gentiles*, (says Jonah), *I shall bring shame on Israel before all people; because a Prophet* is gone from them for their obstinacy, choosing rather to preach to uncircumcised Gentiles than to them, as if there were more hope of the Gentiles than of them. So Jonah more fears the children's disgraces than the Father's dishonor, and their despite than His displeasure. Satan is too well acquainted with man's nature, and so more certainly knows than we wisely consider, that all Adam's sons are from labor easily brought to loiter; more willingly from fear and pain to security and pleasure; therefore seldom or never does he in tempting omit this enticement: It will be for your ease, for your delight, for your security. Therefore he says to Jonah, not only, The way to Nineveh is long and dangerous, your person and message odious, therefore your travel has to be tedious, your troubles grievous, *etc.* But also, he is tempted with *Your passage to Tarshish is easy, your security there sure, your pleasures many, your delight great.* Yes, with this he assaulted Christ Himself, saying, when he had showed Him all the kingdoms of the world, and the glory of them, "All these will I give You," *etc.*, (Matt. 4:8-9). And does he not so also evermore persuade us, *This good, this gain, this glory, this pleasure, or this preferment shall you get, if you so and so deal?* If you will leave the society, the exercises, the profession, and the company of the children of God, and serve me, and worship me; preferring your covetousness, your pride, your lust, before the service of God; not being scrupulous to swear for your gain sometime, nor to lie for your pleasure, nor to cozen for riches; then you shall not only be free from the reproaches wherewith professors are overwhelmed, and the contempt in which they are had, and. the many heavy sighs that they are forced to fetch; but you shall also grow rich soon, and so be well thought of, and had in estimation, and by your wealth live in ease, with all pleasure, procuring everything at your heart's desire.

So Jonah, whichever way he looked, is tempted on every side: tempted to sin, but not constrained; urged, but not compelled; for the devil has power to entice to sin mightily, but not to enforce violently. Lo! then comforts against this cross. Our enemy's power is in our Father's hands; and our

Savior prays for us being most glorious in heaven, as He on earth in humility prayed for His Apostles, that our faith does not fail us, (Luke 22:32). Behold then also encouragements to fight against his assaults: yet see a greater. God has given us this privilege, this promise have we, "Resist the devil, and he will flee from you," (James 4:7). God has given no promise to the devil, that if he persuade, he shall prevail; if he urge, we shall yield. What a shame is it to us that Satan is bolder in tempting, than we are in resisting! Is he not? Oh that we could truly say, *We are as wise, as watchful, as thoughtful to withstand Satan's assaults, as he is wily, vigilant, and more than diligent, to assault!*

But what does Jonah do; so as we have heard by Satan assaulted? Does he resist him as manfully as the devil has set on him cunningly? Alas! no; Jonah is no sooner dissuaded to go to Nineveh, than he is persuaded it were great folly: he is as soon resolved, as he is enticed, to go to Tarshish, thinking it a chief point of wisdom to seek his own ease, his own pleasure, his own sweet delight. Once it is said, "God spoke, and it was done," (Psa. 33:9). Surely the devil also but speaks, and it is done; for he is such an orator as no man can deny him: for who can gainsay him that counsels as a special friend, yes, as a most holy angel? For he would seem to is not only careful both to keep us from danger and the fear of it, and to procure us all good, but also jealous of God's honor, fearful lest men should despise the Word, and so their own salvation. Therefore he made not only Gehazi to take a bribe, (2 Kings 5:22-23), Demas to embrace the world, (2 Tim. 4:10), Judas to betray his Master, (Matt. 26:48-49), and Cain to kill his brother," (Gen. 4:8); but Rebekah also to persuade Jacob, and Jacob to be bold by lying to seek for the blessing," (Gen. 27, *etc.*); Yes, the father of the faithful to commit folly with Hagar," (Gen. 16); as here Jonah not to go to Nineveh, lest, forsooth, God should not is true of His word: as if what to man seems unlikely, that were with God impossible; and He could not be righteous, unless we show ourselves impious.

We have seen some causes why Satan assaulting us, straight overcomes us: would any see more? We have been taught his power, malice, watchfullness, and wiliness: we have most fit and sufficient armor ministered to us, (Eph. 6:11, *etc.*); we have a promise that, resisting him, we shall make him fly from us, (James 4:7). Therefore surely we forget our enemy, or neglect the promise, or take not to us the whole armor of God; specially we like not that armor-bearer, humility: Submit yourselves to God, and then resist the devil. But moreover, we to our own certain peril and pain (so corrupt are we) join with our enemy, more ready to do his will than God's Word. Hereof, no doubt, foolish Balaam asked again and again, until God seeing him bent contrary to that he had been commanded, left him to himself; and so Balaam went on in sin so long, until the very ass whereon he rode was constrained to reprove him. But would you, howsoever Satan tempts, not to be turned by him out of the right way? howsoever he fights, not to be foiled by him? would you have him soon to forsake you, speedily to fly from you? that is, would you resist him? for when we begin valiantly to fight, then forthwith he flies! Consider how shameful a thing it is, being every way encouraged to fight, to show ourselves most dastardly cowards; how dishonorable to our Captain Christ, to yield the victory to His deadly enemy; how dangerous for ourselves, knowing he is a most cruel tyrant, and most inexorable, that most glories and specially takes pleasure in putting us to the most bitter pain that possibly he can, and therefore having overcome us, will forever continue us in most intolerable torments! Yes, you say, these things considered would make us courageously to encounter with Satan, and so soon to conquer him; but he comes often as a friend, as an angel of light; how shall I then descry him, that I may defy him, and make him to fly? How? here indeed is the hardness; for he is a notable hypocrite, the father of hypocrisy: but you must follow the counsel of Christ. you must anoint your eyes with eye-salve, that you may see, (Rev. 3:8). you must be filled with the knowledge of God's will in all wisdom and spiritual understanding, (Col. 1:9), and moreover watch and be sober, (1 Peter 5:8). And lastly, consider, first, how your spirit is affected; for our own spirit, (by nature evermore hard), if it is moved by the Spirit of God, is sad, and soft, and slow; but if it is moved by the spirit of Satan, is proud, boisterous, and stout. Then, whether that which you are indeed moved to be good or evil: if good, that is, agreeable to God's Word, then acknowledge it comes from God; for all good motions are the work of the Spirit of God, howsoever they seem to proceed of ourselves; but if it is evil, that is, not agreeable with the Word of God, then it is always either a lust of our corrupt nature, or a suggestion of Satan. Wherefore it is a sure way to say when we are tempted to evil, This motion is of the devil, for even our corruption came of his suggestion: for the spirit of man is always tossed between these two contrary spirits,—the Spirit of God procuring our salvation, and the spirit of Satan seeking our condemnation. So that if any will get the victory of Satan, he may not be without the spiritual sword, which is the Word of God, (Eph. 6:17). Yes, he must have the *word of God dwell in him richly*, (Col. 3:16), and cry still, *Open mine eyes, O Lord*, (Psa. 119:18), Give me understanding, (verse 34), and incline mine heart to Your testimonies, (verse 36), and beware that he submits himself duly, and that he diligently watches.

So Jonah tempted has consented to neglect his charge: and does he forthwith repent? No, he prepares himself to his purposed journey. *But Jonah rose up to flee to Tarshish.* As Jonah was no sooner tempted to go to Tarshish but he yielded; so, as soon as he had yielded, forthwith he goes. So Jonah made himself a run-away, and showed himself a disobedient servant to his God. And in the meanwhile Nineveh set on the score, and had no hindrance with them in working wickedness; but still filling the cup of all abominations, ran down to hell with as much force and speed as they could. So Nineveh is still Nineveh, *but Jonah is not like Jonah*; for the Prophet is flying and sin is crying, and so all falls to confusion.

But Jonah rose up to flee to Tarshish, etc. Jonah flies to Tarshish before he would go to Nineveh: and everyone is like that son which said he would not, before he went: and so sin is born first, as Esau was born before Jacob, (Gen. 25:25-26).

Therefore if evil may compare with goodness in particular actions, Evil may stay in all mankind corrupt, he is the ancienter. But as soon as you perceive any evil cogitation or motion in yourself, you should be angry with it, nip it in the head, put it to death; and then the unclean spirit, that has long been strong, and with delight dwelt in you, will soon be weary of your house, and say as the evil spirit said, Here is no dwelling for us, let us go into yonder herd of swine, (Matt. 8:31).

But Jonah rose up to flee to Tarshish, etc. Jonah was sent to Nineveh, but he went towards Tarshish. And so it is always with us, we are ever doing that we should not do: for either we do nothing, or that which we are not commanded, or else otherwise than we are commanded. Sometime most rebelliously we do that which we know the Lord straightly forbids; and as Jonah took Tarshish for Nineveh, so we take the devil for an angel, darkness for light, *etc.*

But Jonah rose up, etc. They that should preach at Nineveh are flying to Tarshish; and though he is like a drone, yet does he, even the non-resident, keep his benefice fasting, feasting himself: but will you keep it still? go and preach at Nineveh, as you have been doubly commanded, or for shame leave your privilege and benefice: but they stand staggering, ashamed to keep it, and loathe to leave it; for the sweet morsels of Baal's priests are pleasant to them, that they cannot find in their hearts to leave them as long as they are able to keep them. But no marvel that Jonah fled to Tarshish, when he should go to Nineveh. For this is a stumbling vocation among men, yes, rejected by the children of this world, which always kick against it; so that if you would ask for a painful vocation, this is it; if for a thankless vocation, this is it; if for a contemptible vocation, this is it: for reproving, we are reproved; blessing, we are cursed; preaching peace, we make war; proclaiming liberty, we are imprisoned; do what we can, we are persecuted: and for our work worthy of love, we receive of the most hatred; of few, yes, very few, not any more than a cold affection. Here it has come to pass, that Moses and Jeremiah, being called, excused themselves, (Exod. 3:11; Jer. 1:6); Ezekiel, having received his charge, went in bitterness and indignation of his spirit, and seven days neglected his charge, as Jonah here does his, (Ezek. 3:14-15); Moses, Elijah, and Jeremiah at length complained, (Exod. 5:22; 1 Kings 19:10; Jer. 20:7). And (which to the best men is the greatest grief) it is as easy almost to wash a blackamoor white, as to convert a sinner; because Satan is ever crossing men doing God's will, but specially hindering the course of right preaching: for the Lord was not so earnest to stop the way of Balaam lest he should commit wickedness, as the devil is earnest to stop the way of every *Jonah* lest he fulfill righteousness, that is, cry against Nineveh, longing and duly, that is, wisely and earnestly, laboring to convert Nineveh.

But Jonah rose up to flee to Tarshish from the presence of the Lord. The righteous fall, and now no less than a Prophet, yes, such a Prophet as was the figure of Christ. But who would have thought that such a Prophet should fly from the Lord, yes, and that when he should do Him most service; who counted that no wickedness now, that he ever thought and taught was rebellion, while he was among the wicked? A fearful example, therefore "let him that thinks he stands, take heed lest he fall," (1 Cor. 10:12); for the way is slippery in which we are to walk. When you remember the fall of the Prophet, then first consider that you are much weaker than a Prophet, and therefore the *easier* to be encountered and overthrown, and the *likelier* to have a most grievous fall, except if the Lord mightily would uphold you, seeing such a one cannot stand in the sight of his so mortal enemy, but by him receives so grievous a fall. Secondly, if you see Jonah fly, Moses murmur, David fall to adultery, Solomon to idolatry, and Peter to forswear his Master, you then may learn not to trust to your own strength, for it is weakness, nor to your own wisdom, for it is sinful; but seek help and crave strength at the hand of Almighty God, who gives to all men liberally, and upbraids not, (James 1:5); which does not "break the broken reed, nor quench the smoking flax," (Matt. 12:20), but does rather increase our zeal than diminish it. Thirdly, judge wisely of the fall of Jonah, not rashly condemning him for his fault; for although David joined murder with adultery, yet he repented, and is the dear child of God.

And he found a ship going to Tarshish. Jonah was no sooner arriving in Joppa, but he goes to the haven, or meets with mariners, and presently finds a ship, not going to Nineveh, but to Tarshish. As soon as he set forward to fly from God, Satan straightaways prepared a ship; so that temptation and occasion of sin always goes together. Shall Judas lack money, or Jonah stay for a ship? No. Satan says by the mouth of his ministers, *Here, Judas, take the money, and betray your Master*; and, Jonah, *here is a ship for you, go, haste you away, and fly from the presence of the Lord.* For the devil is always a very serviceable and pleasant devil to such as fly from God; he can find occasion at all times, and means and instruments fit for that purpose. If you will fly from God, the devil will lend you both spurs and a horse, yes, a post horse, that will carry you swiftly and lustily away to all vanity and ungodly lusts. Therefore if any will ask what the devil's occupation is,—it is, to tempt, to entice by all means, to provoke to sin; and then to provide us of the means to practise our purpose, to commit and (as James speaks) to bring forth sin.

And he paid the fare of it. This money was cast into the sea, it did him as little good as if he had utterly lost it: it had been good for him if he had lost it, for it did him much harm. There are many that will spend and waste and they do not care how much on cards and dice, and unlawful games: this money also is cast into the sea, for it does them much more harm than they know of, it does them no good; it were good for them they had not a penny to lose. And so men care not what they pay for vanities and braveries, the most part of which is unprofitable, and rather hurtful than necessary for them, but only for the vain use of the present time, and for some vain respect; this also is cast into the sea, and better should they are if they had it not to lavish, and to their own and many others hurt so to garnish themselves. Men do not care what they pay for their vanity, so it does please their mind for the present, without consideration of the end and use of it: but they will give little or nothing to do good with; so that Lazarus can get nothing, (Luke 16:21), and David can get no meat, (1 Sam. 25:11). Shall I take my bread and my water, and the flesh which I have hilled for my shearers, and give them to one whom I do not know? says churlish Nabal. We can be content to give anything, or do anything, to win the world; but we will give nothing, nor do nothing, thereby to win the kingdom of God.

We have heard Jonah confessing that he received a charge to go to Nineveh, but he arose and fled toward Tarshish, and went to Joppa, and found a ship going to Tarshish, and paid the fare of it, and went down into it: hereafter we shall hear, that being entered the ship, he went to sleep, and slept soundly, and being awakened, he did not confess his sin, but suffered the mariners to devise, to find out for whose cause they were so troubled, and at length also the lots to be cast; never confessing it, until he was forced to it. What did he need to rehearse all this? had it not been enough to have said, that he left his business undone, he was a sinner? No. God would have men to know the stubbornness and disobedience of Jonah, in that this thing was not done on the sudden, but on deliberation, and in no short time, but in some continuance, while he went from Samaria to Joppa, and thence was departed, and had some while sailed; in which space he had leisure enough to have repented, *but did not*. Jonah confessed his sin, that he should not once have listened to Satan's assaults, or reasons of the flesh; and when he had listened, he should not have liked them; and when he had liked them, he should not have consented to obey them; and when he had consented, he should not have put them in practice, he should not have fled toward Joppa; and when he had come to Joppa, he should not have gone to the haven; and when he came to the haven, he should not have paid the fare; and when he had paid the fare, he should not have entered the ship; and when he was entered the ship, he should not have hoisted up the sails, and sailed, and gone to sleep. But this he did, teaching that sin runs on wheels, as it were, down a hill in all post-haste, and never stays until it arrives *even in hell*. For Jonah thought, because he came safe to Joppa, therefore he might go to the haven; and because he came well to the haven, therefore he might pay the fare; and because he paid the fare in peace, therefore he might take shipping; and because he entered the ship in safety, therefore he might hoist up the sails to go; and because he hoisted up the sails without danger, therefore he might go securely to sleep, and safely sail to Tarshish. So sins follow one another like links of a chain, until the tempest of destruction break it in two. So says the forlorn sinner, I have sworn, and God did not punish me, therefore I will steal: I have stolen, and God did not punish me, therefore I will kill: I have killed, and God did not punish me, then why may I not do what I list? I may do this as well as I have done other things heretofore. But if Jonah had considered with himself that God is the Lord, who is all-seeing and almighty, from whom nothing can be concealed, he would never have taken his journey to Joppa; or when he came to Joppa, he would not have paid the fare; or when he had paid the fare, he would not have entered the ship; or when he was gone into the ship, he would not have hoisted the sails, but rather would have leaped out from that ship that would carry him from his God, carry him from his duty; for he forgets himself, thinking the creatures can hide him from the Creator; which is an absurd thing to think, seeing nothing can be hid from Him, (Heb. 4:13). Neither would any, I say, add drunkenness to thirst, or heap sin on sin, or suffer any evil thought to take place in him, if they considered that the just Jehovah beheld them in all their very thoughts. All those that pity Jonah, let them pity themselves: for if we consider our own estate, we have as many and as foul sins in us as there were in Jonah, yes, in Nineveh. Jonah confessed his sin, that we might confess. He confessed it freely, he confessed it fully, that he knew his Master's will, but not only did he not do that, but also took another course quite contrary to that which He commanded; and that not in purpose only, but in *deed* also; not for an hour, *but a long time*;

not in struggling with his weakness, but in a profound ungodly carelessness, or in striving to overmaster his conscience accusing him for his wickedness. And wherefore has he written it, but to admonish us narrowly to look to ourselves, and manfully to fight, that we may stand where he fell; and when we have fallen, as freely and fully to confess it to God always, and to man also when wisdom commands. *Amen.*

THE PUNISHMENT OF JONAH: THE FIRST SERMON

"But the Lord sent out a great wind into the sea, and there was a mighty tempest in the sea, so that the ship was like to be broken. Then the mariners were afraid, and cried every man to his god, and cast forth the wares that were in the ship into the sea, to lighten it of them: but Jonah was gone down into the sides of the ship; and he lay, and was fast asleep. So the shipmaster came to him, and said to him, What meanest thou, O sleeper? arise, and call on your God, if so be that God will think on us, that we perish not."—Jonah 1:4-6

The sin is past, but the punishment is to come; for after disobedience follows wrath, the heavy companion of wickedness: for although she does not love sin, yet she will be always where wickedness is; yes, also full of strength, like a lion which will not be tamed.

He that made the winds commands them, and they obey His voice: the winds and the waters obey Him; but man will not obey Him. He does not say that a wind arose, but says, The Lord sent out a great wind. Therefore we see the cause of this tempest, and so of Jonah's punishment. The just Judge of the whole world may not suffer sin unpunished, therefore he says, *The Lord sent out a great wind.* Then it was not by chance, nor yet by witchcraft; for the mariners (notwithstanding they were infidels) were not so gross as to ascribe it to any such cause; but rather thought it to be sent from some revenging power, being provoked to indignation by some particular person among them, that committed some heinous fact: else why did they cast lots to know him, and find him out that had sinned, and whose sins did procure this tempest to be sent? Though this wind had almost drowned Jonah, yet he said, The Lord sent it; so the Lord sends wind to bring ships to land in safety, (Psa. 107:25-31), and the same Lord sends wind to drown and break and sink other ships. Therefore Job said, when he was bereft of all his substance at once, and left as poor as might be, that the Lord had taken them from him, who had first given all to him; adding also thanksgiving, even for the persecuting hand or God which did so molest him. If some had so much loss by tempest as Job, and such dangers as Jonah, they would surely say with Job, "Blessed be the name of the Lord," (Job 1:21): but more (it is to be feared) would say with Job's wife, "Curse God, and die," (Job 2:9).

And there was a mighty tempest in the sea. First God spoke gently to him, *Arise, go to Nineveh*; then he would not go: but seeing words would not serve, the Lord would take another way, and try whether that could make him obedient to His voice. So the Lord caused a mighty tempest to arise in the sea, like the messengers that were sent to compel folks to come to the banquet, that seeing the commandment could not, the tempest might bear rule: for unless it is an imperious cross, we will not yield; so headstrong is sin. Therefore it is said that God sent out a great wind, so that there was a mighty tempest, that sin might have the foil, and God the victory.

He that sails to Tarshish, or wherever he is forbidden to go, would have as good a wind as he that sails to Nineveh, or whither he is commanded to go; but he that does one thing for another shall receive one thing for another; as Ahab did, who hoped, according to the saying of four hundred false prophets, to go up and prosper; but he went up and perished. As surely as Jonah thought to arrive at Tarshish, so surely the Spaniards thought to arrive in England; but as Jonah's company wondered at this tempest, so at these Spaniards' destruction their fellows at home wondered, yes, were astonished how their invincible power could be destroyed. But God is strong enough for them that kick against Him, and disdained to be crossed of dust and ashes.

And there was a mighty tempest in the sea. The ship went on roundly for a time, the prophet sleeping, the mariners sporting, their sails flaunting, the waters calming, the winds guiding; so merrily sin goes on before the tempest comes. The wind does not blow yet; therefore go on yet a little, and yet a little more; but suddenly the tempest rushes on them before they are aware of it, and tumbles them up and down, and suddenly all is like to be undone. He came to the haven, and paid the fare, and entered the ship, and hoisted up sails, and went on forward: and all to fly from God; but now it appears be fled not from Him, but to Him. Therefore David says, "If I take the wings of the morning, and dwell in the uttermost parts of the sea; even there shall Your hand lead me, and Your right hand shall hold me, therefore whither shall I flee from Your presence?" (Psa. 139:9-10). So that when we think that we fly from God, in running out of one place into another, we do but run from one band to the other; for there is no place where God's hand is not; and wherever a rebellious sinner runs, the hand of God will meet with him to cross him, and hinder his *hoped for* good success, although he securely prophesies never so much good to himself in his journey. What? had he offended the winds or the waters, that they bare him such enmity? The winds and the waters, and all God's creatures are to take God's part against Jonah, or any rebellious sinner: for though God in the beginning gave power to man over all his creatures to rule them; yet when man sins, God gives power and strength to His creatures to rule and bridle man. Therefore he that even now was lord over the waters, now the waters are lord over him. But if Jonah had thought that God would have so brought things to pass, he would not have been so bold in this enterprise. Therefore we may see that sin has no eyes while it is doing. Tush, (says the fool), it is fair weather yet, while he goes to the stocks, (Prov. 7:22).

So that the ship was like to be broken. We have heard of the cause and greatness of this tempest: the effects follow, whereby the greatness of it is the better expressed; first in the ship, then in the mariners.

The ship was like to be broken. The ship was fair and goodly, so strong that it might have encountered with instruments of war, and so sure made that it might have endured great tempest, and made many voyages. Yet now with one tempest, and at one voyage, it was so deformed, so weakened, in such a taking, that it was like to be shivered in pieces; and all because Jonah was in it. Such strife is always between God's wrath and man's disobedience. When God's Word will not turn us, God's winds and other instruments of His wrath must threaten to overturn us.

Then the mariners were afraid, and cried every one to his god, and cast the wares out that were in the ship, to lighten it of them. The effects of this tempest in the mariners were two: first, they were afraid; then used means to appease the tempest, and save themselves.

Then the mariners were afraid. Mariners living in the sea almost as fishes, having the waters as their most necessary element, are commonly men *void* of fear, venturous, and condemners of danger; yet now seeing the tempest so vehement on a sudden, that their goodly and tall ship was tossed almost to a cock-boat, and cracked so that it was like to be torn all to pieces, and thereby were fully persuaded it was no common nor ordinary storm, but a revenging tempest, for some extraordinary cause sent out on them by some great power provoked; now they are afraid, they tremble for fear, (like women that shrink at every stir in the wherry, and like little children, when they are frightened), lest their ship break or leak and so sink, and they lose their goods, their ship, their lives and all. Now these nothing-fearing fellows, these high-stomached men, which *desire danger*, are brought down by danger, fear and quake like a young soldier, which startles at the sound of a gun.

And cried every man to his god, and cast forth their wares into the sea, etc. The means which the mariners use to save themselves are divers: first, they cry to their gods; then when that appeased not the tempest, they cast out their wares.

They prayed. This is then a manifest sign that the heathen acknowledged there is a Divine power seeing and governing the whole world; for they would not have prayed at all, but that they were convinced there was a God who beheld the affairs of men, and could in extreme danger deliver whom

He would. Nature convinced them, the works of God made them to acknowledge it. For in man, though the lamps be wasted since Adam consulted with the devil to be a god, yet there is some little light left, which dwells in darkness, like a spark hid in the ashes, whereby the stately and most glorious frame of the world, with all the wonderful variety of the singular effects of all the excellent creatures in that, considered, man cannot but acknowledge there is a God. Yes, His mighty power the blinded Gentiles saw so expressly in all the creatures, that they imagined it to be impossible for one God to work them all: therefore they thought that there were divers gods, as there were divers seasons, divers nations, divers trades, divers languages, divers and sundry kinds of all things; and so divers nations worshipped divers gods. When the wicked see that all their inventions will not bring their enterprise to pass according to their mind, but they are in extremity, and like to be cast away for want of succor, then they fly to God, being driven by compulsion, as a bear to a stake; and they couch and kneel, and make great shows outwardly of humiliation and piety, all in hope of help from God, and as it were thinking to deceive Him by their hypocrisy.

Everyone to his god. This shows that they were of divers nations; for among the Gentiles every nation had a several god to worship. Chemosh was the god of the Moabites, (1 Kings 11:7), Beelzebub the god of the Ekronites, (2 Kings 1:2), Dagon the god of the Philistines, (1 Sam. 5:2), and the Ephesians worshipped Diana, (Acts 19:35). In our necessity we fly everyone to his god; that is, in the time of necessity everyone does fly for help and ease to that which most feeds his own sickness, or best pleases him, that in which he reposes most confidence, persuading themselves of sufficient relief from that: some run to their coffers, thinking that there it is that is able to procure ease from any troubles; other some turn to their delights and wanton sports, supposing that there is no trouble so great but they will cause them to forget it; some to their glorious attires and costly jewels, imagining they will now as well rejoice their hearts, remedying their grief, as at other times they have delighted others' eyes, pleasing their sight; some to their dainty meats, and some to their soft beds and easy standing, hoping by those to feel relief. In sickness we cry, *Come, physic, help me*; in heaviness we call, *Come, music, cheer me*; in war we sound, *Come, soldiers, succor me*; in quarrels we say, *Come, law, defend me*: evermore leaving the Creator, which is all goodness and powerful in Himself, running to the creatures, which have no goodness nor power save that they receive of Him; neither by their goodness can they do us good, but by His blessings.

And cried every man to his god. They did well in that they prayed, but they prayed not well; for they prayed every man to his god: that is, to feigned gods,—gods in *name*, but not in *nature*; and gods they were that could not help so much as themselves.

Every man to his god. Every of these mariners did now in their extremity call on his god, everyone on that god which he thought most highly of, and whom he had in his prosperity reposed most confidence in. Now while none could help but one, they cried to many; and by this means, while they sought to lay the tempest, they stirred it more; for their prayers being idolatrous, were so wicked, that the Lord had utterly destroyed them, if His mercy had not been wonderful over all His works, (Psa. 145:9). They prayed much like the Papists, which in extremity cry out, some to one saint, some to another, some to saints of this place, others to saints of that place, thinking, as these mariners did, if one will not help, another will.

They cried, etc. They prayed, and their prayers beat the sky, though they could not stop the tempest. They were not, as many of us be when we pray to God, without a sense of their danger, or without great desire to obtain their requests. What an hypocrisy is this that is common among us, to have vehement speeches, and loud cries, and long prayers, without lively affection within!

47

They cried. Here is a distinction of crying to be observed.
The righteous cry, and as well when they are in prosperity as
when they are in calamity, though many nothing so fervently;
but the ungodly then only when the hand of God is on them,
and then also like bears without their prey, always much
doubting, sometimes despairing of help, although they cry for
it. And therefore blessed is he that has the Lord for his God:
and let them know that cry without faith, without confidence
in God, they do but cry in vain. Let not the wavering-minded
man think to receive any good of the Lord, (James 1:6-7) and
cast forth the wares that were in the ship into the sea. Here is
the second means which they used to help themselves. Now
the mariners are content to cast their wares into the sea, in
hope of some furtherance to save their lives thereby; for though
many will venture their lives for riches, yet they rather part
with all their riches than with their lives. But they cast them
out to appease the tempest, or lighten their ship: but it was sin
that procured danger, and being cast away would have saved
all, which being retained, the tempest abating not, the ship is
not the safer, though it is the lighter. "If I regard iniquity in my
heart, (says David), the Lord will not hear me," (Psa. 66:18).
Paul says, Though I cast my life into the fire, if I have no
charity, if I retain malice in my heart, "it profits me nothing," (1
Cor. 13:8). If I do not cast away sin, I cast away all. Some will
give to the poor, and yet use extortion and usury to get money
by: but God says to such, that if they regard wickedness in
their hearts, it profits nothing; though they part with all that
they have, and bestow it on never so good actions, they do but
as the mariners did, cast all away, their desire nothing
satisfied. For though they think themselves beneficial to the
poor thereby, and hope for reward therefore; yet God will
accept of them but as hypocrites: He will respond to none of
their oblations, He *abhors* their very prayers, (Prov. 15:8), until
they have humbled themselves, and reformed their own hearts
before Him from such uncleanness.

They cast forth the wares that were in the ship into the
sea. They would fain have laid the tempest, that so readily lose

their wares, and cast out their very tackling into the sea: but the sea will not be satisfied; the waters must wash the sinner, or there is no safety: *no*, the danger is greater, the sea continually more and more troublesome, vexing them. But Jonah was no sooner cast into the sea, but all was quiet, the winds are calm, and the sea ceases from her raging, (Jonah 1:15). Oh that justice were executed, and he that troubles the ship were in the sea! he that troubles, not he that against all reason is thought to trouble; then should all be safe, yes, peradventure Jonah too.

And they cast forth the wares that were in the ship into the sea. Observe here, that oftentimes many are punished for one man's sin; as all the host of Israel were punished for the sin of Achan, (Josh. 7:12), and here all the mariners and owners of ship or wares for Jonah's sin, *etc.*, to the end that men may learn thereby to admonish one another, when they see they do amiss, with love, and not to say, with Cain, "Am I my brother's keeper?" (Gen. 4:9): for he that is not careful to keep his brother from sin, is not careful to keep himself either from sin or from sorrow. Therefore let us take heed that a wicked one is not found among us unadmonished. I would hope there were not many worse than Jonah among us. Will you know what I think of you? I think you are worse than infidels, Turks, or pagans, that in this wonderful year of wonderful mercies are not thankful, do not believe in God, do not trust in Him, do not glorify His name; but like Pharaoh's sorcerers, who, seeing the great works of God which Moses wrought passing their skill, confessed, saying, "This is the finger of God," (Exod. 8:9): for you confess it is the great work of God, (as you must), but where are the fruits it has brought forth in you? The captain says, *I have done nothing*; the soldier says, *I stirred not*; but the Lord sent out a mighty tempest on them, and after that they escaped our hands, the Lord stretched out His mighty arm against them, and Pharaoh is drowned in the sea; so that he never attained the Land of Promise which he gaped for, and made full account to possess. Further, here we may note that extremity is God's opportunity; for when the wind had almost

49

overturned all, and the waters had almost drowned all, and destruction had almost devoured all, then, and not before, was God's opportunity to set forth His glory.

First, they used prayer to the Divine powers for assistance; then they used such ordinary means as they knew best in such a time, by casting out their wares, to lighten the ship of them; which order is necessary to be used of all Christians in their necessity: first, to seek for aid and assistance at the hands of God; and then to use all such good means to help themselves as God shall enable them to, trusting that of His goodness He will bless their endeavors; or else may they go over all the earth to seek help, and have none; for there is no other way. God indeed is the last refuge, but He is also the first refuge which is to be sought to; for He will have us to acknowledge that man lives not by bread alone, (Matt. 4:4), and, a horse is a vain thing for safety, (Psa. 33:17), and, "Except the Lord keep the city, the watchman wakes but in vain," (Psa. 127:1); no means can help without His blessing. But then He will not have us careless and negligent to use lawful means; for He never or very seldom works without means, when the means may be used by us. Danger then we have seen made them to fear, but fear astonished them not, but gathered their wits together; for they used means with wisdom to save themselves. But when the Lord sends calamity on many of the ungodly, they have so guilty a conscience, that while they feel the great hand of God, they are even distraught of their wits, and made as it were senseless, that they do not know what they do: Yes, when troubles come, it makes them like a headless bee, which buzzes about she knows not whither; or like the swallow, which, by compulsion of the wind, flies backward and forward until it fall into the sea; or like Cain, whose head was fraught with fears, so that he knew not whither to go, doubting to be slain of everyone whom he saw, (Gen. 4:14). But whatsoever befalls the child of God, he has ever matter of consolation, and some moderation of mind to bear it with, expecting a joyful issue of all. Therefore blessed is he that has the Lord for his God.

But Jonah, was gone down into the sides of the ship and he lay, and was *fast asleep*. They prayed to their gods, and their gods were now deaf, while they were so tossed; and Jonah is gone to sleep, when he should have been better occupied. We come here to church to hear the Word, and here we fall asleep; but it would be far better we were away: for we sleep when we should hear, and so sleeping sin, and sleep in sin. Therefore let them now give ear that are asleep, for we have come to Jonah's sleeping, not that we should sleep with him, but by his sleeping to be warned of our security; and we shall see him waked, that we may learn to wake with him. Jonah's fast sleeping is noted, to declare the occasion of the shipmaster's speech to Jonah; but chiefly to note the dead security of Jonah in his sin: forasmuch as though the mariners cried for fear, and cast out their goods, *no*, the very senseless ship seemed to feel the anger of God, and to cry to Jonah by rolling and cracking; yet Jonah was not once moved by it, but lay still fast asleep. So by Jonah's sleeping we see the nature of all the sons of Adam; when they listen to the serpent, they are like changelings, they are cast into a dead sleep; for when they forget God and His Word, and bid conscience *adieu*, they sleep in sin, and that to death, like one sick of the lethargy.

Jonah signifies a dove: Jonah therefore was now indeed Jonah; I mean, like the dove which Noah sent forth of the ark: for as the dove, being gone out of the ark, could find no rest for the sole of her foot, until she returned into the ark again; so when Jonah rose up from the presence of the Lord, he could find no rest for his mind, neither by sea nor land, until he returned again to the Lord. For the cause of Jonah's going down to sleep was, it seems, to ease his mind; for it was disquieted, he felt it grievously troubled, the conscience of his sin tormented it. Therefore now, Oh! that Jonah could sleep until the tempest were past! But it will not be, for the tempest is sent purposely *to wake him*.

And he was fast asleep. See how little Jonah is ashamed of his sin; the entire world smarted for it, and yet he sleeps. As if he should say, Neither the winds blowing, nor the waters roaring, nor the ship reeling, nor the wares casting, nor the mariners crying, with all the stir could move him, waken him from his sleep, or raise him from his sin. Now Jonah might say, I was asleep, and all might have perished for me, if one God had not helped more than all the rest: for Jonah slept, but God waked, and called to the winds and the waters, saying, Toss him, but you shall not drown him; fear him, but you shall not kill him; whip him, and when you have whipt him, send him to Me, that I may send him to Nineveh. Jonah was fast asleep, when the winds over him were blowing, the waters under him tossing, the ship about him reeling, the mariners by him crying, the wares overboard casting: in all the stir Jonah felt nothing, but slept, as if there were no stirring. Yet we go far beyond Jonah in security: for the Lord causes the tempest to blow down houses beside us, the heavens to thunder over us, the earth to quake under us, the water to overflow the land about us, the fire to consume all that we have before us, the air with cold ready to kill us, and all things in an uproar round about against us, thereby always crossing us one way or another; and all to put us in mind of our duty, the neglect whereof is the cause of all these troubles which the Lord does send us: but we sleep more deadly than Jonah in our negligence, void of feeling, because we consider not what we have done, we do not look back on our sin; yet every cross should cause us to examine ourselves thoroughly, and leave no sin unviewed, that we might lively feel our wickedness, and so duly repent it, and soon find release of our miseries. Therefore if we sleep still, and will not be wakened, God will deal more roughly with us than He did with Jonah: for the Lord caused a fish to swallow him, and afterward to cast him up again; but we shall be swallowed of that serpent which never restores again. He should have been their teacher, if he had not been asleep; he should have taught them to pray aright, if he had had any good feeling in him: but all this while we do not read that Jonah once condemned his thoughts, nor so much as once said to himself, Jonah, take heed what you do, you knowest how God may handle you on the waters; though you fly, He can overtake you;

though you hide yourself, He will find you out; though you give yourself to sleep, He shall give you no rest, and awake you to your greater woe. How should we be strong, if a Prophet, and such a Prophet as was the figure of Christ, could not withstand this one temptation, but suffer himself to be led away so far, that when he should run, he lay still, and when he should cry, he held his peace, and when he should zealously bestir himself, he is fast asleep!

In Jonah's sleeping we observe two things. The first is, that when we think ourselves most at rest, then we are in greatest danger. When shipwreck is most likely, then Jonah is asleep; when Herod is vaunting, then he is stricken, (Acts 12:21-23); when Nebuchadnezzar is in his greatest pride, then he is turned-out, (Dan. 4:29-33); when Belshazzar is banqueting, the hand writ his condemnation, (Dan. 5:4-5); when the rich man says to his soul, "Thou have much goods, then his soul is taken from him," (Luke 12:19-20); when the Philistines are sporting, then the roof is falling, (Judg. 16:25-30). So destruction overtakes sinners when they *least* think of it; like a leopard which is taken while he sleeps, or a bird when she sings; therefore suspect your pleasure like a bait.

The second note is the nature of sin, which is here expressed (while it is a-doing) to is not bitter, but sweet; not painful, but pleasant; like a harlot which shows nothing but her bravery and beauty. Adam swallowed the forbidden fruit with pleasure, (Gen. 3:6); Gehazi lied for gold with gladness, (2 Kings 5:24); Noah drank his wine with mirth, (Gen. 9:21); David committed whoredom with delight, (2 Sam, 11:4); so sinners go on merrily, until wrath overtakes them at unawares; like the fool, I will sleep a longer, and fold my hands together a little, yet a little and a little longer, until poverty comes as an armed man, and God's just judgment as the whirlwind, suddenly and irresistibly, (Prov. 24:33-34). Then though you have gotten gold with Gehazi, or honors with Haman, or Naboth's vineyard with Ahab, or all the delights of the world; if you do not have an assurance of your own salvation, if sin is still pleasant, if it is not bitter in your belly, though it is sweet in your mouth, do not deceive yourself, believe God, your hope is but doubting, your strongest confidence but a vain trust.

So the shipmaster came to him, and said to him, *What meanest you, O sleeper? arise, call on your God.* Here Jonah is taken napping: sin has brought him asleep, and now the shipmaster wakens him. The mariners may do him more good than the tempest. Whom sin should waken, peril cannot waken: the winds are not loud enough, nor the waters rough enough, therefore the shipmaster must waken him; else all shall be endangered. If the winds will not waken him, let the waves waken him: if the waves will not waken him, let the mariners waken him: if he will not be wakened, let him perish in his sleep, and die in his sin.

Now mark who is asleep, and who wakens him. Jonah is asleep, and the *mariners* waken him; an Israelite, an infidel. What a thing is this, that he which is the son of Abraham, who is wiser than a thousand mariners, is now wakened and told his duty by a mariner! This is a shame for Jonah, that he which had taught princes, should now be told his duty by mariners. He that long had and should still wake others, needs oftentimes to be wakened by others; and he that should reprove sinners, is often reproved of sinners. And so the Lord sometimes shames His servants, and does vex them with a foolish nation: as He reproved Abraham by Abimelech, (Gen. 20:9), and Balaam by an ass, (Num. 22:28).

Now we might ask Jonah, saying, *Why did you write that you fled from God,* or that when you had most need to pray you did sleep? If you had not so laid open your own shame, you might have been reckoned as one of the best Prophets: therefore why did you do it? Jonah did it to this end,—that in him we may see the reward of disobedience; for, as Paul says, whatsoever is written, "is written for our instruction," (2 Tim. 3:16, 17); and Jonah would never have written it, had it not been for our sakes. If he have done so much for us, which way shall we requite him? That which he would have us to do for him is this,—to be warned by him to suppress all evil motions, not suffering them to take effect, as he did.

What meanest you, O sleeper! Arise! As if they should say, O reckless, altogether careless, quite senseless man! Are you dead, that you do not awake; or benumbed, that you do not feel; or deaf, that you do not hear anything? or do you not care whether you live or die? Have not the winds nor waters raging, nor our loud cries so long thundering, wakened you? Can you sleep in all this stir? Do not our troubles, nor labors, nor losses, nor the common danger, move you? *What meanest thou?* Why do you not come and labor with us in this dangerous time? Is this a time to sleep in, when we are all in peril of our lives? Shall we cry, and you hold your peace? shall we labor, and you rest? shall we cast away all our goods, and you lie sleeping, caring for nothing? This is no time to sleep; it is a time to pray to your God for His assistance, and to use the means that may save our lives: up, arise, help what you can. Jonah hearing this, did not snap like some currish dogs, and bite him that wakened him; neither did he (as in public danger most are likely) sit still, devising with himself to shift for himself, neglecting others; but he arises, he thanked him that waked him.

Many of you come to hear the Word, and here you fall asleep when you have most need to be waking: but I am glad I have now gotten a text to waken you, for now I cannot read my text but I must say, *What meanest you, O sleeper? arise.* But I pray you, have I not wakened you, and yet you sleep again? If you mark not what is said to you, you are asleep, though your eyes are open. But if you were as wise as Jonah, you would not sleep here in the sight of all the people, but would rather get you to sleep in some corner; for Jonah went under the hatches to sleep, and would not sleep in the sight of the mariners. If you were as wise as Jonah, you would thank him that wakened you; no doubt Jonah did. Solomon says, that he which reproves a man afterward shall have more favor than he which flatters, (Prov. 28:23). The Lord Jesus says, "Woe be to that servant, that when his Master comes He shall find sleeping," (Luke 12:45, 46). "Can you not watch one hour?" (Mark 14:37), says He to Peter. Can you not wake while I speak to you? You would all be found in the Church when the Lord comes, but you would not be found sleeping in the Church. You are watched, (though I do not see you below); and none of you can steal a nap, and not be seen; but when your eyes are most shut, and see least, then most eyes are on you: and I can as well stand in the pulpit unseen, as you can sit and sleep there and not be seen. I marvel how you can sleep having so many eyes looking on you, so many clamours in your ears, and God Himself speaking to you. Shall I continue jogging until you are wakened? How long shall I preach afore I can convert the usurer, the extortioner, the drunkard, or the blasphemer, seeing I speak so long, and cannot convert you from your sleeping? What would you do if I read some homilies to you; whereas you cannot wake while I preach to you, and speak against you? If you should see a traitor sleep on the hurdle, or if you should see men sleep with meat in their mouths, would you not marvel? Yet even so do you: while I denounce the great judgments of God against you, and while I am feeding some of you, you fall asleep, and so I preach in vain. There is a country whereof it is said, that it is night with them when it is day with us. I think that country is here: for how many are here which have lost their eyes and their ears since they came here? If all of you were as many of you be, (I mean asleep), the strangers which came here to hear would think that you were all dead, and that I preached your funeral sermon: therefore for shame you should leave off your sleeping. *What meanest you, O sleeper? arise*, sleep no more, and I will waken you no more.

  Arise! and call on your God, if so be that God will think on us, etc. This is another means which they use, Jonah being wakened, to appease the tempest; now that they see they cannot themselves allay the winds, nor assuage the waters, they desire, they exhort Jonah to try what he can do by calling on his God. *Arise, call on your God, etc.* After that the shipmaster had wakened Jonah, he bids him to call on his God; as if he had said, Watch and pray. He speaks like a saint, yet he is an infidel: he did not say, Call on gods; but, Call on *your God*. The shipmaster would not call on his god; but, he says, *Call on your God*, and it may be that your God will help us. If he had said, *Call on our god*, when he said, *Call on your God*, and if he had said, He will help us, when he said, *If so He will help us*; then he had showed some spark of faith. Because he wanted help and comfort, he bids him arise; and because he was fearful, he bids him pray. It may be (he says) He will think on us, that we do not perish. As if he had said, Jonah, we know that you have a God as well as we do, and therefore we say, Call on your God, for now every god is to be tried; therefore if ever you did pray in your life, fall to it now. So Satan leads men a blind way with zeal, in hope of some relief, being in trouble. They called on them for help which were neither willing to assist them, nor able to hear them: and when they perceived by woeful experience that there was no kind of succor to be had that way, they fly to God; and then Satan labors to undermine the confidence and expectation of help, and to place instead of it doubtfulness and infidelity. So Satan will be sure to lose nothing by this bargain any way. Jonah, (they say), call on your God; for if He cannot help us, we are all undone and lost: for we have called on our gods, we have labored hard to amend our state, we have cast away our goods to lighten the ship, but all in vain, for we are no way the better; like the woman which had spent all her substance about medicine, yet all the doctors could not help her until Christ came, (Luke 8:43). So the Papists, while they are well, they pray to every saint and angel for succor against the troublesome times; but in extremity, or at the point of death, none of them can help, so that then they are fain to fly to God, or be destitute: as like idolaters as one fly is like another. They are like the heathen, which worship Juno, Venus, Neptune, Pallas, Jupiter, and the rest: some hold on the one, and some on the other. Some say, *If Jupiter is with me, I do not care for all the petty gods, because I hold him chief*: so another says, *If St. Gabriel is with me, I do not care for the rest*. And some raise great disputations whether this saint or that saint, this angel or that angel, is better; whether our Lady of Bullen or our Lady of

Rome is most sure; whether St. James of Callis, or St. James of Compostella is strongest; and so, like beggars which run from door to door, they run from one saint to another. If one god will not help, another will, think these: as though the gods were contrary one to another, and where the one bids, the other forbids. So some thought that Venus was a friend to the Trojans, and Pallas was not their friend: as fools think of witches, one strikes! another heals.

Call on your God. They bid him call on his God, before they knew Him; but the faithful will not worship a false god, though they may be helped by him. By the example of these mariners, if they thought that their god was the true God, (and why else did they worship him?) we may learn the substance of every temptation that does undermine us, namely, that it will bid us do this evil, that good may come of it: mark, whensoever you are motioned to evil, if it do not promise you some goodness to come of it. But the servants of God ought not to do that which is evil, though they were sure to gain all things that can be wished by so doing; for they have learned their lesson, and how to answer Satan at such times, Why do you tempt me, Satan? for it is written, "Thou must not do evil that good may come," (Rom. 3:8). And this is the armor called *Scriptum est*, wherewith the Lord overcame the devil in the wilderness.

Here also we may see the difference between the faithful and infidels: for, *Call on your God,* says the shipmaster and the rest. The mariners bid Jonah pray to his God in their behalf; but Jonah does not say to the mariners, Pray to your gods in my behalf. And this is also manifest, that a Papist will say to a Protestant, and one that lives well, Pray for me; but a Protestant, if he is anything zealous, will not say to a Papist, *Pray you for me;* knowing that when a Papist does pray, he does it to idols, saints, or angels, or at least without faith, and therefore their prayers are abominable in the sight of God; and therefore they will not bid them do it, because they will not do evil to the intent that good may come of it. Whereby it is manifest that our religion is the true religion, our adversaries themselves being judges. And so Pharaoh said to Moses, "Pray for me," (Exod. 8:8); but Moses said not to Pharaoh, Pray for me. Saul said to Samuel, "Pray you for me," (1 Sam. 15:25); but Samuel said not to Saul, Pray you for me. Therefore the mariners had need of Jonah to pray for them; but Jonah had no need of ignorant idolaters to pray for him. And why should not all pray to Jonah's God, and Pharaoh pray to Moses' God, seeing God has said, "Call on Me in the day of trouble; I will deliver you," (Psa. 50:15). Call on your God (they say) when they cried and saw no help; they distrusted their gods, they thought they would not help; indeed, they could not; therefore they ran to another whom they did not know, hoping to be helped by Him; because they thought some God there was that could do it. So the Papists run from one god to another, from St. Dominick to St. Francis; and why should they run from St. Dominick to St. Francis, but that they mistrusted Dominick? they think he will not hear them, and so they go forward. But in the end the unknown God is thought to be the best. Yet the Lord did not teach Peter one prayer, and John another, but taught them all one prayer to one God only, and to wait still on Him, praying still, with assurance that He will be a help in due time.

If so be that God will think on us, that we perish not. This if, perhaps, and peradventure, cost Adam Paradise. God said to Adam, If you do eat of this tree, "you shall surely die," (Gen. 2:17). Then Eve reported these words this way, "Lest you die," (Gen. 3:3). The Serpent seeing her in such a mind, so careless or forgetful of the commandment, he came and quite changed the matter, and said, you shall not die. So sin creeps on us, while doubtfulness remains in us. So God says, *You shall be saved:* the trembling flesh says, *Peradventure I shall, etc.;* then comes Satan, and he says, you shall die. So that if you will ask what is the faith of sinners, or if you would have it defined; it is this, peradventure, yes, peradventure no. If you will ask me whereon this faith is grounded; it is on ifs and ands: this is the faith of the ungodly, to say, *If so be God will help us;* for they cannot assure themselves of any help. But we may not doubt of our God, and say, It may be, or, If peradventure: for we may freely pray to our God with confidence; and may say, *Our God, and the God of Jonah, will surely help us, and has helped us*. But yet let us know that we have sinned like infidels, and so deserve to be punished like the Egyptians.

If so be that God will, etc. So it comes in like a little leaven which sours the whole lump of dough; and like the moth, which eats the whole wedding-garment: and this same little thief has stolen away all the Papists' faith. Therefore with them wickedness lies sick in bed, and calls to everyone that comes by, Call on God, and pray for me, if so be He will look on me and help me: and so their hope, when the tempest comes, is either an easeless horror, or a comfortless doubting.

If so be that God will think on us. Our God thought on us in the time of trouble: He thought on us, and laid the tempest, when our enemies called on their gods, saints, and angels. But what do we mean, (beloved), when mercy has come, to send for judgment? For though we be saved with Israel, we deserve to be plagued with Pharaoh, because we are not thankful for this, namely, that the Lord has thought on us in our distress: for He travels with mercy, and labors until we be delivered; He goes laded like a bee, but wants a hive. There are two hands, a hand to give, and a hand to receive; God's hand to give, and man's hand to receive. The hand of God is a bountiful and a merciful hand, a hand loaden with liberality, full of gracious gifts; therefore let us stretch forth the good hand to receive it, thankfully to embrace it, cheerfully to entertain it, and carefully to keep it; let us receive it by the hand of faith, the hand of love, and the hand of prayer; for whoso comes with this hand shall be filled, and whoso comes without it shall go empty away, because they have despised the ways of God; *for when I instructed them they would not hear, and what I taught them they would not learn, says the Lord*, (Prov. 1:24-25). Jonah wakened in this way, and so exhorted to call on his God, soon no doubt perceived his danger, and partly with the horror of his sin, partly for fear of the deserved, and so threatened, drowning and other punishments, without question was grievously vexed. For he could not but see that the very dumb creatures were bent against him for his disobedience: the wind blows, as though it would overturn all; the waters roar, as though they would drown all; the ship tumbles, as though she were weary of all; and albeit the mariners had cried, and cast out the wares, as though they would lose all, yet the tempest rages still, their danger is greater than ever.

Wherefore now one might have said to Satan, Satan, you persuade him to fly from his defense for his safety, and made him believe that he should come safe to Tarshish, and them live at liberty and ease, enjoying all temporal benefits at his pleasure; but now you have brought him into the prison of the ship, and it is tossed so by this tempest likely to destroy him, you leave him in the greatest danger, and rejoices that Jonah quakes at the tempest, and has his heart aching for fear of the danger so threatened due to rebellion, yes, seek also to drown him, and that also in hell, howsoever you pretend a desire to preserve him from troubles, and procure him many pleasures, with much security. O most wretched and deceitful liar! he that trusts his enemy, and he that believes you, shall ever be deceived. And now might Jonah say, Beware, by me, for so has the tempter deceived me then has allured me with flattering fantasies, and persuaded me that it was but an easy thing to fly from the presence of the Lord, that sees always all things, and from whom no man, no, nor secret lurking in any man's heart, can be hid, but all are always in His presence. He made me believe that light could be brought out of darkness, that good may come of evil; for he assured me, that if I would set forth towards Tarshish, I should not only shun the presence of the Lord, but should live at ease like one unknown, both for my vocation, and also for my behavior in the execution of it; and so I might creep into a familiarity with these people, and enjoy the benefit of their society. Otherwise, if I went to Nineveh, as the Lord commanded, they would hate and persecute me, yes, and so I should end my life in misery; both because they areing Gentiles, and I a Jew, they cannot abide me, for the one holds the other in contempt; and also because of my message, namely, a prophecy of destruction, grounded on a reproof of their vile and sinful pleasures: which message Satan persuaded me would be so heinously taken, that no death nor torment that they could devise for me would be thought sufficient, and so I should be sure never to escape their hands alive, if I went: as though the eternal and most glorious God, which sent me there, were not able to defend me from all evil when I came there, as well as He did Daniel in the den of lions, and Christ in the wilderness among the savage beasts. And when Satan had so persuaded me, I believed him, and so took my journey to fly from the presence of the Lord, if I could have performed my intention. But the Lord has beheld the stubbornness and disobedience of my heart, and therefore follows me with great displeasure: He has sent out this tempest on the sea, whereby we are like to be overwhelmed; and so near as we are to the water, so near we are to death by all likelihood.

THE PUNISHMENT OF JONAH
THE SECOND SERMON

"And they said everyone to his fellow, Come, and let us cast lots, that we may know for whose cause this evil is on us. So they cast lots, and the lot fell on Jonah."—Jonah 1:7

Now follows another manner in which the mariners use to appease the tempest. They cast lots. But first they consult and consent to cast lots. The tempest was so strong, that they concluded with themselves it was the revenging power of some angry God, for the sin of some notorious wretch that was among them.

Seeing therefore neither they nor Jonah praying had appeased the tempest, but it was rather increased, and no man confessed he was the sinner, they take counsel, and agree to find him out by lots. In which let us observe, first, never a one of them is of David's spirit, who, when he saw the people plagued, said, *Lord, it is I.* Every man excuses himself: for every man would extenuate his own sin and diminish it, and everyone thinks his sin is soothed when he has excused himself. Let Adam be his own judge, and he will say, the woman tempted him to sin; and let the woman be her own judge, and she will say, that serpent persuaded her to it. Let everyone be his own judge, and there will be such posting off of sin, that never a one will be found guilty. There is none that will be so impudent as to say he has no sin at all; yet few that will freely confess they have grievously sinned. Therefore these here say, every man within himself, though he is a sinner, yet he is no great sinner. None are accounted sinners, unless they are openly detected of some notable and heinous crime. If they are dicers, swearers, drunkards, brawlers, pickers, flatterers, profaners of the Sabbath, sleepers at Church, and such like, they are not thought sinners; these actions are counted no sins, but rather recreations: for the multitude count none sinners, unless they are thieves, traitors, open and gross idolaters, and taken with such like capital crimes; no, nor these neither, were it not for fear of the law: as none among the Jews but the publicans were counted sinners; all the rest were good fellows, and just men.

The Papists say, some thoughts, affections, words, and outward actions not agreeing with the law of God, are easily washed away with a little holy water, *etc.* They are not deadly, they deserve not the wrath of God, they are but venial. Did you ever read of these venial sinners in the Scripture? But do you think they have nothing but Scripture? Yes, they have decrees, they have decretals, the ceremonies whereof observed, these venial sins are soon pardoned: and they have a Pope that can forgive any sins. So they lessen sins, so they abate the price of sins, and they can buy out sins with money, or redeem them with masses, and by a little short penance purchase a large and long pardon.

And as the mariners every man thought he was no great sinner; so Jonah thought with himself, *Though I am a great sinner, yet am I not so grievous a sinner as these idolatrous heathens.* Or if he thoroughly condemned himself; yet, unwilling to be known such a rebel, he thought, it may be, and it is most likely, they are many, I but one, peradventure therefore the lot will not fall on me. Like a thief, which, notwithstanding in his own heart he acknowledge himself guilty of that wherewith he is charged, yet will not confess, until the matter be thoroughly sifted, and clearly proved to his own face, in such sort that he cannot for shame (though with shame he confess) deny it. Therefore if God had not sifted out this sinner the better, Jonah would not have been known the man, and the mariners would still have contended who was the lesser sinner: therefore they consult to cast lots.

Let us cast lots. They did not use to cast lots, this was no custom among the mariners; but the tempest was so wonderful that it made them seriously to think of God, and willing to use the means prescribed by God for the ending of doubtful matters, acknowledging that He orders all, and the "lot is the sentence of God," (Prov. 18:18); by the falling of the lot He reveals the truth, (Prov. 16:33). These, like worldlings, never confess God but when He comes in a tempest; they will not see His mercy, until His justice appear; they will not acknowledge God's government, before He bring on them some judgment: like Pharaoh's sorcerers, who confessed not God's majesty while they lived at ease; but when the Lord plagued them, they cried out. "This is the finger of God, (Exod. 8:19).

Let us cast lots, that we may know for whose cause this evil is on us. Why? what are they the better when they know him? What would they do with him on whom the lot should fall? Surely they supposing, or rather clearly seeing, this tempest to be sent from some wrathful power, and that for some one man's sin among them, they determined, having found him, to sacrifice him to the God that was so offended by him. God turns evil into good; but the devil turns good into evil. The Gentiles had a custom in the time of the common plague, to sacrifice one for the rest. This custom they took by imitation of the Jews in offering beasts, and of Abraham in offering his son; the devil, that father of lies and schoolmaster of all mischief, teaching them. So the devil took advantage to do evil by the service of God, in moving the Gentiles to work abomination by offering men, imitating the Jews' commanded sacrifices. But if they had rightly known the true God, they would have taken their sins by the throat, and have sacrificed them.

Come let us cast lots. The mariners were not so wise to prevent the tempest before it came, as they are diligent to allay the tempest when it may not be laid. We, once overtaken with God's just judgments, are very careful always to use all means to be rid of them; but who keeps a watch of his own ways, and diligently labors to keep himself free from that which necessarily draws on itself God's judgment? who purges himself of his sins, lest he is sick? who lets or fetches out his corrupt blood of pride, lust, covetousness, lest he is sore? who keeps a good diet, and makes his choice of holy exercises, godly companions, religious conferences, *etc.*? But we know, he is not safe that is sound, neither he sound that is intemperate.

So they cast lots. Whether it is lawful to cast lots it is not evident by this example, because they were Gentiles, and therefore no precedent for us; but so far may we use them as the Word does lead us, and no further. There are two goats brought to Aaron, that he might cast lots to see which goat should be killed, and which should not, (Lev. 6:8). These goats signify Christ: for as He died, He lived again; and as He was buried, He rose again. Again, the land of Canaan parted by lots, to see what part each tribe should inhabit, (Josh. 14:2). Again: that thief Achan is found out by lots, first by his tribe, then by his family, and lastly, by his particular person, (Josh, 7). Again: it is said that Saul was chosen king by lots; and lest any should have said, that it was his good luck, his good lot or chance, to be king, therefore the Lord appointed that he should be anointed before he was chosen by lots, (1 Sam. 10:2). Again: Matthias is chosen by lots to the apostleship instead of Judas, (Acts 1:26). So that it is lawful in some cases to cast lots, so that they do attribute nothing to them, and acknowledge that the lot is cast into the lap, but the whole disposing of it is of the Lord, (Prov. 16:33): for they must not say that it is their chance, fortune, or good luck; for so they make an idol of it, and rob God of the honor due to Him. For it was not Saul's fortune to be king, but God's mercy: it was not Achan's chance to be caught, but God's judgment. Lots may be used to prevent strife, when all other means have been used; and sometimes before all other means, when in wisdom it is thought the best means. Brethren often, and godly men at first, divided their inheritance by lots; as the children of Israel divided the land of Canaan. Therefore in the church of Geneva there is an order, that in the time of plague there should be a house set apart for the sick to lodge in; and lest they should be uncomforted, they choose out a minister by lots to do it.

So they cast lots. Now we are come to put up ourselves to the court of law, to see if they will do anything for God, for conscience, or for love; namely, that they would end men's suits quickly, and let the poor clients have equity. Some say that lawyers be good until they are counsellors; like lions, which will be gentle until their talons grow. Is not offended, but amend, for malice speaks not. I am persuaded that if the lots were cast to see who troubles the ship, it would fall on the lawyers. Is not offended, but amend, for malice speaks not, A poor client comes forth, accusing one, and going home accuses a hundred; for so few seek to further him, and so many seek to hinder him, that all his gain is but labor and loss. For a small matter many will come to law, to strive for that which with reason might easily be attained without such contention; and others seek to enrich themselves with contending for a small matter with their neighbors, yet in the end lose that they nothing, and that they had beside; and so they contend and strive about a thing commonly, until the lawyer has gained more by them than the thing which is in controversy is worth. These are like the mouse and the frog, which strove so long about marsh ground, that at length the kite came and took them both from it. Others will come up to law about a small matter, and in it so entangle themselves, that they cannot rid their hands of it until it have almost undone them; like a silly sheep that is hunting a fly, which runs from bush to bush, and every bush catches a lock of him, so that the poor sheep is threadbare ere he has done, and has not a fleece left him to cover himself with. So he runs from court to court, to sue, to complain, to plead until he have spent his cloak and his coat: were it not better to have cast lots for the coat at first? For the law is like a butler's box; play still on, until all come to the candlestick. Therefore it is lawful, to end any controversy in a hard matter, to use this means.

Now whether it is lawful to cast dice: If lots may not be used (as Solomon's words, Prov. 18:18, The lot causes contention to cease, compared with Heb. 6:16, prove) but in hard matters and weighty causes, when the thing is doubtful, and all good means are tried before to avoid strife; that question is decided which none but voluptuous men make question of, namely, whether dice-play be a meet exercise for a Christian soul. Solomon says, "The lot causes contention to cease," (Prov. 18:18); therefore lots are to end strife: but these lots make strife; for before you take the dice, you know your own, and no man strives to take it from you but when you casts the dice, you do (as it were) ask whether your own be your own, and makes a strife of no strife. Are you not worthy to lose the gifts of God, which ventures to lose them when you need not? Do you not deserve to forego your own, which are so greedy of another's, that you would have his living for nothing but for turning of a die? Esau did not sell his birthright so lightly, but he had somewhat for it which refreshed his hunger; but God has given you a living, and you spend it for nothing. The mariners did cast lots to find out the sinner; they did not cast dice to see who should win, as dicers do: for to whom the lot falls, he takes all, which deserves to lose all as well as the other, and has no right to it by any law. For God has not allowed one man to take another's goods for the tripping of a die; but either they must be merited, or they must be given, or they must be bought; or else it is unlawful, ungodly, unconscionable, to take them. Besides the brawls, the cozenages, the oaths annexed to this game, which would not agree with it, unless it had been a meet companion for them. you take another man's goods for nothing, whereas God has appointed you to get your living with the sweat of your brows; for you take away that which others sweat for: and whereas you should live by working, you seeks to live by playing, like as the ape, which lives by toying. Does any dicer think he does well? Tell me, what are you thinking? for every sinner condemns in his prayer to God that which he excuses before men. If they which are gamesters repent it, how can they which are gamesters defend it? you should do nothing but that you would have God find you doing, if He should come to judgment. Would you have Him take you at dice? I am sure you would not have God see you so vainly occupied. Neither can you think that Christ, or His Prophets, or Apostles, or Evangelists, were dicers; for no such lots are named in the Holy Scripture: and yet the Lord's day is most profaned with this exercise,—cards and dice, as though they kept all their vanities to celebrate holy days. What have you to allege for dice, now evidence is given up against them? Have you any patron to speak for them, but your vain pleasure and your covetousness, which are condemned already, and therefore have no voice by law? Take away these, and take away dice. The patron condemns the clients, when one vice condemns another. If the exercise were lawful, such patrons as pleasure and covetousness would not speak for it. Take your pleasure therefore in that which is good, and the angels will rejoice with you. If this were good, God would prosper them better that use it: but neither winners nor losers are gainers. I do not know how, but there is not so much won as lost, as though the devil did part stakes with them, and draw away with a black hand when no man sees; for the winner says, he has not won half so much as the loser has lost. One would think that one of them should flow, when so many ebb: there is never an ebb without a flowing, never one loses but another wins, but at dice. What a cursed thing is this, that turns no man to good, which robs others, and beggars themselves! The school of deceit, the shop of oaths, and the field of vanities! you do not only hazard your money in this game, but ventures your salvation, and casts dice with the devil who shall have your soul. For everything that comes well to man he gives thanks; but for that which comes by dice, he is ashamed to give thanks; which shows, that in conscience that gain is evil gotten, and that he sought it without God. Can this be good, when worst men use it most? If it were good, the evil would like worse of it than the good: but the more a man savors of any goodness, the more he begins to abhor it, and his conscience does accuse him for it, as for sin. They which doubt whether God does allow it, need but look how He does prosper them that use it: but they trust not in God, (the terms of their occupation descry), for they call all their cast-chances, as though they relied not on God, but on chance. Therefore if dice make strife without cause; if they take away others good for nothing; if we may not live by playing; if they which have been dicers repent it among their sins; if the holy men never used this recreation, but the worst most delight in it; if you would not have God see you when you

69

plays at dice, nor take you at it when He comes to judgment; if nothing but pleasure and covetousness speak for them; if they do not prosper which take pleasure in it; if they trust not on God, but rely on chance; if you do not only venture your money, but hazard your soul; then the best cast at dice is, to cast them *quite away*.

And the lot fell on Jonah. The lot fell on Jonah, not because he was the greatest sinner of them all, for so is the opinion of the common people, to censure them worst whom they see most afflicted, (Luke 13:2, *etc.*). If anyone be seen to bear his cross, then many will say, *This is a wicked man*; and so think well of themselves, supposing that God is not bent against them to punish them as well, but because Jonah should feel the hand of the Lord both punishing and preserving him, and be reformed. For God corrects all as He did His Son, to learn them obedience, (Heb. 5:8). But if judgment begin at the house of God, what shall become of the ungodly? (1 Peter 4:17-18).

And the lot fell on Jonah. Now when the sinner that troubled the ship is taken, Jonah can hide himself no longer. Now he might also fear to be sacrificed by the mariners presently: for the mariners, partly for the pain they had endured, partly for the loss they had sustained, partly for the danger in which they remained, were no doubt as the she-wolves robbed of their whelps, out of measure furious, and fully bent to sacrifice him on whom the lot fell, to appease the wrathful God. But God stayed and restrained the rage of the mariners, and made them afterward willingly to abide the tempest a while, and put themselves to more pain to save him, endeavoring by rowing to recover land: for having heard of the true God, and, though they lost their goods, having found who is all good, Shall we (they say) destroy him that has saved us? Shall we give him up to death unnecessarily, that has brought us to life, and assured us to reign with God in all glory everlasting? Surely the thankless are graceless; especially they that love not, and show not forth the labor of love for their gracious guide to God. But therefore we may see that the hearts of men are in the hands of God, and "He turns them which way He will," (Prov. 21:1); "he fashions their hearts alike," (Psa. 33:15); Yes, even kings' hearts as rivers of water He turns to water and makes fruitful His vine, to pity and to persecute, to honor and to shame, to love and hate His people, to deliver their power to the beast, (Rev. 17:13), and again to eat the whore's flesh, and to burn her with fire, (Rev. 17:16). Therefore let us never fear to perform our duties whatsoever, to whomsoever: for He forms the hearts of all, who has promised to honor them that honor Him, but to make them contemptible that do despise Him, (1 Sam. 2:30). Neither let us put "confidence in man, nor in princes," (Psa. 146:3); for their hearts are rivers of waters of themselves, fleeting easily, as they are led following. But especially let us not forget chiefly to make prayers, supplications, intercessions, and to give thanks, for all those on the godliness or profaneness of whose hearts the flourishing or defacing of the Gospel of Christ Jesus and the chosen of God does most depend, (1 Tim. 2:1).

And the lot fell on Jonah. Now Jonah could not deny he was that sinner, unless he would accuse God of unrighteous judgment; for the lot is cast into the lap; but the whole disposing of it is of the Lord. Now therefore he must needs confess it. The winds thundering, the waves tumbling, the ship cracking, the mariners quaking, on their gods crying, their wares forth casting, Jonah's prayers requesting, to cast lots consulting, Jonah kept himself close; he would not be thought that sinner. The wind said, I will overturn you: the water said, I will drown you: the ship said, I cannot hold you: the mariners said, We cannot help you: his prayers said, We cannot profit you: his conscience within bleeding, and God at the door of his heart knocking, and the lots now ready for casting, said threateningly, For you the tempest has come, you fugitive! and we will discover you. Yet Jonah conceals his sin; so much did he abhor the shame of men, of strange men, a few men, frail men, or the fear of the fury of the flesh. Therefore after the winds had roared, the waves raged, the ship reeled, the mariners cried, and the lot, his conscience, and God Himself

71

threatened him; the lot also condemned him, and the fear of being sacrificed by sinners to Satan terrified him, so that he forthwith repented thoroughly, he declared it openly, and confessed his sin freely. Such a stir has God before He can come by His own: He must cross us, set Himself and all His creatures against us, strain our bodies, or leave our souls, and constrain us to it, before we will return from our wicked ways and thoroughly humble ourselves to yield Him due obedience. Oh the goodness of the great God! Oh long-sufferance and bountifulness unspeakable, which not only leads, but also in the chains of love draws us to true repentance!

It was God's great goodness to Jonah, that the mariners did not sacrifice him; it is greater that he truly repented; that God *continued him in his calling*, (whose flying from God deserved flying to Satan), and blessed his, not so much solemn preaching, as sudden confession, and short denunciation of vengeance; Yes, made it so powerful, that it converted idolatrous heathens, most hardened idolaters; first mariners, then Ninevites.

For what a blessing felt Jonah, God vouchsafing him of this honor, to offer them a lively, holy, and acceptable sacrifice to God, by whom he presently before greatly feared to have been offered a dead, unholy, and so a delightful, sacrifice to Satan! This fear banished, and that joy possessing him, what a mercy of the Almighty did Jonah think it! But before he converted the Ninevites, he was more to be humbled, fuller to be strengthened, better every way to be prepared. Therefore God would have the sea to wash him, the great fish to fast him, and yet miraculously safe to preserve him, that, being purified, he might pray fervently; and being delivered, find power, comfort, and courage abundantly. Therefore when by lot being taken, and by his own confession found the man that procured the tempest, the mariners, in love and compassion of him, had essayed by rowing to get to land, but could not, the sea raging more and more, and Jonah himself professed he knew the tempest was sent for his cause, and would be laid, he being cast into the sea; Jonah at length was cast out of the ship into the swelling surge of the tempestuous sea. What hope of life then left? is there any? To swallow up all, soon after he is swallowed whole of a great fish. Here let us mark, that after the tempest had terrified Jonah, the mariners reproved him; when they had reproved him, his conscience pricked him; when his conscience had pricked him, the consulting to cast lots grieved him; after grief for consulting, their concluding to cast lots vexed him; vexed at the conclusion, the lot condemns him; the lot having condemned him, in what an agony think we was Jonah? partly, that he should be held that notorious wretch that had brought this woe; partly, lest they in their raging grief, for their great trouble of body, loss of goods, and danger of life, should forthwith kill him for a sacrifice, to appease the unknown angry God! But after this agony the terror of drowning followed, and after that the horror of that huge fish; first, lest it tear him in pieces; then, lest it melt him; afterward, lest it poison him: lastly, three days and three nights the comfortless horror of darkness and noisome stink in the fish's belly tormented him!

First then see, the winds could not further him, the waters could not bear him, the ship could not hold him, the mariners could not help him; and, being cast out, lest all for him be cast away, the great fish would not spare him, the stench would ill feed him, the darkness would less glad him, and light might not visit him. Now see then what Jonah got by his journey: notwithstanding all the promises of which Satan assured him, and all the furtherances which the serpent procured him, he lost his labor, lost his money, lost his joy, lost his credit, lost his quiet, and saw no hope but to lose his life too, finding plentifully and bitterly feeling dreadful fears. He trusted to the winds, the winds could not save him: he trusted to the ship, the ship could not keep him: he trusted to the mariners, the mariners could not help him; he trusted to the lot, the lot would not spare him: he trusted to the waters, the waters could not bear him: neither would the great fish forbear him; neither did any *thing* make show of likelihood to save him. Therefore we may see in Jonah what it profits a man to fly from

God, forsaking his calling, and so practicing the evil motions of Satan instead of the known will of God. Assuredly, if we follow his flatteries, as Jonah did, we shall have, as he had, accusing consciences, fearful hearts, and the wrath of God on our heads: for he has nothing to give us, although he promise and make us believe he has kingdoms. Yet indeed, he has horror of mind for all that obey him, and hell for the reward of his, which will make all their hearts ache which receive it.

See, secondly, in this punishment of Jonah the justice of God. The bee, when she has once stung, loses her sting, so that she can sting no more: so does not God's justice punishing sin; for it retains power, it has store of stings to vex still. When one judgment is executed, He ever has others enough ready, either of the same kind in another degree more sharp, or of another sort: for all the creatures, with their several powers, are God's darts to strike us when He commands. Therefore if we are sick, sickness is not dead with us: if we be poor, poverty ends not: if we are in danger, danger is not therefore put down forever after: and if we be vexed, vexation has not therefore lost his sting. His dart, His weapons also are as sharp now as they were at first; and sharper too, because we are more sinful: for according to the sickness is the medicine; and wounds more dangerous require more *dolorous plaisters*. And if you are disobedient, then He will lead you through them all, until He has humbled you, and made you to glorify Him with obedience, or utterly destroyed you, (Lev. 26:16, *etc.*).

Thirdly, let us not forget neither lightly think of this, that God knows how to punish for sin, yes, most severely to correct His children, though repenting. If our Prophet Jonah here may not keep you some good while in a due meditation of it, let that man after God's own heart, the sweet Prophet of Israel, come to your mind, and in him see whether God pampers all his friends, or does not something sharply, if not bitterly, handle them, if they settle themselves in their dregs, or securely serve the Lord, (2 Sam. 12 and 18).

Lastly, yet consider *God is rich in mercy*, and full of compassion; loathe to punish, unless too far provoked; content to shake His rod over us, to make us fear only, and keep us free from feeling His strokes, if that may have His due work in us, that is, recall, reform, and confirm us. For as the winds could not overthrow Jonah, nor the waters drown him; so neither could the great fish consume, poison, or annoy him, or aught but fear him, though it had swallowed him: for Jonah remembering God, God showed He forgot not Jonah. Therefore when and where Jonah thought verily and speedily to have perished, then and there God caused him to be three days and as many nights most safely preserved. O power omnipotent! O goodness all-sufficient, in all things, at all times! God then as well knows to deliver His out of all distress in due time, as to reserve the wicked to the Day of Judgment to be punished. And in what danger shall we despair? in what extremities ought not we to hope in our most mighty Savior, remembering Jonah in the great fish's belly, (Jonah 2:10), Jeremiah in the mire of the deep dungeon, (Jer. 38:13), Daniel among the fierce lions, (Dan. 6:23), his three companions in the hot burning furnace, (Dan. 3:26), no, 600,000 men of war, and three times as many more, men and women, young and old, in the wilderness, lacking now drink, (Exod. 17:6), then meat, (Exod. 16:13); and all these delivered out of all danger, these last miraculously satisfied with drink out of the rock, and with meat abundantly from heaven?

Though Jonah be cast into the troublous sea, and swallowed of a huge fish, yet he must preach at Nineveh: though Moses flies out of Egypt, yet he must be the leader of God's people after, (Exod. 3:10): Joseph is in prison, but he must be the lord of Egypt, and preserve the Church alive, (Gen. 45:11). Who would have thought that Saul should become Paul, (1 Cor. 15:10), or forswearing Peter a faithful preacher? (Mark 14:71). Suspend then your judgment, and wonder at God's works, whether of mercy or justice: and do not think the worse of a man, though he were cast out of the sea, as Jonah, (Jonah 2:10); or basely brought up, as Amos, (Amos 1:1); for the deliverer of Israel was brought out of the flags, (Exod. 2:3); and the converter of Nineveh out of a great fish, (Jonah 2:10); and the salvation of the whole world out of a *stall*, (Luke 2:16).

And the lot fell on Jonah. The lot fell on Jonah, that he might be cast out of the ship: that as the ship was almost broken, but not altogether; so Jonah might be almost drowned, but not altogether; almost consumed, almost poisoned in the belly of the great fish, but not altogether: that being in the double deep duly humbled, and as gold in a furnace fined and fitted for God's works, he might thence in a miraculous manner come forth, like Lazarus in his winding-sheet, that he might glorify God once again, and courageously cry against Nineveh.

And the lot fell on Jonah. The lot fallen on Jonah, the justice of God (both manifesting the truth incorruptly, and chastising His disobedient servant severely) appeared out with all singular mercy shined; and the mariners' minds were mollified, in that they did not sacrifice him to Satan: but much more was God's mercy, that he by that means truly repented; insomuch that the old idolatrous mariners presently by him were converted; and he, cast into the sea, was not drowned, swallowed of the great fish, and three days continuing in it and did not perish, but miraculously was preserved, and most graciously cast on land safe; and, lastly, crying against Nineveh, that sinful city, had his preaching be mightily prevailing, that he wonderfully humbled them all. This mercy was marvelous, this goodness of God to Jonah most glorious: for the Ninevites hearing, *Yet forty days, and Nineveh shall be overthrown*, first, as the mariners had before done, believed the Word of God, though they had never heard it before. If we heard the Word of God preached, as the mariners and Ninevites did, with trembling hearts in the sense of God's majesty, it would not be but we should feel the power of it lively, and filled with all joy in believing speedily; but ineffectual and fruitless is preaching, because there is nothing almost but irreverent and senseless hearing. And why should God teach the heedless to learn? Why should He give pearls to dunghill cocks, *no*, to very swine? But they believed the Word as soon as they heard it, though they never heard it before. What does that argue? Surely it shows, that the foolish and simple are more diligent and ready, both to hear and receive the Word of God, than those that are wise in their own conceit, or also in the view of the world. What does Christ say? The poor receive the Gospel, (Matt. 11:5). What does Paul say? Not many rich, not many wise, (1 Cor. 1:26). For though we have knowledge, if our knowledge be like the Pharisees', that is, in show of sincerity only, in counterfeit holiness, and hollow-hearted friendship through hypocrisy, it had been better for us that we had been ignorant, for it will but leave us the more inexcusable; it will be found insufficient to save us, but sufficient the more fearfully to condemn us, because we know our Master's will, and do it not, (Luke 12:47, 48). Therefore as Peter said to Simon Magus, "Your money perish with you," (Acts 8:20): so will the Lord say to such, *Your knowledge perish with you, seeing it is fruitless.*

But when Nineveh had believed God, what did they do secondly? They speedily, they notably *repented*; they proclaimed a fast, they put on sackcloth, they humbled themselves before the Lord, they earnestly besought Him to turn away His wrath from this woeful city. Jonah preached at Nineveh, "crying against it," (Jonah 3:4); it seems to have humbled them, and that without a miracle, (without which scant any doctrine is of credit among the Gentiles): for not only within forty, but within four days, much within forty days, he converted Nineveh, ruffling Nineveh, old and idolatrous Nineveh; long before forty days be ended, the seed is sown, grown, increased mightily, and full ripe, in a soil in reason most barren. Sow therefore, you seedsmen, where you are set. If you sow cheerfully, you shall reap plenteously in due time: *faint not.* Do not say, *I have a stony, or a starved, or a thorny ground*: Nineveh repents in sackcloth.

In which willing submission of theirs, and speedy lively repentance at the words of the Prophet, (after he had been three days and three nights in the great fish's belly), the calling of the Gentiles by Christ (after He had been three days and three nights in the bowels of the earth) might well be signified:

for they no less willingly than the Ninevites submitted themselves to the Gospel preached; no less speedily, and peradventure more truly, repented. For though they now so wonderfully humbled themselves, not the fearful multitude only, but the richest and greatest, the nobles and king also, and so all escaped now, (Jonah 3:5-6): yet soon after they returned to their vomit, and never ceased to add sin to sin, until they were by open wars miserably weakened, and at length, fulfilling the prophecy of Nahum, utterly consumed, (Nah. 3). Therefore, first, for the comfort of the godly, since Ahab humbled himself before the Lord; Ahab, I say, that had done exceedingly abominable in following idols, and sold himself to work wickedness in the sight of the Lord, submitted himself under the hand of God, fasting in sackcloth, though he did all this in hypocrisy, and had not the evil threatened brought on him in his days, (1 Kings 21:25-29), seeing Rehoboam and the princes of Israel, who had forsaken the Lord, and the whole tribe of Judah, which wrought wickedness in the sight of the Lord, and provoked Him more with their sins than all that their fathers had done, (1 Kings 14:21-22), humbling themselves before the Lord, and confessing Him just, had not the wrath of the Lord poured on them by Shishak king of Egypt, were not destroyed, but shortly delivered, yes, also things prospered in Judah, though the Lord had threatened to leave them in the hands of Shishak, albeit they truly repented not, (2 Chron. 12). Lastly, forasmuch as Nineveh, that bloody city, full of lies and robbery, the beautiful harlot, with multitude of fornications, that mistress of witchcrafts, which sold the people through her whoredoms, and the nations through her witchcraft, (Nah. 3:1, 4), humbling themselves with fasting, and putting on of sackcloth, the Lord repented of the evil He had threatened them, and did not do it, (Jonah 3:10). How assured may we be, that whatsoever judgment the Lord threatens us, and howsoever He threatens it, it shall not light on us, when we unfeignedly humble ourselves in true fasting, turning from our evil ways, and from the heart vowing to serve God in all holiness! For this is the clear promise of the faithful God: If I shut up heaven, that there is no rain; or if I command the locust to devour the land; or if I send pestilence among My people, "if My people, called by My name, humble themselves, and pray, and seek My presence, and turn from their wicked ways; then will I hear in heaven, and forgive their sins, and heal their land," (2 Chron. 7:13-14). Again, as generally most plainly says just Jehovah, "I will speak suddenly against a nation, or against a kingdom, saying, I will pluck it up, and root it out, and destroy it: if this nation against which I have pronounced turn from their wickedness, I will repent of the plague that I thought to bring on them," (Jer. 18:7-8). Let us then, (O beloved of the Lord), whosoever love the Lord Jesus, be careful to fulfill the condition; and then be confident, not doubting of the performance of the promise, by so much the more, by how much the fewer we be, and by how much the longer and clearer the Lord has threatened most terrible judgments.

Now for the terror of the ungodly, as many of them as repent only when God's hand is on them, and then humble themselves outwardly only, and that but only when the fierceness of His wrath appears, or else after they have escaped the feared judgment fall to their wickedness which they are accustomed again; let them be sure, the strong and just God, that consumed Nineveh slid back, will overtake them also in wrath, and forever turn them over to ceaseless woe. For the greatness, the beauty, the strength and riches of Nineveh could not withstand the hand of God, or keep it from destruction, but rather furthered and hastened it. For with the more excellent ornaments that it was adorned by the Lord, the more heinous and grievous in His sight was the abuse of them. Therefore the hugeness or the strength of this or any other city cannot save it from the judgment of God, being sinful in His sight. Great Sodom is destroyed, great Jericho is destroyed, great Nineveh is destroyed, great Jerusalem is destroyed; and great Rome, the room of all unclean spirits, stays for her destruction, like a whore that stays for her punishment until she be delivered: and these were and shall be punished for unthankfulness and contempt of the Word of God. Yet

Nineveh, Jericho, Sodom, nor Rome, have had half the preaching that we have had; yet we are unthankful too: then what have we to look for? But when Sodom was burned, Zoar stood safe: when Jerusalem was destroyed, Bethlehem stood still. So the Lord always provides for His people, though He never makes so great a slaughter and destruction among His enemies: for the Lord, because of His covenant, always provides for His chosen, although they are only a remnant, like the gleaning after harvest, or like a cluster of grapes on the top of the vine after the vintage, and though there are never so great calamity or trouble: as we see in the Book of Genesis, when there was a great time of dearth and scarcity to come on the land where Jacob was, the Lord had sent Joseph to provide for his father Jacob, lest he should want bread, he or any of his sons and folks, and so ordered the matter that Joseph was treasurer over all the com in Egypt. And so among the Turks and Spaniards and infidels, the Lord will find means to do them good which unfeignedly love Him; and in the dungeon, in prison, and in bonds, yes, and in death, the godly shall find God.

THE TRUMPET OF THE SOUL
SOUNDING TO JUDGMENT

"Rejoice, O young man, in your youth; and let your heart cheer you in the days of your youth, and walk in the ways of your own heart, and in the sight of your eyes: but know you, that for all these things God will bring you into judgment."—Eccl. 11:9

When I should have preached under the cross, I thought about what text to take in hand, to please all, and to keep myself out of danger; and in thinking, I could not find any text in the Scripture that did not reprove sin unless it were in the Apocrypha, which is not of the Scripture. This text bids them that are voluptuous, be voluptuous still; let them that are vain-glorious, be vain-glorious still; let them that are covetous, be covetous still; let them that are drunkards, be drunkards still; let them that are swearers, be swearers still; let them that are wantons, be wantons still; let them that are careless prelates, be careless still; let them that are usurers, be usurers still; but (says Solomon) *Remember your end*, that you shall be called to judgment at the last for all together. This is the counsel of Solomon, the wisest man then living says. What a counsel is this for a wise man, such a one as was Solomon!

In the beginning of his book, he says, "All is vanity," and in the end he says, *Fear God, and keep His commandments*; in the twelfth chapter he says, *Remember your Creator in the days of your youth*; but here he says, *Rejoice, O young man, in your youth*. Here he speaks like an *epicure*, which says, *Eat, drink, and be merry*; here he counsels, and here he mocks; yet after the manner of scoffers, although they deserved it in showing their foolishness, as in the first of the Proverbs, *He laughed at the wicked in derision*; and as in the second Psalm, *God seeing us follow our own ways*. For when He presses us to pray, we play; and when He presses us to run, we stand still; and when He presses us to fast, we feast, and send for vanities to make us have fun; then *He laughs at our destruction*. Therefore when Solomon gives a sharp reproof, and makes you ashamed in one word, he scoffingly bids you do it again, like a schoolmaster which beats his scholar for playing the truant, he bids him play the truant again. Oh this is the most bitter reproof of all! But if any libertine should misconstrue Solomon, and say, that he presses us to be merry and make much of ourselves, therefore he shuts us up with a watchword, and sets a bridle before his lips, and reproves it, as he speaks it, before he goes any further, and says, *But you know, that for all these things God will bring you into judgment*. But if we will understand his meaning, he means when he says, *Rejoice, O young man; Repent, O young man, in your youth*; and when he says. *Let your heart cheer you; let your sins grieve you*; for he means otherwise than he speaks: he speaks like Micaiah in the Book of Kings, the second chapter, *Go up and prosper*; or like as Ezekiel, *Go up and serve other gods*; or as St. John speaks in the Revelation, *He that is unjust let him be unjust still*. But if there is no judgment day, that would be a merry world; therefore, says Solomon, when you are in your pleasures, flaunting in the fields, and in your brave ruffs, and among your lovers, with your smiling looks, your wanton talk, and merry jests, with your pleasant games, and lofty looks, know you that for *all these things* you shall come to judgment.

While the thief steals, the hemp grows, and the hook is covered within the bait; we sit down to eat, and rise up to play, and from play to sleep, and a hundred years is counted little enough to sin in; but how many sins you have set on the score, so many kinds of punishment shall be provided for you. How many years of pleasure you have taken, so many years of pain; how many drams of delight, so many pounds of *dolour*. When iniquity has played her part, vengeance leaps on the stage,— the comedy is short, but the tragedy is longer; the black guard shall attend on you, you shall eat at the table of sorrow, and the crown of death shall be on your heads, many glistering faces looking on you, and this is the fear of sinners; when the devil has enticed them to sin, he persuades like the old Prophet in the Book of Kings, who, when he had enticed the young Prophet contrary to the commandment of God, to turn home with him and to eat and drink, he cursed him for his labor, because he disobeyed the commandment of the Lord, and so as a lion devoured him by the way. The foolish virgins think that their oil will never be spent; so Dinah straggled abroad, while she was deflowered. What a thing is this to say, *Rejoice*, and then *Repent*! what a blank to say, *Take your pleasure*, and then you *shall come to judgment*! It is as if he should say, *Steal and be hanged, steal and you dare*; strangle sin in the cradle, for all the wisdom in the world will not help you out; but you shall be in admiration like dreamers, which dream strange things, and do not know how they come. He says, *Remember judgment*. If you remember always, then you shall have little inclination to sin. If you remember this, then you shall have little inclination to fall down to the devil, though he would give you the entire world, and the glory of it. Solomon says, *The weed grows from a weed to a cockle, from a cockle to a bramble, from a bramble to a brier, from a brier to a thorn*; lying breeds perjury, perjury breeds haughtiness of heart, haughtiness of heart breeds contempt, contempt breeds obstinacy, and brings forth much evil. And this is the whole progress of sin: he grows from a liar to a thief, from a thief to a murderer, and never leaves until he has searched all the room in hell, and yet he is never satisfied; the more he sins, the more he searches to sin: when he has deceived, *no*, he has not deceived you; as soon as he has that he desires, he has not what he desires; when he has left fighting, he goes to fighting as gain; yet a little, and a little more, and so we fly from one sin to another. While I preach, you hear iniquity building up within you, and will break out as soon as you are gone. So *Christ wept*, Jerusalem laughed; Adam broke one, and we break ten; like children which laugh and cry, so as if we kept a shop of vices, now this sin, and then that, from one sin to another. Oh remember your end, (says Solomon), and that you must come to judgment! What shall become of them that have tried them most? Be condemned most.

But if you mark Solomon, he harps on one string, he doubles it again and again, to show us things of his own experience, because we are so forgetful of it in ourselves, like the dreamer that forgets his dream, and the swearer his swearing. So we beg of every unclean spirit, until we have bomb-basted ourselves up to the throat, filling every corner of our hearts with all uncleanness, and then we are like the dog that comes out of the sink, and makes everyone as foul as himself; therefore, says Solomon, If any one will learn the way to hell, let him take his pleasure.

I think I see the dialogue between the flesh and the spirit: the worst speaks first, and the flesh says, *Soul, take your ease, eat, drink, and go brave, lie soft*; what else should you do but take your pleasure? you know what a pleasant fellow I have been to you; you know what delight you have had by my means. But the soul comes in, burdened with that which has been spoken before, and says, I pray you remember judgment, you must give account for all these things; for unless you repent, you shall surely perish. No, says the flesh, talk not of such grave matters, but tell me of fine matters, of soft beds and pleasant things, and talk to me of brave pastimes, apes, bears, and puppets; for I tell you, the forbidden fruit is sweetest of all fruits, for I do not like of your telling me: of judgment; but take you your jewels, your instrument, and all the strings of vanity will strike at once, for the flesh loves to be brave, and tread on corks; it cannot tell what fashion it should be of, and yet to be of the new fashion.

Rejoice, O young man, in your youth. Oh, this goes brave! for while wickedness has cast his rubs, and vengeance cast his spurs, and his foot, and so she reels, and now she tumbles, and then she falls; therefore this progress is ended. Pleasure is but a spur, riches but a thorn, glory but a blast, beauty but a flower; sin is but a hypocrite, honey in your mouth, and poison in your stomach; therefore let us come again and ask Solomon with good intentions, whether he means in *good earnest*, when he spoke these words: "Oh, (says Solomon), it is the best life in the world to go brave, lie soft, and live merrily, if there were no judgment." But this judgment mars all, it is like a damp that puts out all the light, and like a box that mars all the ointment; for if this is true, we have spun a fair thread, that we must answer for all that are not able to answer for one; why, Solomon makes us fools, and gives us gaudies to play with; what then, shall we not rejoice at all? Yes, there is a godly mirth, and if we could hit on it, which is called, *Be merry and wise*. Sarah *laughed*, and was reproved; Abraham laughed, and was not reproved. And so much for the first part.

But know that for all these things *God will bring you into judgment*. This verse is as it were a dialogue between the flesh and the spirit, as the two counsellors: the worst is first, and the flesh speaks proudly; but the spirit comes in burdened with that which has been spoken. The flesh goes laughing and singing to hell; but the spirit casts rubs in his way, and puts him in mind of judgment, that for all these things he now ends with *Rejoice*, and here it comes in, but if this were not coming, we might rejoice still; if young men must for all the sports of youth, what then shall old men do, being as they are now? Surely, if Solomon lived to see our old men live now, as here he says of young men, so high as sin rages, yet vengeance sits above it, as high as Babel.

I think I see a sword hang in the air by a twine-thread, and all the sons of men labor to burst it in sunder. There is a place in hell where the covetous judge sits, the greedy lawyer, the griping landlord, the careless bishop, the lusty youth, the wanton dames, the thief, the robbers of the commonwealth; they are punished in this life, because they ever sinned as long as they could, while mercy was offered to them; therefore, because they would not be washed, they shall be drowned. Now put together, *rejoice and know*, you have learned to be merry, now learn to be wise. Now therefore, turn over a new life, and take a new lesson, for now Solomon did not mock as he did before; therefore this is a check to your ruffs, a check to your cuffs, a check to your robes, a check to your gold, a check to your riches, a check to your beauty, a check to your muck, a check to your graves. Woe from above, woe from below, woe to all the strings of vanity! Do you not now marvel, that you have not a feeling of sin? for now you see Solomon says true; your own heart can tell you that it is wicked, but it cannot amend; therefore it is high time to amend: as Nathan comes to David after Beelzebub, so comes accusing conscience after sin. I think that everyone should have a feeling of sin, though this day be like yesterday, and tomorrow like today; yet one day will come for all, and then *woe, woe, woe, and nothing but darkness!* And though God did not come to Adam until the evening, yet He *came*; although the fire did not come on Sodom until evening, yet it *came*; and so comes the Judge, although He is not yet come, though He have leaden feet, He has iron hands; the arrow slays and is not yet fallen, so is His wrath; the pit is dug, the fire kindled, and all things are made ready and prepared against that day, only the final sentence is to come, which will not long tarry. You may not think to be like to the thief that steals and is not seen: nothing can be hid from Him, and the Judge follows you at the heels; and therefore whatsoever you are, look about you, and do nothing but that you would do openly, for all things are opened to Him. Sarah may not think to laugh, and not be seen; Gehazi may not think to lie, and not be known; they that will not come to the banquet, must stand at the door. What? Do you think that God does not remember our sins, which we do not regard? for while we sin, the score runs on, and the Judge sets down all in the table of remembrance, and His scroll reaches up to heaven. Item, for lending to usury; item, for racking of rents; item, for deceiving your brethren; item, for falsehood in wares; item, for starching your ruffs; item, for curling your hair; item, for painting your face; item, for selling of benefices; item, for starving of souls; item, for playing at cards; item, for sleeping in the church; item, for profaning the Sabbath day: with a number more has God to call to account, for everyone must answer for himself. The fornicator for taking the fill of your pleasure. O son! remember you have taken your pleasure, *take your punishment*: the careless prelate, for murdering so many thousand souls: the landlord, for getting money from his poor tenants by racking of his rents. See the rest, all they shall come like sheep, when the trumpet shall sound, and the heaven and earth shall come to judgment against them, when the heavens shall vanish like a scroll, and the earth shall consume like fire, and all the creatures standing against them; the rocks shall cleave asunder, and the mountains shake, and the foundation of the earth shall tremble; and they shall say to the mountains, *Cover us, fall on us, and hide us from the presence of His anger and wrath, whom we have not cared for to offend.* But they shall not be covered and hid; but then they shall go the black-way, to the snakes and serpents, to be tormented of devils forever. O pain unspeakable! and yet the more I express it, the more horrible it is; when you think of torment passing all torments, and yet a torment passing all that; yet this torment is greater than them, and passing them all!

Imagine you see a sinner going to hell, and his summoner gapes at him, his acquaintance looks at him, the angels shout at him, and the saints laugh at him, and the devils rail at him, and many look him in the face, and they that said they would live and die with him, forsake him, and leave him to pay all the scores! Then Judas would restore his bribes; Esau would cast up his pottage; Achan would cast down his gold; and Gehazi would refuse his gifts; Nebuchadnezzar would be humbler; Balaam would be faithful, and the prodigal would be tame. I think I see Achan running about, *Where shall I hide my gold, that I have stolen, that it might not be seen, nor stand to appear as a witness against me?* And Judas running to the high priest, saying, *Hold, take again your money, I will none of it, I have betrayed the innocent blood.* And Esau crying for the blessing when it is too late, having sold his birthright for a mess of pottage. *Woe, woe, woe, that ever we were born!* Oh where is that Dives that would believe this before he felt the fire in hell, or that would believe the poorest Lazarus in the world to be better than himself, before the dreadful day come when they cannot help it, if they would never so fain, *when repentance is too late!* Herod shall then wish that he were John the Baptist; Pharaoh would wish that he were Moses; and Saul would wish that he had been David; Nebuchadnezzar, that he had been Daniel; Haman to have been Mordecai; Esau would wish to be Jacob; and Balaam would wish he might die the death of the righteous; then he would say, I will give more than Hezekiah, cry more than Esau; fast more than Moses; pray more than Daniel; weep more than Mary Magdalen; suffer more stripes than Paul; abide more imprisonment than Micaiah; abide more cruelty than any mortal man would do, that *go you cursed*, might be, *come you blessed*. Yes, I would give all the goods in the world, that I might escape this dreadful day of wrath and judgment, and that I might not stand among the godless, Oh that I might live a beggar all my life, and a leper! Oh that I might endure all plagues and sores from the top of the head to the sole of the foot, sustain all sickness and griefs, that I might escape this judgment!

The guilty conscience cannot abide this day. The silly sheep when she is taken will not bleat, but you may carry her and do what you will with her, and she will be subject; but the swine, if she be once taken, she will roar and cry, and thinks she is never taken, but to be slain; so of all things, the guilty conscience cannot abide to hear of this day: for they know that when they hear of it, they hear of their own condemnation. I think if there were a general collection made through the whole world, that there might be no judgment day, then God would be so rich, that the world would go a begging, and be as a waste wilderness. Then the covetous judge would bring forth his bribes; then the crafty lawyer would fetch out his bags; the usurer would give his gain, and the idle servant would dig up his talent again, and make a double of it. But all the money in the world will not serve for our sins, but the judge must answer for his bribes; he that has money, must answer how he came by it; and just condemnation must come on every soul of them. Then shall the sinner be ever dying, and never dead, like the salamander that is ever in the fire and never consumed!

But if you come there, you may say as the queen of

Sheba said of king Solomon: "I believed the report that I heard of you in mine own country, but the one half of your wisdom was not told me." If you come there, to see what is done, you may say, *Now I believe the report that was told me in my own country concerning this place; but the one half, as now I feel, I have not heard of.* How do you choose whether you will rejoice, or not; whether you will stand among you blessed, or among you cursed; whether you will enter while the gate is open, or knock in vain when the gate is shut; whether you will seek the Lord while He may be found, or be found of Him when you would not be sought, being run into the bushes with Adam to hide yourselves; whether you will take your heaven now here, or your hell then there; or through tribulation, to enter into the kingdom of God, and so to take your hell now here, or your heaven then there in the life to come, with the blessed saints and angels, so that hereafter you may lead a new life, putting on Jesus Christ and His righteousness?

FOOD FOR NEWBORN BABES

"As newborn babes, desire the sincere milk of the Word, that you may grow thereby."—1 Peter 2:2

This Scripture (beloved in the Lord) contains an exhortation to incite and stir up the believing Jews, that as God had enlightened them with some knowledge of His truth, and sanctified them in some measure with the grace of His Spirit; so they would proceed and go on, and daily increase more and more in the faith and fear of Jesus Christ; like the glorious sun, which still augments and redoubles his heat and light, until it has come to the midst of heaven, where is perfect day. Now the means whereby we receive all our growth and increase in God, is the lively preaching of the Word of truth. And therefore the Apostle, by a figurative and borrowed kind of speech, earnestly presses them to thirst and long for the Word of God, even the food of their souls, as little infants (which are newborn) cry for the mother's milk to nourish and sustain them. For there are two births mentioned in the Scripture: the one fleshly and natural, by propagation, from the first Adam, whereby original and our birth-sin, as it were a serpent's poison, passes and transfuses itself into us; the other heavenly and spiritual by renovation, from the second Adam, which is Jesus Christ, whereby grace and holiness are derived and brought to us.

In this latter and better birth God is our Father to beget us, (1 Peter 1:3); the Church, His spouse, our mother to conceive, us, (Gal. 4:26); the seed whereby we are bred and born again is the Word of God, (1 Peter 1:23); the nurses to feed and to wean and to cherish us are the ministers of the Gospel, (1 Thes. 2:7); and the food whereby we are nourished and held in life is the milk of the Word, as in this place. And therefore, inasmuch as children which are newborn cannot increase in growth and stature, but would die and come to dissolution, unless they are continually fed and nourished with wholesome food; it behoves all the faithful and godly, who are quickened and revived in the life of God, as newborn babes *to desire the sincere milk of the Word, that they may grow thereby*. I do not think we need many words to clear the general drift and scope of this Scripture; as we do not need many fingers to point at the shining sun. Let us now therefore descend to the particular doctrines which issue and spring from the several branches of this Scripture.

First, here is noted a preparation: if we will be bettered and increased by the Word, *we must be as newborn babes*. Secondly, our affection and duty when we are newborn, we must *desire*. Thirdly, the matter and object of our desire, the *milk of the Word*. Fourthly, the *quality* of the milk, it must be *sincere*. Lastly, the end and use for which we desire it, *that we may grow thereby*. For the first point, we must be as newborn babes. Children (we know) are principally commended for simplicity and harmlessness, (Matt. 18:4; 1 Cor. 14:20); and therefore all those which will profit in the school of Christ, and receive light and comfort by the preaching of the Word, are here taught to become as babes, to lay aside all maliciousness, and to bring holy and sanctified hearts to the hearing of it. "Suffer little children to come to Me, (says our Savior), and forbid them not; for of such is the Kingdom of heaven," (Luke 18:16); as if we were never fit to hear and learn of Christ, until we are reformed, and newly changed into little babes again. "For the secret of the Lord (as the Psalmist speaks) is with them that fear Him," (Psa. 25:14); to teach us, that as David would admit no vile person into his counsel, so God will admit no sinful souls into His secrets. "If any man will do God's will, (says our Savior), he shall know of the doctrine, whether it is of God or no," (John 7:17); because no man can learn this doctrine but he that does it; as no man could learn the virgins' song but they which sang it, (Rev. 14:3). And Solomon to the same effect says, "The fear of the Lord is the beginning of knowledge," (Prov. 1:7); as if the first lesson to be wise were to be holy. And therefore Christ is said to have expounded all things to His disciples apart; to show, that if we will have

Christ to teach us, we must go apart from the world. So that as a man slips off all his clothes when he goes into a bath to wash him; so we must slip off all our sins when we come to the Word to feed us; for wisdom will not rest in the defiled soul, nor in a body that is subject to sin. As the devil would not dwell but in a house that was swept from godliness, (Luke 11:25), so the graces of God will not come into the heart which is not cleansed from wickedness; for God will not pour new wine except it is poured into new bottles, (Matt. 9:17). Therefore unless you have prepared new hearts, look for no new blessings to be poured on you. The Jews read the Scriptures daily in their synagogues to find Christ; but all in vain, because their veil is not taken away in reading them: even so do we preach in vain, and you hear in vain, because the veil of sin, which is drawn like a curtain over your hearts, hides and eclipses the glorious light of the Gospel from you. And therefore (beloved brethren) if you will have the Lord to bless your hearing, and to prosper our preaching, you must wash and rinse out the dregs of sin that are frozen in you; you must purge the leaven of maliciousness that sours your souls; you must cast up your covetousness, and your pride, and your slothfulness, and your partial prejudice, like the serpent which spews up his poison when he goes to drink; for this is the cause why there are so many fruitless and non-proficient hearers, because there are so many sinful and wicked hearers. It is said of Christ, that He did not do "many great works in His own country, because of their unbelief," (Matt. 13:58); so it may be said that God conceals many great mysteries of faith from us for our sins' sake. Our wickedness stops Christ's mouth that He will not speak; as the Jews' incredulity chained His hands that He would not work. Will an embroiderer teach another man's servant his trade, if he knows he will hurt him? No more will God teach the devil's servants His truth, because He knows they will offend Him. The seed which fell into the thorny ground sprang up very cheerfully for a time, that it might seem to give a great hope of a joyful harvest; but because thorns grew up with it, "at length they choked it," (Matt. 13:7);

so that unless we cut up the thorny sins which naturally sprout and spring up in us, they will overthrow all the good plants of holy doctrine that are grafted in us. And therefore the Prophet Jeremiah wants us to break up the fallow ground, and "sow not among thorns," (Jer. 4:3); as if the heart must first be sanctified, and afterwards instructed; as iron must first be heated, and afterwards be fashioned. In regard of this, I beseech you, (my beloved), in the fear and reverence of God's blessed name, look to your feet when you enter into the house of God; press not into this marriage-feast without a wedding garment; tread not in the holy sanctuary to hear the Word with an unsanctified and defiled your soul.

A man will not keep the Sabbath in his working apparel, but will put on his richest jewels, and array himself in his best attire; and yet we make no scruple at all to come to the Sabbath's exercise with a profane, and a wicked, and our working-day heart. When Nadab and Abihu offered strange fire before the Lord, God said, "I will be sanctified in them that come near Me," (Lev. 10:3); to show, that the Lord does then look for more holiness at our hands, when, by practice of His service, and the duties of holy religion, we approach and draw more near to Him. Wherefore, to shut up this point, as the beggar (in the Gospel) cast off his cloak to come to Christ, so must we cast off the cloak of our wickedness when we come to hear the word. We must be as babes if we will be Christ's pupils, because He reveals knowledge and wisdom to none but babes, (Matt. 11:25). And yet we must not be babes only, but newborn babes, which have a new soul, a new life, new members, new affections imparted to them. Whereby we learn, that it is not enough, in our regeneration, to redress and reform some specific disordered affection in us; but we must be changed and newly fashioned in every part. As Saul, when the kingly spirit came on him, was turned as it were into another man, (1 Sam. 10:9); so we, when the Word begets us anew, must be turned and changed into other men; and therefore they which are implanted into Christ are called "new creatures," (2 Cor. 5:17); because neither the old heart, nor the old hand, nor the old ear, nor the old eye, will serve the turn; but all must be molten and newly framed again. For that which is "born of the flesh is flesh," (John 3:6): if we will have it in spirit, (that is, fit for God's Worship, who is a Spirit, and must be worshipped in spirit and in truth, John 4:24), it *must* be born again of the Spirit. The sense of this made the Prophet David cry out, "Create in me a clean heart O God; and renew a right spirit within me," (Psa. 51:10). And therefore we must not patch and piece out our hearts for God, like a beggar's cloak, which is made of shreds; but we must be renewed, and thoroughly changed in the spirit of our mind, (Eph. 4:23). When Naaman the leper had washed in Jordan, his flesh came again like the flesh of a young child: if the leprosy of sin be washed and purged from us, all our affections, all our desires will be altered and changed like the flesh of a child; and therefore if we will fit ourselves to be good hearers, we must not entertain friendship with any sin. As the snake slips off her skin, and the eagle casts her bill; so we must quite strip ourselves of all our lusts, when as newborn babes we come to hear.

"Touch not the unclean thing," says the Lord, (2 Cor. 6:17). Because sin will cling to the conscience like bird-lime to a feather; therefore we must not touch it, it must not have a finger of us. When the devil made his reentry, he took to himself seven other spirits worse than himself, (Matt. 12:45). So one devil brings more devils, and one sin pulls on more sins, as one crow calls many crows to a dead animal. And therefore as the "leaven was hid in the meal until all was soured," (Matt. 13:33); so let us never rest seasoning our souls until we are all sanctified; for then we are fit to understand every part of God's will, when we are in every part newborn again.

Furthermore, this point discovers and cries out in gross error within Popery concerning the works of nature, which are wrought and effected by the single virtue and power of our own free will, without the finger and grace of God. For whereas the Papists acquit many of them, and clear them from sin, (as if an unregenerate man, by the strength and ability of his own will, as it were mounted on his own wings, were able to aspire to the accomplishment of holy desire); we see that the Apostle in this place makes no other account of the unregenerate than of dead men, and therefore that they must be quickened and newborn again, before they can practise or perform any vital action in the life of God. Christ is resembled to a vine, and we to the branches, (John 15:5); for as all the juice and sap, whereby the branches spring and live, issues and arises from the root of the vine; so all the grace and goodness that is in us drops and distills from the riches of the person of Jesus Christ. Before God blessed Sarah, she was barren and childless; so until God bless our hearts, they are wicked and fruitless. And therefore as an unclean fountain cannot send forth sweet water, nor "a bad tree bring forth good fruit," (Matt. 12:33); no more can the corrupt and wicked heart of the unregenerate bud and bring forth any good and virtuous actions. So much of our condition and preparation, whereby we have learned with how holy and with how sanctified affections we ought to repair to the hearing of the Word. Now follows our duty and affection when we are newborn.

As newborn babes *desire*. We must not be children in wavering and inconstancy: because the Apostle says, that God has furnished His Church with pastors and teachers, that we are no more children, tossed to and fro, and carried about with every wind of doctrine, (Eph. 4:11), reeling from faith to faith, from religion to religion, like a drunken man from wall to wall. Nor must we be children in understanding and knowledge; because the same Apostle says, Brethren, is not children in understanding: howbeit in malice are you children, but in understanding be men, (1 Cor. 14:20). But we must be children in an ardent and burning affection, in thirsting and longing for the Word of God. "Blessed are they which do hunger and thirst after righteousness; for they shall be filled," (Matt. 5:6); because God fills the hungry with good things; but the rich He sends empty away, (Luke 1:53). "The kingdom of God suffers violence," (Matt. 11:12); because none can enter at the narrow gate, but such as strive, and throng, and thrust to enter. And therefore as when the mother-bird feeds her young, every young-bird gapes, and struggles, and stretches out the neck to receive the food; so when we come to hear, every man must reach and stretch out his heart to receive the Word. For then indeed the Word works most effectually in us, when our hearts before are kindled and inflamed with desire of it; like wax which receives any stamp after it is heated. The Shunammite's child which was raised by Elisha, so soon as his flesh began to wax warm, sneezed, and opened his eyes, and revived again; so when we wax warm in the spirit, and conceive a desire and a thirst of the Word of God, it is an undoubted token that we are born again, and there is breath and a soul within us, and we are not utterly dead in the life of grace. As contrariwise, they which have not a sharp and hungry appetite to be fed and satisfied with the milk of the Word, are but dead carcasses, and skins full of rotten bones. So that the city, which should be the glory of the kingdom, may well be termed Golgotha, the place of dead men's shills, in regard there are so many thousand souls dead in sin, dead in desire, who have no thirst and hunger for the Word of God. If they have a bare reading minister, as children have a puppet to play with, they think themselves in a happy estate; as if Elisha's staff could raise the dead child without Elisha, and the Word give life without a preacher. It may be they can be content, with Micah, to accept a Levite, if they light on him; but who will send to Jerusalem, the school of the Prophets, as Saul sent to Bethlehem, to fetch David for his comfort? I think you know my meaning: I would not wish you wait until preachers offer themselves to instruct you, but to bend to the schools of learning, to provide godly and able men, who may minister the Word in due season. Balak, because he longed for Balaam, went to the utmost coast of the country to meet him. The father, because he longed for his prodigal son, ran to kiss him a great way off. David, because he longed for the ark, went and brought it up from Kirjath-jearim. So then indeed we desire the Word of God, when we will not stay until it come to us, but we will prevent it, and go to the utmost borders of our country to fetch it home to us.

We must desire the milk of the Word, and we must desire it as babes; that is, in three respects. First, they say, children, so soon as they are born into the world, presently cry out for the mother's breast; so must we, so soon as we feel the grace of God to have renewed us, while we are yet hot from the womb, hunger and thirst for the milk of the Word. If the mother should defer to give her child suck, would it is able to live a month, or a week, or a day? No more is our faith able to sustain and support itself, unless it is presently nourished with the food of life. Christ, so soon as He had raised up Jairus' daughter, commanded her meat, (Mark 5:43); as if it were in vain for us to be quickened by the finger of His power, unless we be fed by the Word of His grace. And therefore Eden was watered so soon as it was planted, (Gen. 2:10); to show, that we must be strengthened so soon as we are instructed. So that it is a great fault among us, when God has quickened us with His Spirit, and we perceive His graces to bud and to blossom in us, that we presently provide not moisture to nourish and to preserve them. We count it a miracle that Elijah lived forty days without food; and yet we, after many years of famine, still post off the feeding of our souls. We think it always too soon to begin, though we begin then when we are ready to end; as the rich man, who then went in hand to enlarge his barns, when he was even at death's door to resign his life, (Luke 12:18). As Christ was sent for to heal the ruler's daughter when she was ready to depart, (Matt. 9:18); so many never desire the preacher's company until they are ready to die. They say that the time is not yet come that the Lord's house should be built, nor is it yet time to sanctify their souls for God, nor yet time to provide for the milk of the Word. And so we post off from day to day, from year to year, until we are arrested by death, as the bad lawyer drives off his client from term to term, until the suit is lost. Lot was so long loitering and trifling in Sodom, that the angel was fain to pluck him out with violence; and certainly unless the Lord by the good means of His providence should pluck us out of ignorance and darkness, in which we use such trifling, and plunging, and delaying, scarce one of a thousand would be saved. Wherefore (beloved in Christ) if Paul have planted you in the true faith, desire also an Apollos to water you. If the foundation be laid by a master builder, seek out a skillful workman who may roof it also. If you have received one grace, speedily desire the preaching of the Word, that it may increase and grow up, by dressing and manuring, to a double grace; for even the best gifts will wither and decay in you, unless they are presently watered with the Word.

Again, we know that children are so greedily carried with a desire of their food, that when hunger assails them, they neither regard leisure, nor necessity, nor willingness of the mothers; but all excuses and business set apart, so soon as they cry for it, they must be fed; even so we must not think it enough to desire the Word, but we must be earnest and fervent and importunate in calling and crying for it. A notable parable it is in Luke, how one called for bread in the night; the other answered, that he was in bed; which seemed a reasonable answer, and yet it would not serve, (Luke 11:5-8). So we have long called, (my brethren), and we have a great while craved the bread of life; though it may seem a reasonable answer, that they cannot give it us without impoverishing themselves and their children, who are fat and enriched with the minister's maintenance; yet we ought not to be daunted and discouraged so, but to continue asking still, as Peter continued knocking until the door was opened, (Acts 12:16). For as Jehu was known by his furious marching; so you may know a faithful and true Christian by his zealous perfecting of holy purposes. The mother does not always feed her child fur love; but many times, to keep it still and quiet, is constrained to leave all, and give it suck; so if our mother neither reverenced God, nor feared men, yet if we would be earnest and importunate with her, if we would continually cry and call for it, as babes do for the milk, she would feed us at last, if not of love, yet at least to be eased of us. It is an old saying, that he which asks faintly teaches us to deny him; if we will teach men to grant us, we must ask with courage and constancy. And therefore as Jacob wrestled with the angel, and said, I will not let you go, except you bless me," (Gen. 32:26); so must our requests wrestle with the governors of our land, and say, "I will not let you rest until you hear me. This doctrine indicts and convinces a great number of us, who, though we have a desire *to* the Word, yet we are so chill, and so cold, and so loose in it, that in every cross event we stand stone still. If it is but a straw, it is a block in our way; because, as Jeremiah speaks, "We are not valiant for the truth on the earth," (Jer. 9:3): we have some love to the truth, but we have no courage to labor and adventure for it; as a merchant that would gladly gain, but dares not venture the seas for fear of drowning. If the people are somewhat backward, or a preacher cannot be procured at the first dash, while the fit is fresh on us, we take our discharge, and cast off the care forever after. The slothful man says, "There is a lion in the way," (Prov. 26:13); and so we discourage ourselves in seeking good things, because there is pain in the way. But if we desire the Word as babes do milk, we must never rest to desire it *until we have it.*

Lastly, we know children are continually craving food; a little pause, and then to the breast again; and therefore we must not be gorged and glutted with once serving, but continually desire it. We must be of Elijah's diet, bread and flesh in the morning, and evening too; so morning and evening our souls must be fed. The Apostle exhorts, "Let the word of Christ dwell in you richly," (Col. 3:16); because it must not take up a night's lodging, and so be gone; but it must have a continual residence and abode in our hearts. Though the ground is good, yet it must have the former and the latter rain to make it fertile; and yet many of us think to grow plants with one shower, and to go to heaven with one sermon. It is reported of the faithful, that they continued daily with "one accord in the temple," (Acts 2:46); as if a Sabbath-day's exercise would not serve the turn, unless we had some ordinary repast on the working-days also. And therefore as the lamp burns continually in the temple without quenching; so the Word must continually sound in our ears without intermission. So you see (beloved) that if you will desire the milk of the word as newborn babes, you must desire it presently, without delay; importunately, without fainting; and continually, without loathing, never being satisfied with it.

Now we come to the matter and object which we must desire, namely, our food and nourishment in Christ, which is here called the milk of the Word. To this our Savior recalls us from all our dainties: "Labor not for the meat which perishes, but for that meat which endures to everlasting life," (John 6:27). For the Word is everlasting food, and immortal seed, (1 Peter 1:23, 25), because it makes us immortal, and to last forever. We desire wealth, honor, pomp, and pleasure, and everything save the milk of the Word, which we should desire; like Adam, who had all trees, and yet liked none but the forbidden tree. There is a desire of the world, but it is a tare to choke the good corn, (Matt. 13:22): there is a desire of money, but it is the root of all evil, (1 Tim. 6:10): there is a desire of the flesh, but it fights and wages war against the Spirit, (Gal. 5:17): there is a desire of preeminence, but it is swelling, and ambitious, (James 4:1): there is a desire of revenge, but it arises from a rash and carnal spirit, (Luke 9:54): there is a desire of praise, but it is cursed and Pharisaical, (John 5:44; 12:43): the blessed and holy desire is to desire the milk of the Word. When Jonathan saw the honey dropping, he has to be licking; so when you see the milk of the Gospel, you must desire to be sucking. Of all the blessings of Canaan this was the chief one, that it flowed with milk and honey; and this encouraged the Israelites to travel through the desert to possess it. The Word is a land flowing with better milk and honey, and we must not think any pains or toil too much to attain it. God has many names in Scripture to make us conceive more honorably of Him; so has the Word many titles to make it more amiable. It is called a lamp, to direct us; a medicine, to heal us; a guide, to conduct us; a bit, to restrain us; a sword, to defend us; water, to wash us; fire, to inflame us; salt, to season us; milk, to nourish us; wine, to rejoice us; rain, to refresh us; a treasure, to enrich us; and the key, to unlock heaven's gates to us. So, the

Word is named by all things, that we should only desire it *instead of all things.* And surely, therefore, the Word is in no great request among us, because we do not know what blessings it brings with it. It is called the Word of salvation, because it saves the soul from pining; as the corn which Joseph sent did Jacob's house from famine. So that as Elisha said of the Jordan, *Wash, and be cleansed*; so may we say of the Word, *Hear it, and be saved.* It is called the Word of life, because it revives the spirit; as Elisha's bones revived the Israelite. It is called the Word of reconciliation, because it is like a golden chain to link God and us together. And in regard hereof it is called "a jewel of inestimable price," (Matt. 13:46); as if all the treasure in Egypt were not wealth enough to buy it. And therefore as David longed for the well of Bethlehem; so we must long and languish for the milk of the Word.

The Word is resembled to milk in three respects. First, because it is the only food of the faithful, as milk is the only and proper food of babes. Secondly, because it is not hard and intricate, but plain and easy to be conceived, as milk is easy to be digested. Thirdly, because it is sweet and comfortable to the soul, as milk is sweet and pleasant in taste.

For the first point: The Lord charges the Israelites to do whatsoever He had commanded, and not to add or diminish anything, (Deut. 12:32). And Josiah, Joshua, Ezra, and the rest, when they would renew the Lord's covenant with the people, read nothing but the law; to show that it was the only rule and square of all their duty. And therefore Isaiah recalls us to the "law and to the testimony, *etc.*," (Isa. 8:20); and Christ sends us to search the Scriptures, because in them we think we have eternal life, (John 5:39). And therefore the Popish Church, which (not content with the milk of the Gospel) has broached many heathen traditions and unwritten trash, does not feed, but choke and poison, her children with them, and deprive the Lord's people of this food of life; and, like cursed Philistines, stopping up the wells of water which others have dug, what do they else but starve and famish so many nations? Well may their hedge-priests, like dry nurses, delight and disport the children for a season; but when hunger bites, when the distressed conscience would be fed and comforted, then they are not able to afford them the very crumbs from Christ's table. And therefore we must needs account the estate of those congregations to be full of dread and horror, which have not this milk of the Word to feed their souls; which want a good steward to give them their meat in due season; which, like the Egyptians, lie crawling in the dark, when other churches enjoy most comfortable light. Jacob forsook the blessed land of Canaan when it had no bread; and can we be enamored of those assemblies where there is no soul's food? If you did consider, (my beloved), that you cannot be nourished to eternal life but by the milk of the Word, you would rather desire your bodies might be without souls, than your churches without preachers. I tremble to think how often you have heard this, and yet how little you have performed it.

For the second point: That the doctrine of the Gospel is plain, appears when the wise man says, "All the words of His mouth are plain, and right to them that find knowledge," (Prov. 3:9). "The testimony of the Lord is sure, making wise the simple," (Psa. 19:7). If our Gospel is hid, (says the Apostle), it is hid to them that are *lost*, (2 Cor. 4:3). For as the sun, which was made to lighten all things, is most light; so the Word, which was made to clear all things, is most clear; so that if there is no communion between light and darkness, and the Word of God be a lamp to "our feet and a light to our paths," (Psa. 119:105); then it is evident that the Word has no darkness in it. If we do not see all things, the fault is not in the light, *but in the eye*; as Hagar could not see the water, which yet was before her. And therefore our adversaries falsely charge the Scriptures of exceeding hardness and intricateness. When the spies were returned from Canaan, they could not say but that it was a good land; but they said it was hard to come by; so the Papists must needs confess that the Scripture is a good Word; and yet, to dissuade the Lord's people from a serious and diligent search of it, they bring up a slander, and say, it has many obscurities and by-paths. But as Elisha saw the horses and fiery chariots which his enemies could not see; so (beloved) if you come with a faithful and a holy heart to the Word and to the Scripture, you shall see that plainness and easiness in the doctrine which our adversaries cannot see.

For the third point: That the Gospel is the only comfort and consolation of a faithful soul, the Prophet Jeremiah says, "Your words were sound, and I did eat them, and Your word was to me the joy and rejoicing of my heart," (Jer. 15:16). "Your testimonies have I taken as an heritage forever; for they are the rejoicing of my heart," (Psa. 119:111). As a man will be glad to be hired to a nobleman; so David, when he had gotten the milk of the Word, rejoiced as much as if he had been hired to God. And therefore in all the story of the Acts, we see joy and comfort to have followed the Word, as Elisha followed Elijah, and would not leave him. As the wise men rejoiced exceedingly, when they saw the star which should lead them to Christ; so you have matter of great joy and comfort, when you hear the Word preached, which shall carry you to heaven, like the chariots which conveyed Jacob into Egypt. There are many Michals in this land, which have mocked king David for dancing before the ark. There are many which term us heady and foolish men, because we come and throng and press this way to a sermon. But as Christ said, "Father, forgive them; for they do not know what they do," (Luke 23:34); so I, God forgive them, they do not know what they say. For if they did feel the calm of conscience, the joy of heart, the consolation of spirit, and the exceeding and everlasting comforts in God, which the faithful possess and enjoy by hearing the Word, they would account us not only fools, but stark mad, if all the pleasures or profits or dangers of the world should withdraw or withhold us from it.

So much for our food: now we come to the quality of our food. It must be *sincere* milk. Sincere, both in its *savor*, and also in *effect* and *operation*. For, as in nourishing our body naturally, our blood cannot be good, if our diet is unwholesome; so in feeding our souls spiritually, neither our hearts, nor affections, nor our words, nor our works, can be good, unless the milk is wholesome whereon we feed; and therefore, as our Savior presses us take heed what you hear, (Mark 4:24); so the Apostle, to the like effect, gives a caveat to take heed on what we feed. For there is a pure and fresh doctrine, in Jer. 1:7, and there is a sour and leavened doctrine, in Matt. 16:6; there is a new wine of the Gospel, in Matt. 9:17; and there is a mixed wine in the cup of fornicators, Rev. 17:2; there are wholesome words, 1 Tim. 1:15; and there are corrupt and unwholesome words, Eph. 4:29; there is a doctrine of God, John 7:16; and there is a doctrine of devils, 1 Tim. 4:1; there is an edifying and a building word, Eph. 4:29; and there is a fretting and cankered word, 2 Tim. 2:17; As the Prophets' children cried out, "Death in the pot," (2 Kings 4:40), so some places may say, *Death in our food*; and therefore it is, that we are so often forewarned in the Scripture to "beware of the leaven of the Pharisees and of the Sadducees," (Matt. 16:6); to beware of false prophets which come to us in sheep's clothing," (Matt. 7:15); to beware that "no man spoil us through philosophy," (Col. 2:8); to "try the spirits whether they are of God," (1 John 4:1); as we must taste our food before we digest it, and try our gold before we treasure it. Christ tasted the vinegar, but would not drink; so when we taste false doctrine, we must reject it. There are many greedy of milk, but it is dragon's milk: they take great pains to learn, but it is to learn the language of Ashdod, and not the language of Canaan: they run to hear, but to hear fables and untruths. Nimrod was as painful in building of Babel, as Solomon in rearing the holy temple. Micah entertained a Levite, and consecrated his silver; but to an idolatrous worship. The Israelites melted their ear-rings; but to erect a calf. Jezebel fed a great rout of trencher-chaplains; but to honor Baal. Many desire to have milk, but they will have it from dragons poisoned; and therefore we are here warned to desire the sincere milk, *etc.*, for the Lord will not have the wine of His Word to be mingled and mashed with the water of human inventions. He that has My word, let him speak My word faithfully. What is the chaff to the wheat? (Jer. 23:28). God would not have one field sowed with two kinds of grain;

to show us that He would not have one heart filled with two kinds of doctrine. Dagon could not stand with the Lord's ark; no more can Christ's truth hold any fellowship with the word of error. And therefore as the ministers must beware that they do not make merchandise of the Word of God; so must the people also, that they drink not any milk but that which is sincere. And here you ought (my beloved) more carefully to behave yourselves, as you see the devil more subtly to assault you; and under the cloak of zeal and reformation, to bring into the Lord's sanctuary most wicked profanation. As a man will be more wary to try every piece of gold, when he cries many counterfeit and Flemish angels to fly abroad; so when you see many sorts of doctrine crawling daily like locusts out of the bottomless pit, you must be more diligent to taste and try which is sound and sincere.

It follows, *That you may grow thereby.* Here is the end of our hearing, *that we may grow in grace, and increase in the faith of righteousness.* For the faithful are called *the trees of righteousness,* (Isa. 61:3), because they must be always springing; *lively stones,* (1 Peter 2:5), because they must grow in the building; *good servants,* (Matt. 25:21, 23), which must trade and traffic the Lord's talents to increase; *fruitful branches,* (John 15:2), which must be purged and pruned by the hand of the heavenly Husbandman. Isaac must not always hang on Sarah's breast, but must be weaned; so we must not always be children, but grow up and increase, and profit more and more. As the star never ceased until it came over Christ, so we must never rest walking until we come to God. If we have faith, we must proceed "from faith to faith," (John 1:16); if we have love, we must "increase and abound in love," (1 Thes. 3:12); if we have zeal, we must endeavor to be consumed with zeal, (John 2:17); if we be liberal to the distressed saints of God, we must double our liberality, (Rom. 12:13), as Elkanah gave Hannah a double portion, (1 Sam 1:5). If we read the Scriptures, (2 Tim. 3:15), we must go on and continue in prayer, (Col. 4:2). If we give alms, we must step on one foot farther, and give them with cheerfullness, (2 Cor. 9:7). And so, as the eagle continually soars until she come to the highest, so must we still increase until we come to perfection. "Let us go on to perfection," (Heb. 6:1); as if a faithful man were like a ship under sail, never anchoring until he arrive at heaven. The greater is our sin, which hear, and hear, but are never the more reformed for our hearing; like Pharaoh's ill-favored kine, which devoured the fat kine, but remained as ill-favored as they were before; so many of us, when we have lugged the breast almost dry, after twenty or thirty years' feeding, are as scragged and lean as we were before. No man almost among us is more zealous, no man more faithful, no man more constant for the truth, no man more fervent in religion, no man more sanctified, no man more diligent in practicing, nor less vicious now, than he was a hundred sermons ago; as if we were night blank ravens, which cannot be washed with all the soap of the Gospel. Though we have long heard, and still desire to hear, jet we do not grow by our hearing; we are very dwarfs in Christ, scant able to go, little in faith, little in love, little in patience, little in obedience, little in zeal; like Zacchaeus, so little that we cannot see Christ. This is an undoubted evidence that we have not fleshy, but stony hearts, which though they are washed, yet they cannot be watered with the sweet showers of the Gospel. For is there not in every tavern, and in every shop, and in every house, and in every hall, as much covetousness, as much bribery, as much cozening, as much wantonness, as much maliciousness, after this long shine of the Word, as there was before? Are we not now as slothful in God's service, as dissolute in the practice of Christian duties, as dishonest in our dealings between man and man, as proud in our attire, as light in our behavior, as hypocritical abroad, as sinful at home, as we were before? And what is the reason of it, but that we come to the fountain rather to draw than to drink; rather to hear, than to be bettered, and sanctified, and increased by our hearing? One sort hears not at all, like Eutychus, which was sleeping when Paul was preaching, (Acts. 20:9); another sort forgets all, as Nebuchadnezzar did his dream; the most part remembers all, but will make no practice of it; as a carpenter, which should square all by rule, sticks it at his back, and works all by aim. But assuredly (my beloved) it were better you never heard, than so, in despite of God, to abuse your hearing. *If I had not come and spoken to them*, (says Christ), *they had not had sin; but now they have no cloak for their sin*, (John 15:22). What cloak can you have, when God offers grace, and you wilfully refuse it? As meat, the more a man receives, the more it distempers, if it is not digested in this way the more you learn, and the more you hear, the greater is your sin, if you grow not by it. If the servant which hid his talent in a napkin was so handled, what shall be done to them which suffer their talent to perish? And therefore every man must beware "how he hears," (Luke 8:18); every man must take heed that he "receive not the grace of God in vain," (2 Cor. 6:1); that he desires the milk of the Word to be bettered and increased by it. Wherefore whosoever you be that hears this, and will hear others, search your conscience, whether you be grown in any virtue since you heard the last sermon consider what sin you had the last Sabbath, which you have not this Sabbath. If you find no change, then the Word has not had its working in you; you are not increased by the food which you receive. Will not a man be angry to set his child to school, and find him always at his *A, B, C*? So God will be displeased if we are negligent and slack, and never take out His lessons, but stand still. I know many of you will give me the hearing of this, as you have done many of my brethren heretofore; but as the worm struck Jonah's gourd, and it died in the morning, so by the next morning a greedy worm or covetousness, or the like sin, will have perished all. If it is so, know the Judge stands at the door, ready every hour to summon you to death, to make your appearance at the bar of justice, and to give up your account for every talent, yes, for every lesson that you have *learned* and *left unpracticed*. As for you, if any of you walk in dutiful obedience to the Word, I beseech you in the fear of God, and in the bowels and love of Jesus Christ, that you will abound and increase yet more and more, and contend by all means to put in practice and exercise those things that you hear; that so at length, when you be ripe for the sickle, and the great day of harvest has come, you may be gathered as good corn into the Lord's garner, and be invested in the holy heavens with that blessed kingdom which God has provided for them that serve and fear Him. *Amen.*

THE BANQUET OF JOB'S CHILDREN

"And his sons went and feasted in their houses, everyone his day; and sent and called for their three sisters to eat and to drink with them. And it was so, when the days of their feasting were gone about, that Job sent and sanctified them, and rose up early in the morning, and offered burnt offerings, according to the number of them all: for Job said, "It may be that my sons have sinned and cursed God in their hearts." So did Job continually."—Job 1:4-5

This book is a story of patient Job, and shows how God can deal with all, and how they should receive all things at His hand; seeing the most innocent man in the world, when God would try him, was brought so low, that the devil had power to lay on him what torment he desired, death only excepted; and yet he stood to it with such constancy, that he says, *Though the Lord slay me, yet will I trust in Him.* Such power was given to his faith and love and patience, that they overcame the devil, which said, that if he might have leave to plague him, he would curse God to His face, (verse 11). Therefore God would have this victory to be recorded of all such as are sick, or sore, or needy, or oppressed; that whatsoever pain we suffer, we may remember that Job's pain was sharper than this, and yet could not make him so impatient, but when like a man he was offended with his torments, like a holy man he was more offended with himself, and angry with his anger. Therefore at last God returned to him, and removed his troubles, and made his end more honorable than his beginning; as if He should say, So it shall be done to the man which is not offended with My chastisements.

Now to our purpose. In the first verse of this chapter the Holy Spirit shows what a good man Job was, saying, that he was *perfect and upright, and one that feared God, and eschewed evil.* In the second verse He shows what store of children Job had, saying, *He had seven sons and three daughters.* In the third verse He

109

shows what store of riches Job had, saying, *His substance was seven thousand sheep, and three thousand camels, and five hundred yoke of oxen, and five hundred she asses, etc.* In the fourth verse He returns again to his children, showing how they were occupied before the wind came, and blew the house on their head, saying, *His sons went and feasted in their houses, everyone his day; and sent and called for their three sisters to eat and to drink with them.* In the fifth verse He comes again to Job, and shows a proof of his virtues, which He commended him for before, saying, *That when his sons had feasted, he sent for them, and sanctified them, and rose up early, etc.*

So if you ask what his sons did, the Holy Spirit says, that they *feasted.* If you ask where, He says, *In their own houses.* If you ask when, He says, *Everyone kept his day.* If you ask who were the guests, He says, *that one invited another, and the other invited him again, and they called for their sisters to them, and so made merry together.* If you ask what further Job did, the narrative says, that after every feast first he sent for his sons, and then he sanctified them, and then he sacrificed for them: the reason is added, because Job thought, *It may be that my sons have sinned, and cursed God in their hearts.* His zeal in this action is declared by three circumstances: first, that *he rose up early in the morning;* secondly, that *he offered so many sacrifices as he had sons;* thirdly, that *he performed this offering every day while the feast lasted.* Of every circumstance a little, because some had rather hear many things than learn one.

First here is to is noted, that among the blessings of Job, his *children* are reckoned first. So soon as the Holy Spirit was past his spiritual blessings, which He mentions in the first verse of all, before all his other blessings, lands, and houses, and goods, and cattle, and friends, and servants, He speaks of his children, as the chief treasure which Job had next to his virtues, although he was counted the greatest man for riches, and cattle, and all things else, in all the East parts, (verse 3). Therefore the devil, when he had taken away all his other riches, took away his children last of all, trying him as it were by degrees; as if he should say, I have a greater plague for him yet: if the losing of his goods, and stealing of his cattle, and burning of his houses, and slaving of his servants, will not move him; yet I know what will rouse him; when his children are all feasting together, I will raise a mighty wind, and blow down the house on their heads, and kill every son and daughter which he has at a clap. Indeed this news frightened him about, as appears in the twentieth verse. His patience was so great, that when they brought him word of his oxen, and camels, and asses, and sheep, he never shrunk, we do not read that he made any answer; as though he cared not for them; but when he had heard that his dear children, seven sons and three daughters, after he had brought them up to ripe years, were slain all at once, then the story says, that he arose, and rent his mantle, and shaved his head, and fell down on the ground, and worshipped, and said, "Naked came I out of my mother's womb, and naked shall I return there," (verses 20-21). So even the devil knows what a man loves, and what a blessing it is to have children. Therefore when God commanded the man and the woman to be fruitful and multiply, it is said before that "God blessed them," (Gen. 1:28), which was the first blessing that was given to man which is called a blessing, the blessing of children. Again, when God spoke the same words to Noah and his sons, it is said before that God blessed Noah and his sons, (Gen. 9:1): so children came still under the name of blessing. So God Himself shows that children are His gifts, to make you thankful for them, and careful of them, as Job was. And therefore some men have more riches, and some less, and some none, because it is the blessing of the Lord (as Solomon says) which makes rich, (Prov. 10:22). So some men have many children, and some few, and some none, because it is the blessing of God (as David says) which sends children, (Psa. 127:3, and 128:3-4). But this is the difference between temporal blessings and spiritual blessings: that spiritual blessings are simply good, and therefore do all men good that enjoy them; as faith and love and patience can never hurt a man, but better him; and temporal blessings are as he which has them. To a good man riches are good, honors are good, health is good, liberty is good, because he does good with them; but to an evil man they are evil, because they make him worse, and he does evil with them; as Jeroboam had not done so much hurt, if he had not been in such honor. Therefore we pray for health, and wealth, and honor, and rest, and liberty, and life, with a caution, *If it is God's will*, as Christ prayed for the removing of His cross; because we do not know whether they are good or evil, whether they will make us better or worse, or whether we shall do good with them or hurt. So when Job had his cattle, and his houses, and his friends, and his servants, and his children about him, he was like a man of whom David speaks, "The righteous shall flourish like the palm tree," (Psa. 92:12). Therefore the devil said, that God had made a hedge about Job, (Job 1:10). As a hedge goes round about a garden, so God's blessings went round about Job; according to that, (Psa. 32:10), *He that trusts in the Lord, mercy shall compost him about.*

So Job was endowed with children; but how his children were affected, we cannot define so well as of their father, because the Holy Spirit does not sayhing of them, but that they feasted; which does sound as though He noted a disparity between Job and his sons, as there was between Eli and his sons; for oftentimes a godly father has toward children, which make him watch, and fast, and pray, and weep, when they little think, while they themselves ruffle, and swear, and banquet, and game, until poverty fall on their purses, as the house fell on their heads. So it seems that Job's sons were secure on their father's holiness, as many are on their father's husbandry, which think, The old man has enough for us, we do not need care to get or save; so they might think, Our father sacrifices for us, we may feast and be merry, his devotion will serve for us; he is an old man, let him pray, and God will hear him. One Lot is enough in a house. But if Job had bred up his sons so, God would not have commended him, but rebuked him, as He did Eli. Therefore this is not spoken against Job's sons, that they feasted, as it is spoken against the Israelites, that they sat down to eat, and rose up to play, (Exod. 32:6).

For, first, it is not like that he which was so commended of God, that He said, There is none like him in the earth, (verse 8), would not teach his children in their youth, as he prayed for them after. Again, if they had been epicures and libertines and bezzlers, God would not have heard his prayer for them, no more than He would hear Samuel's prayer for Saul. Again, if they had despised that God which their father worshipped, he would never have said as he says, It may be that my sons have cursed God, as though some fault might escape them by ignorance or rashness; but he would have said, My sons are blasphemers, and therefore I must punish them. For that which the law said against blasphemers after, that Job understood by the law of conscience, written in his heart, as Paul says, (Rom. 2:15).

Again, if they had used their feasts for their lusts, like them which say, *Let us eat and drink, for tomorrow we shall die*, it had been vain for Job to speak to them of sanctification, for they would not have sanctified themselves at his bidding. But it is said, that before Job offered sacrifice for them, they were sanctified; that is, they considered the faults which they had committed, and repented for them, and reconciled themselves, and then Job sacrificed for them. Again, if their feasts had been surfeiting and disorders, like our wakes and revels, Job should have forbidden their feasts, and not prayed God to pardon their sins which they committed in feasting, and suffer them to sin still; for that were to mock God, as though he desired not pardon for their sins past, but rather leave for them to sin still.

Lastly, we do not see by any circumstance of the story that they abused their feasts, either in suspected houses, or profane company, or corrupt speeches, or impure gestures, or wanton dancings, or unlawful dalliances, or vain superfluities; but that our feasts might be allowed, if they were like to theirs. For, first, they did feast in their own houses: they did not run to ordinaries, or ale-houses, or taverns, as they which seek for the strongest wine, or hunt after news, or worse purposes; but, like good neighbors, they invited one another borne, and kept their hospitality in their own houses, as our gentlemen should do that lie about London, which are a kind of non-residents from their poor neighbors. Secondly, they did not feast every day, like the rich glutton in (Luke 16); but everyone kept his day in the year when their feastings came. So it is not meant that the sons did nothing but feast, and the father nothing but pray; but, as the feasts of the Jews came at certain times of the year, to celebrate some blessings of God, so they observed their feasting-times, to celebrate their good-wills one to another. Lastly, they did not join themselves with ruffians, and swearers, and tipplers, as all are likely to meet together at a feast; neither did they invite the rich to their tables, as James says, which are feasts of flattery; but they were all one kin, and one heart, brethren and sisters, like the disciples which sat down together.

All this shows that their meetings tended to nourish amity, and that they had respect to the continuance of their peace, and increase of their love one towards another; which was the first cause that feasts were instituted in the Primitive Church, and therefore called the feasts of charity, only that friends and kinsmen and neighbors might meet one with .another to receive the blessings of God, and rejoice together like Joseph and his brethren, lest Christian familiarity should wear out of use and be forgotten. For you may see in Eccl. 2:24, and 3:12, and 5:18, where Solomon speaks of the joy and pleasure and delight which we may take in God's creatures; and again in Psa. 104:15, where David says, that as bread was made to strengthen, so wine was made to comfort the heart; that God would not only have us fed, but of His exceeding goodness He would have us cheered and comforted beside; as He shows by this abundance of His creatures, in that He has ordained so many things more than we need. Why did God create more things than we need, but to show that He allows us needful and comfortable things? for all the good things which were not created for need, were created for delight. Therefore even the Scriptures have commended solemn feasts, in Lev. 23, Num. 28 and 29, and Exod. 13, where you may read of sundry feasts commanded by God Himself; as the feasts of gathering fruits, the feasts of trumpets, the feasts of tabernacles, the feasts of new moons, the feasts of reconciliation, the feasts of dedication of the temple, *etc.* Beside it is said that Abraham made a great feast the same day that Isaac was weaned, (Gen. 21:8). So it is said of Samson, that he made a feast when he was married, (Judg. 14:10). And at a feast in Cana Christ showed the first miracle that ever He wrought, turning water into wine, (John 2:11). If feasts had been unlawful, Christ would not have been there: therefore the wise man says, "There is a time to laugh," as well as he says, "There is a time to weep," (Eccl. 3:4). When he says there is a time both to laugh and weep, he implies that the time to laugh is not every day, as it is said of Dives, that he fared sumptuously every day, (Luke 16:19), for then there were a time to laugh, but no time to weep. Therefore if you will know the time when to laugh, and when to weep, God has set Uriah for an example. When the Church was quiet, and his country safe, Uriah could rejoice as well as others; but when the Church was troubled, and his country in danger, though the king bade him go home, and eat, and drink, and solace with his wife, he would not do so, but said, *The ark and Israel and Judah abide in tents; and my lord Joab and the servants of my lord are encamped in the open field; shall I then go to mine house to eat, and to drink, and to lie with my wife? As you live, and as your soul lives, I will not do this thing*, (2 Sam. 11:11). See what a sin he counted it to feast then, which at another time he counted no sin! Therefore if you ask when it is time to feast, and when to fast, learn of Uriah: he forbad not to feast; but if he should see your feasting now, he would say, as Elisha said to Gehazi, "Is this a time to take a reward?" (2 Kings 5:26). Is this a time to make feasts? No, the father and the sons both had need to arise early now, and sacrifice together; for if ever the house were falling on our heads, as it did on theirs, now the devil has sent forth his winds, now the Pope has laid his ordinance, *no*, our own hands, which should prop it, are digging as busily as the enemies, with reproaches, and slanders, and suggestions, to undermine the Church, which is falling already, that we might die like the Philistines, with the temple on our heads. Is this a time to feast, Uriah, when the house of God is beset like the house of Lot; when the armies Of Antichrist are preparing against God's people? As the voice asked Zechariah, and Amos, and Jeremiah, what they did see; so if you ask your prophets what they do see, they may say, they do see the wolf devouring the lambs. We see a dark ignorance running over the land, like the blackness of Egypt: we see the Romans coming in again, as they came to Jerusalem, and sacking the temple: we see the Papists carving of images, and the people kneeling before them: we see the professors of the Gospel shrink away, as the disciples fled from their Master when He was taken. Is this a time to feast, Uriah? is this a time to flatter? is this a time to dissemble? is this a time to loiter? is this a time to keep silence? is this a time to gather riches? is this a time to revenge wrongs? is this a time to set forth pageants? No, says Hezekiah, (2 Kings 19:3), This is a time of trouble, in which the prince and nobles and people should humble themselves, as the citizens of Nineveh, lest the ark be taken from England as the ark was taken from Israel; which God grant that our eyes never see.

So much of Job's children, how everyone had his several house; which shows how God blessed them with riches, as he did their father, and what care Job had, like a father, to provide for them: then how they feasted together; which shows how good and how pleasant a thing it is for brethren to dwell together in unity, (Psa. 133:1).

Now you shall see what the old man does, which was so commended in the first verse: the story says, that he sent for his sons, and sanctified them, and sacrificed for them. In which words the Holy Spirit shows the pattern of a holy man and good father, which kept the rule that God gave to Abraham, to bring up his children in the fear of the Lord. Job does not as some, which, when they have passed their bounds, set all at random, and say with Cain, "My sin is greater than can be forgiven," (Gen. 4:13); but he goes to the remedy, as the Jews, when they were stung, went to the brazen serpent: albeit my children have not done their duties in all points, but offended in their feastings, yet am I sure that God will have mercy on them, and on me, if we ask Him forgiveness. Therefore he sent for his sons like a father, and then he taught them like a preacher to sanctify themselves, and then he offered sacrifice for them. First, we will speak of the cause which moved Job to sacrifice for his sons, set down in these words,—Job said, *It may be that my sons have sinned, and cursed God in their hearts*. He was glad, good man, to see his children agree so well together; but he would have them merry, and not sin; and therefore he puts them in mind every day while they feasted, to sanctify themselves. He does not condemn honest mirth, and sober feasts, to maintain amity and peace; but (being thoroughly acquainted with man's infirmity) he showed that he never had observed any feasts so duly celebrated, but some disorder or other has crept in, whereby God has been dishonored at His own table, either for superfluity of meat, or excess of drink, or unchaste songs, or corrupt speeches, or wanton dancings, or unseemly dalliances. The devil has been still at one end, and is lightly the master of the feast. Therefore Job thought with himself, *It may be that my sons have committed some scape like other men*: I cannot tell they are but men; it is easy to slip when occasion is ready, though they think not to offend. He had no apparent cause to suspect them, and therefore he speaks in the doubting phrase, *It may be that they have sinned*. It is better to be fearful than too secure: that which happens often in the like case, he might well doubt it, though he had warned them before; therefore his heart was not quiet, but still this ran in his mind all the while they feasted, It may be that my sons sin. How wary was Job over himself, which was so jealous over his sons, lest one sin should slip from them! *no*, if you mark, he speaks not of any open or gross sins which he feared; but he speaks of a sin in the thought. It may be that my sons have cursed God in their hearts. Blasphemy is properly in the mouth, when a man speaks against God, as Rabshakeh did; but Job had a farther respect to a blasphemy of the heart, counting every sinister affection of the heart as it were a kind of blasphemy, or petty treason. So the penitent man does aggravate his sins, and stretch them as it were on the rack, to make his small sins seem great sins, that he might beware as well of small as great. Contrariwise, the profane and carnal-minded man does mince, and flatter, and extenuate his sins, as though they were no sins, because they should not trouble him. For this sin which Job calls blasphemy, which is the highest name of sin, the Papists call but a venial sin, that is, but a slight sin, because it is in the thought: so Job and they differ in judgment.

Now concerning this speech of Job, *It may be that my sons have sinned*, or, It may be that myself have sinned, which I may properly and rightly term the jealousy of a holy man; herein Job shows in what fear he stood of his sons so long as their feast lasted, even as a merchant does until his ship come home. First, we may see this,—that the best things may soon be corrupted by the wickedness of men: such is our nature, ever since Adam chose evil before good, good has been turned into evil, notwithstanding that our intent and meaning be good. As for example, when a husband loves his wife, or a father loves his children, these are good and holy and commendable things; yet there is no man can be found that does love his wife or his children with that evenness (as I may call it) or just proportion, but that there is some odds in the balance when his affection is weighed, which may crave pardon, like the feasts of Job's children. If these odds are in all our measures, then it is no strange case, that Job thought with himself, that his children might offend God in the thing that of itself does not offend. Therefore it is good for man, so long as he lives in this world, to remember still that he is among temptations, and sits at a feast like Job's children, where he may soon take too much. If the fish did know the hook, and the bird had seen the net, though they have but the understanding of fishes and birds, yet they would let the hook alone, and fly over the net, and let the fowler whistle to himself. So we must look on our riches as we look on snares, and behold our meats as we behold baits, and handle our pleasures as we handle bees, that is, pick out the sting before we take the honey; for in God's gifts Satan has hid his snares, and made God's benefits his baits; that, as Adam said, "The woman whom you gave to be with me she gave me of the tree and I did eat," (Gen. 3:12); so they may say, The riches, or the honors, or the liberty, or the wife, or the servants, or the children, or the meats, or the wit, or the beauty which you have given me, tempted me to sin. So many sins lie in wait for us about our meats, and drinks, and beds, and ways, that, unless we watch, pray, and look about us at every time, it may be, (as Job says), that we may sin in our doings, or in our sayings, or at least in our hearts, as he thought of his sons. Therefore no doubt but as Job thought that his sons might offend in their feastings; so he taught them even when they were feasting, and when they sat at the table, and when they drank one to another, to think oftentimes, We may sin, as our father told us; which bridled their mirth, and stopped many words at the door, even when sin was at the tongue's end. You are not Job's sons; but you are come to be Job's scholars; therefore learn that which his children learned. If a man did but carry this watch-word with him, whensoever he eats, or speaks, or bargains, it would cut off a thousand idle words and wicked acts in one year, for which he shall give account.

The second lesson which Job seems to point us to is, to prepare ourselves before we eat the communion; that is, to sanctify ourselves and meats as Christ did; when they had nothing but a few fishes and bare bread, yet there was prayer before they did eat. For, as Paul says, "Every creature of God is good, for it is sanctified to us by prayer and thanksgiving," (1 Tim. 4:4-5). He that does not pray to God for his daily bread, nor thank Him for it, does not receive the creatures of God, but steals them from Him, as a man which takes a thing without asking or thanking. There is a kind of men which I speak of, which hold it too sad a matter to say a short grace before they begin their meal, lest it should forespeak their mirth, and keep them in a sober mind until they rise again. I have heard many say, that they cannot be merry unless they swear, and whoop, and carouse, and dally, and gibe; therefore, if they can choose, they will never be a guest where any godly man is present, lest his countenance or word should dash their sport; and if any matter of God happen to come in while they are in the vein, it is like a damp which puts out their lights, and turns their mirth into heaviness, as the hideous hand which wrote on the wall cast Belshazzar into a dump. These men needed to leave their feasting, and go to praying; for they desire to die, like the Jews, with the quails in their mouths. It may be (thought Job) that my sons have a spice of this vanity. If it is so with the godly sort, as Job's children were, that they may forget themselves at such a time, and step too far, and slip a sin; what shall we say of them I that drive God out of their company when they banquet, and say that Scripture does not become the table? as though we should forget God while we receive His benefits. We do not need say as Job said, *It may be that they have cursed God in their hearts*; for they blaspheme Him with their mouths: we do not need say, It may be that they do sin; for they do nothing but sin, and their feast is a feast of sins, as if the devils should banquet together. But they which feast as Job would have his children, sanctify themselves before, and eat as in the presence of God, and are merry as it were with the angels: when they take their bread, they think with themselves, *What a goodness is this, that God gives such virtue to bread to sustain life, which has no life in itself!* and when they see so many things before them prepared for the flesh, they consider with themselves, What care God has of my soul, which cares so much for my body, which shall ultimately go to dust!

There is yet another lesson which will stand you in great stead, if you mark it, when Job here says, *It may be that my sons have sinned*; hereby he teaches us to suspect the worst of the flesh, and to live in a kind of jealousy of ourselves, as he says that his manner was, (Job 9:28), I am afraid of all my sorrows; that is, he did mistrust himself, and washed his hands, and his feet, and his eyes, and his ears, and his tongue, lest they should sin; as a mercer mistrusts his prentice lest he should filch; so he thought not only whether his sons sinned, but he thought of his own sins too. When you see some selling in their shops, some tippling in the taverns, some playing in theatres, then think of this with yourself, It is very like that these men swallow many sins, for God is never so forgotten as in feasting, and sporting, and bargaining; then turn to your compassion, and pray for them, that God would keep them from sin when temptation is at hand, and that He would not impute their sins to their charge: so we should do for our brethren as Job did for his children. Again, so we ought to think when we ourselves come from places of temptation which infect like a corrupt air, It may be that I have sinned: have I seen and heard all this, and not slipped my foot with them? come I home sound and whole? have I drawn none of the infected air? does none of the dust stick on my garments? Look about, my soul, and if you remembers any sin which slipped from you, then pray for yourself, as Job did for his children. If you will not pray for yourself, who shall pray for you? If you will not repent yourself, who shall repent for you? Do not look for Job to sacrifice for you: Job cannot sacrifice for you; but you may sacrifice yourself, and none but you. This should be the thought of every Christian, not whether we have pleased, nor whether we have revenged, but whether we have sinned; for if Job was so jealous of his children, how should we be of ourselves!

SATAN'S COMPASSING THE EARTH

"And the Lord said to Satan, "Whence comest thou?" Then Satan answered the Lord, and said, "From going to and fro in the earth, and from walking up and down in it." And the Lord said to Satan, "Have thon considered My servant Job, that there is none like him in the earth, a perfect and an upright man, one that fears God, and eschews evil?""—Job 1:7-8

I have spoken of the question already, now of the answer. Going to and fro here does signify tempting, and the earth does signify all the people of the earth; as if he should say, I come from tempting all men. It is some vantage to us to hear that the Spaniards are coming, before they come; and what number they have, and how they are appointed, that we may levy our forces accordingly. But, (beloved), there is a greater adversary than the Spaniard, which brings in the Spaniard, your adversary the devil, (1 Pet. 5:8). It is good for us to hear when he comes, that we may be in readiness against him, as we prepare against them. Therefore this Scripture and this time accord well. In Rev. 12:10 the devil is called *the accuser*; and now I am an accuser of the accuser: he accuses us to God, and God accuses him to us, that when he comes like an angel, yet we may say to him like Christ, "Get you hence, Satan," (Matt. 4:10). First, give me leave to say to you as Christ said to His disciples, *Take heed how you hear*; for that which I am to speak to you of the devil, the devil would not have you hear. And therefore as he is a *compasser*, so he will compass your eyes with shows, and your ears with sounds, and your senses with sleep, and your thoughts with fancies, and all to hinder you from hearing, while the articles are against him: and after I have spoken he will compass you again with business, and cares, and pleasures, and quarrels, to make you forget that which you have heard, as he has made you forget that which you have heard before; or else to condemn it, as though you might do well without it; as he has compassed them which do walk in the streets while the voice of God sounds in the churches as they pass by. Therefore before every sermon you have need to remember Christ's lesson, *Take heed how you hear.*

Now to the matter: *Satan, whence comest thou? From going to and fro in the earth.* Here the devil is called in like a jailer, which keeps some in perpetual prison, and some are bailed, and some return to prison again, and some are executed. They which sin fearfully stay as it were about the prison, but are not bound; they which sin wittingly are under lock; they which sin greedily are under lock and bolts; they which die in their sin are like them which are condemned: this is the bondage which we have brought ourselves to for a fair apple. When the tempter overcame us, we were removed out of Paradise, where we were seated; when we have overcome the tempter, we shall be translated into heaven, where he was seated. Heaven-door was wide, and the way was broad, before the rebellion; but when we knocked at the cannel-door, then the good door was shut. Heaven is large, but the way to heaven must be narrow; therefore God has set our enemies in the gate to fight with us before we enter, that this saying might be verified, *The kingdom of heaven suffers violence.* So soon as we rise in the morning, we go to fight with two mighty giants, the world and the devil; and whom do we take with us but a traitor, this brittle flesh, which is ready to yield up to the enemy at every assault? only He which suffers Satan to compass us, does stay him from destroying us. When God asked Cain, *Where is your brother?* Cain lied, and said, *I cannot tell*: when God asked Sarah why she laughed; Sarah lied, and said, *I laughed not*: but when God asked the devil from whence he came; he answered truly, *From going to and fro in the earth.* And yet he which speaks truth himself taught them to lie; as he is called the father of liars, because he teaches all others to lie. How then? Was Cain worse than the devil, because he lied, and the other told truth? By this you may see, that carnal men do not know so much of God as the very devil knows; for he knew that God could tell where he had been, but Cain doubted whether God could tell what he had done, and

123

therefore he made a lie. So the devil teaches his scholars to do worse sometimes than he will do himself; even as he would bring them (if it were possible) into a worse plight than he is in himself. The devil's faith cannot save us, no more than it can save him: the devil's knowledge cannot convert us, no more than it does convert him; and yet he would not have men believe that which he believes himself, nor have us understand so much as he understands himself. For if Cain had understood so much as he, that God knew whether he lied or no, he would have answered God truly, as Satan did. But the devil knew that there was no dissembling with God, who knows what He asks before He asks; therefore he told the truth to God, though he lied to man; for to lie to Him which knows, is as if one should lie to himself. But Cain was not so well learned: he thought peradventure God might understand his murder, as a thief suspects in his heart that the judge may know his theft; but he doubted whether God did know it, and therefore he denied it, like one which is guilty, but thinks that if he confess, he shall be hanged; and therefore, though evidence and witness accuse them, yet you see many will not accuse themselves.

From going to and fro in the earth. He which was called *Satan* before, which signifies an *adversary*, is here said to compass the earth, which is to say, being put together, an adversary compassing the earth; and therefore let the earth beware, like a city which is besieged with the adversaries. The devil has more names than any prince has titles: some God has given to him, and some he has given to himself. But this is to is noted in the devil's names, that he never calls himself a liar, nor a tempter, nor an accuser, nor a slanderer, nor a deceiver, nor a devourer, nor a murderer, nor a master, nor an adversary, nor a viper, nor a lion, nor a dragon, nor a wolf, nor a cockatrice, nor a serpent. But when Christ asked him his name, he called himself Legion, which imports a multitude, as if he should brag of his number: and here he calls himself in effect the compasser of the earth, as if he should brag of his power. And in Luke 4:6 he calls himself the *possessor of the earth*, as if he should brag of his possessions; and in the same he calls himself the giver of the earth, as if he should brag of his liberty. So he which is evil itself does shun the name, because he would not be hated; and therefore no marvel if men call evil good, and would be counted honest, though they are never so lewd, for so will the devil. But as God never calls the devil but by those names which the devil hated; so he never calls sinners by those names which they call themselves: for if you observe the Scripture, there is no name of the devil, but in some place of Scripture or other, the wicked are called by the same name. He is called a liar, and they are called liars: he is called a tempter, and they are called tempters: he is called a murderer, and they are called murderers: he is called a slanderer, and they are called slanderers: he is called a viper, and they are called vipers: he is called a lion, and they are called lions: he is called a wolf, and they are called wolves: he is called a serpent, and they are called serpents. So God would they that shall be damned should have the name of him which is damned, to put him in mind. Now none of the devil's names are in the book of life; and therefore liars, and tempters, and slanderers, and murderers, and defainers, are not: therefore these are devil's names. This I note, to show you how deadly God hates sin, that neither the devil nor his followers could ever get a good name of Him; for all this compassing, he could never compass this,—to shuffle any praise of himself into this book of life: for he does not compass heaven, but earth, though he would compass both. The devil himself tells us here that he compasses, and he does not tell why he compasses; but his name *Satan*, that went before, which he did not speak of, this tells us why he compasses: because it signifies an *adversary*, it gives us to understand that he compasses the earth like an adversary. God compasses the earth like a wall to defend it: the devil compasses the earth like an enemy to besiege it: for enemy is his name; he is envy even to the name.

Three things I note wherefore the devil may be said to go to and fro in the earth. First, because *he tempts all men*. Secondly, because *he tempts all to sin*. Thirdly, because he tempts *by all means.* So whosoever sins, in whichsoever he offends, whereby soever he is allured, the sin, the sinner, and the bait, are compassed and contrived by the arch politic, which calls himself a compasser. Many have their names for nothing, because they do nothing for them; like Laban's images, which were called gods, though they were but blocks; but the devil deserves his names. He is not called a tempter, a liar, a slanderer, and an accuser, and a deceiver, and a murderer, and a compasser, in vain; like St. George, which is always on horseback, and never rides: but he would do more than by his office he is bound to. Others are called officers, because they have an office; but he is called an enemy, because be shows his envy. Others are called *justicers*, because they should do justice; but he is called a tempter, because he practices temptations. Others are called pastors, because they should feed: but he is called a devourer, because he does devour; and we call him a compasser, because that he does compass. Ever since he fell from heaven he has lived like Cain, which cannot rest in a place, but is a runagate over the earth, from door to door, from man to man, begging for sins as the starved soul begs for bread. He should have dwelt in heaven, and not been compassing the earth; he should have sung with the angels, and not been quarrelling with men: but he has changed his calling, and has become a compasser, that is, to lay fetters on men, as God has fettered him, lest they should ascend to the place from whence he is fallen. Therefore in this the liar spoke truth, when he said, *From going to and fro in the earth*: as if he should say to God, I come from the slaughter of Your servants; not to ask forgiveness for all the souls which he has slain already, but to get a commission that God would make him knight-marshal over the world, to slay and kill as many as he hated; like the bramble which set itself on fire first, and then fired all the wood. Peter, describing the devil's walk, says, that he goes *about*; the devil says, that he goes *to and fro*. Peter put in, *seeking whom he may devour*: the devil leaves out *devour*, and says no more but that he *goes*. This *circular walk* is peculiar to the devil, and therefore may be called the devil's circuit. All other creatures go forward, but the devil goes about; which may well be applied to the crafty devil, because to go about is commonly taken to undermine; when any means to destroy you, then we say, he will compass you; so when the devil compasses, then beware lest he devour. For the devil goes about men as the fowler goes about the lark to snare her, as the thief goes about the house to rob it, as the ivy goes about the oak to kill it. The devil's walk is a siege, which goes about but to find an issue to go in; for he goes about but until he can get in to be a possessor. He is content to be a compasser. The first name the devil has in Scripture is a serpent: he is a serpent, and so are his ways like a serpent, which winds himself like a circle. As God is said to make an hedge about men, so here the devil is said to make an hedge about men; but this is an hedge of temptations, and that is an hedge against temptations. As David says, the angels compass us, so might he say, the devils compass us. Satan compasses, and man is compassed; Satan is like the circumference, and man is as it were the center; that is, temptations go round about him, and he dwells in the midst of them. So much of compassing: now what he does compass.

From going to and fro in the earth. This is the devil's pilgrimage, from one end of the earth to the other, and then to the other again, and then back again; like a wandering merchant, which seeks his traffic where he can speed cheapest. I have heard of some travellers which have gone about the earth; but I never heard of any that had seen all parts of the earth, but this old pilgrim Satan, which has been in heaven, and in paradise, and in the earth, and in the sea, and in hell, and yet has not done his walk; but, like the sun which courses about the earth every day, so there is not one day but Satan sees every man on earth: as a compass has no end, so he makes no end of compassing. Because he is such a compasser of the world, therefore Paul calls him the "god of this world," (2 Cor. 4:4); not a piece of the world, as England, or Ireland, or France, or Germany, or Spain; but of *the world*, that is, of all the countries, and cities, and towns, and villages, and houses. The

Pope talks of his kingdom, how many provinces are under his dominion; but the devil's circuit is greater than the Pope's. One would think that he could never tend half his flock, because he is vicar of so great a monarchy; and yet he is never non-resident. You may see his steps everywhere so broad and fresh, as though they were printed in ashes. If God makes you see your country naked, your temples desolate, your cities ruined, your houses spoiled, you will say the Spaniards have been here; so, when you see your minds corrupted, your hearts hardened, your wills perverted, your charity cooled, your judges bribers, your rulers persecutors, your lawyers brabblers, your merchants usurers, your landlords extortioners, your patrons simonists, your pastors loiterers, you may say the devil has been here. Seeing then these weeds grow in every ground, you may bear the devil witness that he does compass all the earth. If a man love his friend, he will say, I will go a hundred miles to do him good; but if the devil hates a man, he will go a thousand miles to do him hurt. The devil does not go his progress like a king, only for delight; but all the way he goes, Peter says, he seeks whom he may devour. The devil goes a-visiting; he will teach the sick how they shall recover their health; he will whisper the poor how they shall come by riches; he will tell the captives how they shall redeem their liberty; but to devour is the end of his visitation. Therefore Peter called him a *lion*; and said, that he went about; and told us that he sought as he went; at last he says, to devour, and there he ends; showing, that devouring is his end.

Now you shall hear whom he compasses, and to what he compasses, and how he compasses. When it is said, that the devil compasses the earth, it is meant that he compasses the men of the earth: out of which I gather, first, of all creatures he compasses man; secondly, that he compasses all men, and by consequence that he compasses good men. The devil is like an archer, and man is his mark, and temptations are his arrows. As Peter is called a fisher of men; so the devil may be called a hunter of men; for of all creatures his envy is only to men, because man was made to serve God, and inherit the joys which he has lost; therefore he is called no slayer, but a manslayer. When there are no men on earth, then the devil will compass the earth no more.

Secondly, he assaults all men, like Ishmael, which was against all. It is said of Saul and David, "Saul has slain his thousands, and David his ten thousands," (1 Sam. 18:7); but if you put in Satan, you may set up the number, and say, *Satan has slain his billions.* As there is a legion of men, so there is a legion of devils; that as they say Peter's angel, so they might say Peter's devil: for Christ would not have called Peter Satan, if Satan had not backed him. As death kills all, so the devil tempts all: when he has Eve, he hunts for Adam; when he has Adam, he hunts for Cain: as the father was tempted, so was the son; as the mother was tempted, so must her daughters. Every man but Christ may say, I have been overcome; but Christ Himself cannot say, I have not been tempted. In the Spanish Inquisition the Protestants are examined, but the Papists slip by; but in the devil's Inquisition Papist, and Protestant, Atheist, and Puritan, and all are examined. He is not a captain of forties, nor of fifties, nor of sixties, nor of hundreds; but he is general over all which fight not under Christ's banner: he possessed the two Gergesenes, which were men; he possessed Mary, which was a woman; he possessed the man's son, which was a child. Nimrod is called a mighty hunter, which killed beasts; but this is a mighty hunter, which killed Nimrod himself. God keep us out of his chase!

Thirdly, he wars against the righteous, even because they are righteous. As God makes the barren fruitful, and the fruitful to bear more fruit; so the devil would have them serve him which serve him not, and they which serve him to serve him more: and therefore as the giant encountered with David, so the devil encountered with David and with David's Lord. He which gave him leave here to tempt Job, was after tempted Himself, although the net brake, and the bird escaped. Yet as he tempted Christ thrice together, and as he desired to sift Peter more than others; so they that follow Christ, and are like Peter, are more sifted than others. For this viper is like the viper which seized on Paul. Among many which stood by the fire, the viper chose but Paul, and lighted on him before all the rest; so if one be holier than another, this viper will battle with him. And there is great reason why the godly are tempted more than the wicked, because the wicked are his servants, and do tempt others.

As he tempts all men, so he tempts to all sins; for hell and the devil are alike; therefore, as hell is never filled with sinners, so the devil is never filled with sins; and therefore when he had made Peter deny his Master once, he made him deny Him twice; and when he had made him deny Him twice, he made him deny Him thrice. For this cause our sins are counted among those things which are infinite, because the devil and our flesh meet together every day to engender new sins. All the devil's riches are in baits: he has a pack full of oaths for everyone which will swear; a pack full of lies for everyone which will deceive; a pack full of excuses for everyone which will dissemble. As he does go through the streets, into every shop he casts a short measure, or a false balance: as he passes by the taverns, he sets dissension between friends: as he passes by every inn, he casts a pair of cards, and a pair of dice, and a pair of tables: as he passes by the courts, and finds the lawyers at the bar, he casts among them false evidences, forged writings, and counterfeit seals. So, in every place where he comes (like a foggy mist) he leaves an evil savor behind him. The murmuring of Moses, the dissimulation of Abraham, the idolatry of Aaron, the incest of Lot, the drunkenness of Noah, the adultery of David, the flight of Jonah, the denial of Peter: name Satan, and you have named the very *spawn of all sins*, which with his tail plucked down the stars from heaven. How many hate their enemies and friends too, and yet embrace this enemy, because he kisses when he betrays, as though he would not betray! Avarice says, *I will make you amiable*: Tyranny says, *I will make you dreadful*: Sloth says, *I will make you beautiful*: Vanity says, *I will make you merry*; Prodigality says, *I will make you beloved*. So the poor sinner stands distracted how he may follow all sins at once; seeking grapes from thistles, and roses from thorns.

As he tempts to all sins, so he tempts by all means; for the name of a compasser does import a cunning tempter. There is craft in compassing. The hunter makes a rail about the deer, as though he would guard them, when he means to take some of them; the fowler goes about the bird as if he did not see her, when he comes to snare her. If men have so many sleights to compass their matters, how can the compasser himself hold his fingers? If the serpent's seed is so subtle, what do you think of the old serpent, who has been learning his trade ever since the creation? If men's trades may be called crafts, the devil's trade may be called craft. Herod is called a fox, but this fox taught him his subtlety. This is he that prepared flatterers for Rehoboam, which prepared liars for Ahab, which prepared concubines for Solomon, which prepared sorcerers for Pharaoh, which prepared witches for Saul, which prepared wine for Benhadad, which prepared gold for Achan, which prepared a ship for Jonah, which prepared a rope for Haman. He goes not about for nothing. But this is the first trick of his compassing,—he marks how every man is inclined, what he loves, what he hates, what he fears, and what he wants; and when he has the measure of his foot, then he fits him. Ask what you will, here is he which offered the whole world. What? shall Jonah stay for want of a ship? *No, here is a ship, go and fly from the Lord.* Shall Esau stay for want of broth? *No,* here is a mess of broth, go and sell your birthright. Shall Judas stay for want of thirty pence? *No,* here is thirty pence, go and betray your Master. Shall Pilate stay for want of a halter? *No,* here is a halter, go and hang yourself. The tyrant shall not want a flatterer, the wanton shall not want a mate, the usurer shall not want a broker, the thief shall not want a receiver; he is a factor between the merchant and the mercer, and the gentleman and the tenant; he is a make-bate between, the man and his wife; he is a tale-bearer between neighbor and neighbor. So, if you ask me what is the devil's trade or occupation, all the day long he is making nets and traps and snares to catch you and me, which gape for the worm.

If then the devil is such a busy-body, who meddles in every man's matter, let us remember what the wise man says, *A busy-body is hated*: the devil is to be hated, because he is a busy-body. The Jews could not abide the Publicans, because they were like sumners and takers, which carried toll out of their country into another: how then can we abide this great Publican, which takes toll over all the world? *No*, not toll of men, but men themselves? He which compasses the earth, compasses us, even us that stand here. Therefore, what shall I say, but as Christ said, *When the thief compasses the house, shall not the owner guard the house?* If the city be compassed and not defended, how shall it stand? As the devil runs round about, so the armor must go round about us; and then though he compass us, yet he shall not overcome us; but as the Israelites were safe, though the water compassed about them; as the three children were safe, though the flames compassed about them; as Daniel was safe, though the lions compassed about him; so they which have Christ's armor are safe, although the devils compass about them. "I will not be afraid (says David) what man can do to me," (Psa. 56:11); *no*, I will not fear what the devil can do to me; for He which is with me is greater than he which is against me. So much of the devil and his compassing.

As the serpent compasses, so does his seed: and therefore Solomon calls the ways of the wicked crooked ways. This is the great compasser; there are little compassers beside; like the Pharisees, of whom it is said, that they compassed sea and land to make one like themselves. Instead of these compassers, we have seminary priests, which compass, from Rome to Tyburn, to draw one from Christ to Antichrist. I will not name all compassers beside, lest I be compassed myself; but this I speak within compass, that there is a craft of compassing, and Satan is the craft-master, and the rest are his prentices, or factors under him. When he compasses some men, he sets them to compass other men; and so he has his compassers and spies in every country, like continual lieges to follow his business for him, which will do it as faithfully as himself. If he appoint them to lie, they will lie as fast as he: if he appoints them to deceive, they will deceive as cunningly as he: if he appoints them to slander, they will slander as falsely as he: if he appoints them to flatter, they will flatter as smoothly as he: if he appoints them to mock, they will mock as scornfully as he: if he appoints them to revenge, they will revenge as spitefully as he: if he appoints them to persecute, they will persecute as fully as he. So if he but says, *Let there be an oath*, straight there is an oath: let there be a lie, straight there is a lie: let there be a flout, straight there is a flout: let there be a bribe, straight there is a bribe: let there be a quarrel, straight there is a quarrel. Therefore in this the liar told the truth, for he has compassed the earth indeed.

So you see what the devil answered, when God asked him from where he came. Now if God should ask you, as He asked the devil, from where you came before you came here to Him, or rather where you will go when you depart from before Him; I do verily think that some here did come from as bad exercises as the devil himself; and that when they do depart from this place, they will return to as bad exercises again as the devil did; some to the taverns, and some to the alehouses, and some to stages, and some to brothels, and some to dicing, and some to quarrelling, and some to cozening. I would eagerly know this. If the devil came from tempting, and you from sinning, who was better occupied; he in commanding you, or you in obeying him? They which come to the church and return to their sins, come to the Lord as the devil came, not to be reformed of his evil, but to have a passport to do more evil.[1] If any such be here, he has learned nothing, but goes empty away; for they which come like Satan, go like Satan. A little water is sprinkled on them, which falls off again to the ground so soon as they are out of the church door: all which they learned is forgotten, like a perfume which savors no longer

---

[1] *Note bene.* Editor.

than they abide in the house where it burns. Therefore, as I warned you at first, Take heed how you hear, so I warn you now, *Take heed lest this compasser come and steal that which you have heard.* For when Judas had almost received the Sacrament, the devil entering into him, after that could never be driven out again; so if the devil enter into you after you have received this warning, he will possess you like Judas, stronger than he did before, and every word shall condemn you. As he which "eats the Sacrament unworthily, eats his own damnation," (1 Cor. 11:29); so he which hears the Word unfruitfully, hears his own damnation; "for the Word which I have spoken, (says Christ), the same shall judge you in the last day," (John 12:48).

AN ALARM FROM HEAVEN: SUMMONING ALL MEN TO THE HEARING OE THE TRUTH

"Go you therefore, and teach all nations, baptizing them in the name of the Father, and of the Son, and of the Holy Spirit."— Matt. 28:19

The Apostle Paul, writing to Timothy, tells him that God would have all men come to the knowledge of the truth, and "be saved," (1 Tim. 2:4). In which words the Apostle gives him to understand, that there is no other way either for priest or people to come to God, but by that ordinary means, which is *the hearing of the Word*; the which the Apostle calls His truth, because it is not only true of itself, but also witnesses of His truth, who is truth itself. By the very same name does our Savior Christ call God's Word, when, making His prayer to His heavenly Father, (for the elect), He says, "Sanctify them through Your truth;" and immediately adds, "Your Word is truth," (John 17:17). The next thing that the Apostle advertises Timothy of is that this truth, being rightly known, brings salvation to them that so know it. And this the Apostle confirms by an argument taken from his own faith, when he says, "I am not ashamed of the Gospel of Christ; for it is the power of God to salvation to everyone that believeth," (Rom. 1:16). And last of all, the Apostle has set down the generality of this truth, both in saying to Timothy, that God would have all men to be acquainted with it; and to the saints at Rome, that it is able to save every believer. Here it comes, that, writing to the Colossians, he exhorts them not so much to the hearing of this truth taught them, as to an inward entertainment of the same, when he says, "Let the word of Christ dwell in you richly, in all wisdom; teaching and admonishing one another," (Col. 3:16). Teaching themselves, because many of the Colossians seemed to be ignorant of that which they should know; and admonishing themselves, because a number of them did know

135

much, but practiced little. So that such is the entertainment that God's Word ought to find among us, as David promised to it, when he said, "Teach me, O Lord, the way of Your statutes, and I shall keep it to the end," (Psa. 119:33). And we are taught to entertain God's Word by the example of John, who, receiving the little book at the hand of the angel, was commanded to "eat that book," (Rev. 10:9); partly to teach us, that God's Word must abide within us; and partly to signify, that our bodily bread serves not our soul's necessity, (Matt. 4:4). Isaiah said that he had carefully carried God's message; for, "I am found (he says) of those that sought Me not," (Isa. 65:3). Howbeit he was not so careful in speaking, but the people were as careless in hearing: for the which cause he utters this complaint, *Who has believed our report? and to whom is the arm of the Lord revealed?* (Isa. 53:1). When Jeremiah had faithfully delivered the message of the Lord his God in rebuking those Jews which burned incense to the idols of Egypt, he says, that all the men that knew that their wives had burned incense to strange gods, and a great many women which stood by gave him this answer, "As for the word which you spoke to us in the name of the Lord, we will not hearken to you," (Jer. 44:16). Such was the wickedness of the people so many years past, as appears in many places of God's Word; among the which that of those in Babylon was not the least; which moved Jeremiah, to send Seraiah to them with the book, and with a strait charge, that when he had read it to them, he should bind a stone to it, "and cast it into the river Euphrates," (Jer. 1:63); this was to teach the Babylonians and all men, that as the hard stone caused the good book to sink in the water, so hardness of our stony hearts is not only the depriving us of many good blessings, but also a violent sinking of our souls in sin. The just consideration of this moved the Apostle Paul to expostulate the matter with every hard-hearted sinner in this sort: "Do you not know that the goodness of God leads you to repentance?" But after your hardness and impenitent heart you treasures up to yourself "wrath against the day of wrath," and revelation of the righteous judgment of God, (Rom. 2:4-5). And yet to see what small preparation there is to repentance! Every godly man wishes, like zealous Jeremiah, "Oh, that my head were waters, and mine eyes a fountain of tears, that I might weep day and night for the slain of the daughter of my people!" (Jer. 9:1). So grievous is the way of the ungodly to the child of God, that he cannot account it any better thing than a race in which they run, striving who shall come first to the devil; when they lead a life as void of repentance, as if sin were seen and allowed, and hell-fire but an old wives' fable. What made Jeremiah so weary of his people, but that he saw them weary of well-doing? For, sighing and sorrowing, so he says, "Oh, that I had in the wilderness a lodging-place of wayfaring men; that I might leave my people and go from them I for they are all adulterers, an assembly of treacherous men," (Jer. 9:2).

So long as Stephen the martyr talked to the Jews of their pedigree, they hearkened to him diligently; but when he rebuked their sins, saying that they were a stiff-necked people, and of a hard heart, resisting the Holy Spirit, in persecuting the Prophets, and putting to death the Lord of life, then they stopped their ears, and, gnashing their teeth, ran on him, and stoned him to death. So it fares at this day among men, that many are as well contented to hear pleasant things, as the Jews were to hearken to Stephen repeating their parentage; but if a man shall hit all sorts of ill manners, as well as speak to all sorts of men, they hold it as a principle, that he forgets his text who remembers their sins: notwithstanding they know, that it is the minister's duty to tell the house of Jacob their sins, and to let Israel hear of their transgressions, (Isa. 58:1); and the people's part, not only to be content, but also desirous, to know their duties, and to show their desire in the forwardness of their coming before him that ought to teach. Otherwise we might imagine that God spoke in sport, when He said by His Prophet, "The priests lips shall keep knowledge, and the people shall seek the law at his moves," (Matt. 2:7). For he thought the evil-disposed people in Ezekiel's time, who used to hear him preach with the like affections that many bring now-a-days. Concerning whose fruitless hearing God informs

Ezekiel, by saying to him, Son of wan, the children of your people still are talking of you by the walls, and in the doors of the houses, and speak one to another, everyone to his brother, saying, Come, I pray you, and hear what is the word that comes forth from the Lord. They come to you as the people come, and they sit before you as My people, and they hear your words, but will not do them: "for with their mouths they show much love, but their heart goes after their covetousness. And lo, you are to them as a very lovely song of one that has a pleasant voice, and can play well on an instrument: for they hear your words, but they do them not," (Ezek. 33:30-32).

These people, and the people which were in the time or Hosea the Prophet, may presently be matched with the men of our age, who were as ready to rail on the priest as he was pressed to reproved their sins: For, says Hosea, "The people areas those that strive with the priest," (Hos. 4:4). It is most true, that the want of salvation proceeds both of the lack of teaching, and of the want of faith to believe rightly that which is taught. The first of these is approved by the words which the Holy Spirit spoke by the mouth of this Prophet last named, so, "My people are destroyed for lack of knowledge," *etc.*, (Hos. 4:6). The other by the testimony of our Savior Christ Himself, who, sending His eleven to preach and baptize, says, "He that believes and is baptized, shall be saved; but he that believes not, shall be damned," (Mark 16:16). Why did the rich man go to hell, but either for one of these causes before named, or for them both? (that is to say) because he never frequented the Word of God, whereby faith is begotten in the hearts of the hearers; or if he heard the same Word, yet it was heard so carelessly, that it took no root at all. And indeed that answer which Abraham made to his request seems to skirt the truth of that which I say; for when request was made by that hell-hound, that a messenger might go from the dead to his five brethren, which were yet at his father's house, *etc.*, Abraham replied this way, "They have Moses and the Prophets, let them hear them," for as Abraham says, if that which Moses has set down of God's justice cannot batter our brazen faces and hearts of adamant, nor the invaluable and most assured promises made by Christ to His elect, and recorded by His Prophets, cannot drive us from sin, and draw us to Himself; then there is no more hope of us in hearing the Word of God than was of Simon and Judas, though they heard the Word, and received the sacraments: for our life is no other way reformed by a careless kind of hearing, than Jeroboam redressed the religion in Israel when he set up two golden calves, the one in Dan, and the other in Bethel, that the Israelites might worship them; or Nebuchadnezzar in his kingdom, when he destroyed idols, that he might be worshipped as God. It is a matter so true, that no man can so much as imagine, much less speak, the contrary without great offence, that God has done so much for His vine as by any means might be, (Isa. 5:4): insomuch that David the King of Israel never had greater cause than the Prince and people of England have, to say of the goodness of God, "He has not dealt so with any nation," (Psa. 147:20), in giving to us so long use of His laws. And yet he that compares the pastor's painful preaching with the people's little profiting, in most places of this land, shall find just occasion to think that the Son of God has pronounced that same curse on this English vine which He uttered against that fruitless fig-tree mentioned by Matthew in these words, "Never fruit grow on you henceforward," (Matt. 21:19). God grant that there are not some men who measure the meat by the man; like those proud citizens which said, "We will not have this man to reign over us," (Luke 19:14); and loathe the message, because they like not the messenger; like those scornful Jews that told Jeremiah to His face, The word which you have spoken to us in the name of the Lord, we will not hearken to you; but we will certainly do "whatsoever thing goes forth out of our own mouth," (Jer. 44:16-17); but that they may know them which labor among them, and are over them in the Lord; and not barely know them, but also love them for their work's sake, (1 Thes. 5:12-13).

So having finished the former circumstances as compendiously as I promised, I proceed to the next words; the ones which contain in them the second part of a Christian minister's duty, which is, *to minister the sacraments rightly*; whereof one is set down in its due order, by the Instituter Christ Himself, when He says, *Baptizing them, in the name of the Father, and the Son, and the Holy Spirit.*

Now because the word *baptism* has diverse significations in the Scripture, I will here set down as many of them as my memory can record. First, the word *baptism*, according to the true meaning of the Greek word *Baptisma*, does not signify only a dipping, but such a dipping in the water as does cleanse the party dipped: and for that the Primitive Church did use to put the party baptized quite under the water; therefore Paul, writing both to the Romans and Colossians, uses these words, *We are buried with Him by baptism into death*: that like as Christ was raised up from the dead by the glory of the Father, even so we also should walk in newness of life, (Rom. 6:4; Col. 2:12). In which words the apostle shows what resemblance their baptism has with Christ's death and resurrection. Secondly, baptism is used for a bare washing: in which sense our Savior spoke when He said to the Pharisees, "Laying aside the commandment of God, you hold the traditions of men, as the washing of pots and cups: and many other such like things you do," (Mark 7:8). And in the same sense we read in the Epistle to the Hebrews, when the author says, that the old tabernacle consisted of many washings and ceremonial rites, until the day of reformation came, (Heb. 9:10). Thirdly, by baptism we may understand affliction; as our Savior Christ did, in saying to James and John, the sons of Zebedee, *Can you be baptized with that baptism wherewith I am baptized?* (Mark 10:38); and to His disciples, I have a baptism to be baptized with: but how am I straitened "till it is accomplished," (Luke 12:50). Fourthly, baptism is a liberal distribution of the graces of God; as appears in these words. "John baptized with water, but you shall be baptized with the Holy Spirit not many days hence," (Acts 1:5). Fifthly, the word baptism is taken for doctrine only; as in that place in which the

Holy Spirit, having occasion to speak of Apollos, a Jew of Alexandria, says, that he was mighty in the Scriptures, and did know only the baptism of John, (Acts 18:24-25). And last of all, baptism is taken for a reverend order of ministering that sacrament in the Church, and the whole sanctification of the parties baptized: as in the words of this present part of Scripture, *baptizing, etc.*

But to speak of the sacrament itself: It has been usual with Almighty God from time to time to confirm His covenants with seals set to the same. For example, we see that there is a rainbow in the clouds: the reason whereof is, that God having in His justice destroyed the old world for sin, (only Noah and his family being excepted), the same God in His mercy made a covenant with Noah, that He would never destroy it so again: for confirmation of it, He set the rainbow in the clouds, as a seal to that covenant between Himself and Noah, (Gen. 9:12, *etc.*). So was circumcision given to Abraham as a seal of confirmation in that promise, that in his seed all nations of the earth should be blessed, (Gen. 17:10-11): so that as many as were circumcised were within compass of that covenant; instead whereof we have baptism, the which whosoever shall refuse, we account him as cut off from God's Church. Christ Jesus gave invisible grace by visible laying His hands on children and other sick people, (Mark 10:16). So He gave the gift of His Holy Spirit to His disciples, when, having breathed on them, He said, "Receive you the Holy Spirit," (John 20:22).

The sacraments were ordained in the Church of God for three uses. First, that we should acknowledge all those to be our fellow-servants whom we see to have to put on the same livery with ourselves: and in this sense said the Apostle Paul, "As many of you as have been baptized into Christ have put on Christ," (Gal. 3:27). Secondly, the sacraments put a manifest difference between the true Church and the false: as Peter has taught us, in saying. Repent and be baptized every one of you in the name of Jesus Christ: "for the promise is to you, and to your children, and to all that are afar off, even so many as the Lord our God shall call," (Acts 2:38-39). And our Savior says, "Of such is the kingdom of God," (Mark 10:14); that is, to such as lead an innocent life. The third use of the Sacraments is, to seal up in the hearts of the elect all those promises which God has made to them in Jesus Christ His Son and their Savior: in the which sense Paul spoke, when he said, that Abraham received the sign of circumcision, as a seal of that righteousness which he had by faith, (Rom. 4:11): and in the very same sense our Savior says, "He that believes and is baptized shall be saved," (Mark 16:16). But it is to be considered, that the Instituter sets down the form of administering the Sacrament, when He says, *Baptizing them in the name of the Father, and of the Son, and of the Holy Spirit.* He commands to baptize in the name of the Father and of the Son, because the Holy Spirit proceeds from the Father and the Son: and in the name of the Holy Spirit; for, except a man be born of water and the Spirit, he cannot enter the kingdom of God, (John 3:5). When our Savior offered to wash Peter's feet, he imagined it to be a needless work, for, you shall never wash my feet, he says: but when Christ answered, that such as are not washed by Him have no part with Him, that is, neither part of His Spirit, nor of His kingdom; Peter, bethinking himself better, would not have his feet only, but also his hands and his head, washed, (John 13:8-9). How is it that it is not necessary to wash any more than is unclean: as Peter's feet defiled with dirt and mire, so our souls spotted with sins must be cleansed by Christ's blood only. And after this manner it is necessary that everyone of us should be washed; whereof the outward putting of water on the party baptized is a lively figure. John the Baptist was sanctified in his mother's womb, as the angel had foreshowed, (Luke 1:15): but when our Savior Christ came to him to be baptized, John forbade Him, saying, "I have need to be baptized of You, and you come to me?" (Matt. 3:14). That kingly Prophet David was a man after God's own heart; yet he says of himself, "I was shapen in iniquity, and in sin did my mother conceive me," (Psa. 51:5). Job was called by God Himself a just and upright man, fearing God, and eschewing evil, whose peer was not found on the face of the earth; notwithstanding all this, he says of himself, "Who can bring a clean thing out of an unclean?" (Job 14:4). The which question is all one with Paul's affirmation, who says, *If the root be holy, so are the branches*, (Rom. 11:16). As if he had said, *If Adam, the father of us all, was undefiled, then are we his sons clean also*; but if he were once dead in sin, being our root, then how could we his imps have life of ourselves? And this was spoken of original sin: as for actual sins, namely, those sins which we continually commit, they are as palpable as the darkness of Egypt, the which (as Moses says) was so gross that it might be felt, (Exod. 10:21). Insomuch that David says, "When the Lord looked down from heaven on the children of men," (that is, when He considered man's conversation), "they were all gone aside, that there was none that did good;" insomuch that the prophet repeats it with an emphasis, and says, "No not one," (Psa. 14:2-3). And the man of God, Moses, says, "When God beheld the boldness of the old world in sinning, it repented Him that He had made man," (Gen. 6:5-6); that is, He was sorry that man, whom He had made to live well, should live so ill. The continual sin of Sodom brought fire and brimstone from heaven to consume them in the same, (Gen. 19:24). David, feeling the burden of his sins, began to sink under them; for he says, "My iniquities are gone over mine head: as a heavy burden they are too heavy for me," (Psa. 38:4). Paul having by the virtue of the law learned his sins, (for he had not known sin, but by the law, Rom. 7:7), fell to lamenting of them this way, "O wretched man that I am! who shall deliver me from the body of this death?" (Rom. 7:24). Where it is to is noted, that he calls his body a body of death in respect of sin, which gives power to death over our bodies. And to conclude, of such force is sin in us, that if the goodness of God had not so preordained, that the unbelieving husband is sanctified by the believing wife, and the unbelieving wife by the believing husband, our children should be very unclean, (1 Cor. 7:14).

Again, being washed or baptized in the name of the Father, Son, and Holy Spirit, we are advertised, that we must give godly, Christian, and holy names to our children, in token of their sacred profession; for holy is He that has called us. And that we may be the more forward so to do, it will be worth our labor to consider of a few examples tending to the same purpose. As of Zacharias, the father of John the Baptist, who being dumb when his son was born, his friends made signs to him how he would have him called; "and asking for a pair of writing-tables, he wrote, saying, His name is John," (Luke 1:63); which word John is as much as to say, Grace; and so was Zacharias commanded by the angel to name him, (Luke 1:13). The Scripture affords plentiful examples of those that have given names to their children according to such occasions as have been offered in the time of their travail. As when Rachel went with her husband Jacob toward Bethel, to build an altar to God, she travailed in child-birth, and in travailing died: but before she departed, "she called his name Benoni," (Gen. 35:18); that is, the son of her sorrow: but his father Jacob called him Benjamin; that is, the son of his right hand. So Leah having borne to Jacob four sons, she said, "Now will I praise the Lord," etc., (Gen. 29:35). And that she might the better bear in mind her promise, she named her last son Judah. When the man of Benjamin came from the Israelites with his clothes rent and dust on his head, in token of heaviness, and certified father Eli, that God's ark was taken by the Philistines, and that his two sons were slain; the old father fell backward out of his seat, and broke his neck: and his daughter-in-law, Phinehas' wife, (1 Sam. 4:18, etc.), being frightened with fear, fell in travail, and died in child-bed; but before her death she called her son Ichabod, that is, "The glory is departed from Israel;" meaning thereby, that she accounted the glory of God to be taken from Israel, when God's ark (which was a figure of His church, in which we glorify His name) "was taken, away by the enemy," (1 Sam. 4:18-22); and secondly, to admonish all parents so to nurture up their children, that they may seek to maintain the glory of God better than Eli did, for the wickedness of whose children, as also for the father's default in not correcting them, God had threatened before, that if He once began with him,

"He would make an end with him," (1 Sam. 3:11-14). So that as the prophet says, "Children, being the fruit of the womb, as they come from God, are a good blessing, and an heritage from the Lord," (Psa. 127:3), because He it is from whom every good and perfect gift proceeds: yet in respect of men, so may the matter be handled, that they shall find no such cross or curse as graceless or unruly children; such as Esau and his two wives, who were a grief of mind and a heart-breaking to Isaac their father, and Rebekah their mother, (Gen. 26:35).

It is true, that the most godly men and women have rather desired sons than daughters at the hands of God; but they did it for good and godly purposes. As when Abraham desired a son, to the end that Eliezer, the steward of his house, being a stranger, namely, a man of Damascus, should not be the heir of his goods, (Gen. 15:2). So did Hannah pray to God for a son, when she said, "O Lord of hosts, if you will indeed look on the affliction of your handmaid, and remember me, and not forget your handmaid, but will give to your handmaid a man-child, then I will give him to the Lord all the days of his life, and there shall no razor come on his head," (1 Sam. 1:11). And as the very name of a son is in price and preferred at this day, so has it been heretofore; as when Phinehas' wife being near her death in travail, the midwife with the rest thinking to comfort her, said, "Fear not, for you have born a son," (1 Sam. 4:20). When the angel said to Abraham, "This time twelvemonth Sarah, your wife, shall bear a son;" *Sarah laughed*, as partly doubting, and partly joying that so aged a woman as she should conceive a son by so aged a man as Abraham was, (Gen. 18:10, 12). The same angel that certified Zacharias that Elisabeth his wife should bear John the Baptist, said, not only that it should be a son, but such a son as should bring joy to him and many more, (Luke 1:13-14). And that angel Gabriel that was sent of God to Mary, the mother of our Savior according to His humanity, says, that instead of fear, she had found favor with God: and his reason is this, "For you shall bear a Son, and shall call His name Jesus," (Luke 1:30-31). As if he had said, *It is a great blessing of God to bear a child, and a greater to bear a man-child*: but to be so far in God's favor as to bear such a Son as shall be the Savior of the world, it is the greatest grace which has been heard of. In this God will make His Church joyful, which is exceedingly special, and for all the rest of His blessings in general, God makes us *thankful. Amen.*

THE SINNER'S CONVERSION

"And He entered and passed through Jericho. And, behold, there was a man named Zacchaeus, which was the chief among the publicans, and he was rich. And he sought to see Jesus who He was; and could not for the press, because he was little of stature. And he ran before, and climbed up into a sycamore tree to see Him: for He was to pass that way. And when Jesus came to the place, He looked up, and saw him, and said to him, "Zacchaeus, make haste, and come down; for today I must abide at your house."'—Luke 19:1-5

In the end of the chapter before going we may see how Christ healed a man blind in his bodily sight, namely, Bartimaeus, whereby He shows Himself to be the Physician of the Body, (Eph. 5:23): here we shall see how He cured one blind in mind, namely, Zacchaeus, where He shows Himself to be the Physician of the Soul, and therefore the Savior of the whole man.

In speaking of Zacchaeus and his conversion, we will observe four circumstances: first, the place where he was called, which was Jericho; secondly, the person that was called, Zacchaeus the publican; thirdly, by whom and how he was called, by the voice of Christ; and lastly, the effect and fruit of his calling, his good confession.

First therefore, for the place where he was converted, it appears to be Jericho, a city not far distant from Jerusalem. It was sometime a notable city, until it was subverted and ruined by the Lord's champion Joshua, (Josh. 6:24). It was built again in the days of Ahab, by Hiel the Bethelite, (1 Kings 17:4), and remains at this day, with the rest of that Holy Land, under the Turkish Empire. To this Jericho the Lord of Heaven and Earth vouchsafes to come in the likeness of a servant. And as Joshua compassed Jericho seven times, minding to destroy it; so Christ, the true Joshua, resorted oftentimes to Jericho, minding to save it. But as in the destruction of Jericho Joshua spared none but Rahab the harlot; so Jesus, in His journey to Jericho, converted none but Zacchaeus the publican. When Joshua had conquered and razed Jericho, he sowed salt in it, to make it barren, and cursed him that should attempt to build it up," (Josh. 6:26); yet in this barren soil Christ has His spiritual harvest; and in this cursed city he has a holy temple, a blessed building. Samaria, that wicked city, affords many that believe in Christ, (John 4:39). And out of Galilee, from whence they thought no good thing might come, (John 1:46; 7:52), Christ called divers of His apostles. And even in Jericho, this cursed city, Christ has a rich man that is to be saved. In every place Christ has His chosen. There is neither Jew nor Gentile, Barbarian nor Scythian, bond nor free, but Christ over all is rich to all that call on Him, (Rom. 10:12).

Now follows the description of Zacchaeus, which is most plainly and fully set forth to us. The Holy Spirit speaking of Zacchaeus and his conversion, comes in with an *Ecce, Behold*, as if it were a wonder that Zacchaeus should be converted. Zacchaeus was a Gentile, a publican, a rich man, and therefore behold a miracle; as if in the conversion of Zacchaeus these three should be converted at once.

Zacchaeus was a Gentile: a marvel to see a Gentile become a Jew, that is, to believe in Christ, (Rom. 2:28). He was a principal publican: a strange thing to see a chief customer to give over his office. And he was rich also: a rare matter to see a rich man to enter into the kingdom of God, (Matt. 19:23). And therefore behold a miracle; as if at this day the Turk, Pope, and the King of Spain, were at once persuaded to forsake their idolatry and superstition. Christ going to Jerusalem converts a Gentile, to signify the calling of the Gentiles: He converts a publican, to show that notorious sinners may hope to be saved, if they repent and amend, as Zacchaeus did: He converts a rich man, to show that all rich men are not excluded from the kingdom of heaven.

He was called Zacchaeus before his conversion, but he was never truly called Zacchaeus, until Christ called him so. His name signified, simple, pure, honest; but his life was subtle, impure, and most detestable. So many are called by honest names whose deeds betray their dishonest natures, and vices oftentimes are shrouded in the habits of virtue: like Aesop's ass masking in the lion's skin, until his long ears detect his folly; or like the crow that is decked in others' plumes, until every bird do pluck his feather.

Zacchaeus by his profession was a publican; and therefore much detested of the Jews: for the publicans were Roman officers, appointed to gather and receive public custom or tribute of the Jews, who were at that time in subjection to the Romans. And among these officers Zacchaeus was the chief, and (as it seems) overseer of the rest that were in Jericho; and therefore in chief hatred among the Jews, as one that chiefly favored the Romans' tyranny, and served to abridge their country's liberty, which ought not to be subject to any nation.

Besides, he condemned the ceremonies of the Jews, and did not regard their religion, nor lived after their law; and therefore, with the rest of the heathen publicans, was excommunicate out of their synagogues, (Matt. 18:17). So was he hated for his profession, because he was a publican; and for his religion, because he was a heathen. Yet was he beloved for his wealth; for the rich, have many friends, (Prov. 14:20). And though they do never so wickedly, yet have they some to take their parts. If they speak never so proudly, yet are there some to praise their saying.

Zacchaeus was a publican, and therefore rich; for publicans had to be rich, and usurers will be wealthy. But rich publicans make poor princes, and wealthy usurers make many beggars. In every province there were many publicans, and therefore much poor people in every place; for where there are many caterpillars, the fruit is soon consumed; and where there are many extortioners, beggars must needs abound. By the law of God there might be no beggars in Israel, (Deut. 15): but when so many publicans were suffered to receive tribute of the Jews, contrary to God's law, no marvel though so many sat and begged, contrary to God's law, (Luke 18:35; John 9:8; Acts 3:2). By the law of God there ought to be no beggars among

Christians, (Psa. 37:25). But when so many usurers are tolerated in a Christian commonwealth, contrary to the law of Christ, (Luke 6:35), no marvel though we have so many beggars, contrary to the mind of Christ. The poor (says Christ) you have with you always, and when you will you may do them good, (Mark 14:7). And we shall be sure to have the poor among us always; but we must make such good provision for them, that they is not fain to beg their bread.

So was Zacchaeus rich to himself for he was a publican; but he was rich towards God also, for he had a desire to see Christ. Almighty God, who is rich in mercy, (Eph. 2:4), has so inspired his heart with the desire of heavenly riches, that whereas before his whole delight was in seeking of worldly wealth, now his greatest care is to seek for heavenly treasure. He now forgets what his profession is, and begins to be of a new profession; and he whose heart was wholly set on earthly profit, is now like old Simeon, most desirous to see his Savior, (Luke 2:29). The tetrarch Herod desired to see Christ, and despised Him when He saw Him, (Luke 23:8, 11); but Zacchaeus the publican desired to see Christ and rejoiced when he saw Him; like Abraham, that desired to see the day of Christ, (John 8:56). And therefore of the servant of Satan Zacchaeus is now become the child of Abraham, which rejoiced to see the day of Christ. Happy were his eyes that saw so blessed a sight; for many prophets and righteous men have desired to see and to hear those things that Zacchaeus both saw and heard, and could not see nor hear the same, (Luke 10:24). If Jacob thought himself happy, if that he might see his son Joseph before his death, (Gen. 45:28); then surely thrice happy Zacchaeus, whose circumstance it was, not only to see, (as Jacob did), but to rejoice (as Mary did) in Christ his Savior.

As Zacchaeus was desirous to see Christ in earth, so I would have the rich men of our time desirous to see Christ in heaven. For although with the eyes of our body we cannot see Christ, as Zacchaeus did; yet with the eyes of our faith we may behold him, as Stephen did, (Acts 7:56). But if our faith be so weak sighted that we cannot see Christ, yet let us have a desire to hear Christ in His Word, whereby our faith may be increased; for faith comes by hearing the Word of God, (Rom. 10:17). And as the Queen of the South desired to hear the wisdom of Solomon, so let us be desirous to hear the wisdom of Christ our Savior. King Solomon left some books in writing, in which is seen some part of his wisdom, (1 Kings 4:32-33); and Christ our King has left to us His most sacred Word, as it were a taste of His wisdom, sufficient matter for our salvation. This is that heavenly food, (Matt. 4:4), whereby our souls are fed to eternal life: let us therefore labor for that heavenly food; and as the Israelites were careful to gather manna to sustain their bodies, (Exod. 16), so let us be as careful to hear the Word to feed our souls. The people, in the time of Christ, took great pains to follow Christ both by land and sea, (John 6:24); and many now-a-days, I confess, are very forward to follow His faithful ministers: but as they followed Christ so fast to fill their bellies, (John 6:26), so these frequent sermons for fashion to serve the time.

Zacchaeus is desirous to see Christ with a godly care: but yet he could not obtain this purpose; a thing common. For everyone that has any good motion, has always some hindrance to cross the same; and Zacchaeus has a double impediment to hinder his honest enterprise; the press of the people, and his little stature. In which the former, that is, the multitude, is always likely to be an enemy to those that would come to Christ.

This hindered the blind man from receiving his sight; for the people rebuked him that he should hold his peace, (Luke 18:39), until Christ called him, and opened his eyes. This hindered them that brought the man sick of the palsy; for they could not come nigh to Christ for the press, (Mark 2:4), until they uncovered the roof of the house, and let down the bed in which the sick of the palsy lay. This hindered the healing of the deaf and dumb, until Christ took him aside from the multitude, (Mark 7:33), and cured him. This hindered the raising of the ruler's daughter, until Christ had thrust out the minstrels and the multitude, and then restored the maid to life, (Matt. 9:25).

Finally, this hindered Zacchaeus here from coming to Christ, until Christ vouchsafed to call him to Himself. So always a multitude that is prone to evil withdraws and hinders us from approaching to Christ; and therefore we must not follow a multitude to do evil, nor decline after many to overthrow the truth, (Exod. 23:2).

The second impediment that hinders Zacchaeus from seeing Christ is his little stature. He was so low of stature, that he could not see Christ above the multitude; but Christ was above the multitude, and therefore could see Zacchaeus, though he were so low of stature: for the Lord looks not on his countenance, nor on the height of his stature; "but the Lord looks on the heart," (1 Sam. 16:7); and prefers little David before Eliab his eldest brother, because He finds in him a better heart to serve the Lord, (1 Sam. 16:12). And Zacchaeus in his little body has a heart and mind prepared to seek and see the Lord. Zacchaeus was so low that he could not see Christ; but many among us fare so high that they will not see Christ. The common people in the time of Christ were so desirous to follow Christ, that neither lameness, nor blindness, nor sickness, could stay them from coming to Him; but the common people in our time are more ready to follow their sport and pastime, than to come to the church to hear of Christ. And as for our rich men, who sees not that they will make great haste to see a commodity, but will scarcely come out of doors to hear a sermon? They come to Christ as Nicodemus came to Christ, by night, (John 3:2), as if they were ashamed to come to church; but they run sifter profit, to get riches, as Gehazi ran after Naaman the Syrian to get a bribe, (2 Kings 5:21).

So has Zacchaeus two hindrances so that he could not see Christ; the one in the people, the other in himself. And we have many lets to withdraw us from Christ: some are external and without us, as the enticements of the world; and some are internal and within us, as the lusts of our own flesh. The press of the people hinders Zacchaeus from seeing Christ in His humility; and the multitude of our sins press us down, that we cannot see Christ in glory. Zacchaeus was a man of little stature, and that hindered him from seeing Christ in earth; and we are men of little faith, and that is the cause we cannot behold Christ in heaven.

Though Zacchaeus was a man of little stature, yet it appears that he was not a man of little wit: for when he could not come to the sight of Christ for the multitude, he had the wit to run before, and to climb up into a tree, to obtain his purpose. And for the most part it falls out, that men of low stature are men of high conceit, and the shortest bodies have the sharpest wits; God so providing, that the defects of their bodies might be supplied with the gifts of their mind. Now Zacchaeus, that before was loathe to move his foot from the custom-house for losing his profit, begins to run after Christ for fear of a greater loss; like Elisha, that left his ploughing, and ran after Elijah, to follow his new vocation, (1 Kings 19:20). But Zacchaeus does not only run, but also climbs up into a tree to see Christ. A strange thing that Zacchaeus, a rich man, and a chief customer, should behave himself so childishly in the sight of so great a multitude: but the desire he had to see Christ made him forget himself, and to commit such things as were not fitting for his state and credit. So they that will follow Christ must make account to do many things contrary to the fashion of the world, and their own liking, (Rom. 12:2). If Christ Himself were content to leave the glory which He had with His Father, to come down to us; shall not we be content to leave the reputation which we have with men, to go up to Him? But, alas! where is there any almost that prefers so, the fruition of this earthly prison before the possession of that heavenly mansion; and had not rather hazard the hope which they have of eternal glory, than lose the present enjoying of their fading pleasure? The ambitious man hunts after honor, and will not lose an inch of his estimation. The covetous man seeks after profit, and counts, like Judas, all lost that comes not to his bags, (John 12:6). And the voluptuous man bestows his time in pleasure, and thinks that his chief felicity. So every man makes his heaven of that in which he most delights, and is content to take great pains to accomplish his fond desires. But here Zacchaeus is of another mind; for, being a public officer, he climbs into a tree, which did not stand with his gravity; and, being a rich man, he runs to see Christ, which was not for his worldly profit; Yes, he takes great pains to see Christ, not respecting his ease or pleasure.

In this way we must be affected, if we desire to come to Christ, that neither honors, nor preferment, nor profit, nor pleasure, nor kindred, nor friends, be able to hold us back. We must be ready not only to run, but also to climb, (if need require), as Zacchaeus did; that is, to take some pain and travail to have a sight of Christ. The Queen of the South undertook a great and tedious journey to hear the "wisdom of Solomon," (Matt. 12:42); but we are loathe to take any pain to hear one that is greater than Solomon. The people in David's time brought so much treasure and so many gifts to the building of God's temple, that the priests were fain to bid them cease, (1 Chron. 29); but a great part of the people in our time are so sparing of their pain and cost, that they think that time very much misspent which is employed in the service of God; and that money ill-bestowed which is given to the maintenance of His ministers.

When Zacchaeus could not see Christ for the multitude, he climbs into the tree that grows in the way where He was to pass, that from a tree he might behold Him which was to suffer on a tree for man's salvation: so when we cannot draw near to Christ by reason of our sins that press us down, we will climb up by a lively faith, which is the tree of life, that grows in the way to eternal life, that so with the eyes of our faith we may behold Him that died for our sins on a tree.

It was a wild fig-tree that Zacchaeus climbed; but not like that unfruitful one which our Savior cursed, (Matt. 21:19); for this bare most precious fruit, even such as Christ Himself vouchsafed to pluck; a happy tree that bare such precious fruit as Zacchaeus was; but thrice happy Zacchaeus, that so happily climbed on that happy tree!

This tree grew in the way that Christ was to pass, for

else Zacchaeus might have climbed to no purpose: so if we desire to find Christ, we must seek Him in the way where He has promised to show Himself to us, that is, in His holy temple, where His Word is duly preached, and His Sacraments reverently administered; for where two or three are gathered together, He has promised to be present among them.

And when Jesus came to the place, He looked up, and saw him. As Zacchaeus ran before Christ, so Christ followed after to see Zacchaeus. Satan for his part went about "like a roaring lion, seeking to devour him," (1 Peter 5:8); but Christ for His part goes about like "a good Shepherd," (John 10:11), minding to save him. And although Satan, a strong armed man, had taken some possession in the heart of Zacchaeus; yet Christ, a stronger than he, comes unarmed, and takes from him his harness in which he trusted, and rescues his spoil, (Luke 11:21-22).

Christ comes to the place where Zacchaeus was, because otherwise it had been impossible for Zacchaeus to come to His presence: for unless the Lord vouchsafe to come to us, we cannot attain to the presence of God. As no man might have any access to King Ahasuerus except he stretched out his golden sceptre, (Esth. 4:11); so no man may come to Christ, unless he is called by the golden sceptre of His sacred Word.

Christ looked up, and saw him, before Zacchaeus could look down to behold Him. So the Lord prevents us with His mercy, whom He might cast off in His justice: and if He perceive in us a willing mind to come to Him, He is content to come first to us; and, like that good father, to behold us while we are yet a great way off, and to have compassion on us, (Luke 15:20).

When Job's three friends, that came to visit him in his great calamity, lift up their eyes afar off, they did not know Job, because he was so sore afflicted, (Job 2:12). But Christ, who is the mirror of true friendship, cannot so soon forget His friends, howsoever they are disguised. He knows His own sheep wheresoever He sees them, (John 10:14), whether they are under the fig-tree, as Nathanael was, or on the fig-tree, as

Zacchaeus was, He has respect to them. And if they have a desire to seek, they shall be sure to find, (Matt. 7:7); and if they labor and are heavy laden, He will refresh them, (Matt. 11:28). Christ is now come to the place where Zacchaeus is to be called; and as Abraham lift up his eyes, and "saw in the bush a ram that was to be sacrificed," (Gen. 22:13); so Christ, lifting up his eyes, saw in the tree Zacchaeus the sinner that was to be converted. And now begins the conversion of Zacchaeus, for now Christ begins to speak to him.

Zacchaeus desired only to see Christ; but now Christ calls him by name, and offers His own self to him. This was more than Zacchaeus expected, and yet no more than Christ vouchsafeth; namely, to give more than is desired. The sick of the palsy, that asked health, obtained also forgiveness of sins, (Luke 5:20). Solomon desired wisdom, and the Lord gave him wisdom, and abundance of wealth beside, (1 Kings 3:12, 13). Jacob asked but meat and clothing, and God made him a great rich man, (Gen. 28:20). And Zacchaeus desired only to have a sight of Christ, and was so happy as to entertain Him in his house. So the Lord, that is rich in mercy to all that call on Him, (Rom. 10:12), uses oftentimes to give more than we ask: and He that is always found of them that seek Him with their whole heart, (Jer. 29:13), is found also sometimes of Gentiles that did not know God, (Isa. 65:1; Rom. 10:20). Let us therefore, that were sometime sinners of the Gentiles, seek the Lord as Zacchaeus did, while He may be found, and call on Him while He is near, (Isa. 55:6). He will be found of them that seek Him heartily, and is near to all them that call on Him in truth, (Psa. 145:18).

Zacchaeus, make haste, and come down. Now Christ begins to call Zacchaeus from the tree to be converted, as God called Adam from among the trees of the garden to be cursed, (Gen. 3:8-9). Before, Zacchaeus was too low, and therefore was fain to climb; but now he is too high, and therefore he must come down. And we, for the most part, are either too high or too low; too hot or too cold; too quick or too slothful in the Lord's business. Sometime we flock together to hear a sermon, like the people that pressed on Christ to hear the Word, (Luke 5:1); and quickly we run to see some pleasant pastime, like the Athenians, whose ears always itched to hear some news, (Acts 17:21). Who make more show of conscience and religion than they that show themselves most irreligious and unconscionable? Who seemed more confident and valorous in Christ's cause than Peter? and not long after, who more traitorous and faint-hearted? (Matt. 26).

Many can say with Peter, that they will not stick to die before they will deny Christ; but when it comes to the trial, they are ready to abjure Christ and His religion, before they will hazard either life or living.

He that will come to Christ, must come at once, without delay; for delays (especially in the matter of our salvation) are most dangerous, and repentance may not be deferred. We must make no tarrying to turn to the Lord, nor put off from day to day; lest the wrath of the Lord break forth suddenly, and we are destroyed in our security, and perish in the time of vengeance. When the Lord is minded to do us good, He will have us come quickly, like Joseph, that in the time of famine would have his father Jacob to come down quickly to him, to sojourn in Egypt, where there was some plenty of food, (Gen. 14:9). As the children of this world are very nimble to work wickedness; so the children of light should be as nimble to follow goodness. Judas was nimble to betray Christ, (John 13:27), and the bad debtors could sit down quickly to misreckon their creditor, (Luke 16:6-7); so let us come quickly to hear of Christ, that Christ may accept of us quickly; let us be nimble to make our account before, that we do not (like the foolish builder) come short of our reckoning, (Luke 14:28-9).

But why must Zacchaeus come down so hastily? Even to entertain Christ in his house; for today (says Christ) I must abide at your house. This was joyful news to little Zacchaeus. Not long before he wanted means to see Christ, but now he has an opportunity to entertain Him in his house.

There was more humanity in Christ than in Zacchaeus; for if Christ had not bidden Himself to dinner, He had not been bidden for Zacchaeus: so if Christ does not offer Himself to us in His afflicted members, (Matt. 25:40), He may go long enough before we will offer Him any entertainment. As often as the poor craves any relief at our hands, let us imagine that Christ asks something of us. But as Zacchaeus must entertain Him presently without delay; so let us be ready to help them presently, because they stand in need of present help: and as he must receive Christ into his house, so we must make account to receive His needy members into our houses. And as the unjust steward procures himself friends with his master's goods, so let us make the poor to be our friends, by our beneficence and bounty towards them; that so receiving them (when they have need) into our earthly houses, they may receive us, when we stand in greatest need, into everlasting habitations.

They that were invited to the marriage, "refused to come," (Matt. 23:3); but Christ is content to come to Zacchaeus' house *before* He was invited. In which also He shows His great humility, in coming before He was requested; as they betrayed their great arrogancy, in refusing to come being solemnly bidden. It was a part of great humility, that He that was most free from sin would vouchsafe to come into a sinner's house: but it was a sign of greater humility, that He would betray His great necessity, and seek for succor at a sinner's hand. Alas, poor humble Savior! who, though you are Lord of heaven and earth, as you are the Son of God, yet, as you are the Son of man, have nowhere to lay Your head, (Matt. 8:20). How justly did Your Prophet Jeremiah wonder at Your humble poverty, saying, O the hope of Israel, the Savior of it in time of trouble, why should you be as a stranger in the land, and as a wayfaring man that turns aside to tarry for a night, (Jer. 14:8). The Son of God vouchsafes to come, and that unrequested, to a sinful man's house; a special favor: but He disdains not to make His necessity known to him.

O strange humility! Here therefore appears the singular humanity and great humility of Christ to sinful men: He offers Himself to be their guest, if He find them willing to entertain

Him for their guest. And Zacchaeus, no doubt, was willing to entertain Him; for although Christ did not hear the voice, yet He heard the affection of Zacchaeus inviting Him to dinner. As therefore Zacchaeus was willing to receive Christ into his house, so let us be ready to receive Him into our hearts: for as Christ said to Zacchaeus, *This day I must abide at your house*; so He says to every one of us, This day I must abide in your hearts. Wherefore as the Prophet David says, "Lift up your heads, O you gates, that the King of Glory may come in," (Psa. 24:7); so I say to you, *Open your hearts*, that the Word of God may enter in. This day the Word of God may abide in your hearts, for this day the Word is preached to you; and who knows whether he shall live to hear it the next Sabbath? "Today, therefore, if you will hear His voice, harden not your hearts," (Psa. 95:7-8), as did the Israelites; lest if you harden your hearts, His voice is heard no more among you. This day you may gather this heavenly manna, as the Israelites might gather their manna six days together," (Exod. 16:4-5); but tomorrow, perhaps, and six days after, you may not gather it; as the seventh day manna might not be found. The Lord grant that you may gather sufficient food for the sustentation of your souls: that as Elijah the Prophet journeyed in the strength of the meat that the angel brought him, even to Horeb the mount of God, (1 Kings 19:8), so you, in the strength of the spiritual meat which here I bring you, may be able to pass through the dangerous ways of this troublesome world to God's holy mountain, the haven of all happiness. Where He bring us that has dearly bought us with His precious blood, even Christ Jesus the righteous: to whom with the Father and the Holy Spirit, three Persons and one God, be given all glory and majesty, world without end. *Amen.*

THE SINNER'S CONFESSION

"And he made haste, and came down, and received Him joyfully. And when they saw it, they all murmured, saying, That He was gone to be guest with a man that is a sinner. And Zacchaeus stood, and said to the Lord; "Behold, Lord, the half of my goods I give to the poor; and if I have taken anything from any man by false accusation, I restore him fourfold." And Jesus said to him, "This day is salvation come to this house, forsomuch as he also is a son of Abraham.""—Luke 19:6-9

You heard the last Sabbath how Zacchaeus the Publican was called to be a Christian: now you shall hear the fruit of his conversion. No sooner had Christ called him from the tree, but that he *made haste*, and *came down*, and *received Him joyfully*. This was the fruit which it had in the heart of Zacchaeus, namely, *obedience to the voice of Christ*: a fruit more precious and acceptable to God than the most pleasant fruits which Eden yielded, and a sacrifice more sweet and acceptable to Him than all the sacrifices which the law required. This is the sacrifice wherewith God is well pleased, (Heb. 13:16), even when His voice is obeyed, (1 Sam. 15:22). The voice of the Lord is a glorious voice, and mighty in operation, dividing the flames of fire, and shaking the cedar trees," (Psa. 29); so the voice of Christ is a glorious voice, His voice is mighty in operation, dividing asunder of soul and spirit, (Heb. 4:12), and shaking Zacchaeus from the wild fig-tree into which he had climbed. The same God to whose command the winds, the sea, the devils, and death itself obey, (Matt. 8:27), here commands Zacchaeus to come down at once; and he comes down hastily to receive Him into his house, and he receives Him *joyfully*. As Zacchaeus could not come at Christ until he was called; so no man *can* come to Christ *except* the Father *draw him*, (John 6:44). And as Zacchaeus could not choose but come when he was called by the voice of Christ; so when any man is called *effectually* by the preaching of the Gospel, he cannot but choose to come to Christ; for where there is an effectual calling, there is grace given also to obey the same, (Rom. 8:30). The Lord is patient sometimes to call us often, because we do not know the voice of Him that calls us; as He called Samuel three times before he answered, because at that time Samuel did not yet know the Lord, (1 Sam. 3:7) but as soon as he understood that it was the Lord that spoke to him, he replied presently, *Speak, for Your servant hears*, (verse 10): so when the Lord calls any man effectually by the preaching of His Word, all the parts and powers of his body yield their obedience; the ear listens, the tongue confesses, the heart believes, the head devises, the hand performs, the foot runs, the eye directs, and all "concur to do Your will, O God," (Psa. 40:8).

Such and so effectual is the voice of Christ in the hearts of His chosen, that it makes Saul, of a bloody persecutor, to become Paul, a painful preacher, (Acts 9); it causes Peter, of a silly fisherman, to become a catcher of men, (Matt. 4:19); and Zacchaeus here, of a vile publican, to become a zealous Christian. And such also is the nature of the Word preached, wheresoever it pleases the Lord to give success and increase thereto, that it is able to transform the minds of men, to beget faith in. the hearts of infidels, and (in a word) to "save such as are ordained to eternal life," (Acts 13:48). This is the power of the Word of God, even to cause a consenting to the truth of it; and this is the property of the children of God, to yield all obedience to the Word of God. As soon as Christ called Zacchaeus, he comes down presently; like the light in the creation, that was made as soon as God said, "Let there be light," (Gen 1:3). Here therefore of Zacchaeus, that obeyed the voice of Christ, let us learn obedience to the voice of Christ! As Christ bids Zacchaeus to come down, because he was too high, so He says to every one of us, *Come down*, because we are too high-minded. But with us the voice of Christ is not so effectual as it was with Zacchaeus; for he was content to come down at the first bidding; but we must be often bidden to beware of pride and ambition, and yet we will still be climbing. There are few so high that are content with their calling: but as Haman was always aspiring, until he came to the gallows; so many among us are always climbing, until we catch a fall.

Again, as Christ says to Zacchaeus, *Today I must abide at your house*; so Christ says to us, *Today My poor afflicted members should receive some succor at your hands.* But as the Priest and the Levite "passed by the wounded man, leaving him half dead," (Luke 10:31-32), so we, for the most part, pass by our needy brethren, leaving them unrelieved. So we are in every way disobedient to the voice of Christ. He teaches us to be humble, as He Himself is, (Matt. 11:29), and we are often proud and insolent, as Satan is. He wants us to be merciful, as our heavenly Father is, (Luke 6:36), and we are cruel and unmerciful, as the rich glutton was, (Luke 16:21). This is the cause why the earth *deceives, and renders not her fruit*, (Isa. 24:4). This is the cause why the sword devours abroad, and why the pestilence destroys at home, (Deut. 28:15, *etc.*; Lev. 26:14, *etc.*). And in a word, this is the cause of all the mischiefs and calamities that are threatened, even because we are obstinate and rebellious against the Lord, We are undutiful and disobedient to the voice of Christ, even though He calls us so lovingly to come to Him, (Matt. 11:28).

Zacchaeus was called but *once*, and he comes *quickly*; but we are called oftentimes, and almost every day, and that by the voice of Christ Himself; "for he that hears you, (says Christ), hears Me," (Luke 10:16); and yet we cannot find the way to Christ. The Word of God, which is a lamp to our feet, and a light to own path, (Psa. 119:105), has been plainly and plentifully preached among us these many years, and yet many among us have not learned yet to come to Christ. Zacchaeus comes quickly when Christ calls him: let us therefore learn of Zacchaeus to come quickly when Christ calls us. We must be quick in the Lord's business, for God cannot abide loiterers standing all the day idle, (Matt. 20:3), and as He loves a cheerful giver, (2 Cot. 9:7), so He likes a cheerful *follower*.

It followed therefore that Zacchaeus received him cheerfully, Still Zacchaeus is a receiver: before he was a receiver of custom, now he is a receiver of Christ. Zacchaeus received Christ two ways: first, into his heart, when he desired to see Him; and then into his house, when he gave Him hospitality. Many received Christ to house, but not into their heart, and therefore received Him grudgingly; but Zacchaeus received Christ first into his heart, and then into his house, and therefore received Him joyfully. Of Zacchaeus' joyfulness, we must learn to be joyful when we do anything for the cause of Christ: we must be glad to harbor Christ in His members, as Zacchaeus was glad to harbor Christ Himself. As before, in coming down from the tree, Zacchaeus showed his obedience; so here, in receiving Christ into his house, he shows the great love that lie bare to Him. If Zacchaeus had not loved Christ, he might have sent Him to some common inn; but Zacchaeus is content to receive Christ in his own house; Yes, he rejoices to have gotten so good a guest; like Abraham, that used to sit at the door of his tent, and rejoiced to entertain strangers that went by the way, (Gen. 18:1). And therefore, though Zacchaeus were a Gentile born, yet herein he shows himself the child of Abraham, because he does the works of Abraham, (John 8:39). So did Abraham, and so must we do, if we will show ourselves to be the children of Abraham. When Abraham thought only to have entertained men, he receives the angels in the shape and likeness of men; and when Zacchaeus thought to entertain the Son of man, he receives the Son of God Himself. Let us therefore (as the Apostle wants us) not to be forgetful to entertain strangers; for thereby some have "entertained angels unawares," (Heb. 13:2). And why should we not hope to entertain the like or better guests, if we be given to hospitality, as those godly fathers were? for as the angels came to them in the likeness of men; so Christ Himself comes to us in the likeness of a poor man, of a lame man, and of a blind man; and when He comes, He comes hungry, or thirsty, or naked, or barbourless, or sick, or imprisoned; and happy are they that feed, or clothe, or harbour, or visit Him, when He comes this way afflicted.

When Abraham entertained the angel, he was not only

busy Himself, but his wife and all his household were careful to make provision for them; so when Zacchaeus received Christ into his house, his whole family, no doubt, were no less willing and careful to entertain Christ than their Master was: and therefore not only to Zacchaeus, but even to his whole house salvation is promised, because the whole family rejoiced at Christ's coming. Let rich men learn of Zacchaeus to entertain Christ in His needy members; and let rich men's servants learn of Zacchaeus' family to show themselves merciful like their merciful masters, that they may receive the reward of mercy and hospitality at the last day, "Come, you blessed; for I was harbourless, and you took Me in," (Matt. 25:34-35). Generally, as Zacchaeus received Christ, so let everyone that is able be glad to distribute to the necessity of the poor saints. If we have much, let us give plentifully; if we have little, let us give gladly of that little; if we is not able to give a penny, yet haply we may afford a morsel of bread; if not that, yet there is none so needy that cannot give a cup of cold water; and even so small a gift shall not lose His just reward, (Matt. 10:42). Zacchaeus received Christ into his heart; but many among us are ready to drive Christ out, and to receive Satan instead of Him. Zacchaeus received Christ into his house; but there are many rich men among us, that, like Dives, will not afford poor Lazarus the crumbs that fall from their table; but, as the damsel opened not the gate for gladness when she knew Peter's voice, (Acts 12:14); so by contrary, these men for very grief shut their gates, when they perceive a beggar there. Finally, Zacchaeus was joyful when he entertained Christ; but many among us are sorrowful when they should relieve the poor; like churlish Nabal that reviled David, when he should have relieved him, (1 Sam. 25:9-12). So long as Job prospered, he kept a worthy and a worshipful house, he did not suffer the stranger to lodge in the streets; but he opened his door to the traveller that went by the way, (Job 31:32). But now many gentlemen of the country are content to suffer the stranger, the fatherless, and the widow, not only to lie, but even to starve and die, in the streets with hunger and cold, and never receive them to house or harbor, nor afford them any relief or succor. But as the voice of Abel's blood cried from the earth to God for vengeance against his brother's cruelty, (Gen. 4:10); so the voice of the poor and their piteous cries shall enter into the ears of the Lord; and their guiltless blood (which is poured forth in every place without all compassion) shall pull down heavy and sudden vengeance from heaven on the heads of those unmerciful cormorants, unless, while this time of mercy lasts, they show mercy to their distressed neighbors.

So you have heard how Zacchaeus behaved himself in entertaining of Christ. Now you shall see the behavior of the Pharisees in disdaining of Christ. When they saw it, they all murmured, saying, *That He was gone to be a guest with a man that is a sinner.* Before they hated Zacchaeus for his vices, because he was covetous; now they envy him for his virtues, because he was given to hospitality: for the wicked will have always something to find fault with in the children of God, like the sons of Jacob that hated their brother Joseph because of his dreams," (Gen. 37:4, 11); and like Saul, that unhappy king, that envied David for his happy victories, (1 Sam. 18:8). So the wicked, when they cannot charge the godly with any grievous crime, they begin to grudge at their well-doing: and therefore not only Zacchaeus is hated for receiving of Christ, but Christ is hated also for being his guest. When they could not accuse Christ for sin, they accuse Him for companying with sinners: for they must be still accusing some or other for one thing or other, like their father the devil, that both by name, and by nature, is a continual accuser of the brethren. It had been the duty of the Pharisees to have received Christ, and made much of him, as Zacchaeus did; but they are so far off from entertaining Him themselves, that it grieves them to see Zacchaeus give Him entertainment. And surely such is the perverse nature of the wicked, that they will neither receive the grace of God when it is offered them, nor willingly suffer any other to embrace the same: like the wicked Jews, that would neither believe the doctrine that Paul preached, nor could abide that the Gentiles should be brought to the faith of

Christ, (Acts 13:60). The high priests thought themselves too high to have poor humble Christ among them; the Scribes and the Pharisees in their own conceit were too good, too wise, and too holy to receive Him into their company; and not content to sequester and estrange themselves from Christ, they disdained also that He should be conversant with publicans and sinners, as though He were not worthy to be conversant among them.

If it were the office of Christ to convert sinners, (Matt. 9:13); why should the Pharisees be offended at Him, if He were sometimes conversant with sinners to work their conversion? If Christ were a physician to cure the sickness of the soul, (Matt. 9:12), that is, to save the people from their sins; why should the Pharisees murmur at Him for keeping of company with Zacchaeus, that was sick in soul? for as it is expedient for the physician to visit his patients for their better recovery; so it was convenient Christ should visit sinners for their speedy conversion. But as the physician that resorts to sick persons is not straightway infected; so the Soul's Physician that converses with sinners is not thereby polluted. And therefore as Christ performed His office, though the Pharisees murmured so let the ministers of God learn, by this example, to perform their duties, though the wicked be offended. It was the office of Christ to call sinners to repentance, (Luke 5:32): Yes, He came to call Pharisee-sinners as well as publican-sinners, if the Pharisees would have confessed themselves to be sinners, as the publicans did; but because they stood so much on their own righteousness, and despised others, therefore Christ denounced so many woes against them, and prefers the penitent publican, that trusted in the Lord's mercy, before the proud Pharisee, that trusted in his own merits.

Though Paul was a Pharisee, and the son of a Pharisee, (Acts 23:6), yet he is not ashamed to confess himself as one of the chief sinners that Christ came to save, (1 Tim. 1:15). So is the Pharisees that murmured at Zacchaeus would have been saved, they should have confessed themselves chief sinners as Paul did. They should not have accused Christ for keeping company with sinners, but they should have accused themselves for not keeping company with Christ. The just man (says Solomon) is the first accuser of himself; but the Pharisees are so far from accusing themselves, that they began to accuse Zacchaeus and Christ together. So the Pharisees of our time, that make religion a cloak to cover their corrupt dealing, have this property,—to think other men to be heinous sinners, and themselves only to be righteous; insomuch as they will not stick to speak like that proud people, that was likely to say, "Come not near me; for I am holier than you," (Isa. 65:5); and like the presumptuous Pharisee, *I thank God, I am not as others are,* extortioners, usurers, adulterers, drunkards, or such like, (Luke 18:11). I sanctify the Sabbath, which other men profane: I frequent sermons, which they neglect: I reverence the name of God, which they blaspheme: I pay tithes, which others withhold; and fast oftentimes, which they do seldom or never. These were the speeches of the Pharisees that lived in the time of Christ, whom He so often called "hypocrites," (Matt. 5:23); and these are the speeches of the hypocrites of our age, that seem to live after the straightest sect of our religion, (Acts 26:5). They make clean the outside of the cup and the platter, (Luke 11:39); that is, they justify themselves and seem marvellously holy in the sight of men, which can discern by the outward appearance only; but to God, that sees and searches the secrets of the hearts and minds, they are like painted sepulchers, "full of dead men's bones, and all uncleanness," (Matt. 23:27); that is, they have their inward parts full of ravening and all kind of wickedness. Wherefore, as Christ said to His disciples, "Except your righteousness shall exceed the righteousness of the Scribes and Pharisees, you shall in no case enter into the kingdom of heaven," (Matt. 5:20); so I say to you, that *except your righteousness exceed the righteousness of these pharisaical hypocrites, you cannot be saved.*

These Holy Pharisees did use to call the publicans, not usurers, nor extortioners, as they themselves were, but by the general name of sinners, as though they themselves were free from sin. So the Papists at this day do not call the most sincere professors of the Gospel Lutherans, Calvinists, Zwinglians, or

Protestants, as they were likely to call them; but now they term us *heretics*,—a name more odious than any other; whereas in the mean season they themselves are of all others are *the greatest heretics*. So the Atheists of our time, when they cannot accuse the godly that are among us of usury, or bribery, or extortion, or drunkenness, or any such notorious sin, they call them *hypocrites*, which is the sum of all: when as in very truth they themselves do best deserve that name. But it makes no matter what they call us, neither are we to be moved at their despiteful speeches; for as the bitter taunts of these murmuring Pharisees could not hinder Zacchaeus in his conversion; so the slanders of these godless men must not discourage the servants of God from their good profession. The Pharisees did Zacchaeus a great wrong in calling him sinner, when he had repented of his sin; and the Atheists at this day do greatly wrong the true professors in calling them hypocrites, which have truly repented of their former sins, and endeavor by all good means to lead a godly life. Therefore as Zacchaeus preferred his soul's health before all their murmuring; so it behoves us to look to our soul's salvation, notwithstanding all the reproaches and slanders that are devised against us. And as the Pharisees might call Zacchaeus sinner, but could not hinder his conversion; so the malicious worldlings may take away our goods or good names, yes, and our lives also, but cannot deprive us of our salvation. Wherefore, as our Savior said to His apostles, "Be not afraid of them that kill the body, and after that have no more than they can do," (Luke 12:4); so I say to you, *Be not afraid of the frowns of the wicked*, for they are not able to hurt your better part; seek not to gain the favor of the world, for the whole world is not able to save a soul: "but fear Him which after He has killed, has power to cast into hell," (Luke 12:5); and seek Him that is able to save you in heaven forever.

Now follows another fruit of Zacchaeus' conversion, namely, his good confession; for as he believed with his heart to righteousness, so he confessed with the "mouth to salvation," (Rom. 10:10). When Zacchaeus was mocked of the Pharisees, it seems that he should stoop down for shame; but when he was this way reproved and reviled by them, the Scripture says, that he stood up, in sign of gladness. As the Apostles departed from the council, "rejoicing that they were counted worthy to suffer shame for His name," (Acts 5:41); so Zacchaeus the publican went forth rejoicing, that he was reproached for the cause of Christ. Before, Zacchaeus was a publican, and therefore stood in sin very dangerously; like the house that is built on the sand, ready to be over-turned with every tempest: but now Zacchaeus is become a true Christian, and therefore stands in righteousness very safely; like the house that is built on a rock, free from any danger of falling, (Luke 6:48, 49).

Behold, Lord, the half of my goods, etc. There are two parts of his confession. The first is his gift to the poor; the second is the restitution of his unjustly-gotten goods. Before Zacchaeus was an oppressor of the poor, now he is a great benefactor of the poor; before he was an encroacher on other men's goods, now he is a distributor of his own goods: before he was a receiver and a taker, now he is a restorer and a giver: "neither does he give sparingly, but he gives liberally, laying up a good foundation against the time to come," (1 Tim. 6:19). Now Zacchaeus found that precious pearl, and for joy of it he is content, not to sell, but to give all that he has to enjoy the same, (Matt. 13:45, 46). When the rich ruler (in the former chapter) was willed to sell all that he had, and distribute to the poor, "he was very sorrowful; for he was very rich," (Luke 18:22-23); but Zacchaeus, perhaps as rich as he, is content of his own accord, and unbidden, to give half his goods to the poor, and that with a cheerful mind. If Zacchaeus had given only the third part of his goods, no doubt but Christ would have accepted it, for He accepted the widow's farthing, because it was given with a willing mind, (Luke 21:3); but if he had given all his goods to feed the poor, as the Pharisees gave their alms, to be seen of men, yes, or his body to be burned, (1 Cor. 13:3), as some Romans have done, to get renown; it should have been to no purpose, because it was done to a wrong end.

Now as Zacchaeus was rich in the goods of this life, so was he rich in faith also: neither was it an idle or dead faith that Zacchaeus had, but it was a fruitful and lively faith, faith which works and labors by love, (Gal. 5:6), such as is required at the hands of Christians. St. James says, "Show me your faith by your works," (James 2:18); and here Zacchaeus shows his faith by his works. Before he was exercised in ungodly works, which are the fruits of infidelity; but now he is exercised in the works of mercy, which are the fruits of a lively faith. Zacchaeus is very liberal in relieving the poor, but he is liberal of that which is his own; so there are many now-a-days that are very liberal, but it is of that which is none of theirs; for as Nadab and Abihu offered strange fire to the Lord, (Lev. 10:1), so these men offer strange goods to the Lord. There are some among us that think to make amends for their unjust dealing, by giving part of that to some good uses which they have gotten by bad means; if they have gotten a pound by usury and oppression, they are content perhaps to give a penny to relieve the poor. But as it was not lawful for the Israelites to bring the price of the hire of an harlot into the house of the Lord," (Deut. 23:18); so it is not lawful for us to apply the gain of our ill-gotten goods to the service of God.

The half of my goods I give, etc. Zacchaeus does not say, I have given, as an upbraider of God; or, I will give, as a delayer, that means to give away his goods after his death, when he can keep them no longer; but he says, I give; to signify that his will is his deed, and that he means not to take any days of payment for the matter. For as before he ran apace to see Christ, and came down quickly to entertain Christ in His own person; so does he here give quickly to relieve Christ in His needy members. This is Zacchaeus' last will and testament that he makes before his death, and sees the same proved and performed before his eyes. If therefore we desire to do any good to any of our poor brethren, let us learn of Zacchaeus to do it quickly, while we are alive; for time will prevent us, and death will prevent us. I know there are many that would be willing to give some part of their goods to the poor before their death, as Zacchaeus did, but that they do not know what need themselves may have of it before they die; and therefore for the most part, they will hardly forsake or leave their goods, until their goods forsake and leave them. But herein they show themselves to doubt of God's providence, and as it were to distrust His payment, who has promised to repay whatsoever is given to the poor, as it were lent to Himself, (Prov. 19:17): and that not secretly, though they did their alms never secretly, but the Lord will reward them openly, as our Savior speaks, (Matt. 6:4). The wise Preacher wants us to "cast our bread on the waters," (Eccl. 11:1), that is, to be liberal to the poor, whose watery eyes betray their great necessity; or, (as others expound it), to hazard and adventure some of our goods on our needy brethren, as merchants do adventure their goods on the seas; for although they may seem to be in great peril and danger of perishing in the waters, yet commonly it falls out that, by the blessing of God, they return with greater profit. So, albeit the relief that is bestowed on our distressed neighbors may seem to be lost; yet, as the wise man says, after a time we shall find it again. And as the precious oil descended from Aaron's beard to the skirts of his clothing, (Psa. 133:2); so certainly the oil of mercy and charity, which we pour into the wounds of our distressed brethren, (Luke 10:34), shall descend into our own souls. And as the widow's oil was increased in the cruse, because she believed the Lord's prophet, (1 Kings 17:16); so shall this precious oil bestowed on the poor be returned on our heads in great measure. So is Zacchaeus liberal, as you see: for he gives away half his goods. But he does not give it to the rich, that might give to him again; but he gives it to the poor, that cannot requite him; to teach us on whom we should bestow our alms. As God, that is rich in mercy, gives all things to us, that cannot requite Him; so the rich men of this world (if they have any spark of mercy in them) should give to the poor, that cannot requite them. But among us, in every place almost, it is far otherwise; for if anything be to be given not they that are poorest and stand in greatest need, but they that can make best friends, are best preferred. So Dives is still enriched, and Lazarus is still rejected. If we send to a great man, we send an ox for a present; but if we send to a poor man, we send a crust for an alms. Therefore, as Christ said to the Jews, that the Ninevites should rise in judgment against them, because they "repented at the preaching of Jonas," (Matt. 12:41); so it may be said to us, that Zacchaeus shall rise in judgment against us, and condemn us; for he showed great mercy on the poor, but we are void of all compassion.

So you have heard the first part of Zacchaeus' confession, in which you see his liberality to the poor. Now you shall hear the second part of his confession, where he promises restitution of his unjustly gotten goods. Before Zacchaeus gave to the poor the half of that which was his own; now he restores that which is none of his to the right owners. And because he had detained their goods so long, to their great loss and hindrance therefore he does not only restore the principal, which he had taken from them; but he allows them their costs and damages that they had sustained. As Jehoram, king of Israel, caused to be restored to the Shunammite her house and land, and all the fruits and profits of the same, which were wrongfully kept from her seven years together, (2 Kings 8:6); so Zacchaeus the customer restores to those that he had oppressed, their goods which he had gotten from them by fraudulent dealing, with all the fruits and profits that might come of it during the time of his unjust possession. So liberal was Zacchaeus to the poor that he gave them half his goods; and so little got Zacchaeus by his usury and oppression, that for every penny he restores four. If the usurers and extortioners of our time would restore four-fold for that they have wrongfully gotten, I fear they would have but a small half to give to the poor, and but a little left to help themselves. There was no law to compel Zacchaeus to make such restitution; except he will confess himself to be a thief, because he was a usurer, and then the Law of God requires such restitution. And surely, Zacchaeus seems after a sort to confess his theft, because he promises four-fold restitution. If a man had stolen a sheep, the Law of God requires that he should restore "four sheep for one," (Exod. 22:1; 2 Sam. 12:6); and the ancient Romans had this law,—that usurers should forfeit four times so much as they took for usury. If the same law were now to use against our thievish usurers, as it was sometime among them, we should not have such complaining of the poor both in prisons and streets. But if these great thieves (I mean our biting usurers) that rob and spoil without ceasing when they have no need, might find no more favor than those petty thieves, which rob and steal sometime when they are driven to it by extreme necessity, then, surely, the Commonwealth would soon be disburdened of that pestilent brood of caterpillars wherewith it is pestered I wish them betimes to look to their own estate, and with Zacchaeus to forsake their damnable trade. If they have lived here by the gain of usury, let them now lament their sin, and call to God for mercy and forgiveness: let them make restitution of that they have wrongfully taken, and grieve that they have so long detained that which is none of theirs. For as no sin is pardoned without repentance to God, so usury is not pardoned without repentance to God; and as the sin of theft is not removed before restitution be made to men, (if the party is able), so the sin of usury (which is a secret theft) is not remitted before restitution be made to those that are oppressed and spoiled by this secret theft.

So you have seen how Zacchaeus, that was once a hoarder of his goods, as our rich men are, is now a liberal disposer of his goods, as I wish they were. He that lately was a camel laden with riches, and therefore unapt to go through a needle's eye, (Matt. 19:24), has now, like the camel, cast off his rich lading, and therefore may enter in at the narrow gate, (Matt. 7:14). Some rich men would rather have lost their lives than foregone their goods, and for half that loss would have proved very pensive: but this was the most joyful news that ever came to Zacchaeus' house, sweeter to him than all his gold and silver; that whereas before he was in the state of damnation, now salvation is promised to him and his house;

and whereas before he was the servant of Satan, now he is become the child of Abraham. Now Zacchaeus' house is become God's house, and Zacchaeus himself is the son of Abraham; and therefore no cause why Christ should not resort to Zacchaeus' house. As Christ said to the penitent thief, "This day shall you be with Me in Paradise," (Luke 23:43); so He says to the penitent publican, *This day salvation has come to your house, and this day you are become a son of Abraham.* Christ loves not to be long in any man's debt: for as He says to Zacchaeus, *Today I must abide at your house;* so He says to the same Zacchaeus, *Today and henceforth forever you and your house must abide with Me in heaven.* Here is a happy change; instead of a little worldly treasure, subject to loss by thieves, and to spoil by rust and moth, to have all store of heavenly treasure, which "neither thieves can steal, nor canker can corrupt," (Matt. 6:19-20); instead of an earthly house, subject to fire and falling, to have "a house given of God, not made with hands, eternal in heaven," (2 Cor. 5:1). Who would not rather choose with Zacchaeus, to give half of his goods to the poor, that he may be an heir of salvation, and the son of Abraham, to rest in his father's bosom, than, with Dives, to keep all from the poor, and be tormented in those eternal flames? That rich glutton, that denied the crumbs from his table, challenged Abraham for his father; but he was refused, because he did not have the faith nor works of Abraham. But Zacchaeus, though by nature he were not the child of Abraham, yet by grace he is become the child of Abraham, because he walked in the steps of that faithful father, (John 8:39). Abraham believed before he was circumcised; so Zacchaeus believed *before he was circumcised,* (Rom. 4:12). As Abraham left his country, and all that he had, when God called him, (Gen. 12:4); so Zacchaeus left his office, and the most part of his riches, when he was called by the Son of God: and as Abraham desired to see the day of Christ, and saw it, and rejoiced, (John 8:56); so Zacchaeus desired to see Christ, and he saw Him, and rejoiced. Now is Zacchaeus, a Gentile, become the child of Abraham: and not only he, but his whole house also is become the house of Abraham; for when Zacchaeus is converted, *his whole house is converted*. As the master is, such are the servants: if he is godly and religious, they prove godly and religious; if he is an atheist, they prove atheists likewise. Therefore do not keep company with the wicked, for it is most pernicious; but associate yourself with those that fear the Lord, that you also may learn to fear the Lord: who for His mercy grant that we may with Zacchaeus be desirous to see Christ, joyful to receive Christ, liberal to relieve the members of Christ, and ready to make amends when we have wronged any of our brethren; that so, with Zacchaeus, we may be heirs of salvation, and the true sons of Abraham, to reign with Christ in heaven forever, by the means and merits of Him that died and rose again for us. To whom with the Father and the Holy Spirit be all glory. *Amen.*

THE WEDDING GARMENT

"Put you on the Lord Jesus Christ."—Rom. 13:14

There are many fashions of apparel, but they are too light, or too heavy, or too coarse, or too stale, and all wear out At last the apostle found a fashion that surpasses them all; it is never out of fashion, meet for all seasons, fit for all persons, and such a profitable weed, that the more it is worn the fresher it is. What fashion have you seen comparable to this? It is not like the clothes of David's ambassadors, which covered their upper parts, (2 Sam. 10:4); nor like Saul's armor, which tired David when he should fight with it, (1 Sam. 17:39); nor like the counterfeit Jeroboam's wife, which disguised herself to go unknown, (1 Kings 14:2); nor like the old rags of the Gibeonites, which deceived Joshua, (Joshua 9:4, 5); nor like the paltry suit of Micah, which he gave once a year to his Levite, (Judges 17:10); nor like the glutton's flaunt, which jetted in purple every day; nor like the light clothes which Christ said are in kings' courts, and make them lighter that wear them, (Matt. 11:8). But it is like the garment of the high priests, which had all the names of the tribes of Israel written on his breast, (Exod. 28:21); so all the names of the faithful are written in the breast of Christ, and registered in the book of his merits, (Mal. 3:16). It is like Elijah's mantle, which divided the waters, (2 Kings 2:8); so he divided our sins and punishments, that they which are clothed with Christ, are armed both against sin and death. It is like the garments of the Israelites in the wilderness, which did not wear; forty years together they wandered in the desert, and yet, says Moses, their shoes were not worn, but their apparel was as when they came out of Egypt, (Deut. 29:5); so the righteousness of Christ does last forever, and his merits are never worn out.

This garment Paul has sent to you, to go before the king of heaven and earth, a holy garment, a royal garment, an immaculate garment, an everlasting garment; a garment whereof every hem is peace of conscience, every plait is joy in the Holy Spirit, every stitch is the remission of some sin, and saves him which wears it. If we put on Christ, we are clothed with his obedience, whereby our wickedness is covered; we are clothed with his merits, whereby our sins are forgiven; we are clothed with his Spirit, whereby our hearts are mollified, and sanctified, and renewed, until we resemble Christ himself. This is the apostle's meaning, to put on Christ, as it is unfolded in Col. 3:12. Where he brings forth all the robes of Christ, and sorts of them, and says, put on mercy, put on meekness, put on humility, put on patience, put on love; all which before he called the new man. So that to put on Christ, is to put on the new man with all his virtues, until we be renewed to the image of Christ, which is like a new man among men. They which labor to be righteous, and yet believe that Christ's righteousness shall save them, have put on Christ as Paul would have them. We are not taught to put on angels, nor saints, nor the Virgin Mary, nor Paul himself, to cover our sins with their righteousness, as the papists do; but we are commanded to put on Christ, and cover our sins with his righteousness. The body has many garments, but the soul has one garment. Every clout will cover our sores, but the finest silk will not cover our sins. Therefore when we seem brave to others, we seem foul to God, because his eye is on our sins, which lie naked when all the rest is covered, until we put on Christ, and then we hear the voice, "Your sins are forgiven," and we have the blessing, "Blessed is the man whose sin is covered." So we are clothed and blessed together.

Now let us see how to put this garment on. Many fumble about it, like children which have need of one to put on their clothes. Some put on Christ like a precious head-attire, which all day is worn, beautified with jewels, and beset with gems, to make the face seem more amiable; but at night that riches is laid aside, and the head muffled with some regardless attire. So do our curious women put on Christ, who when they hear the messengers of grace offering this garment, and preparing to make the body fit to be garnished with so glorious a vesture, as Paul did the Romans, first washing away

177

drunkenness and gluttony, then chambering and wantonness, then strife and envy, and so sin after sin, they seem like the stony ground to receive it with joy, and think to beautify their heads with this precious ointment; but when he tells them there is no communion between Christ and Belial, that if this garment be put on, all other vanities must be put off; they then turn their day into darkness, and reject Christ, that would be an eternal crown of beauty to their heads, and wrap their temples in the uncomely rags and refuse of every nation's pride. In these toys they cause their servants to spend many hours on every day in the week, but especially on the Sabbath day, to deck their bodies, as if they were but little children, which had need of one to put on their clothes. Some put on Christ as a cloak, which hangs on their shoulders, and covers them: when they go abroad to be seen of men, they can cast on the cloak of holiness, and seem for a while as holy as the best; but so soon as they come home the cloak goes off, and the man is as he was, whose vizard was better than his face. So hypocrites put on Christ, as many retain to noblemen, not to do them any service, but to have their countenance. Many put on Christ like a hat, which goes off to everyone which meets them; so every temptation which meets them, makes them forget what they heard, what they promised, what they resolved, and change their way as though they had not repented at all. So the common people (like yourselves) put on Christ: they are zealous so long as they are in the church, and beat their breasts, and cast up their eyes like the publican, (Luke 18:13), when they hear a sentence which moves them; as though they would do no more against that saying whiles they live; but the next business puts all out of mind until they come to the church again. Some put on Christ as a glove, which covers only the hand; so they put on the face of Christ, or the tongue of Christ; but their hands work, and their feet walk, as they did before. So many professors of religion put on Christ, which call but for discipline and reformation, that they might get a name of zeal and sincerity to cover some fault which they would not be suspected of. So every man would cover himself with

Christ, but they do not have the skill, or they do not have the will to put him on.

Now hear how Christ must be put on. As the angel taught John to read the book when he exhorted him to eat it, so must we put on Christ, as if we are eating him. As the meat is turned into the substance of the body and goes through every part of man, so Christ and his word should go from part to part until we are of one nature with them.

So we must put on Christ; for the word signifies *to put him on*, as you would put him in, that he may be one with you, and you with him, as it were in a body together. As he has put on all our infirmities, so we must put on all his graces, not half on, but all on, and clasp him to us, and gird him about us, and wear him, even as we wear our skin, which is always about us. Then there shall be no need of wires, nor curls, nor periwigs; the husbands shall not be forced to rack their rents, nor enhance their fines, nor sell their lands to deck their wives; but as the poor mantle of Elijah seemed better to Elisha than all the robes of Solomon, (2 Kings 2:13), so the wedding garment shall seem better than all the flaunts of vanity, and put every fashion out of fashion, which is not modest and comely like itself.

So have you heard what is meant by putting on Christ: first, to clothe ourselves with righteousness and holiness like Christ; and then, because our own righteousness is too short to cover our arms, and legs, and thighs of sin, but still some bare place will peer out, and shame us in the sight of God, therefore we must borrow Christ's garments, as Jacob did his brother's, (Gen. 27:15), and cover ourselves with his righteousness; that is, believe that his righteousness shall supply our unrighteousness, and his sufferings shall stand for our sufferings, because he came to fulfill the law, and bear the curse, and satisfy his Father for us, that all which believe in him might not die, but have life everlasting, (John 3:16).

Now I have showed you this good garment, you must go to another to help you to put it on; and none can put this garment on you. Only Christ, who is the garment, the Lord Jesus Christ can help you. Therefore let us pray to Him.

You must put him on as Lord; that is, your ruler to command you, your tutor to govern you, and your master to direct you; you must be no man's servant but his, take no man's part against him, but say with the apostles, "Whether is it meet to obey God or you?" (Acts 4:19). You must put him on as Jesus, that is, your Savior in whom you trust, your protector on whom you depend, your Redeemer on whom you believe; you must not look for your salvation from angel, or saint, nor anything beside him. For the name of Jesus signifies a Savior, which is given to none but him, and he is not only called the Savior, but the *Salvation*, in the Song of Simeon, (Luke 1:69), to show that he is the *only* Savior; for there are many saviors, but there can be but one salvation; as there may be many tortures, and yet but one death. Therefore, when he is called the Salvation, it implies that there is no savior beside him. You must put him on as Christ, that is, a king to rule, a prophet to teach, a priest to pray and sacrifice, and pacify the wrath of God for you. For this name Christ does signify that he was anointed a king, a priest, and a prophet for man: a king to rule him, a priest to offer sacrifice for him, a prophet to teach him. So that he puts on Christ as Lord, which worships none but him; he puts on Christ as Jesus, which believes in none but him; and he puts on Christ as Christ, which worships none but him, believes in none but him, and hears *none but him.*

A PREPARATIVE TO MARRIAGE

You have come here to be contracted in the Lord; that is, of two to be made one, Gen. 2:18; for as God has knit the bones and sinews together for the strengthening of men's bodies, so he has knit man and woman together for the strengthening of their life, because "two are firmer than one," (Eccles. 4:9). And therefore, when God made the woman for man, he said, "I will make him a help," showing that man is stronger by his wife. Every marriage, before it is knit, should be contracted, as it is showed in Exod. 22:16, and Deut. 22:28: which stay between the contract and the marriage was the time of longing, for their affection to settle in, because the deferring of that which we love does kindle the desire, which, if it came easily and speedily to us, would make us set less by it. Therefore we read how Joseph and Mary were contracted before they were married, (Matt. 1:18). In the contract Christ was conceived, and in the marriage Christ was born, that he might honor both estates: virginity with his conception, and marriage with his birth. You are contracted, but to be married. Therefore I pass from contracts to speak of marriage, which is nothing else but a communion of life between man and woman joined together according to the ordinance of God.

First, I will show the *excellency* of marriage; then the *institution* of it; then the *causes* of it; then the *choice* of it; then the *duties* of it; and lastly, the *divorcement* of it.

Well might Paul say, Heb. 13:4, "marriage is honorable;" for God has honored it himself. It is honorable for the author, honorable for the time, and honorable for the place. Whereas all other ordinances were appointed of God by the hands of men, or the hands of angels, (Acts 12:7, Heb. 2:2), marriage was ordained by God himself, which cannot err. No man or angel brought the wife to the husband, but God himself, Gen. 2:22; so marriage has more honor of God in this than all other ordinances of God beside, because he solemnized it himself.

Then it is honorable for the time, for it was the first

ordinance that God instituted, even the first thing which he did, after man and woman were created, and that in the state of innocency, before either had sinned: like the finest flower, which will not thrive but in a clean ground. Before man had any other calling, he was called to be an husband; therefore it has the honor of antiquity above all other ordinances, because it was ordained first, and is the more ancient calling of men.

To honor marriage more yet, or rather to teach the married how to honor one another, it is said that the wife was made of the husband's rib, (Gen. 2:22); not of his head, for Paul calls the husband the wife's head, (Ephes. 5:23); not of the foot, for he must not set her at his foot The servant is appointed to serve, and the wife to help. If she must not match with the head, nor stoop at the foot, where shall he set her then? He must set her at his heart, and therefore she which should lie in his bosom was made in his bosom, and should be as close to him as his rib, of which she was fashioned.

Lastly, in all nations the day of marriage was reputed the most joyful day in all their life, and is reputed still of all; as though the sun of happiness began that day to shine on us, when a good wife is brought to us. Therefore one says, that marriage does signify merry-age, because a play-fellow has come to make our age merry, as Isaac and Rebekah sported together.

Solomon considering all these excellencies, as though we were more indebted to God for this than other temporal gifts, says, "Houses and riches are the inheritance of the father, but a prudent wife comes of the Lord," (Prov. 19:14).

Houses and riches are given of God, and all things else, and yet he says, houses and riches are given of parents, but a good wife is given of God, as though a good wife were such a gift as we should account comes from God alone, and accept it as if he should send us a present from heaven, with this name written on it, the gift of God.

Beasts are ordained for food, and clothes for warmth, and flowers for pleasure, but the wife is ordained for man; like little Zoar, a city of refuge to fly to in all his troubles, (Gen.

19:20); and there is no peace comparable to her but the peace of conscience.

Now it has to be, that marriage, which was ordained of such an excellent author, and in such a happy place, and of such an ancient time, and after such a notable order, must likewise have special causes for the ordinance of it. Therefore the Holy Spirit shows us three causes of this union.

One is, the propagation of children, signified in that when Moses says, Gen. 1:27, "He created them male and female," not both male nor both female, but one male and the other female; as if he created them fit to propagate other. And therefore when he had created them so, to show that propagation of children is one end of marriage, he said to them, "Increase and multiply," (Gen. 1:28); that is, bring forth children, as other creatures bring forth their kind.

For this cause marriage is called matrimony, which signifies *motherage*, because it makes them mothers which were virgins before, and is the seminary of the world, without which all things should be in vain, for want of men to use them; for God reserves the great city to himself; and this suburbs he has set out to us, which are regents by sea and by land.

The second cause is to avoid fornication. This Paul signifies when he says, "For the avoiding of fornication, let every man have his own wife," (1 Cor. 7:8). He does not say for avoiding of adultery, but for avoiding of fornication, showing that fornication is unlawful.

The third cause is to avoid the inconvenience of solitariness, signified in these words, "It is not good for man to be alone;" as though he had said, *This life would be miserable and irksome, and unpleasant to man, if the Lord had not given him a wife to company his troubles.* If it is not good for man to be alone, then it is good for man to have a help-meet; therefore as God created a pair of all other kinds, so he created a pair of this kind. We say that one is none, because he cannot be fewer than one, he cannot be less than one, he cannot be weaker than one, and therefore the wise man says, Eccles. 4:10, "Woe to him that is alone," that is, *he which is alone shall have woe*. Thoughts, and cares, and fears will come to him because he has none to comfort him, as thieves steal in when the house is empty; like a turtle which has lost his mate; like one leg when the other is cut off; like one wing when the other is clipped; so had the man been, if the woman had not been joined to him; therefore for mutual society, God coupled two together, that the infinite troubles which lie on us in the world might be eased with the comfort and help one of another, and that the poor in the world might have some comfort as well as the rich; for "the poor man," says Solomon, "is forsaken of his own brethren," (Prov. 19:7); yet God has provided one comfort for him, like Jonathan's armor bearer, that shall never forsake him, (1 Sam. 14:7), that is, another self, which is the only commodity (as I may term it) in which the poor match the rich; without which some persons should have no helper, no comfort, no friend at all.

But as it is not good to be alone, so Solomon shows that "it is better to be alone than to dwell with a froward wife," (Prov. 21:9), which is like a *quotidian ague*, to keep his patience as usual. Such furies haunt some men, like Saul's spirit, (1 Sam. 16:14), as though the devil had put a sword into their hands to kill themselves; therefore choose whom you may enjoy, or live alone still, and you shall not repent you of your bargain.

That you may take and keep without repentance, now we will speak of the choice, which some call the way to good wives' dwelling, for these flowers grow not on every ground; therefore they say, that in wiving and thriving a man should take counsel of all the world, lest he light on a curse while he seeks for a blessing. As Moses considered what spies he sent into Canaan, (Deut. 1:23), so you must regard whom you sends to spy out a wife for you. Discretion is a wary spy, but fancy is a rash spy, and likes whom she will mislike again.

To direct you to a right choice herein, the Holy Spirit gives you two rules in the choice of a wife, godliness and fitness; godliness, because our spouse must be like Christ's spouse, that is, graced with gifts and embroidered with virtues, as if we married holiness itself. Secondly, the mate must be fit.

It is not enough to be virtuous but to be suitable; for divers women have many virtues, and yet do not fit to some men; and divers men have many virtues, and yet do not fit to some women; and therefore we see many times even the godly couples jar each other when they are married, because there is some unfitness between them, which puts them at odds. What is *odds*, but the contrary to even? Therefore make them even, says one, and there will be no odds. From hence came the first use of the ring in weddings, to represent this evenness; for if it is straighter than the finger it will pinch, and if it is wider than the finger it will fall off, but if it are fit it neither pinches nor slips; so they which are alike, strive not; but they which are unlike, are fire and water. Therefore one observes that concord is nothing but likeness; and all that strife is for unfitness, as in things when they fit not together, and in persons when they suit not one another. How was God pleased when he had found a king according to his own heart? (1 Sam. 2:35). So shall that man be pleased that finds a wife according to his own heart; whether he is rich or poor, his peace shall afford him a cheerful life, and teach him to sing, "In love is no lack." Therefore a godly man in our time thanked the Lord that he had not only given him a godly wife, but a fit wife; for he had said, not that she was the wisest, nor the holiest, nor the humblest, nor the most modest wife in the world, but the most fit wife for him in the world, which every man should think when that knot is tied, or else so often as he sees a better, he will wish that his choice were to make again. As he thanked God for sending him a fit wife, so the unmarried should pray to God to send him a fit wife; for if they is not like, they will not like.

There are certain signs of this fitness and godliness, both in the man and in the woman. If you will know a godly man, or a godly woman, you must mark five things: the report, the looks, the speech, the apparel, and the companions, which are like the pulses, that show whether we will be well or ill with them. The *report*, because as the market goes, so, they say, the market-men will talk. A good man commonly has a good name, (Prov. 10:7), because a good name is one of the blessings which God promises to good men.

The next sign is *the look*; for Solomon says in Eccles. 8:1, "Wisdom is in the face of a man;" so godliness is in the face of a man, and so folly is in the face of a man, and so wickedness is in the face of a man. And therefore it is said in Isa. 3:9, "The trial of their countenance testifies against them;" as though their looks could speak. And therefore we read of "proud looks," and "angry looks," and "wanton looks," because they betray pride, and anger, and wantonness.

I have heard one say, that a modest man dwells at the sign of a modest countenance; and an honest woman dwells at the sign of an honest face, which is like the gate of the temple that was called Beautiful, (Acts 3:2); showing, that if the entry be so beautiful, within is great beauty. To show how a modest countenance and womanly shamefacedness commends a chaste wife. It is observed that the word *nuptice*, which signifies the marriage of the woman, declares the manner of her marriage; for it imports a covering, because the virgins which should be married, when they came to their husbands, for modesty and shamefacedness covered their faces, as we read of Rebekah, (Gen. 24:65), which as soon as she saw Isaac, and knew that he should be her husband, she cast a veil before her face, showing that modesty should be learned before marriage, which is the dowry that God adds to her portion.

The third thing is her *speech*, or rather her *silence*, for the ornament of a woman is silence; and therefore the law was given to the man rather than to the woman, to show that he should be the teacher and she the hearer. Solomon describing a right wife says, "She opens her mouth with wisdom and the law of grace is in her tongue." A wife that can speak this language, is better than she that has all the tongues.

The fourth sign is the *apparel*; for as the pride of the glutton is noted, in that he went in purple every day, (Luke 16:19), so the humility of John is noted, (Mark 1:6), in that he went in haircloth every day. A modest woman is known by her sober attire, as the prophet Elijah was known by his rough garment, (2 Kings 1:8). Do not Look for something better within the person than you see outside of the person, for everyone seems better than she is; if the face is vain, the heart will be filled with pride.

The fifth sign is the *company*; for birds of a feather will fly together, and fellows in sin will be fellows in league, even as young Rehoboam chose young companions, (1 Kings 12:8). The tame beasts will not keep with the wild, nor the clean dwell with the leprous. If a man can be known by nothing else, then he may be known by his companions; for like will be drawn to like.

All these properties are not seen at three or four times with a few meetings or courtings, for hypocrisy is spun with a fine thread, and none are deceived so often as lovers. He which will know all his wife's qualities before he is married to her, must see her eating, and walking, and working, and playing, and talking, and laughing, and chiding, or else he shall have less with her than he looked for, or more than he wished for.

When these rules are warily observed, they may join together, and say, as Laban and Bethuel said in Gen. 24:50, "This comes of the Lord, therefore we will not speak against it." How happy are those, in whom faith, and love, and godliness are married together, before they marry themselves! For none of these martial, and cloudy, and whining marriages can say, that godliness was invited to their bridal, and therefore the blessings which are promised to godliness flies from them.

In Matt. 22 Christ shows that before parties married they were likely to put on fair and new garments, which were called wedding garments; a warning to all which put on wedding-garments, to put on truth and holiness too, which so precisely is resembled by that garment more than other. Miserable is that man which is chained with a woman that does not like his religion; she will be nibbling at his prayers, and at his study, and at his meditations, until she has tired out his devotion, and turned the edge of his soul, as David was tried of his malapert Michal: she mocked him for his zeal and liked herself in her folly, (2 Sam. 6:16); many have fallen at this stone. Therefore, is not twenty wedded to her which has not the wedding garment; but let unity go first, and let union follow after, and hope not to convert her, but fear that she will pervert you, lest you say after, like him which should come to the Lord's banquet, "I have married a wife, and cannot come," (Luke 14:20).

Yet the chief point is behind, that is, our duties. The duties of marriage may be reduced to the duties of man and wife, one toward another, and their duties toward their children, and their duty toward their servants. For themselves, says one, they must think themselves likened to birds: the one is the cock, and the other is the hen; the cock flies abroad to bring in, and the hen sits on the nest to keep all at home. So God has made the man to travel abroad, and the woman to keep house; and so their nature, and their mind, and their strength are fitted accordingly; for the man's pleasure is most abroad, and the woman's within.

Love is the marriage virtue which sings music to their whole life. Wedlock is made of two loves, which I may call the first love and the after love. As every man is taught to love God before he is bid to love his neighbor, so they must love God before they can love one another. To show the love which should be between man and wife, marriage is called *conjugium*, which signifies a *knitting or joining together*; showing, that unless there is a joining of hearts, and a knitting of affections together, it is not marriage in deed, but in show and name, and they shall dwell in a house like two poisons in the stomach, and one shall always be sick of the other.

Therefore, first, that they may love, and keep love one with another, it is necessary that they both love God, and as their love increases toward him, so it shall increase each to other.

To pass over sleights, which seldom prosper unless they have some warrant, the best policy in marriage is to *begin well*; for as boards well joined at the first fit close ever after, but if they square not at the first they warp more and more, so they which are well joined are well married; but they which offend their love before it is settled, fade every day like a marigold, which closes her flower as the sun goes down, until they hate one another more than they loved at first.

To begin this concord well, it is necessary to learn one another's natures, and one another's affections, and one another's infirmities, because you must be helpers, and you cannot help unless you know the disease. All the problems almost which trouble this band rises of this, that one does not hit the measure of the others heart, apply themselves to either's nature, whereby it comes to pass that neither can refrain when either is offended, but one sharpens another when they have need to be calmed. Therefore they must learn of Paul, (1 Cor. 9:20), to fashion themselves one to another, if they would win one another; for if any problems arise, one says, in no way divide beds for it, for then the sun goes down on their wrath, Eph. 4:26, and the means of reconcilement is taken away. Give passions no time; for if some men's anger stands but a night, it turns to malice, which is incurable.

The apostle says that there will be offences in the church, (1 Cor. 11:19); so sure there will be many offences in marriage; but, he says, these are trials who have faith, these are but trials who are good husbands and who are good wives. His anger must be in such a mood as if he chides with himself, and their strife as it were a sauce made of purpose to sharpen their love when it becomes unpleasant; like Jonathan's arrows, which were not shot to hurt, but to give warning, (1 Sam. 20:20). Knowing once a couple which were both choleric, and yet never fell out, I asked the man how they did order the matter that their infirmity did not make them discord? He answered me, *When her fit is on her, I yield to her, as Abraham did to Sarah; and when my fit is on me, she yields to me; and so we never strive together, but asunder.* I thought this was a good example to commend to all married folks.

His next duty to love, is a fruit of his love; that is, to let all things be common between them, which were private before. The man and wife are partners, like two oars in a boat;

therefore he must divide offices, and affairs, and goods with her, causing her to be feared, and reverenced, and obeyed of her children and servants, like himself, for she is an under officer in his commonwealth, and therefore she must be assisted and borne out like his deputy; as the prince stands with his magistrates for his own quiet, because they are the legs which bear him up. To show this community between husband and wife, he is to maintain her as he does himself, because Christ says, Mark 10:8, "They are no more two, but one." Therefore, when he maintains her, he must think it to be but one charge, because he maintains no more but himself, for the two are now one. He may not say, as husbands are likely to say, that which is yours is mine, and that which is mine is mine own; but that which is mine is yours, and myself too. For as it is said, Rom. 8:32, "He which has given us his Son, can he deny us anything?" So she may say, He which has given me himself, can he deny me anything? The body is better than the goods; therefore if the body be mine, the goods are mine too.

Lastly, he must tender her as much as all her friends, because he has taken her from her friends, and covenanted to tender her for them all. To show how he should tender her, Peter says, "Honor the woman as the weaker vessel," (1 Peter 3:7). As we do not handle glasses like pots, because they are weaker vessels, but touch them nicely and softly for fear of cracking them, so a man must entreat his wife with gentleness and softness, not expecting that wisdom, nor that faith, nor that patience, nor that strength in the weaker vessel, which should be in the stronger; but think when he takes a wife he takes a vineyard, not grapes, but a vineyard to bear him grapes; therefore he must sow it, and dress it, and water it, and fence it, and think it a good vineyard, if at last it bring forth grapes. So he must not look to find a wife without a fault, but think that she is committed to him to reclaim her from her faults; for all are defective. And if he finds the proverb true, that in space comes grace, he must rejoice as much at his wife when she amends, as the husbandman rejoices when his vineyard begins to bear fruit. Abraham said to Lot, "Are we not brethren?" Gen.

13:8, that is, may brethren have problems? But they may say, Are we not one? Can one chide with another? Can one fight with another? He is a bad host that welcomes his guest with stripes. Does a king trample his crown? Solomon calls the wife, "the crown of her husband," Prov. 12:4; therefore he which wounds her, wounds his own honor. She is a free citizen in your own house, and has taken the peace of you the first day of her marriage, to hold your hand until she releases you again.

Paul says, Col. 3:19, "Be not bitter to your wives," noting, that anger in a husband is a vice. Does the cock spur the hen? Every man is ashamed to lay his hands on a woman, because she cannot match him; therefore he is a shameless man which lays hands on his wife. The hand does not buffet its own cheek, but stroke it. If a man be seen raging with himself, he is carried to bedlam; so these madmen which beat themselves should be sent to bedlam until their madness is gone. Solomon says, Prov. 5:19, "Delight continually in her love," that is, begin, proceed, and end in love. In revenge, therefore, he shows that delight is gone, because he calls love their delight. So we have sent letters to husbands to read before they fight. Now let us go home to love again. Would you learn how to make your match delightful? Solomon says, "rejoice in her love continually," (Prov. 5:19). As though you could not delight without love, and with love you may delight continually, therefore love is called the thankful virtue, because it renders peace, and ease, and comfort to them that make use of her. So much for husbands.

Likewise the woman may learn her duty of her names. They are called *goodwives*, as good wife A and goodwife B. Every wife is called a good wife; therefore if they are not good wives, their names lie of them, and they are not worth their titles, but answer to a wrong name, as players do on a stage. This name pleases them well. But besides this, a wife is called a yoke-fellow, to show that she should help her husband to bear his yoke, that is, his grief must be her grief; and whether it is the yoke of poverty, or the yoke of envy, or the yoke of sickness, or the yoke of imprisonment, she must submit her neck to bear it patiently with him, or else she is not his yoke-fellow, *but his yoke*; as though she were inflicted on him for a penalty, like to Job's wife, whom the devil left to torment him when he took away all he had beside.

Besides a yoke-fellow, she is called a helper, (Gen. 2:18), to help him in his business, to help him in his labors, to help him in his sickness, like a woman-physician, sometime with her strength, and sometime with her counsel.

Beside a helper, she is called a comforter too; and therefore the man is pressed to rejoice in his wife, (Prov. 5:18); which is as much as to say, that wives must be the rejoicing of their husbands, even like David's harp to comfort Saul, (1 Sam. 16:23).

The daughters of Sarah are bound to call their husbands lords, as Sarah called her husband, (Gen. 18:12, 1 Peter 3:3, 6); that is, to take them for lords, for heads and governors. If you disdain to follow Abraham's spouse, the apostle bids you follow Christ's spouse; for he says, Eph. 5:24, "Let a wife be subject to her husband, as the church is to Christ." "A greater love than this," says Christ, "no man can have," (John 15:13); so a better example than this no woman can have. That the wife may yield this reverence to her husband, Paul would have her attire to be modest and orderly, (1 Tim. 2:9); for garish apparel has taught many gossips to disdain their husbands. This is the folly of some men, to lay all their pride on their wives; they care not how they sloven themselves, so their wives jet like peacocks. But Peter does commend Sarah for her attire, and not Abraham, (1 Peter 3:5), showing that women should brave it no more than men; and God made Eve's coat of the same cloth that he made Adam's, (Gen. 3:21). They covered themselves with leaves, and God derided them, (Gen. 3:7); but now they cover themselves with pride, like Satan which is fallen down before them like lightning, (Luke 10:18). Ruff on ruff, lace on lace, cut on cut, four-and-twenty orders, until the woman is not so precious as her apparel; that if any man would picture vanity, he must take a pattern of a woman, or else he cannot draw her likeness. As

Herodias was worse for her fine dancing, (Matt. 14:6), so a woman may have too many ornaments. Frizzled locks, naked breasts, painting, perfume, and especially a rolling eye, are the forerunners of adultery; and he which has such a wife, has a fine plague. Once women were married without dowries, because they were well nurtured; but now, if they weighed not more in gold than in godliness, many should sit like nuns without husbands. So we have shadowed the man's duty to his wife, and the woman's to her husband.

After their duties one to another, they must learn their duties to their family. One compares the master of the house to the seraphin, which came and kindled the prophet's zeal; so he should go every day? Therefore Paul is so earnest with Philemon to make much of Onesimus his servant, that he desired Philemon to receive him as he would himself, (Philem. 17). Therefore, because cruel and greedy masters should not use them too hardly, God remembered them in his creation, and made every week one day of rest, in which they should be as free as their masters, (Gen. 2:2); so God pities the laborer from heaven, and every Sabbath looks down on him from heaven, as if he should say, One day your labors shall have an end, and you shall rest forever, as you rested this day.

By this we see, as David limited Joab, that he should not kill Absalom, (2 Sam. 18:5), so God has bound masters, that they should not oppress their servants. Shall God respect you more than them? Are you made fresher to your labor by a little rest? And is not your servant made stronger by rest to labor for you? How many beasts and sheep did Laban lose, only for hardly entreating of a good servant, (Gen. 31:9); therefore that is the way to lose, but not to thrive.

Our Lord is called a servant, (Isa. 42:1, Matt. 12:18), which teaches Christians to use their servants well for Christ's sake, seeing they are servants too, and have one master, Christ. As David speaks of man, Psa. 8:6, saying, "thou have made him a little lower than the angels," so I may say of servants, that God has made them a little lower than children; not children, but the next two children, as one would say, inferior children, or sons in law. And therefore the householder is called *pater familias*, which signifies the father of his family, because he should have a fatherly care over his servants, as if they were his children, and not use them only for their labor, like beasts.

Lastly, we put the duty towards children, because they come last to their hands. In Latin, children are called *fiignora*, that is, pledges; as if I should say, A pledge of the husband's love to the wife, and a pledge of the wife's love toward the husband; for there is nothing which does so knit love between the man and the wife as the fruit of the womb. Therefore, when Leah began to conceive, she said, "Now my husband will love me," (Gen. 30:20); as though the husband did love for children. If a woman have many defects (as Leah had), yet this is the amends which she makes her husband, to bring him children, which is the right wedding-ring, that seals and makes up the marriage. When their father and mother fall out, they perk up between them like little mediators, and with many pretty sports make truce, when others dare not speak to them.

Therefore, now let us consider what these little ones may challenge of their parents that stand them instead of lawyers. Before we teach parents to love their children, they had need be taught not to love them too much, for David's darling was David's traitor; and this is the manner of God, when a man begins to set anything in God's room, and love it above him which gave it, either to take away it, or to take away him, before he provoke him too much. Therefore, if parents would have their children live, they must take heed not to love them too much; for the giver is offended when the gift is more esteemed than he.

The first duty is the mother's, that is, to nurse her child at her own breasts, as Sarah did Isaac, (Gen. 21:7); and therefore Isaiah joins the nurse's name and the mother's name both in one, and calls them "nursing mothers;" showing that mothers should be the nurses. So when God chose a nurse for Moses, (Exod. 2:8), he led the handmaid of Pharaoh's daughter to his mother, as though God would have none nurse him but his mother. After, when the Son of God was born, his Father thought none fit to be his nurse but the virgin his mother, (Matt. 2:14). The earth's fountains are made to give water, and the breasts of women are made to give suck. Every beast and every fowl is bred of the same that did bear it, only women love to be mothers, but not nurses. Therefore, if their children prove unnatural, they may say, you follow your mother, for she was unnatural first, in locking up her breasts from you, and committing you forth like a cuckoo, to be hatched in a sparrow's nest. Hereof it comes that we say, "He sucked evil from the dug;" that is, as the nurse is affected in her body or in her mind, commonly the child draws the same infirmity from her, as the eggs of a hen are altered under the hawk. Yet they which have no milk, can give no milk. But whose breasts have this perpetual drought? In the same way, it is like the gout; no beggars may have it, but citizens or gentlewomen. In 1 Kings 2:2, we have David instructing his sons; in Gen. 49, Jacob correcting his sons; and in Job 1, Job praying for his sons. These three put together,—instructing, correcting, and praying,—make good children, *and happy parents.*

Once Christ took a child, and set him in the midst of his disciples, and said, "He which will receive the kingdom of heaven, must receive it as a little child," (Luke 18:17); showing that our children should be so innocent, so humble, and so void of evil works, that they may be taken for examples of the children of God. Therefore, in Psa. 127:3, children are called "the heritage of the Lord," to show that they should be trained as though they were not men's children, but God's, that they may have God's heritage after. So if you do, your servants shall be God's servants, and your children shall be God's children, and your house shall be God's house, like a little church, when others are like a den of thieves, (Col. 4:15).

If you have read all this book, and are never the better, yet catch this flower before you go out of the garden, and peradventure the scent of it will bring you back to smell the rest. As the corpse of Asahel made the passengers to stand, (2 Sam. 2:23), so I placed this sentence in the door of your passage, to make you stand and consider what you do before you marry. For this is the scope and operation of it, to call your mind to a solemn meditation, and warn you to live in marriage as in a temptation, which is like to make him worse than he was, as the marriage of Jehoram did, (2 Chron. 21:6), if he does not use Job's preservative, to be jealous over all his life, (Job 9:28).

The allurements of beauty, the troubles about riches, the charges of children, the losses by servants, the unquietness of neighbors, cry to him that he is entered into the hardest vocation of all other; and therefore they which have but nine years' apprenticeship to make them good mercers or drapers, have nineteen years before marriage to learn to be good husbands and wives; as though it were a trade of nothing but mysteries, and had need of double time over all the rest.

Therefore, so often as you think on this saying, think whether you are examples of it, and it will waken you, and chide you, and lead you a straight path, like the angel which led the servant of Abraham, (Gen. 24:40).

So have I chalked the way to prepare you to marriage, as the Levites prepared their brethren to the Passover, (2 Chron. 35:6). Remember that this day you are made one, and therefore must have but one will. And now the Lord Jesus, in whom you are contracted, knit your hearts together, that you may love one another like David and Jonathan, (1 Sam. 18:1); and go before you in this life like the star which went before the Gentiles, (Matt. 2:9), that you may begin, and proceed, and end, in his glory! To whom be all glory forever! *Amen.*

THE TRUE TRIAL OF THE SPIRITS

"Quench not the Spirit. Despise not prophesying. Try all things, and keep that which is good. Abstain from all appearance of evil."—1 Thes. 5:19-22

At the last time when I spoke of these words, "In all things give thanks," and "Quench not the Spirit," touching the first, I showed you that it is an easier thing to obtain of God than to be thankful to him; for more have gone away speeders than have gone away thankful, (Luke 17:17).

After speaking of those words, *Quench not the Spirit*, I showed you that the Spirit does signify the gifts and motions of the Spirit. The Spirit in the 3rd of Matthew is likened to fire; and therefore Paul says well, "Quench not the Spirit," because fire may be quenched.

Then I showed you how the Spirit is quenched, as a man quenches his reason with too much wine; and therefore we say, *When the wine is in, the wit is out*; because before, he seems to have reason, and now he seems to have none; so our zeal, and our faith, and our love, are quenched with sin. Every vain thought, and every idle word, and every wicked deed, is like so many drops to quench the Spirit of God. Some quench it with the business of this world; some quench it with the lusts of the flesh; some quench it with the cares of the mind; some quench it with long delays, that is, not plying the motion when it comes, but crossing the good thoughts with bad thoughts, and doing a thing when the Spirit says, *Do not do it*; as Ahab went to battle after he was forbidden. Sometimes a man shall feel himself stirred to a good work, as though he were led to it by the hand; and again, he shall be frightened from some evil thing, as though he were reproved in his ear; then, if he resists, he shall immediately feel the Spirit going out of him, and hear a voice pronouncing him guilty, and he shall hardly recover his peace again. Therefore Paul says, "Grieve not the Spirit," (Eph. 4:30); showing that the Spirit is often grieved before it is quenched; and that when a man begins to grieve, and check, and persecute the Spirit lightly, he never ceases until he has quenched it; that is, until he seems to have no spirit at all, but walks like a lump of flesh.

After *Quench not the Spirit*, follows *Despise not prophesying*. In the end of this epistle, Paul speaks like a father which has come to the end of his life; who, because he has but a little while to speak, heaps his lessons together, which he would have his sons remember when he is gone. So Paul, as though he were set to give good counsel, and had not leisure to speak that he would, send the Thessalonians a brief of his mind, which their meditation should after amplify and expound to them.

His first advice is, "Quench not the Spirit;" that is, when a good motion comes, welcome it like a friend, and do not cross it with your lusts. The second admonition teaches how the first should be kept, "Despise not prophesying;" and the Spirit will not quench, because prophesying kindles it. The third admonition teaches how to make fruit of the second. Try the doctrines of them which prophesy, and you shall not believe error for truth, but hold to the best. The fourth admonition is the sum of all, and it comes last, because it is longest in learning; that is, "Abstain from all appearance of evil." This is the sum of all.

If you mark, Paul does not say, despise not prophets, but *prophesying*; signifying, that from the contempt of the prophets, at last we come to despise prophesying too, like the Jews, who, when they were offended with the prophet, charged him to prophesy no more, (Jer. 11:21). Therefore, as Christ warned his disciples to hear the Scribes and Pharisees, although they did not as they taught, (Matt. 23:3); so Paul warned the Thessalonians, that if any prophets among them do not as they teach, and therefore seem worthy to be despised, like the Scribes and Pharisees, yet that they take heed that they do not despise prophesying for the prophets. Because the preachers are despised before the word be despised, therefore we will speak first of their contempt.

Christ asked his disciples what they thought of him,

(Matt. 16:13), so I would ask you, what do you think of preachers? Is he a contemptible person which brings the message of God, which has the name of an angel, (2 Cor. 5:20), and all his words are messengers of life? Prophets are of such account with God, that it is said, Amos 3:7, "God will do nothing before he reveals it to his prophets;" so prophets are, as it were, God's counsellors. Again, kings, and priests, and prophets, were figures of Christ; all these three were anointed with oil, to show that they had greater graces than the rest; but especially the prophets are called men of God, (1 Kings 13:1), to show, that all which are of God will make much of prophets for God's sake. Therefore when the prophet Elisha would send for Naaman the leper to come to him, these were his words, Naaman "shall know that there is a prophet in Israel," (2 Kings 5:8); as though all the glory of Israel were chiefly in this, that they had prophets, and others had none; as if one parish should triumph over another, because they have a preacher, and the other have none. Therefore when this prophet was dead, Joash the king came to his corpse, and wept over his face, and cried, "O my father, my father! the chariots of Israel, and the horsemen of the same!" (2 Kings 13:14); showing that the chariots, and horses, and soldiers, do not so safeguard a city, as the prophets which teach it, and pray for it. Therefore when God would mark the Israelites with a name of greatest reproach, he calls them a people which rebuke their priests, as if he should say, usurpers of the priest's office, for they rebuke their priests, which are appointed to rebuke them.

As Paul shows the Thessalonians how the preachers of the word should be honored, so he teaches the Philippians how to honor their teachers, saying, "Receive him in the Lord with great gladness, and make much of such," (Phil. 2:29); that is, show yourselves so glad of him, that he may be glad of you. Have you need to be taught why Paul would have you make much of such? Because they are like lamps, which consume themselves to give light to others, so they consume themselves to give light to you; because they are like a hen, which clucks her chickens together from the kite, so they cluck you together from the serpent; because they are like the shout which did beat down the walls of Jericho, Josh. 6:20, so they areat down the walls of sin; because they are like the fiery pillar which went before the Israelites to the land of promise, so they go before you to the land of promise; because they are like good Andrew, which called his brother to see the Messiah, (John 1:41), so they call on you to see the Messiah; and therefore make much of such.

If we should make much of prophets, how much should we make of prophesying! If we should love our instructors, how much should we love instruction! Simeon keeping in the temple met with Christ, (Luke 2:28); so many hearing the word, have met with knowledge, have met with comfort, have met with peace, have met with salvation; but without the word no one was ever converted to God. Therefore, whensoever the word is preached, everyone may say to himself, as the disciples said to the blind man, "Be of good comfort, he calls you," Mark 10:49; be of good comfort, the Lord calls you; but when the word is not preached, then every man may say to himself, Beware, the devil calls you. When the prophets went from Jerusalem, the sword, and famine, and pestilence, and all the plagues of God rained on them, even as fire came on Sodom so soon as Lot was gone out, (Gen. 19:24); therefore what may those lands fear, which use their prophets as the Jews used those which were sent to them? Amos calls it an evil time, in which the prudent keep silence, chap. 5:13, therefore this is an evil time, in which the prudent are silent. Once Paul said to Timothy, "Let no man despise your youth," (1 Tim. 4:12), showing that preachers should not be despised for their youth; but now they despise the young prophets and the old too. How is the double honor turned to single honor! No, how is our honor turned to dishonor! "If I be a master," says God, "where is my fear?" (Mal. 1:6); so, if we be prophets, where is our reverence? Does not the contempt of the prophets cry to God, as well as the blood of Abel? (Gen. 4:10). When the messengers which were sent to the vineyard for fruit were beaten of them which should have laden them, then it is said that the lord of the vineyard became angry, and said that he would let out the vineyard to others, which should yield him the fruits of it, (Matt. 21:43). The meaning of this is that when the preachers and teachers which Christ sends to his church for fruits are abused and persecuted of those who they call to the banquet, then he will remove their light and his gospel to others, which will yield him the fruits of it.

Has not this despising of the preachers almost made the preachers despise preaching? The people's neglect of the prophets has made the prophets neglect prophesying. The nonresident keeps himself away, because he thinks the people like him better because he does not trouble them; and the drone never studies to preach, for he says that an homily is better liked of than a sermon; and they which would study divinity above all, when they look on our contempt, and beggary, and vexation, turn to law, to physic, to trades, or anything, rather than they will enter this contemptible calling. And is not the ark, then, ready to depart from Israel?

The second thing which makes prophets and prophesying despised, is the lewdness and negligence of them that are able to do well in their ministry, and yet do what is contrary. It is said of Hophni and Phinehas, that by their corrupt sacrificing they made the people abhor the sacrifice, (1 Sam. 2:17); so many, by their slubbering of the word (for want of study and meditation), make men think that there is no more wisdom in the word of God than they show out of it; and therefore they stay at home, and say, they know as much as the preacher can teach them.

There is a kind of preacher risen up lately, which shroud and cover every rustical, and unsavory, and childish, and absurd sermon, under the name of the simple kind of teaching, like the popish priests, which make ignorance the mother of devotion. But indeed, to preach simply is not to preach rudely, nor unlearnedly, nor confusedly, but to preach plainly and perspicuously, that the simplest man may understand what is taught, as if he did hear his own name. Therefore, if you will know what makes many preachers preach so barely, and loosely, and simply, it is your own simplicity, which makes them think, that if they go on and say something, all is one, and no fault will be found, because you are not able to judge in or out; and so because they give no attendance to doctrine, as Paul teaches them, (1 Tim. 4:16), it is almost come to pass, that in a whole sermon the hearer cannot pick out one note more than he could gather himself. Wheat is good, but they which sell the refuse of wheat are reproved, (Amos 8:6); so preaching is good, but this refuse of preaching is but like swearing: for one takes the name of God in vain, and the other takes the word of God in vain. As every sound is not music, so every sermon is not preaching, but worse than if we should read an homily. In Jeremiah 48 there is a curse on them which do the business of the Lord negligently. If this curse does not touch them which accomplish the chief business of the Lord negligently, truly I cannot tell whom the prophet means. These would not have prophesying despised, and yet they make it despised themselves.

The last thing which makes prophets and prophesying despised is, the diversity of minds. While one holds one way, and another *another* way, some leave all, and will be of no religion, until both parties agree; as if a patient should suffer himself, and eat no meat at all, because one physician says that this meat will hurt him, and another says that meat will hurt him. These are the three enemies which make us and our labors despised.

After *Despise not prophesying*, follows *Try all things*, as if he should say, *Despise not prophesying, but for all that try prophesying lest you believe error for truth; for as among rulers there are bad rulers, so among prophets there are false prophets*. The men of Berea would not receive Paul's doctrine before they had tried it; and how did they try it? It is said they *searched the Scriptures*. This is the way which Paul would teach you to try others, whereby he was tried himself; whereby we may see that if you read the Scriptures you shall be able to try all doctrines: for the word of God is the touchstone of everything, like the light which God made to behold all his creatures. A man tries his horse, which must bear him, and shall he not try his faith which must save him?

Now, when we have tried by the word which is truth and which is error, what should we do then? We are to "Keep that which is best." This means *stay at the truth*, as the wise men stayed when they came to Christ. We must keep and hold the truth, as a man grips a thing with both his hands; that is, defend it with your tongue, maintain it with your purse, further it with your labor, in danger and trouble, and loss and displeasure, come life, come death; think, as Christ sealed the truth with his blood, so you must seal it with your blood, or else you *Do not keep it*, but let it go. Well does Paul put *try* before *choose*, for he which tries may choose the best, but he which chooses before he tries takes the worse sooner than the best, and therefore the pope's priests, because the people should take superstition before religion, will never let them have the touch-stone. They but keep them from the Scripture, and lock it up in an unknown tongue, which they cannot skill of, lest they should try their doctrines, like the men of Berea, (Acts 17), making religion a craft, as men call their trades. Therefore, as Josiah rejoiced that the book of God was found again, so we may rejoice that the book of God is found again, for when the people might not read it, it was all one as if they had lost it.

After *Try all things* and keep the best, follows *Abstain from all appearance of evil*; as if he should say, That is like to be best which is so far from evil that it has not the appearance of evil; and that is like to be the truth, which is so far from error that it has not the show of error; whereby he shows that nothing should be brought into the church, or added to our religion, but that which is undoubted truth, without suspicion of error. It is not enough to be persuaded of our faith, but we must be assured of it; for religion is not built on doubts, but on knowledge. Here we may marvel why Paul bids us abstain from all appearance of evil, because sin, and heresy, and superstition are hypocrites; that is, sin has the appearance of virtue, and heresy has the appearance of truth, and superstition has the appearance of religion. But by this the apostle does note that there is no sin, nor heresy, nor superstition, but, if the visor be taken away from it, it will appear to be a sin, and heresy, and superstition, though at the first sight the visor do make it seem none, because it covers the evil, like a painted sepulcher on worms and rotten bones.

Hereby we are taught to judge of all things as they are, and not as they seem to be. As we draw aside the curtain before we behold the picture, so we must remove our prudence and all surmises, and then behold the thing naked as it is, if we will know it indeed.

A DISSUASION FROM PRIDE, AND AN EXHORTATION TO HUMILITY

"God resists the proud, and gives grace to the humble."—1 Pet. 5:5

Saint Peter teaching every man his duty, how one should behave himself to another, exhorts all men to be humble, and abstain from pride; as though humility were the bond of all duties, like a list, which holds men in a compass, and pride were the make-bait over all the world: to which Solomon gives witness, (Prov. 13:10), saying, "Only by pride man makes contention;" because pride makes everyone think better of himself than of others, whereby he comes to give place to the other; and therefore, when neither party will yield, as Abraham did to Lot, (Gen. 13:2), how should there be any peace? So pride breaks the peace, and humility sets it again; therefore, to toll men from pride to humility, as it were from the concubine to the right wife, the apostle shows how God is affected to pride, and what mind he bears to humility: "God resists the proud, and gives grace to the humble;" as if he should whisper in men's ears and say, *Take heed how you company with pride, or give entertainment to her, for she is not Caesar's friend*; the king counts her his enemy, and all that take her part; she has been suspected ever since the angels rebelled in heaven, and Adam sought to be equal with God, (Gen. 3); therefore, his majesty has a stitch against her, as Solomon had to Shimei, (1 Kings 2:36), and would not have her favorites come in his court unless they hold down their mace, stoop when they enter. But if you can get in with humility, and wear the colors of lowliness, then you may go boldly, and stand in the king's sight, and step to his chamber of presence, and put up your petitions, and come to honor. For humility is very gracious with him, and so near of his counsel, that as David and Solomon say, he commits all his secrets to her, (Prov. 3:32, Psa. 25).

Many sins are in this sinful world, and yet, as Solomon says of the good wife, Prov. 31:29, "Many daughters have done virtuously, but you surmount them all." So I may say of pride, many sins have done wickedly, but you surmount them all; for the wrathful man, the prodigal man, the lascivious man, the surfeiting man, the slothful man, is rather an enemy to himself than to God; the envious man, the covetous man, the deceitful man, the ungrateful man, is rather an enemy to men than to God; but the proud man sets himself against *God*, because he goes against his Laws; he makes himself equal with God, because he does everything without God, and craves no help of him; he exalts himself above God, because he will have his own will, though it is contrary to God's will. As the humble man says, "Not to us, Lord, not to us, but to your name give the glory," (Psa. 115:1); so the proud man says, *Not to him, not to him, but to me give the glory.*

Men will praise you, not when you reform yourself to God, but when you *Do form yourself to your lusts*; that is, they which will be strutters shall not want flatterers, which will praise everything that they do, and everything that they speak, and everything that they wear, and say it becomes them well to wear long hair; that it becomes them well to wear bellied doublets; that it becomes them well to jet in their going; that it becomes them well to swear in their talking; that it becomes them well to boast in their talking. Now, when they hear men soothe them in their follies, then, they think, *we have nothing else to commend us, if men will praise us; for our vanities we will have friends now.* So the sickness swells and thinks with itself, *if they will look on me when I set a stout face on it, how would they behold me if I were in apparel! If they do so admire me in silks, how would they cap me, and curtsey me, and worship me, if I were in velvets! If I be so brave in plain velvet, what if my velvet were pinked, or cut, or printed!* So they study for fashions, as lawyers do for delays, and count that part naked which is not as gaudy as the rest, until all their body be covered over with pride, as their mind with folly. Therefore David says in Psa. 73:6, that pride is as *a chain to them*, that is, it goes round about them like a chain, and makes them think that all men love them, and praise them, and admire them, and worship them for their bravery. Therefore, as Saul said to Samuel, "Honor me before this people," so the proud man says to his chain, and his ruffs, and his pinks, and his cuts, *Honor me before this people.* All that he speaks, or does, or wears, is like Nebuchadnezzar's palace, which he built for *his* honor, (Dan. 4). This is their work so soon as they rise, to put a peddler's shop on their backs, and color their faces, and prick their ruffs, and frizzle their hair, and then their day's work is done, as though their office were to paint a fair image every morning, and at night to blot it out again. From that day that pride is born in the heart of man, as the false prophets were schooled to speak as the king would have them, so their eyes, and feet, and tongues are bound to speak, and look, and walk, as the proud heart prompts them. If God were in love with fashions, he were never better served than in this age; for our world is like a pageant, where every man's apparel is better than himself. Once Christ said that soft clothing is in king's courts, (Matt. 11:8); but now it is crept into every house; then the rich glutton jetted in purple every day, (Luke 16), but now the poor unthrift jets as brave as the glutton, with so many circumstances about him, that if you could see how pride would walk herself, if she wore apparel, she would even go like many in the streets, for she could not go braver, nor look stouter, nor mince finer, nor set on more laces, nor make larger cuts, nor carry more trappings about her, than our ruffians and wantons do at this day. How far are these fashions altered from those leather coats which God made in paradise! (Gen. 3:21). If their bodies changed forms so often as their apparel changes fashions, they should have more shapes than they have fingers and toes. As Jeroboam's wife disguised herself that the prophet might not know her, (1 Kings 14:2); so we may think that they disguise themselves that God might not know them; no, they disguise their bodies until they do not know themselves; for the servant goes like the master, the handmaid like her mistress, the subject like the prince, as though he had forgotten his calling, and mistook himself, like a man in the dark, which puts on another man's coat for his own, that is too wide, or too side for his body; so their attires are so unfit for their bodies, so unmeet for their calling, so contrary to nature, that I cannot call them fitter than the monsters of apparel.

But for pride, noblemen would come to church as well as the people; but for pride, gentles would abide reproof as well as servants; but for pride, you would forgive your brother, and your brother would forgive you, and the lawyers should have no work. But when you think of these things, pride comes in, and says, Will you go like a haggler, will you follow sermons, will you take the check, will you put up wrong? What will men say? That you are unknown, and a coward, and a fool, and no man will reverence you, but every man will condemn and abuse you. So men are fain to put on the livery of pride, as they put on the liveries of noblemen, to shroud and defend them from the contempt of the world. Who has not felt these counsels in his heart, which would not believe that any pride was in him? Yet as Absalom was a worse son than Adonijah, because Adonijah rebelled against his brother, (1 Kings 1:5), but Absalom rebelled against his father, so pride has worse children than vanity of apparel. Tyranny in princes, ambition in nobles, rebellion in subjects, disobedience in children, stubbornness in servants; name pride, and you have named their *mother*; therefore shall not God resist pride which has sowed so many tares in his ground?

Absalom thought that rebellion would make him a king, (2 Sam. 15:2); but God resisted his pride, and his rebellion hanged him on a tree. Nimrod thought that Babel should get him a name, (Gen. 11); but God resisted his pride, and the name of his building was called confusion ever since. Nebuchadnezzar built his palace for his honor, (Dan. 4); but God resisted his pride, and his palace spewed him out when his servants remained in it. Shebna built a sepulcher for his memorial, (Isa. 22); but God resisted his pride, and buried him in another country, where he had no sepulcher provided. Herod hoped when the people cried at his words, "It is the voice of God," that he should be worshipped ever after as God; but God resisted his pride, and before he descended from his throne, the worms so defaced his pomp, that none which called him God would be like to him. So when women take more pains to dress themselves than they do all the year after, and pay dearer to maintain one vice than they need to learn all virtues, they think to please men by it; but God resists their pride, and all that see them, though they cap and curtsey to them, yet they think worse of them, and think that they would not wear these signs of lightness and pride, unless they were light and proud indeed. So if their apparel condemns them before men, how will it condemn them before God! If sin did not blind them, would they so deceive themselves to take the contrary way, and think that should honor them which disgraces others? But as Balaam was stopped and did not know who stopped him, (Num. 22), so they are resisted, and do not know who resists them. Though they do all to please, yet they can please none: they do not please God, for God resists them; they do not please the humble, for the humble are contrary to them; they do not please the proud, for the proud do envy them which strive to be as proud as they; they do not please themselves, because they cannot be so proud and brave as they would be; only they content and please the devil, because their pride does entitle him to them.

So much of God's battles against the proud. Here Peter leaves the proud with this brand in their forehead, "This is the man whom God resists;" then he turns to the lowly, and comforts them, "but he gives grace to the humble;" as if he should say, *You are like John the beloved disciple, which leaned on Christ's bosom, (John 13:23); though God resists the proud, yet he will not frown on you, but when he resists them, he will give grace to you*; as if he should say, *The proud are without grace, for God gives not grace to the proud, but to the humble*, according to that of Isa. 66:2, "To him will I look, even to him that is poor, and of a contrite heart, and trembles at my words;" therefore "learn of me," says Christ, (Mat 11), "to be humble and meek," as though the humble and meek were his scholars. Therefore God must out of necessity love the humble, because they are like his Son. They shall have his best gifts, of which he says in 2 Cor. 12:9, "my grace is sufficient;" as he should say, *He which has given you his grace, can he deny you anything?* As Paul says, "he which has given us his Son, will he not give us all things with him?" Therefore grace may be called the gift of gifts, because all gifts come with grace, as the court goes with the queen. Therefore fear not to be humble, lest you be condemned; for all the promises of God are made to humility.

This is the ladder whereby we must ascend, (Gen. 28:12). Pride does cast us down, and humility must raise us up. As the way to heaven is *narrow*, (Matt. 7:13), so the gate is low, and he had need to stoop which enters in at it; therefore such a man is not proud, lest God oppose himself against you; but be humble, and the grace of God be longs to you. "He resists the proud and gives grace to the humble." If you disdain to learn humility of man, learn it of God, who humbled himself from heaven to earth, to exalt you from earth to heaven, to which kingdom (when the proud shall be shut out) the Lord Jesus bring us for his mercy's sake! *Amen.*

THE YOUNG MAN'S TASK

"Remember your Creator in the days of your youth."—Eccles. 12:1

Among the rest, I may call this Scripture *The Young Man's Task*, in which the wise man shows us when is the best time to sow the seed of virtue, that it may bring forth the fruit of life, and make a man always ready to die. Let him *remember his Creator in the days of his youth*, and all his life shall run in a line, the middle like the beginning, and the end like the middle; as the sun sets against the place where it rose.

After Solomon had described man, like Martha, troubling and toiling herself about many things; at last he brings him to that one thing necessary, which Christ taught Mary, and shows him that if he had begun there at first, he had found that which he sought without trouble, and been happier many years since than he is now. Therefore to them which are young, Solomon shows what advantage they have above the aged; like a ship which seeing another ship sink before her, looks about her, pulls down her sail, turns her course, and escapes the sands, which would swallow her, as they had done the other.

So they which are young do not need to try the snares and allurements of the world, or the issues and effects of sin, which old men have tried before them, but take the trial and experience of others, and go a nearer way to obtain their wished desires. That is this, says Solomon: if you would have any settled peace or hearty joy in this vain or transitory world, which you have been seeking all the time since you were born, you must "remember your Creator," which *made* you, which has *elected* you, which has *redeemed* you, which daily *preserves* you, which will forever *glorify* you. And as the kind remembrance of a friend recreates the mind, so to think and meditate on God who will supply your thoughts, dispel your grief, and make you cheerful, as the sight of the ark comforted David; for joy, and comfort and pleasure is where God is, as light, and cheerfullness, and beauty is where the sun is. Now, if you would have this joy, and comfort, and pleasure to be long, and would escape those thousand miseries, vexations, and vanities, which Solomon, by many weary and tedious trials, sought to make naked before you, and yet held all but vanity when he had found the way, you must "remember your Creator in the days of your youth" at the first spring-time, and then your happiness shall be as long as your life, and all your thoughts while you remains on earth a foretaste of the glory of heaven. This is *the sum* of Solomon's counsel.

"Remember, O young man, in your youth." No more *rejoice*, but *remember*. Solomon mocked before, and showed what they did remember; here he shows what they should *remember*. Lest any libertine should misconstrue him, and say, Solomon taught to *rejoice*, Solomon gave us leave to sin, Solomon said, *Do as you list, for you are young men, and have a privilege to be lascivious and vain; he recants with a breath, and denies forthwith his word, even where he spoke it.*

What did I say? "Rejoice, O young man, in your youth?" I would say, "Remember, O young man, in your youth." So God mocks us while we sin, like Micaiah, which bid Ahab fight against Aram, and then forbade him again; so he bids them rejoice, and forbids them again. Rejoice not in your youth, but *repent* in your youth. One would think that Solomon should have given this memorandum rather to old men than to young men, *Let them repent which look to die.* "Oh," says Jeremiah, (Lam. 3:27), "It is good for a man to bear the yoke I in his youth." If it is good to suffer in youth, it is better to learn in youth. Therefore, if David wished that his tongue might cleave to the roof of his mouth if he forgot Jerusalem, (Psa. 137:6), what are they worthy which forget God, the King of Jerusalem? Can a child forget his father? Is not God our Father? Therefore, who is too young to remember him, seeing the child does know his father? As the deepest wounds had need to be first tented, so the most unstable minds have need to be first confirmed. In this extremity is youth, as Solomon shows them before he teaches them; for in the last verse of the former chapter he calls youth "vanity," as if he should speak completely about evil in a *word*, and say that youth is *even the age of sin*. Therefore, when he had showed young men their folly under the name of vanity, like a good tutor he takes them to school, and teaches them their duty, "Remember your Creator," as though all sin were the forgetfulness of God; and all our obedience came from this remembrance, that God created us after his own image, in righteousness and holiness, to serve him here for a while, and after to inherit the joys which he has himself, which if we did remember, doubtless it would make us ashamed to think, and speak, and do as we are likely. For what man does remember his Creator, or why he was created, while he swears and forswears, and makes his trade of sin, as though there were no God to judge, nor hell to punish? This is because the remembrance of God, which would wake sinners, is so chased from the mind of men, for fear it should curb them of their pleasures, that they dare not think of such things, but they strive to serve him *hereafter*. So he stands as it were at the ladder foot and keeps us off with these weapons, that we cannot get on the first staff, but one thought or other pulls us back, when the foot is in the stirrup ready to ride away from all our sins at once. So we have long purposed to serve God, and every man thinks that he should be served, but we cannot accord of the time when to begin: one says, *When I am rich*; another says, *When I am free*; another says, *When I am settled*; another says, *When I am old, then my pleasure will leave me, and I shall are fitter to fast and pray, and sequester myself, but now I shall be mocked if I am not like others*. So, like bad borrowers, when our day is past already, we crave a longer, and a longer, and yet a longer, until we be arrested with death; so the, prince of creatures dies before he considered why he lived; for as no discipline is used where Christ's discipline is neglected, so no time is observed where God's time is omitted.

It is an old saying, Repentance is never too late; but it is a true saying, *Repentance is never too soon.* Therefore, we are commanded to "run that we may obtain," (1 Cor. 9:24), which is the swiftest pace of man. The cherubims were portrayed with wings before the place where the Israelites prayed, (Exod. 25:20), to show how quickly they went about the Lord's business. The hound which runs but for the hare, girds forth so soon as he cries the hare start; the hawk which flies but for the partridge, takes her flight so soon as she spies the partridge spring; so we should follow the word so soon as it speaks, and come to our Master as soon as he calls. For he which will not come when God calls, whatsoever he says, it is impossible that he should resolve to come hereafter; for he which is evil, how should he resolve to be good? Therefore now or never; *now and ever*, the tree which does not bud in the spring is dead all the year. When a married man is first married, he may use the matter so to win his wife to him, or estrange her heart forever. When a pastor comes first to a place, with a small matter he may make the simple people like him, or dislike him, so long as he stays; when the heir comes to his lands, lightly all his tenants begin to speak well of him, or evil of him; when a prince comes to the crown, by the laws which he makes first, the people guess how he will rule ever after, and either dispose their hearts to love him, or wish his death.

And if we can say of others, when we see a graceless boy, you will prove a wag-string if you live to be older; why should we, if we begin as ill as he, think that we shall be better and better, which judge that he will be worse and worse? As the arrow is directed at the first, so it flies all the way, over or under, or beside, but it never finds the mark, unless it is leveled right in the hand; so they which make an evil beginning, for speak themselves at the first, and wander out all their race, because when they should have leveled their life, they took their aim amiss. Therefore happy are they which have their arrow in their hand, and day before them, for they do not need wish to be young again. Now kill the serpent in the egg, for when he is a serpent he will kill you; if you cannot overcome sin in the infancy, before the root fasten, and the fence be made about it, how will you struggle with the lion, when he uses his paws, and sin is become like an old man, so tough and froward, that he will not hear?

There was a pool in Jewry where the sick and leprous lay, (John 5:2); for at one time of the day the angel came and stirred the water, and then he which stepped in first was healed of his disease. He which stepped in first was healed, says John; none but he which stepped in first; so he which takes time is sure, but he which foreslows time often fails rather than speeds. For when golden opportunity is past, no time will fit for her. If Elijah would be served before the widow, when she had but a little cruse of oil, which was not enough to serve herself, will God be served after Elijah? Will God be served after you? *no*, after the flesh, and after the devil? There are not many Simeons, but many as old as Simeon, which never yet embraced Christ in their hearts. They thought to repent before they were so old, yet now they dote for age, they are not old enough to repent yet. No, I answer, many masters of Israel, mayors, aldermen, sheriffs, justices, bailiffs, constables, gentlemen, know no more what it is to be born again, than Nicodemus which came by night; line after line, sermon after sermon, and the black-moor like himself. All their terms are vacations, all their religion promises, and all their promises hypocrisies. Instead of catechizing their children, as Solomon teaches them, they catechize them to hunt and hawk, to ride and vaunt, to ruffle and swear, to game and dance, as they were catechized themselves, lest the child should prove better than his father, and then he is qualified like a gentleman. *Is this to seek the kingdom of heaven first, or last, or not at all?* Woe to the security, woe to the stubbornness, woe to the drowsiness of this age. The thief comes at midnight, and we sleep until the dawning of the day; we let in Satan before we bid him avoid; we sell our birthright before it come to our hands; we seek for oil when our lamps should burn; this day passes like yesterday, and tomorrow we shall spend like this day! If youth had need of legs, age had need of wings to fly to God. But as Christ said, "The poor receive the gospel," though the rich be more bound;

so we may say, the young men receive the gospel, though the old men have more cause.

The young men follow Christ, the young men hear the word, the young men sanctify themselves, the young men stand for the church, the young men bear the heat of this day; old Noah is drunk, old Lot is sleepy, old Samson has lost his strength. Once the younger brother stole the blessing from the elder, and now he has got it again, as the malice of Esau shows, which persecutes him for it. I speak it to their shame, they that wear the furs and scarlets, as though they were all wisdom, and gravity, and holiness, even to the skirts, may say as Zedekiah said to Micaiah, "When did the Spirit depart from me and go to you?" When did zeal depart from us and go to you? They are so nestled in the world, and acquainted with sin, that it is too late now for the word to speak to them; they may look on the signs of wisdom, and gravity, and holiness when they see their long beards, and grey heads, and side gowns, and ask, *Why is this bush hanged out, and no wine within?* Why marvel then, if they are not reverenced but mocked and pointed at when Shem and Japhet had need to come again and cover their nakedness? What a shame was it to the Israelites when Christ said by a Canaanite, "I have not found so great faith in Israel!" So what a shame is it to the elders, that Christ may say again, *I have not found so great faith, nor knowledge, nor zeal in masters, and fathers, and rulers, as in servants and children, and apprentices*; which made an old father of this city say, which now is with God, that if there were any good to be done in these days, *it is the young men that must do it*; for the old men are *out of date*, their courage stoops like their shoulders, their zeal is withered like their brows, their faith staggers like their feet, and *their religion is dead before them. Amen.*

THE TRIAL OF THE RIGHTEOUS

"Many are the troubles of the righteous, but the Lord delivers him out of them all."—Psalm 34:19.

This verse has three parts, for here the righteous are the agents, their condition troubles, and the Lord their deliverer. So many things fall out contrary to our minds every day. That which wants patience in this world, is like a man which stands trembling in the field without his armor, because everyone can strike him, and he can strike none. So the least push of pain, or loss, or disgrace, does trouble that man more which has not the skill to suffer, than twenty trials can move him which is armed with patience, like a golden shield in his hand, to break the stroke of every cross, and though the heart and the body suffer; for while the heart is whole, all is well. "A sound spirit," says Solomon, "will bear his infirmity, but a wounded spirit what can sustain?" (Prov. 18:14). Therefore, as the lid is made to open and shut, to save the eye, so patience is set to keep the soul, and save the heart whole, to cheer the body again. Therefore if you mark, when you can go by an offence, and take a little wrong and suffer trouble quietly, you have a kind of peace and joy in your heart, as if you have gotten a victory, and the more your patience is, still the less your pain is. For as a light burden, borne at the arm's end, weighs heavier by much, than a burden of treble weight, if it is borne on the shoulders, which are made to bear; so if a man set *impatience* to bear his cross, which is not fit to bear, it will grumble, and murmur, and start, and shrink, and let the burden fall on his head, like a broken staff, which promises to help him over the water, and leaves him in the ditch. But if you put it to patience, and set her to bear it, which is appointed to bear, she is like the hearty spies that came from Canaan, and said, "It is nothing to overcome them," (Joshua 2). So patience says, *It is nothing to bear, it is nothing to fast, it is nothing to watch, it is nothing to labor, it is nothing to be envied, it is nothing to be back-bited, it is nothing to be imprisoned.* "In all these things," says Paul, "we are more than conquerors," (Rom. 8:37).

Patience has a device to draw such a skin over our sores that shall make our poverty seem riches, our reproaches seem honor, our bondage seem liberty, our labor seem rest, our sorrow seem joy, our pain seem ease, our sickness seem health, and all that hurt us rejoice us, until we say with David, "Your judgments are pleasant," showing that God's justice is as pleasant to the patient as his mercies to others. Therefore what a peacemaker were this in the commonwealth, if the magistrate had patience to bear his envy, if the preacher had patience to bear his study, if the creditor had patience to bear his losses, if the bondman had patience to bear his service, if the husbandman had patience to bear his labor, if the sick man had patience to bear his pain, if the poor man had patience to bear his wants. For want whereof many think themselves in hell, and say that no man's pain is like their pain, no man's wants like their wants, no man's foes like their foes, no man's wrongs like their wrongs, when they can scarce tell where their pain holds them. Therefore, albeit few can talk of humility, and charity, and meekness, and thankfulness, and temperance, and those severe virtues which pull from pleasure; yet every man wishes for patience, like a physician, to ease his grief by all means that they can. So they which are wicked, although they cannot see the goodness of other virtues, yet can see the goodness of patience, and perceive when they see a patient man and an impatient man both sick of one disease, yet both are not troubled alike, but that he which has most patience has most ease, and he which is most impatient is most tormented, like a fish which strives with the hook. Therefore even those which cannot suffer that they might have rest, yet sing the patient proverb, "In sufferance is rest."

"Many are the troubles of the righteous, but the Lord delivers him *out of all*." Here are the two hands of God, like a wound and a plaster; one casts down, and the other raises up. It is good for a man to know his troubles before they come, because afflictions are lightened in the expectation; therefore,

God says of Paul, (Acts 9:16), "I will show him how many things he shall suffer for me." God deals plainly, and tells us the worst first; what we shall trust to, as Christ told his disciples at the first, "If you will be my disciples, you must take up the cross," (Matt. 16:24); cold entertainment, to break their fast with the rod! Other feast makers, says Christ, broach the best wine first, but Christ keeps the best until the last, (John 2:10). This is the manner of God's proceedings, to send good after evil, as he made light after darkness, (Gen. 1:3); to turn justice into mercy, as he turned water into wine, (John 2); for as the beasts must be killed before they could be sacrificed, so men must be killed before they can be sacrificed; that is, the knife of correction must prune and dress them, and lop off their rotten twigs before they can bring forth fruit. These are the cords which bind the ram to the altar, lest when he is brought there he should run from thence again; this is the chariot which carries our thoughts to heaven, as it did Nebuchadnezzar's, and our assumption before our assumption. This is the hammer which squares the rough stones until they are plain, and smooth, and fit for the temple; this is the first messenger which is sent to compel them to the banquet, which will not come when they are invited. Because we are naturally given to love the world more than is good for us, therefore God hath set an edge of bitterness on us to make us loathe it.

The cross is one of our schoolmasters in this life, and the best wisdom is dearest bought. Prosperity seeks for nothing, but necessity seeks, and studies, and labors, and prays for her wants. As the rod makes the scholar to ply his book, so all our knowledge is beaten into us; some learn their goodness of poverty, some of sickness, some of troubles. Adversity is the fit time to learn the justice, mercy, power, and providence of God; a fit time to learn the patience, wisdom, faith, and obedience of man; a fit time to learn the subtlety, frailty, and misery of this world.

When God does visit the wicked, his punishments are called plagues, and curses, and destructions; the plagues of Egypt, the curse of Cain, the destruction of Sodom. But when he does visit the righteous, his punishments are called corrections, and chastisements, and rods, which proceed from a Father, not to destroy us, but to try us, and purge us, and instruct us; therefore, when we are afflicted, one says, That God lets us blood to save our lives, for our lives are rank, and must be lopped. And as Jacob was blessed and halted both at one time, so a man may be blessed and afflicted both together. Afflictions do not hinder our happiness, but our happiness comes by affliction, as Jacob's blessing came with halting. As Christ was no sooner born but Herod sought his life, (Matt. 2), so the new man is no sooner born of the Spirit but the serpent is ready to devour him, his brethren to banish him, and hell to swallow him. In the entire world he has no friend but he which made the world. This is the state of the church militant; she is like the ark floating on the waters, like a lily growing among thorns, like the bush which burned with fire, and was not consumed, (Exod. 3:2). So the city of God is always besieged, but never ruined. Christians and persecutions close together like Christ and his cross. As Christ was made to bear his own cross, (Luke 23:33, John 19:17), so they are made to hold their cheeks to the nippers, their faces to be buffeted, their backs to be scourged, their eyes to be pulled out. Their peace is persecution, their rest labor, their riches poverty, their glory reproaches, their liberty imprisonment. Although they are the sons of God, the brethren of Christ, the only heirs of heaven, yet because they suffer their hell here, they must be content to be subject to their enemies, to be objects to their kinsmen, to be hated of most, to be condemned of all, to be persecuted over the earth, a very haven and receptacle of troubles.

When David spoke of troubles, he spoke of troops, and heaps, and stars, and sands; and therefore he says many, as though he were fain to lay them down in the gross sum, not reckon them. By "many tribulations," says Paul, (Acts 14), but how many he could not number; for, except our sins, there is not such plenty of anything in the world as there is of *troubles* which come from sin. As one heavy messenger came to Job after another, see chapter 1:14-16, so now since we are not in paradise, but in the wilderness, we must look for one trouble after another. Therefore afflictions are called *waters*, because as one wave falls on another, so one trouble falls on another, (Psa. 42:7-9).

As a bear came to David after a lion, and a giant after a bear, (1 Sam. 17:34), and a king after a giant, and Philistines after the king, so when they have fought with poverty, they shall fight with envy; when they have fought with envy, they shall fight with infamy; when they have fought with infamy, they shall fight with sickness, like a laborer which is never out of work. So you see the righteous in troubles, like the Israelites in exile, (Exod. 3:10). Now the Lord comes like Moses to deliver them. Adversity seeks out the promise, the promise seeks out faith, faith seeks out prayer; then God hears, and mercy answers. All this while Christ seems to sleep, as he did in the ship; now he rebukes the winds and waves, (Matt. 8:26), and troubles fly before him like a troop of wolves before the shepherd.

This should content the righteous, to be delivered at last; as David quieted himself, saying, (Psa. 41:11), "By this I know the Lord favored me, because mine enemies do not triumph over me;" not because I have no enemies, or because I have no troubles which would overcome me.

Therefore when he wrote down many troubles, he blotted it (as it were) with his pen again, as a merchant razes his book when the debt is discharged; and instead of many troubles, he puts in, the Lord delivers. Because he forgives all sins, he is said to deliver from all troubles; to show that we have need of no Savior, no helper, no comforter, but him.

The lawyer can deliver his client but from strife; the physician can deliver his patient but from sickness; the master can deliver his servant but from bondage; but "The Lord," says David, "delivers out of all." As when Moses came to deliver the Israelites, he would not leave a hoof behind him; so when the Lord comes to deliver the righteous, he will not leave a trouble behind him. But even as they pray in Psalm 25, "Deliver Israel, O Lord, out of all his troubles;" so he will answer them, "Be you delivered out of all your troubles;" that is, this, and this, and this (that trouble that you think intolerable, that trouble which you think incurable); the Almighty has might against all. When Job is tried, not a sore shall stick on him. Therefore, as Elisha did not fear when he saw as many angels as enemies, (2 Kings 6); so, when you see as many mercies as troubles, let the comfort satisfy you, which satisfied Paul, "Fear not; for I am with you," (Acts 27:24), your pardon is coming; like the angel which stayed the sword over Isaac's head, (Gen. 22). Read on but a little further, and you shall hear the voice which proclaimed war proclaim peace; many troubles in the beginning of the verse, and no troubles in the end. What physician has been here? The Lord, says David. "The Lord was in this place," says Jacob, "and I knew it not," Gen. 28:16; so the Lord is in affliction, and men did not know it. He which says, I put away your iniquities, (Isa. 43:25), must say, I put away your infirmities. For there is no Savior but one; which says to death, "I will be your death." As the woman was sick until Christ came, (Matt. 9:19); so until the Lord comes, there is nothing but trouble. Many are the troubles of the righteous, but there is One deliverer of the righteous; many terrors, but one Comforter. Troubles come in an hundred ways, like water through a grate; but mercy enters always at one door, like a pardon which comes only from the prince. Therefore, says God, "In me is your help," (Hosea 13:9). "I create comfort," (Isa. 65). Note that he calls himself a *Creator of comfort*; that is, as there is but one Creator, so there is but one comforter; and as he created all things of nothing, so he creates comfort of nothing; that is, when all comfort is worn out, and no seed of joy left to raise up comfort again, then he brings comfort out of sorrow, as he brought water out of the rock, (Exod. 17:6, 8, 14); that we may say, "The finger of the Lord has done this."

So Moses describes the journey of the righteous, as if they should go through the sea and wilderness, as the Israelites went to Canaan, (Exod. 13:18). Do not look for ease nor pleasure in your way, but for beasts, and serpents, and thieves; until you are past the wilderness, all is strait, and dark, and fearful; but as soon as you are through the narrow gate, all is large, and goodly and pleasant, as if you were in paradise. Seeing then your kingdom is not here, look not for a golden life in an iron world; but remember that Lazarus does not mourn in heaven, though he suffered pains on earth, (Luke 16); but the glutton *moumeth* in hell, that he did not stay for the pleasures of heaven. To which pleasures the Lord Jesus bring us, when this cloud of trouble is blown over us! *Amen.*

THE GODLY MAN'S REQUEST

"Teach us, O Lord, to number our days, that we may apply our hearts to wisdom."—Psa. 90:12

Five things I note in these words: first, that death is the haven of every man; whether he sits on the throne of a kingdom, or keeps in a cottage, at last he must knock at death's door, as all his fathers have done before him. Secondly, that man's time is set, and his bounds appointed, which he cannot pass, no more than the Egyptians could pass the sea; and therefore Moses says, "Teach us to number our days," as though there were a number of our days. Thirdly, that our days are few, as though we were sent into this world but to see it; and therefore Moses, speaking of our life, speaks of days, not of years, nor of months, nor of weeks; but "Teach us to number our days," showing that it is an easy thing ever for a man to number his days, they are so few. Fourthly, the aptness of man to forget death rather than anything else; and therefore Moses prays the Lord to teach him to number his days, as though they were still slipping out of his mind. Lastly, that to remember how short a time we have to live will make us apply our hearts to that which is good.

The first point is that as everyone had a day to come into this world, so he shall have a day to go out of this world. When Moses had spoken of some which lived seven hundred years, and other which lived eight hundred years, and other which lived nine hundred years, showing that some had a longer time, and some a shorter, yet he speaks this of all, *mortuus est*; at last comes in *mortuus est*, that is, *he died*, which is the epitaph of every man. We are not lodged in a castle, but in an inn, where we are but guests, and therefore Peter calls us strangers, (1 Peter 2:2). We are not citizens of the earth, but citizens of heaven, and therefore the apostle says, "We have here no abiding city, but we look for one to come," (Heb. 13:14). As Christ says, "My kingdom is not of this world," (John

18:36), so we may say, My dwelling is not in this world, but the soul soars upward whence she came, and the body stoops downward whence it came; as the tabernacles of the Jews were made to remove, so our tabernacles are made to remove. Every man is a tenant at will, and there is nothing sure in life but death. As he which wrote this is gone, so I which preach it, and you which hear it, one coming in, and one going out, is to all. Although this is daily seen, yet it had need be proved, *no*, every man had need to die, to make him believe that he shall die.

Before sin nothing could change us; now everything changes us; for when winter comes we are cold, when age comes we are withered, when sickness comes we are weak, to show that when death comes we shall die. The clothes which we wear on our backs, the sun which sets over our heads, the graves which lie under our feet, the meat which goes into our mouths, cry to us that we shall wear, and fade, and die, like the fishes, and fowls, and beasts, which even now were living in their elements, and now are dead in our dishes. Every thing every day suffers some eclipse, and nothing stands at a stay, but one creature calls to another, *Let us leave this world*. Our fathers summoned us, and we shall summon our children to the grave; first we wax old, then we wax dry, then we wax weak, then we wax sick, and so we melt away by drops; at last, as we carried others, so others carry us to the grave. This is the last bed which every man shall sleep in; we must return to our mother's womb. Therefore Jacob calls his life but a pilgrimage; therefore Paul called his life but a race, (2 Tim. 4:7); therefore David calls himself but a worm, (Psa. 22:6). A pilgrimage has an end, a race has a stop, a worm is but trodden under foot, and dead straight; so in an hour we are, and are not. Here we are now, and then we are separated; and tomorrow one sickens, and the next day another sickens; and all that are here never meet again. We may well be called earthen vessels, (2 Cor. 4:7), for we are soon broken; a spider is able to choke us, a pin is able to kill us, all of us are born one way, and die a hundred ways. As Elijah stood at the door of the cave when God passed by, (1 Kings 19:9), so we stand in the passages of this world, ready to go out whensoever God shall call. We lose first our infancy, and then our childhood, and then our youth; at last, as we came in the rooms of others, so others come into our rooms. If all our days were as long as the day of Joshua, when the sun stood still in the midst of heaven, (Joshua 10:13), yet it will be night at last, and our sun shall set like others. It is not long that we grow, but when we begin to fall, we are like the ice which thaws sooner than it froze: so these little worlds are destroyed first, and at last the great world shall be destroyed too; for all which was made for us shall perish with us. What do you learn when you think of this, but that which Moses says, to apply your hearts to wisdom? Death comes after life, and yet guides to the whole life, like the stern of a ship; but for death there would be no rule, but every man's lust should be his law; he is like a king, which frightens afar off, though he defer his sessions, and stay the execution, yet the very fear that he will come makes the proudest peacock lay down his feathers and is like a damp which puts out the lights of pleasure.

David numbered his days by a measure: "My life," he says, "is like a span long," (Psa. 39:5). When he measured his life, he took not a pole, or a long measuring rod, nor a yard to measure it by, but a short measure, his short span, "My life is like a span long." So you have learned to number your days, or rather the hours of your days. As some came into the vineyard in the morning, and some at noon, and some at night, so some go out of this vineyard in the morning, some at noon, and some at night. Some men's life has nothing but a morning, some have a morning and noon; he which lives longest, lives all the day, and therefore the youngest of all pray but for this day, and if he lives until tomorrow, then he prays for that day, saying still, "Give us this day our daily bread." So that a pleasant life may be compared but to a glorious day, and a sorrowful life to a cloudy day, and a long life to a summer's day, and a short life to a winter's day. How comes it to pass, that when a man dies, all his years seem but so many days, and before he dies, all his days seem so many years? Job speaks of all alike, "Man which is born of a woman has but a short time to live," (Job 14:1). Jacob was one hundred and thirty years old, and yet when he came before Pharaoh, he said, "Few and evil have my days been." Though Pharaoh did not speak of days, but asked him "how old he was," yet he answered of days, to show that not only his years but his days were few. Our fathers, marveling to see how suddenly men are, and are not, compared life to a dream in the night, to a bubble in the water, to a ship on the sea, to an arrow which never rests until it fall, to a player which speaks his part on the stage, and straight he gives place to another; to a man which comes to the market to buy one thing and sell another, and then is gone home again; so the figure of this world passes away. This is our life; while we enjoy it, we lose it.

Of those who have a skill in numbers, not one can determine the number of our days. We can number our sheep, and our oxen, and our coin; but we think that our days are infinite, and therefore we never go about to number them. We can number other men's days and years, and think they will die ere it is long, if we see them sick, or sore, or cold; but we cannot number our own. When two ships meet on the sea, they which are in one ship think that the other ship does sail exceeding fast, but that their ship goes fair and softly, or rather stands still, although in truth one ship sails as fast as the other; so every man thinks that the others post, and run, and fly to the grave, but that himself stands stock still, although indeed a year with him is no longer than it is with the others. Besides that, we are given to forget death, we strive to forget it, like them which say, "We may not remember," (Amos 6:10).

Two things I note in these words: first, that if we will find wisdom, we must apply our hearts to seek her; then, that the remembrance of death makes us apply our hearts to it. Touching the first, Moses found some fault with himself, that for all that he had heard, and seen, and observed, and was counted wise, yet he was new to begin, and had not applied his heart to learn wisdom, like the wise man, which says, "I am more foolish than any man; I have not the wisdom of a man in me," Prov. 30:2. So insatiable and covetous, as I may say, are the servants of God, the more wisdom, and faith, and zeal they have, the more they desire. Moses speaks of wisdom as if it were physic, which does no good before it is applied; and the part to apply it to is the heart, where all man's affections are to love it and cherish it, like a kind of hostess. When the heart seeks it finds, as though it were brought to her, like Abraham's ram. Therefore God says, "They shall seek me and find me, because they shall seek me with their hearts," (Jer. 29:13), as though they should not find him with all their seeking unless they did seek him with their heart. Therefore the way to get wisdom is to apply your hearts to it, as if it were your calling and living, to which you were bound prentices. A man may apply his ears and his eyes as many truants do to their books, and yet never prove scholars; but from that day which a man begins to apply his heart to wisdom, he learns more in a month after than he did in a year before, *no*, than ever he did in his life. Even as you see the wicked, because they apply their hearts to wickedness, how fast they proceed, how easily and how quickly they become perfect swearers, expert drunkards, cunning deceivers, so if you could apply your hearts as thoroughly to knowledge and goodness, you might become like the apostle which teaches you. Therefore, when Solomon shows men the way how to come by wisdom, he speaks often of the heart, as "Give your heart to wisdom," "let wisdom enter into your heart," "get wisdom," "keep wisdom," "embrace wisdom," (Prov. 2:10, 4:5, 13:8), as though a man went a-wooing for wisdom. Wisdom is like God's daughter, that he gives to the man that loves her, and sues for her, and means to set her at his heart. So we have learned how to apply knowledge that it may do us good; not to our ears, like them which hear sermons only, nor to our tongues, like them which make table-talk of religion, but to our hearts, that we may say with the virgin, "My heart does magnify the Lord," (Luke 1), and the heart will apply it to the ear and to the tongue, as Christ says, "Out of the abundance of the heart the mouth speaks," (Matt. 12:34).

I can but teach you with words, as John baptized with

water. As Moses prayed the Lord to teach him to number his days, so you must pray the Lord to teach you to number your days. And now I lead you to number your days. It may be that you have but twenty years to serve God; will you not live twenty years like a Christian, that you may live a thousand years like an angel? It may be that you have but ten years to serve him; will you not serve ten years for heaven, which would serve twenty years for a farm? It may be that you have but five years to serve God; will you not spend five years well, to redeem all your years for five? Yet God knows whether many here have so long to repent for all the years which they have spent in sin. If you were born today, your journey is not a hundred years; if you are a man, half your time is spent already; if you are an old man, then you are drawing to your inn, and your race is but a breath; therefore, as Christ said to his disciples when he found them sleeping, "Could you not watch one hour?' so I say to myself, and to you, Can we not pray? Can we not suffer a little while? He which is tired can crawl a little way, a little further, one step more for a kingdom. For this cause God would not have men know when they shall die, because they should make ready at all times, having no more certainty of one hour than another. Therefore our Savior says, "Watch," because you do not know when the Lord will come to take you, or to judge you; "Happy are they which hear the word and keep it." So you see that death is the last on earth, that the time of man is set, that his race is short, that he thinks not of it, that if he did remember it, it would make him apply his mind to good, as he does to evil. And now I end as I began, "The Lord teach us to number our days, that we may apply our hearts to wisdom." *Amen.*

THE ART OF HEARING

"Take heed how you hear."—Luke 8:18

There is no sentence in Scripture which the devil had rather you should not regard than this lesson of hearing; for if you take heed how you hear, you shall not only profit by this sermon, but every sermon after this shall leave such instruction, and peace, and comfort with you as you never thought the word contained for you; therefore no marvel if the tempter do trouble you when you should hear, as the fowls cumbered Abraham when he should offer sacrifice. First, he labors all that he can to stay us from hearing; to effect this, he keeps us at taverns, at plays, in our shops, and appoints us some other business at the same time, that when the bell calls to the sermon, we say, like the churlish guests, *We cannot come*, (Matt. 22). If he cannot keep us away with any business or exercise, then he casts fancies into our minds, and drowsiness into our heads, and sounds into our ears, and sets temptations before our eyes; that though we hear, yet we should not mark, like the birds which fly about the church. If he cannot keep our ears, nor slack our attention as he would, then he tickles us to mislike something which was said, and by that make us reject all the rest. If we cannot mislike anything which is said, then he infects us with some prejudice of the preacher; he does not as he teaches, and therefore we less regard what he says. If there are no fault in the man, nor in the doctrine, then, lest it would convert us, and reclaim us, he courses all means to keep us from the consideration of it, until we have forgot it. To compass this, so soon as we have heard, he takes us to dinner, or to company, or to pastime, to remove our minds, that we should think no more of it. If it stays in our thoughts, and likes us well, then he has this trick; instead of applying the doctrine, which we should follow, he turns us to praise and extol the preacher. He made an excellent sermon! He has a notable gift! I never heard any like him! He which can say so, has heard enough; this is the repetition which you make of our sermons when you come home, and so to your business again until the next sermon come; a breath goes from us, and a sound comes to you, and so the matter is ended. If all these comers hear in vain, and the tempter be so busy to hinder this work more than any other, Christ's warning may serve for you, as well as his disciples, "Take heed how you hear," (Mark 4:24). There is a hearing, and a preparative before hearing, (Eccles. 5:1); there is a praying, and a preparative before praying; there is a receiving, and a preparative before receiving, (1 Cor. 11:28). As I called examination the fore-runner, which prepares the way to the receiver, so I may call attention the forerunner, which prepares the way to the preacher: like the plough, which cuts up the ground, that it may receive the seed. As there is a foundation, on which the stones, and lime, and timber are laid, which holds the building together; so, where this foundation of hearing is laid, there the instructions, and lessons, and comforts do stay and are remembered; but he which leans his ears on his pillow, goes home again like the child which he leads in his hand, and scarce remembers the preacher's text. A divine tongue and a holy ear make sweet music, but a deaf ear makes a dumb tongue. There is nothing so easy as to hear, and yet there is nothing so hard as to hear well. The Jews did hear more than the entire world beside, yet because they took no heed to that which they heard, therefore they crucified him which came to save them, and became the most cursed people on the earth, which were the most blessed nation before; therefore the *ABC's* of a Christian is to learn the *art of hearing*. We care how we sow, lest our seed should be lost; so let us care how we hear, lest God's seed be lost.

As children play the truants in the school, so men play the truants in the church. How many come to hear me, and yet, peradventure, some do not hear, while I speak of hearing! One has no pitcher, another has left his pitcher behind him, another has brought a broken pitcher which will hold no water; therefore Christ calls us fishers; for as a fisher takes but a few in respect of those which go by, so we reform but a few in respect of them which go as they came.

Now of Christ's hearers. We find in the Gospel that Christ had four sorts of hearers; while I count them to you, think of what sort you are, for I doubt not but that there be here of all sorts. Some heard him to wonder at him, like Herod, which was moved with the fame that went of him. Some came to hear, because they would know all things, that they might be able to talk of them. It seems that Judas was such a scholar, for he had learned to preach, but not to follow. Some came to cavil and to trip him in his speeches; of these hearers were the scribes and Pharisees, which would make him an enemy to Caesar. Some were like to the good ground, which came to know what they might do, and how they should believe; like the humble scribe which inquired the way to heaven.

Now to our hearers. As there were wise virgins and foolish virgins, so there are wise hearers and foolish hearers. Some are so nice that they had rather pine than take their food of any which is licensed by a bishop, as if Elijah should refuse his food because a raven brought it to him, and not an angel; some come to the service to save forfeiture, and then they stay the sermon for shame; some come because they would not be counted atheists; some come because they would avoid the name of papists; some come to please their friends. One has a good man to his friend, and lest he should offend him, he frequents the preachers, that his friend may think well of him; some come with their masters and mistresses for attendance; some come with a fame; they have heard great speech of the man, and therefore they will spend one hour to hear him once, but to see whether it is so as they say; some come because they are idle; to pass the time they go to a sermon, lest they should be weary of doing nothing; some come with their fellows; one says, *Let us go to the sermon*; *Content*, he says, and he goes for company; some hear the sound of a voice as they pass by the church, and step in before they are aware; another has some occasion of business, and he appoints his friends to meet him at such a sermon, as they do at Paul's. All these are accidental hearers, like children which sit in the market and neither buy nor sell. But as many foxes have been taken when they came to take, so they which come to spy, or wonder, or gaze, or scoff, have changed their minds before they went home, like one which finds when he does not seek.

As you come with divers motions, so you hear in divers manners: one is like an Athenian, and he hearkens after news; if the preacher say anything of our armies beyond the sea, or council at home, or matters at court, that is his lure. Another is like the Pharisee, and he watches if anything be said that may be wrested to be spoken against persons in high place, that he may play the devil in accusing of his brethren; let him write that in his tables too. Another smacks of eloquence, and he gapes for a phrase, that when he comes to his ordinary he may have one figure more to grace and worship his tale. Another is malcontent, and he never pricks up his ears until the preacher come to gird against some whom he spites, and when the sermon is done, he remembers nothing which was said to him, but that which was spoken against others. Another comes to gaze about the church; he has an evil eye, which is still looking on that from which Job averted his eye. Another comes to muse; so soon as he is set, he falls into a brown study; sometimes his mind runs on his market, sometimes on his journey, sometimes of his suit, sometimes of his dinner, sometimes of his sport after dinner, and the sermon is done before the man thinks where he is. Another comes to hear, but so soon as the preacher has said his prayer, he falls fast asleep, as though he had been brought in for a corpse, and the preacher should preach at his funeral.

This is the generation of hearers. Is not the saying of Christ fulfilled now, "Hearing you hear not?" because we hear and hear not; like a covetous churl which goes by a beggar when he cries in Christ's name for relief, and hears him cry, but will not hear him, because he craves that which he will not part with. May we not say again with Christ, "What went you out to see," rather than, "What went you out to hear?" seeing you remember that which you see, and forget all that which you hear. So you depart from our sermons like a slide-thrift's purse, which will hold no money.

One thing is necessary, and all unnecessaries are preferred before it. The greatest treasure in the world is most despised, the star which should lead us to Christ, the ladder which should mount us to heaven, the water that should cleanse our leprosy, the manna that should refresh our hunger, and the book that we should meditate on day and night, (Psa. 1:2), lies in our windows, no man reads it, no man regards it; the love of God, and the love of knowledge, and the love of salvation is so cold, that we will not read over one book for it, for all we spend so many idle times while we live.

This age has devised divers methods to learn many things in shorter time than they were learned of old. A man may spend seven years in learning to write, and he may meet with a scribe which will teach him as much in a month. A prentice may spend nine years in learning a trade, and some master (if he were disposed), would teach him as much in a year. A man may fetch such a compass that he may be a whole month in going to Berwick; and another, which knows the way, will go it in less than a week; so to everything there is a further way, and a nearer way, and so there is to knowledge. You do not remember the hundredth part of that which you have heard, and tomorrow you will not remember the tenth note which you have heard this day. It may be that some will remember more; and why not you as well as he? Because one uses a help of his memory, which the other uses not. If you will use his policy, you shall remember as well as he; for let him neglect his help, and the best memory here shall not carry away half which he marks now, until it is night. When the woman of Samaria heard Christ speak of water, of which "he that drinks shall thirst no more," *Oh,* (says she), "give me of that water." So, now you hear of such a way, you would fain know it, but will you use it? I wish that I were such a messenger, that I could compel you to it; for truly until you use it, you shall never learn faster than you do. Now I think you have a desire to hear it, I will show it to you; first, in mine opinion two things out of every sermon are especially to is noted; that which you did not know before, and that which speaks to your own sin; for so you shall increase your knowledge, and lessen your vices.

Now if you would remember both these a year hence as fresh as now, this is the best policy that ever you shall learn, to put them presently in practice; that is, to send them abroad to all the parts of your soul and members of your body, and reform yourself in resemblance to them, and you shall never forget them, for your practice remembers them. But before this you must use another help, that is, record every note in your mind, as the preacher goes; and after, before you Do eat, or drink, or talk, or do anything else, repeat all to yourself. I do know some in the university, which did never hear good sermon but as soon as they were gone they rehearsed it this way, and learned more by this (as they said) than by their reading and study; for recording that which they had heard when it was fresh, they could remember all, and hereby got a better facility in preaching than they could learn in books. The like profit I remember I gained, when I was a scholar, by the like practice.

What a shame is this, to remember every clause in your lease, and every point in your father's will; *no*, to remember an old tale so long as you live, though it is long since you heard it; and the lessons which you hear now will be gone within this hour, that you may ask, What has stolen my sermon from me? Therefore, that you may not hear us in vain, as you have heard others, my exhortation to you is, to record when you are gone that which you have heard. If I could teach you a better way, I would; but Christ's disciples used this way when their thoughts ran on his speech, and made them come again to him to ask the meaning; the virgin his mother used this way when she pondered his sayings, and laid them up in her heart; the good hearers of Berea used this way, when they carried Paul's sermon home with them, that they might examine it by the Scripture.

If you will know why many preachers preach so barely, loosely, and simply, it is your own simplicity which makes them think that if they go on and say something, all is one, and no fault will be found; because you are not able to judge in or out; and so because they give no attendance to doctrine, as Paul teaches them, it is almost come to pass, that in a whole sermon, the hearer cannot pick out one note more than he could gather himself; and many loathe preaching, as the Jews abhorred the sacrifice for the slubbering priests, which cared not what they offered; and the greater sort imagine that there is no more wisdom in the word of God, than their teachers show out of it. What a shame is this, that the preachers should make preaching be despised! In Jeremiah 48 there is a curse on them which do the business of the Lord negligently; if this curse does not touch them which do the chief business of the Lord negligently, it cannot take hold of any other. Therefore let every preacher first see how his notes move himself, and then he shall have comfort to deliver them to others, like an experienced medicine, which himself has proved.

THE MAGISTRATES' SCRIPTURE

"I have said, you are gods; and you are all the children of the Most High: but you shall die as a man, and your princes shall die like others."—Psa. 82:6-7

I may call this text, *the Magistrates' Scripture*; considering the state of kings and governors, how much good they might do, and how little they perform, God becomes a remembrancer to them. And first, shows what a high calling princes and rulers have, and then, lest they should be proud of it, and make their magistracy a chair of ease, he turns on them again, as though he had another message to them, and tells them, that though they are above others, yet they shall die like others; and though they judge here, yet they shall be judged hereafter, and give account of their stewardship, how they have governed, and straightway their subjects, how they have obeyed. A good memorandum for all in authority, so to deal in this kingdom, that they lose not the kingdom to come.

I have said, you are gods, etc. How can he call them gods, which calls himself the only God? and says, "There are no more gods but he," (Isa. 44:6, 45:21). "I have made you Pharaoh's god," says God to Moses, (Exod. 7:1), because he had given him power to speak to Pharaoh in his name, and to execute his judgments on him; so he calls magistrates *gods*, because he has given them power to speak to the people in his name, and to execute his judgments on them. Out of this name rulers may learn how to govern, and subjects how to obey. As the inferior magistrates do nothing but as the superior magistrate prescribes, so they which rule under God, for God, must rule by the prescript of God, and do nothing but as their conscience tells them that God would do himself. Therefore they which use their power against God, which bear the person of God and execute the will of the devil, which make laws against God's law, and are enemies to his servants, are worse than Balaam, which would not curse whom God blessed, (Num.

22:18); and so much as in them lies, make God a liar, because they cannot so well be called gods, as devils. Such gods go to hell.

This extols the calling of magistrates. As Jacob honored Joseph's children, when he said they should be called after his name, (Gen. 48:16); so God honors the magistrates when he gives them his own name, calling them gods, as though they were a kind of godhead in them.

"These things pertain to the wise," (Prov. 24:23), and they themselves do not always see it; yet he which has a spiritual eye, and carries the pattern of God in his heart, may see another likeness of God in magistrates, than in common persons. As the builders of the temple had a special wisdom and spirit, which God gave them for that work which they were chosen to, (Exod. 31:3 and 35:31), so when Samuel had anointed David, he says, that "the Spirit of the Lord came on David from that day forward," (1 Sam. 16:13), as though he had another spirit after than he had before. There is a difference between kings and inferior magistrates; for the prince is like a great image of God, the magistrates are like little images of God, appointed to rule for God, to make laws for God, to reward for God, to punish for God, to speak for God, to fight for God, to reform for God, and therefore their battles are called "The Lord's battles;" and their judgments, "The Lord's judgments;" and their throne, "The Lord's throne;" and the kings themselves, "His kings," to show that they are all for God, like his hands. By some he teaches mercy, by some justice, by some peace, by some counsel, as Christ distributed the loaves and the fishes by the hands of his disciples, (Matt. 14:18). This God requires of all when he calls them gods, to rule as he would rule, judge as he would judge, correct as he would correct, reward as he would reward, because it is said, that they are instead of the Lord God; that is, to do as he would do, as a scholar writes by a copy. This is a good study for magistrates in all their judgments, to consider what God would do, because they are instead of God, I rule for God, I speak for God, I judge for God, I reward for God, I correct for

God; then as he would do and determine, so must be my sentence.

They are called gods, to encourage them in their office, and to teach them that they do not need dread the persons of men; but as God does that which is just and good without the jealousy of men, so they, on the bench, and in all causes of justice, should forget themselves to be men, which are led by the arms between favor and fear, and think themselves gods, which fear nothing. This boldness is so necessary in them which should judge all alike.

This is the religion of these times: they fear nothing more than to be counted too precise; but God does call them more than precise, for he calls them gods; of all men they should not forget his name. Princes and rulers have many names of honor, but this is the most honorable name in their titles, that they are called gods; other names have been given them of men for reverence, or flattery, but no man could give them this name but God himself. Therefore their name is a glass in which they may see their duty.

So their name tells them how they should rule, and by consequence teaches how we should obey. God calls them gods, therefore he which condemns them, condemns God; God calls them fathers, therefore we must reverence them like fathers; God calls them kings, princes, lords, judges, powers, rulers, governors, which are names of honor; and shall we dishonor them whom God does honor? Our first lesson is, "Fear God;" the next is, "Honor the king," (Prov. 24:21, 1 Peter 2:17); that is (as Paul interprets it), we must "obey for conscience," (Rom. 13:5), not against conscience; for that were to put a stranger before the king, and the king before God, which, Christ says, *have no power but from God*, (John 19:11); and therefore cannot make themselves magistrates, (Heb. 5:4), no more than they can make themselves gods. As none could give this name but God, so no man which exalts himself can challenge this honor, no more.

It follows, but you shall die as a man. Here he distinguishes between mortal gods and the immortal God. You have seen their glory; now behold their end, "They shall all die like others." Though they are never so rich, so goodly, so mighty, so honorable while their date lasts, yet they may as truly as Job call "corruption their father, and the worm their mother," (Job 17:14); for the grave shall be the last bed of all flesh. As they were born like men, so they shall die like men; the same coming in and going out is to all. When Isaiah had said that "all flesh was grass," as though he would correct his speech, he adds, "and the glory of it is as the flower of the field," (Isa. 40). As if he should say, *Some men have more glory than others, and they are like flowers*; the others are like grass: no great difference, the flower shows fairer, but grass stands longer; one scythe cuts both down, like the fat sheep and the lean, that feed in two pastures, but are killed in one slaughter. So, though the great man lives in his palace, and the poor man dwells in his cottage, yet both shall meet at the grave, and vanish together. Even they which are lords, and judges, and counsellors now, are but successors to them which are dead, and are nearer to death now than when I began to preach of this theme. It had been a great sessions for all others to die; but for magistrates, princes, for kings, for emperors to die as they die, what a battle is this that leaves no man alive! Shall the gods die too? He gives them their title, but he tells them their lot. Though their power, though their wealth, though their honor, though their titles, though their train, though their friends, though their ease, though their pleasures, though their diet, though their clothing is not like others', yet their end shall be like others', "I have said that you are gods, but you shall die like other men." But for this die, many would live a merry life, and feast, and sport, and let the world slide; but the remembrance of death is like a dampening cone, which puts out all the lights of pleasure, and makes him rub, and frown, and whine which thinks on it, as if a mote were in his eye. Oh how heavy these tidings are to hear you shall die, from him which has life and death in his own hands, when the message is sent to them which reigned like gods! as if he should say, *Even you which glister like angels, whom all the world admires, and sues and bows to, which are called honorable, mighty and gracious lords, I will tell you to what your honor shall come*: first, you shall wax old like others, then you shall fall sick like others, then you shall die like others then you shall be buried like others, then you shall be consumed like others, then you shall be judged like others, even like the beggars which cry at your gates: one sickens, the other sickens; one dies, the other dies; one rots, the other rots: look in the grave, and show me which was Dives and which was Lazarus. This is some comfort to the poor, that once he shall be like the rich; one day he shall be as wealthy, as mighty, and as glorious as a king; one hour of death will make all alike; they which crowed over others, and looked down on them like oaks, others shall walk on them like worms, and they shall be gone as if they had never been.

Where are they which founded this goodly city, which possessed these fair houses, and walked these pleasant fields, which erected these stately temples, which kneeled in these seats, which preached out of this place but thirty years ago? Is not earth turned to earth? And shall not our sun set like theirs when the night comes? Yet we cannot believe that death will find us out, as he has found out them; though all men die, yet every man dreams, I shall escape; or at the least, I shall live until I am old. This is strange, men cannot think that God will do again that which he does daily, or that he will deal with them as he deals with others. Tell one of us that all others shall die, we believe it; tell one of us we shall die, and we believe it sooner of all than of one; though we are sore, though we be weak, though we be sick, though we be elder than those whom we follow to the ground. So they thought which lie in this mold under your feet, as you do. If wisdom, or riches, or favor, could have entreated death, those which have lived before us would have kept our possessions from us; but death would take no bail, we are all tenants at will, and we must leave this cottage whensoever the landlord will put another in our room, at a year's, at a month's, at a week's, at a day's, at an hour's warning, or less. The clothes which we wear on our backs, the graves which are under our feet, the sun which sets over our heads, and the meats which go into our mouths, do cry to us that we shall wear, and set, and die like the beasts, and fowls, and fishes, which now are dead in our dishes, and but even now were living in the elements. Our fathers have summoned us, and we must summon our children, to the grave. Everything everyday suffers some eclipse, nothing standing at a stay; but one creature calls to another, *Let us leave this world.* While we play our pageants on this stage of short continuance, every man has a part, some longer, and some shorter; and while the actors are at it, suddenly death steps on the stage, like a hawk which separates one of the doves from the flight; he shoots his dart; where it lights, there falls one of the actors dead before them, and makes all the rest *aghast*; they muse, and mourn, and bury him, and then to the sport again! While they sing, play, and dance, death comes again and strikes another; there he lies, they mourn for him, and bury him as they did the former, and play again. So one after another until the players be vanished, like the accusers which came before Christ, (John 8:9); and death is the last on the stage, so "the figure of this world passes away." Many which stand here may lie here or elsewhere within this year. But you think it is not I, and he thinks it is not he; but he that thinks this comes soonest to it. If I could make you believe that you have but a year to live, and that all which hear me this day shall come to the bar before this day another year returns again, you would prepare yourselves to die, and leave your sins behind you, and depart Christians out of the church, with a mind to do all that God would have you. So, I have proclaimed to all kings, princes, judges, counselors, and magistrates, that which Isaiah foretold to one, "Set your things in order, for you shall die." *Amen.*

THE LADDER OF PEACE

"Rejoice evermore. Pray continually. In all things give thanks."—1 Thes. 5:16-18

When I spoke last of these words, I showed you how the apostle commends to us three virtues, of greater price than the three presents which the wise men brought to Christ: the first is, "Rejoice evermore;" the second is, "Pray continually;" the third, "In all things give thanks." All three are of one last, for we must rejoice continually, because he says, Rejoice evermore; and we must pray continually, because he says, Pray continually; and we must give thanks continually, because he says, In all things give thanks. These are the three things which, one says, all men do, and no man does, because every man does them, and scarce one does them as he should; therefore the apostle, to show us how we should do them well, does put continually to them, as though continuance were the perfection of all virtues. I chose this scripture for a consolation to them which are afflicted in conscience, which is commonly the disease of the most innocent soul, for they think that they do well to mourn continually; and Paul says, *Rejoice continually*; and therefore I will speak a little more of these words than I did before. If you mark it, it may well be called *The Ladder of Peace*, for it stands on three steps, and every step is a step from trouble to peace, from sorrow to joy; for he which can rejoice, is past grief; and he which can pray, is passing from his grief; and he which can give thanks, has obtained his desire. A man cannot rejoice and mourn; a man cannot pray and despair; a man cannot give thanks and be offended; therefore keep still on one of these three steps, and you shall never sorrow too much. If you cannot rejoice, as if your pain were past, then give thanks, because your pain is profitable. If you cannot think that your pain is worth thanks, then pray that you may have patience to bear it; and it is impossible in praying, or thanking, or rejoicing, that any grief should want patience enough to bear it. But when you forget to rejoice in the Lord, then you begin to muse, and after to fear, and after to distrust, and at last to despair, and then every thought seems to be a sin against the Holy Spirit.

The Son of God is called, "The consolation of Israel," (Luke 2:25), to show that he brings consolation with him, and that joy is where Christ is, as light is where the sun is; therefore the chief joy is called "The joy of the Holy Spirit," (Rom. 14:17), to show that they have the chief joy which have the Holy Spirit; therefore the greatest peace is called "The peace of conscience," (Phil. 4:7), to show that they have the greatest peace which have a good conscience; therefore the faithful are said to be "anointed with the oil of joy," (Isa. 59:3), as though joy were in their countenance; therefore they are said to be "clothed with the garment of gladness," as though gladness did compass them like a garment; therefore Paul, in all his epistles, does join "grace and peace" together, (Rom. 1:7, 1 Cor. 1:3, 2 Cor. 1:2, Gal. 1:3, Eph. 1:2, Col. 1:2, 2 Thes. 1:2, Titus 1:4, Philemon 3), and show that the peace of God does follow them which have the grace of God. It is not in vain that the Holy Spirit, when he named Barnabas, interpreted his name too, because it signifies "the son of consolation," (Acts 4:36); as though he delighted in such men as were the sons of consolation. "Comfort one another," says Paul, (1 Thes. 4:18). How shall we comfort one another without comfort? Therefore Paul says, "God comforts us, that we may be able to comfort others, by the comfort whereby we ourselves are comforted of God," (2 Cor. 1:4), showing that we cannot comfort others unless we be comfortable ourselves; and therefore, that we may perform this duty, we are bound to nourish comfort in ourselves. Paul says, "I am full of comfort," (2 Cor. 7:4); who then can say, I am full of sorrow, but he must be contrary to Paul? As the body may not offend the soul, so the soul may not injure the body, because it is the body's keeper; but a pensive man does injure the body and the soul too; for Solomon says, "A sound spirit will bear his infirmities, but a wounded spirit who can bear?" (Prov. 18:14), as if he should say, *The heart must be kept courageous, and strong, and lively, like an instrument which is tuned to tune all the rest, or else every grief will make you impatient.* In (Deut. 30:9) it is said, that God "rejoices to do us good;" and therefore, in (Deut. 28), the Jews are reproved, because they rejoiced not in the service of God. As he loves a cheerful giver, so he loves a cheerful *server*, and a cheerful preacher, and a cheerful hearer, and a cheerful worshipper; and therefore David says, "Let us sing heartily to the Lord," (Psa. 95:1); showing, as it were, the tune which delights God's ears. Therefore, let us pray God every day to turn all our joy into the joy of the Holy Spirit, and all our peace into the peace of conscience, and all our sorrow into the sorrow for sin, and all our fear into the fear to sin, that so we may sorrow and rejoice together, fear and hope together; that is, have one eye to the law, to keep us from presumption, and another eye to the gospel, to keep us from despair; and then this comfort is sent to us, "Rejoice evermore," or else we have nothing to do with it.

Secondly, It is such a pleasant thing, that Paul joins pray continually with rejoice continually, to show that no man has such joy, as he which is often talking with God by prayer; as if he should say, If you have the skill to pray continually, it will make you rejoice continually; for in the company of God is nothing but joy and gladness of heart.

Who *ever* fell into heresy, or into apostasy, or into despair, before he fell *from* prayer, the preservative of the soul? "If you hadst been here," says Martha to Christ, "my brother had not died," (John 11:32); so if prayer had been here, these evils had not happened. This is the holy water which drives away unclean spirits, as Christ shows when he speaks of the devil, which is "not cast out but by fasting and prayer," (Matt. 17:21). This is the cross which saves us from evil, as Christ shows when he teaches us to pray (as it is written in the 11th of Luke), "Deliver us from evil." This is the oil which heals our sickness, as James shows in his 5th chap. ver. 25, when he says, "The prayer of faith shall save the sick." It has such a hand in all things, that it is like the sanctifier of everything. It blesses our thoughts, and blesses our speeches, and blesses our actions. As Abraham blessed his servant before he went from him, (Gen. 24), so prayer blesses our works before they go from us. Whatsoever you do before you have blessed it with prayer, you have no promise that it shall prosper or do good, because he which should bless it is not made a counsel to it. Therefore we should not presume to use any of God's gifts, or any of God's graces, without prayer, lest that which is good does not good but hurt to us.

For this cause St. Paul, in the 14th chapter of the Romans, and the 6th verse, teaches us to pray before we eat. For this cause Paul prayed before he journeyed, (Acts 20:26, 38); for this cause Elijah prayed before he sacrificed, as it appears in the 1st book of Kings, 18:36; for this cause the Israelites prayed before they fought; and for this cause we pray before we preach. It is a good thing to preach, and yet you see we do not presume to preach before we pray; because "Paul plants, Apollos waters; but God gives the increase," (1 Cor. 3:6). Even so, we should not presume to give alms, nor to give counsel, nor to give help, before we have prayed that it may do good. *no*, we should not presume to exercise our faith, nor our repentance, nor our obedience, without prayer; because there is no faith so perfect but it had need of prayer to strengthen it. Also, there is no love so perfect but it had need of prayer to confirm it. There is no repentance so perfect but it had need of prayer to continue it; there is no obedience so perfect but it had need of prayer to direct it. Therefore he does sin which presumes to do any good work without prayer, because he seems to do it by his own power; for he that craves not assistance from God, which gives power to faith to bring forth works, as well as he does to trees to bring forth fruits, or to medicine to bring forth health. Therefore no virtue has done so much as prayer has done, for all virtues have had their power from prayer; and therefore one says, that prayer has done as many exploits as all virtues beside.

I have known many wicked men hear sermons, and I have known many wicked men study, and I have known many wicked men fast, and I have known many wicked men preach, and I have known many wicked men counsel; but I did never know any wicked man that could pray well, nor any that could pray well, live wickedly. This Peter proves in his first epistle and fourth chapter, when he says, "Be sober and watchful in prayer," showing, that all cannot pray, but they which are sober and watchful.

St. Paul, in (Rom. 12), teaches us a reasonable service of God. Here he seems to enjoin us an unreasonable service of God. For whoever prayed continually? Or if we should pray continually, when should we hear, or preach, or when should we study, or when should we work? So one service seems to hinder all services; but indeed it does further all services, and therefore we are commanded to pray continually, because we can do nothing without prayer. But if you imagine that this commandment is broken if your lips are not always going, which was the heresy of the Messalians, or if you do not dwell always in the church, like the golden candlesticks, then you are out of Paul's mind, for Paul did not pray continually with his lips, and therefore he does not mean a lip prayer; neither did Paul live day and night in the temple, and therefore he does not mean a church prayer; and further, it seems that the Jews were not appointed to pray at all times, for they had set times of prayer; and therefore we read how "Peter and John went up to the temple at the time of prayer," (Acts 3:1); therefore to pray continually, is to lift up our hearts continually to God, and to pray in our thoughts, as Moses did, though we open not our lips; and so we pray continually. As when a good man is to answer before his persecutor, a thought prays in his heart that he may answer wisely; when he is to give alms, a thought prays in his heart that it may do good; when he is to give counsel, a thought prays in his heart that it may prosper; when he is to hear a sermon, a thought prays in his heart that he may be edified and sanctified by it. So we may pray and hear, pray and speak, pray and eat, pray and study, pray and work together, as the Jews built and fought together, (Neh. 4:7). And therefore prayer seems a harder thing than it is. For if it had been irksome for any to pray, Paul would not have joined praying and rejoicing together. It is not hard which a man may do and rejoice too. If a man love entirely, he has no such delight as to talk often, and to confer daily with him whom he loves; for by this his love is increased, and his joy is doubled; but the seldomer we commune together, little by little our affections abate, until at last we become strange one to the other, as though we had never been acquainted. Even so our affections and familiarity does grow towards God by often praying to him; and when we leave off to pray, then our affections draw from him, and his affections from us.

Seeing, then, that prayer is such an excellent thing, that it is given to none but to him which is called excellent and such a pleasant thing, that Paul joins pray continually with rejoice continually; and such an heavenly thing, that it makes us like the angels which are in heaven; and such a necessary thing, that God built a house for it, and made a day for it; and such a holy thing, that none but the holy can deal with it; and such a strong thing, that it overcomes God which overcomes all; how is it, then, that our fathers spent so much time in prayer, and we make no account of it? Have we nothing to pray for as well as they? *no*, they prayed for nothing but we had need to pray for the like. The Turks and idolaters pray to them that cannot hear; but he which says, "I will hear," has not so many supplications to him as noblemen. What will we give God, if we will not afford him thanks? What will we do for him, if we will not praise him? "If you be wise," says Solomon, "you are wise to yourself;" so if we do pray, we do pray for ourselves. Shall the birds sing to God, and not they for whom he created birds? What a fool is he which will fight, and travel, and watch for himself, and will not speak for himself! If God had required such costly sacrifices of us as he did of the Jews, it is to be feared that he would not be served at all; for we are such Gergesites, that we would not part from our beasts to sacrifice to him. Therefore, let us not say, God will not hear, but let us say, *We do not ask*; for God is more ready to give than we to ask. Therefore, let us pray that our neglect of prayer may be forgiven.

A LOOKING-GLASS FOR CHRISTIANS

"I say, through the grace that is given to me, to everyone that is among you, that no man presume to understand above that which is meet to understand; but that he understand according to sobriety, as God has dealt to every man the measure of faith."—Rom. 12:3

First of the preface, and then of the counsel. In the first verse of this chapter Paul persuades the Romans "by the mercy of God" towards them; here he persuades them "by the grace of God towards him Paul speaks like a man on his death-bed, which is set to give good counsel, and goes from one lesson to another, as though he would speak all with a breath. First, he counseled them to make their bodies serve God, because the body is a servant as well as the soul; then he forbade them to fashion themselves to the world, because no man can serve two contrary masters; then he advised them to renew their minds, because, except the mind be reformed, the body will serve but a while; and he sets them to seek God's will, because the will of man does seduce him. And now, to make up his testament, as it were, he admonishes them to rest in the knowledge of God's will, and not to search farther, nor to be proud of their knowledge, but to use their knowledge to humble their pride.

Five things, in my judgment, are to be noted in these words: The first is, that wisdom is a thing to be desired, for when he says, not above sobriety, he would have us wise within sobriety. The second is, that every man affects a kind of wisdom, either according to sobriety, as Paul counseled the Romans, or above sobriety, as the Romans did before. The third is, few are wise, as God counts wisdom; and therefore Paul speaks to all, as though all were to learn this lesson. The fourth is, that sobriety shows, *like a glass*, who are wise, and who are not. The last is, that the wisdom which goes beyond sobriety does hurt him which has it, and others; for when Paul says, "Be wise to sobriety," he implies, that who is not so is in a

250

kind of distemper, like one scarce sober. Paul makes a general charge, "I say to everyone, be wise according to sobriety;" as though everyone had too much wisdom, or too little. Virtue is a means between two vices, which sits so close beside her, that one can scarce see her; covetousness on the one side, and prodigality on the other side, and charity in the midst; pride on the one side, rusticity on the other side, and comeliness in the midst; flattery on the one side, malice on the other side, and love in the midst; carefulness on the one side, carelessness on the other side, and diligence in the midst; diffidence on the one side, presumption on the other side, and faith in the midst; superstition on the one side, atheism on the other side, and religion in the midst; ignorance on the one side, curiosity on the other side, and knowledge in the midst; so that there is but one virtue still for two vices; therefore extremities bear rule in this world. Either we cry *Hosanna*, or else *Crucifige* either Christ must not wash our feet, or else he must wash our feet and body too; either we will have Paul a god, or else we say he is cursed of God, (Acts 28:4, 6); either we say, "Touch not, taste not," for it is unclean, or else we say, "Let us eat and drink, for tomorrow we shall die." If we love, we do over-love; if we fear, we over-fear; if we are careful, we are over-careful; if we are merry, we are over-merry; if we are solemn, we are over-solemn; if so, we cannot be wise, but we are over-wise; so soon as we are thought to know something, we would be thought ignorant of nothing. There is a kind of down or curdle on wisdom, like the train of gentlewomen, which is more than needs, which we call the crotchets of the brain, which must be weeded out, as the tree is lopped when it grows too thick; or else they will perish in the brain, like a scum which sees into the broth. The Scripture speaks of many ancient, and many rich, and many strong, and many mighty; but of one wise man, and yet that wise man, too, before he died, stepped beyond sobriety. Therefore, even as you look, lest other men's wisdom should deceive you, so look lest your own wisdom deceive yourselves. There is a kind of wisdom which is more contrary to wisdom than ignorance. As good corn and bad corn come both to the market to be sold, and the bad would like to have as much money as the good; so true wisdom and false wisdom come both, show both, offer both, praise both.

Therefore, as God appointed the people their bounds which they might not pass, when he talked with Moses on the mount; so he has appointed certain precincts of wisdom, which when we transgress, we may be said to exceed our commission; like Shimei, when he went beyond the river, which Solomon forbade him. The rail or pale of wisdom is sobriety. As wisdom is made overseer of all other virtues, so sobriety is made overseer of wisdom, to measure it forth in even portions and due seasons, that none of God's gifts be lost. As water is to the wine, to allay the heat of it, and salt is to meat, to make it savory; so sobriety is to wisdom, to make it wholesome and profitable to him which has it, and them which seek it of him. "If you have found honey," says Solomon, "take not too much, lest you surfeit," (Prov. 25:16). *no*, if you have found wisdom, take not too much, lest you surfeit. There is a surfeit of wisdom, which is the most dangerous one of all others; when a man begins, like Paul, to be puffed up, which was Aaron's and Miriam's disease, when they murmured against Moses, because they thought themselves fitter to govern than he, (Num. 12:2). No virtue is better than wisdom and humility; but if a man be proud of his wisdom and humility, then the virtue is turned into vice. "If the light be darkness," says Christ, how great is that darkness! So if our humility be pride, how great is that pride! If our knowledge be ignorance, how great is that ignorance! Therefore, as we remember, be wise as serpents; so let us remember, be simple as doves; or else we drown in our wisdom, like a light that quenches in its own tallow.

Now, that you may know how to be wise according to sobriety, there are certain properties of this sober wisdom which I will show you.

The first is, not to arrogate to ourselves more than God has given us. As the man said, "I believe, Lord, help my unbelief;" so the wise man may say, I understand, Lord, help my ignorance. For one thing which we know, we are ignorant of a thousand things which *we should know*; yet the foolish virgins would be thought as wise as their sisters.

No man can abide to be disgraced in his mind; we had rather seem wicked than simple. As every bird thinks her own birds fairest, so every man thinks his own wit ripest. "There is a generation," says Solomon, "which are pure in their own conceit, but they are not cleansed from their filthiness," (Prov. 30:12). So there is a generation which are wise in their own conceit, but they are not cleansed from their foolishness.

The second property is, not to glory of anything in ourselves.

The third property is, not to despise others.

The fourth property is, to keep within our calling. He which meddles with that which he has not to do with is compared to one that catches a dog by the ears, and dares neither hold him still nor let him go; so that he can neither go forward for want of skill, nor backward for shame. God has given certain gifts to certain callings; as no man can exceed his gifts, so no man should exceed his calling. It is not meet that he should be a freeman which was never a prentice, nor that he should leap into Moses's chair that never sat at Gamaliel's feet. If you never do so well, and are not called to it, the Scripture says plainly, "Who has required this of you?" you are an usurper of another's office. "A fool," says Solomon, "is meddling;" showing that a wise man meddles not but where he has to do. We are compared to a body; some men are like the head, and they must rule; some are like the tongue, and they must teach; some are like the hand, and they must work. When this order is confounded, then that comes to pass which we read of Eve; when the woman would lead her husband, both fell into the ditch, (Gen. 3). Therefore, as Christ said, "Who has made me a judge over you?" (Luke 12:14), so they which are not judges should say, *Who has made me a judge?* He which is not a teacher should say, *Who has made me a teacher?* He which is not a ruler should say, *Who has made me a ruler?* And this is a better peace-maker than the lawyer.

The fifth property is, not to be curious in searching mysteries. This Paul means when he says, "Let no man presume to understand above that which is meet to understand." The star, when it came to Christ, stood still, and went no farther; so when we come to the knowledge of Christ, we should stand still and go no farther; for Paul was content to not know anything but "Christ crucified." It is not necessary to know that which God has not revealed; and the well of God's secrets is so deep, that no bucket of man can sound it; therefore we must row in shallow waters, because our boats are light, and small, and soon overturned. They which have such crotchets and circumstances in their brain, I have marked this in them, that they seldom find any room for that which they should know, but go to and fro, seeking and seeking, like those which sought Elijah's body, and did not find it. Let men desire knowledge of God as Solomon did; but not desire knowledge as Eve did.

Curious questions and vain speculations are like a plume of feathers, which some will give anything for, and some will give nothing for. Paul rebuked them which troubled their heads about genealogies; how would he reprove men and women of our days, if he did see how they busy their heads about vain questions, tracing on the pinnacles, where they may fall, while they might walk on the pavement without danger? Some have a great deal more desire to learn where hell is, than to know any way how they may escape it; to hear what God did purpose before the world began, rather than to learn what he will do when the world is ended; to understand whether they shall know one another in heaven, than to know whether they are longing to heaven. This rock has made many shipwrecks, that men search mysteries before they know principles; like the Bethshemites, which were not content to see the ark, but they must pry into it, and finger it. Commonly the simplest men busy their heads about the highest matters; so that if they meet with a rough and crabbed question, like a knob in the tree, and while they hack and hew at it with their own wits to make it plain, their saw sticks fast in the cleft, and cannot get out again; at last in wrath they come like malcontents with God, as though the Scripture were not perfect, and either fall into despair, or into contempt of all. Therefore it is good to leave off learning where God has left off teaching; for they which have an ear where God has no tongue, hearken not to God, but to the tempter, as Eve did to the serpent. This is the rule whereby a man may know whether his wisdom stand right.

I cannot tell how it comes to pass that no man can serve God unless he know God (for none do obey him except they which do know him), and yet it is said that there was never so much knowledge and so little goodness. Surely as Christ said to his disciples, "O you of little faith!" So he might say to us, O you of little understanding! for there is not too much wisdom, but too much ostentation; humility is none of our virtues. They which should teach others to be wise according to sobriety, pass the bounds of sobriety themselves. Every man has a commonwealth in his head, and travails to bring forth new fashions. As the Jews were not content with such rules as God had appointed them, but would have a king like the Gentiles; so the wisdom of this world is to devise better orders, better laws, better titles, better callings, better discipline than God has devised himself. "Every plant," says Christ, "which my Father has not planted shall be rooted up;" that is, every title, and every office, and every calling which God has not planted, shall be rooted up. To be wise according to this book, is to be wise according to sobriety. Therefore seek the wisdom of Christ, for the wisdom of the serpent is turned into a curse, the wisdom of the Pharisees is turned into a woe, the wisdom of Ahithophel is turned into folly, the wisdom of Nimrod is turned into confusion, the wisdom of the steward is turned into expulsion, the wisdom of Jezebel is turned into death. This is the end of the deceiver's wisdom, of the extortioner's wisdom, of the usurer's wisdom, of the persecutor's wisdom, of the flatterer's wisdom, of the sorcerer's wisdom, of the hypocrite's wisdom, of the Machiavellian's wisdom. As Moses' serpent devoured the sorcerer's serpent, so

God's wisdom shall devour man's wisdom.

Wherefore, "By the grace of God which is given to me, I say to every one of you," with Paul, "Be wise to sobriety." Do not be not ashamed to seem ignorant of some things, but remember that it is better to seem ignorant, than to be proud. So, you have heard what wisdom is; now let us pray to God for it. *Amen.*

A CAVEAT FOR CHRISTIANS

"Let him that thinks he stands take heed lest he fall."—1 Cor. 10:12

Here the apostle warns us, that we are all in a house ready to fall, all in a ship ready to sink, and all in a body ready to *sin*. Who can say what he will do when he is tried? Therefore Paul does not say, Let him that stands take heed lest he fall, but "Let him that thinks he stands take heed lest he fall," warning us before that we take heed of falling, and to examine how we stand, whether we stand or not. For when he makes his speech of them which "think they stand," not of them which stand, he intends that few stand in comparison of them which think they stand. Many think themselves wise, that are fools like others; as many think themselves pure, which are profane like others. Solomon notes, (Prov. 30:12), "There is a generation which are pure in their own conceit, and yet are not washed from their filthiness, as though there were a generation or sect of such men. And again, (Prov. 20:6), "Many men will boast of their goodness, but who can find a faithful man?" So, many seem to stand, which stand not; many think they believe, which do not know what faith means; many look to be saved, which cannot tell who shall save them, no more than Nicodemus knew what it was to be born again. The reason is, many are afraid to sound too deep, and examine their conscience, lest it should upbraid them with the most noise of their sins. Therefore, as a favorable judge, which would save the malefactor, will ask him so cunningly, that he will answer for him too; and then he will say, I find no fault in this man, let him pay his fees and be gone; so will such a man say, I find no fault in this faith; I think it is a sound faith, I think it is a good faith, I think it is religion enough, when I come to the church, and love my neighbor, and obey my prince, and give every man his own, and pay my tithes, and fast twice a week, as the Pharisee did; I think this is well, what would you have more?

Have I not kept all the commandments? Luke 18:21. "No," says Christ, "there is one thing behind;" examine yourself, and still you shall find something behind, like a cobweb in the top of an house when the floor is swept. Therefore well does Paul say, "he that thinks that he stands," not he which stands; for he which stands in Christ falls not; but he which thinks he stands falls suddenly, and may finally, unless he stand on his watch. *Take heed* is a good staff to stay upon, and so often a man sins as he casts it from him; all go astray.

But this is the difference between the sins of them which have faith, and them which have no faith. They which have no faith fall like an elephant, which, when he is down, rises not again; they which have faith do but trip and stumble, fall and rise again. Their falls teach them to stand, their weakness does teach them strength, their sins do teach them repentance, their frailness teaches them constancy, as Peter was better after his denial than he was before. Judas did never stand, but seemed to stand; the disciples knew not that he was a thief, for they asked, "Is it I? Is it I?" Christ knew, as it appears, when he gave him the bread, and said, "That which you do, do quickly." If ever he had stood, he could not have been termed "the son of perdition." Many did seem to the world to go out of the church, but John says they were never of the church; meaning, that if they had been of the church, they could not have gone out of it; for the true vine could not leave her grapes, nor the olive her fatness, nor the fig-tree her sweetness, so they which stand in the faith do not fall away, but seem to fall, as hypocrites seem to stand. The best men have had their slips, but always they rose again, as though they had sinned to teach us repentance; therefore their sins are written, which else should have been concealed for their honor.

"How are the mighty overthrown," says David. Like Peter, which said he would never forsake Christ, and forsook him first. The strong men are fallen, even Solomon himself, and David, and Noah, and Lot, and Samson, and Peter, the lights of the world, fell like stars of heaven. These tall cedars, strong oaks, fair pillars, lie in the dust, whose tops glittered in the air, that they which think they stand, may take heed lest they fall. Who am I that I should stand like a shrub when these cedars are blown down to the ground, and showed themselves but men? Let no man say what he will be, before he has examined what he is, but run his course with a trembling fear, always looking down to the rubs which lie before him and the worthies that are slain already.

This is the profit we should make of other men's faults, like a pearl which is taken out of the serpent; when we see our brother's nakedness, it should move us to compassion of him, and a fear of ourselves. For when we rejoice at another's fall, like Ham, as the leprosy went from Naaman to Gehazi, so God "turns his wrath from them," and it lights on us, (Prov. 24:17, 18), and such as have despised others without remorse, have fallen in the like, or more shamefully, themselves, and never rose again. What shall we do then when we hear of other men's faults? Not talk as we do, but beware by them, and think, *Am I better than he? am I stronger than Samson? am I wiser than Solomon? am I more chaste than David? am I soberer than Noah? am I firmer than Peter, if God should leave me to myself, if he should withdraw his hand which holds me? Into how many gulfs have I been falling, when God has prevented me of occasion, or delayed the temptation, or wonderfully kept me from it, I do not know how? for he delivers me from evil, as he delivered David from the blood of Nabal by Abigail, which came unlooked for.* So he has prevented many wonderfully, when they were assaulted so hardly, that they thought to have yielded to the enemy. Sometimes I may say there wanted a tempter, sometime I may say there wanted time, sometimes I may say there wanted place; sometimes the tempter was present, and there wanted neither time nor place, but God held me back that I should not consent: so near we have glided by sin, like a ship which rides on a rock, and slips away, or a bird which escapes from the fowler when the net is on her. There is no salt but may lose his saltiness, no wine but may lose his strength, no flower but may lose his scent, no light but may be eclipsed, no beauty but may be stained, no fruit but may be blasted, nor soul but may be corrupted. We stand all in a slippery place, where it is easy to slide, and hard to get up; like little children, which overthrow themselves with their clothes, now up, now down at a straw, so soon we fall from God, and slide from his word, and forget our resolutions, as though we had never resolved. Man goes forth in the morning, weak, naked, and unarmed, to fight with powers and principalities, the devil, the world, and all their adherents; and whom does he take with him but his flesh, a traitor, ready to yield up at every assault to the enemy? So man is set on the side of a hill, always declining and slipping; the flesh muffles him to make him "stumble, the world catches at him to make him fall, the devil undermines him to make him sink, and cries still, *Cast yourself down*; and when he falls, he goes apace, as Peter, who denies three times together; and when he is fallen, is like a stumbling-stone in the way for others, that they may fall too. Therefore, "Let him that thinks he stands, take heed lest he fall." So earnestly must we call on our souls, that we are not weary of well-doing; for happier are the children that never began, than Judas, whose end was worse than his beginning. Wisdom and righteousness are angry with him that leaves his goodness to become worse. If you were like the vine, or the olive, or the fig-tree, they would not leave their grapes, or their fatness, or their sweetness, to get a kingdom, but the bramble did. If you be like the bramble, what will you do when the fire comes? As this is a memorandum to all, so especially let him that rules, and him that teaches, take heed lest he fall; for if the pillars shrink, the temple shakes. As when a great tree is hewn down, which is a shadow to the beasts, and a nest to the birds, many leaves, and boughs, and twigs fall with it; so many stand and fall with them whose lamps give light to others, even as Jeroboam's sin made Israel to sin. Therefore Paul has given you a watchword, which everyone should write on his table, on his bed, and on his nails, lest he forget in one hour; for he which stands now may fall before night. Sin is not long in coming, nor quickly gone, unless God stop us, as he met Balaam in his way, and stay us, as he stayed the woman's son, when he was a-bearing to his grave. We run over reason, and tread on conscience, and fling by counsel, and go by the word, and post to death, as though we ran for a kingdom. Like a lark, that falls to the ground sooner than she mounted up; at first she retires as it were by steps, but when she comes nearer the ground, she falls down with a jump; so we decline at first, and waver lower and lower, until we are almost at the worst, and then we run headlong, as though we were sent quickly to hell: from hot to lukewarm, from lukewarm to key-cold, from key-cold to stark dead; so the languishing soul bleeds to death, and does not see his life go, until he is at the very last *gasp*. Woe to him that is guilty of this murder! If the blood of Abel cried for vengeance against his brother Cain, which slew his body, shall not God be revenged for the death of his soul? "Where is your brother?" says God. No, where is your soul? Have you slain it, which was my spouse, my temple, mine own image? *Amen*.

JACOB'S LADDER; OR, THE WAY TO HEAVEN

"Thus run, that you may obtain."—1 Cor. 9:24

Because I have but one hour to teach you all that you must learn of me, I have chosen a text which is like Jacob's ladder, that shows you the way to heaven. This is all that you would know; and it may please God to open your eyes, that you may know it before you depart. Hear to practice; do not hinder the Spirit, but let it work without resistance; record when you are gone, and you shall see the great power of God, what he is able to do for you by one sentence of this book, if you digest it well. "So run, that you may obtain." If many run and do not obtain, how easy is it to run in vain! And how happy is he which obtains that, that all men wish, when so many miss it for nothing but for this, because they run out of the way! You have heard, read, and done much, and would do more, to obtain eternal life with the angels in heaven; for this you pray, and fast, and watch, and obey the laws of God, and come together every Sabbath to hear, to pray, to praise, and serve him which gives it. How many prayers, how many fasts, how many watches, how many works, how many hours in reading the word, in hearing the word, in receiving the sacrament, in examining your heart, in chastening your flesh, were spent and lost, if you should run in vain! As Esau hunted for a blessing, and went without it. Therefore the Holy Spirit does say nothing, but it is like a mark in our way, to show us when we are in, and when we are out; for God would not have us lose our labor, like Laban, which could find in his heart, after Jacob had served him twenty years, to send him away empty; but he would have you to "seek and find," to "ask and receive," to "run and obtain;" therefore he says, "So run, that you may obtain." As there is a heaven, so there is a way to heaven; one way Adam came from paradise, and by another he must return to paradise. The passage is not so stopped but

262

there is a way, though a strait way, and a door, though it is a narrow door, and therefore only a few find it; only they which are like Jacob see a ladder before them, as Jacob did. He had many dreams before, and did not see it; at last "he dreamed, and, behold, a ladder which reached from earth to heaven, and all the angels descended and ascended by it," to show that no man ascends to heaven but by that ladder. This *ladder* is *Christ*, which says, "I am the way," and therefore he presses us to follow him. If we must follow Christ's steps, let us see how he went to heaven. He began early, for at twelve years of age he said, "I must go about my Father's business," Luke 2:49. He made speed; for John says that "He spoke and did more good things," in three and thirty years, "than could be written," John 21:25. He kept the right way; for when he said, "Who can accuse me of sin?" none could accuse him of any, though they watched him for that purpose. He continued well; for he died like a lamb, and prayed to his Father, and forgave his enemies. Therefore we will call the steps of this ladder, *Mature, propere, recte, constanter*; that is, *Begin betime, Make haste, Keep the way*, and *Hold to the end*, and you shall go after your Master.

Touching the first, *Begin early*. God requiring the first-born for his offering. The best season to seek God is to seek him *early*. And therefore *Wisdom* says, "They that seek me early shall find me;" but to them which defer, Wisdom says, "Ye shall seek me but shall not find me." Who is so young that has not received some talent or other? Therefore youth cannot excuse him, because the talent requires to be used of everyone that has it. This made David to cry, "Remember not the sins of my youth," (Psa. 25:7), which he would not have spoken, if God did not mark the sins of youth as well as age. Therefore the fathers were charged to teach their children the same law which they had themselves, (Deut. 6:7). Therefore Christ rebuked the disciples which forbade the little children to be brought to him, (Matt. 19:14); for, should children honor their father, and not honor God? It was a sweet concert when the children went before Christ to the temple and sung their

Hosanna, to make their fathers ashamed, which did not know the Messiah when he came, when their little children knew him. It is written, when Christ heard a young man answer that he had kept the commandments from his youth, Christ began to love him, (Mark 10:20, 21); (which, shows how Christ loves these timely beginnings), when we make him our nurse, and draw our first milk from his breasts. There is not one confession for old men, and another for young men; in the Creed, the old man does not say, "I did believe in God," and the young man does not say, "I will believe in God;" but both say, "I do believe in God." For he which is called *I am*, (Exod. 3:14), loves I am, and cares not for I was, nor I will be. When Christ asked Peter, "Do you love Me?" (John 21:15), he looked that he should answer him, "Yes, Lord, I love you;" and not drive off as Felix did Paul, (Acts 24:25), "I will hear you," I will love you, when I have time convenient: no, when you do not have convenient time, for if this be the convenient time, after this the convenient time is past. Manna was gathered in the morning, because when the sun arose it melted away; so virtue must be gathered ahead of time, for if we stay until business and pleasures come on us, they will melt it faster than we can gather it. If you lack a spur to make you run, see how every day runs away with your life; youth comes on childhood, age comes on youth, death comes on age, with such a swift sail, that if our minutes were spent in mortifying ourselves, yet our glass would be run out before we had purged half our corruptions. So much of the first step.

The second step in your journey is, to *keep the way*. As God taught the Israelites the way to Canaan, sending a fiery pillar before them, which they did follow wheresoever it went; so when he ordained a heaven for men, he appointed a way to come to it, which way he that misses shall never come to the end. As Herod sought Christ over all the land of the Jews, but none found him but *those which followed the star*, (Matt. 2); so there is something still that leads men to Christ, which we must follow, or else we cannot come where he is. There are many wrong ways, as there are many errors; there is but one right way, as there is but one truth. And, therefore, Jacob did not see many, but one ladder, which reached to heaven; and John the Baptist is said, not to "prepare the ways of the Lord," but "the way" showing that there is but one right way in this life; which; Solomon understands for the means, and therefore he said, "Turn not to the right hand nor to the left," implying that we may err as well of the right hand as of the left. As if he should say, *Some are too hot, as others are too cold*; some are too superstitious, as others are too careless; some are too fearful, as others are too confident; there is a zeal without knowledge, a love without singleness, a prayer without faith, and a faith without fruits. Therefore the apostle does warn us to "examine whether we are in the faith," (2 Cor. 13:5); not whether we have a kind of faith, but whether we are in the faith, *i.e.* the true faith. Therefore Paul says, *Run so*. It is not enough to run, but we must know how we run; it is not enough to hear, but we must care how we hear; it is not enough to believe, but we must care how we believe; it is not enough to pray, but we must care how we pray; it is not enough to work, but we must care how we work, for we cannot do good unless we do it well.

Now when you are in the way, it's good to make speed; therefore the next step in your journey is, *Make haste*. For this cause Paul says, *Run*, which is the swiftest pace of man; as though he should go faster to heaven than to any place else in the world. His meaning is this, that as a man watches, and runs, and labors, to be rich quickly, so he should hear, and pray, and study, and use all means, to be wise quickly. This the apostle understands when he bids us to add, as if he should say, *When you are in the way, and know good from evil, every day kill some vice, and every week sow some virtue, and make your two talents five talents, your five talents ten talents, and ever be doing; and at last it shall be opened to you, because you have knocked.* Christ says, "The kingdom of heaven is got by violence," (Matt. 11:12); therefore a man must be earnest and zealous in the religion that he professes, or else it makes no matter of what religion he is, for, if he is only lukewarm, God threatens to *spew him out of his mouth*, (Rev. 3:15, 16). Every man has a kind of religion, and the religion of most is to be like one another,—as merciful as others, as humble as others, as devout as others; but God says, "Be holy, as I am," not as others are; for Christ says, "Except your righteousness exceed the righteousness of the Pharisees," although they were holier than others, "ye shall not enter into heaven;" that is, except you be more than statute-protestants, which go to the church, and hear an homily, and receive once a year, but will not offend any person, nor leave any custom, nor bear any charge, nor suffer any trouble for the glory of God, you shall come to heaven when the Pharisees come out of hell. As love delights men, so zeal pleases God, for zeal is the love of God. Therefore every sacrifice was offered with fire, to show with what zeal they should burn which come to offer prayer or praise or thanks to the Lord; therefore the Holy Spirit descends in fire, to show the fervency of them on whom the Holy Spirit rests; therefore the cherubims were portrayed with wings before the people, to show that they should be as earnest and quick about the Lord's business as the cherubims; therefore God would not take a lame nor halting sacrifice, to show how he abhors slackness in all our duties; therefore St. James says, "Be swift to hear," (James 1:19). We must be swift to pray, swift to obey, swift to do good; for he is not cursed only which does not the Lord's business, but he which "does it negligently," (Jer. 48:10), *i.e.* he which does anything before it, like him that would bid his friends farewell, and follow Christ after, (Luke 9:61). The hound, which runs but for the hare, runs as fast as possibly he can; the hawk, which flies but for the partridge, flies as fast as she possibly can; and shall he which runs for heaven creep more slowly than the dial?

The fourth step in this happy journey is, *Persevere to the end*. There is nothing in our life which suffers so many eclipses and changes as our devotion; hot and cold, in and out, off and on, not in one mood so long as the sparrow sits on the ground, but looking like the chameleon, of the color of that which we see: if we see good, it puts us in a good thought; if we see or hear evil, it turns us from good to evil again. So man is rolled on a wheel that never stands still, but turns continually about, as though he were giddy and treading the maze. He is on the side of a hill where it is easy to slide, and hard to get up the flesh. Therefore the apostle, moved with pity, seeing man stand on such a slippery ground, as it were in a ship ready to sink, or a house bending to fall, he cries to them that stand surest, "Take heed lest you fall;" *i.e.* when you have put on your "armor of light," and are in the spiritual field to fight the Lord's battles against the world, the flesh, and the devil, turn not back like Demas, but remember the comfort of Elisha, that "there are more with you than against you," and that the tempter can overcome none but them which yield. Other servants change their masters for better masters; but all that serve God are like the servant which received an earring or mark in his ear after the manner of the Jews, in token that he would serve his master forever, like the vestures which bare their own mark. Therefore the Holy Spirit cries so often, "Be faithful even to the death," "Is not weary of well-doing," "Take heed lest you fall." For when you are weary of your godliness, God does not count you good, but weary of goodness; and when you decline from righteousness, God does not count you righteous, but revolted from righteousness. Therefore Paul says, "Pray continually," as though prayer were nothing without continuance. Jacob did not overcome God so soon as he began to wrestle with him, but when he had wrestled with him all night. And it is said that Christ took pity of them that stayed with him. "I will not leave you," says Elisha to Elijah; so we should not leave God. Some came into the vineyard in the morning, and some at noon; but none received any reward but they which stayed until night. As God's mercy endures forever, so our righteousness should endure forever. Every thought, and word, and deed of a faithful man is a step towards heaven; in every place he meets Christ, everything puts him in mind of God; he seeks him to find him, and when he has found him, he seeks him still; he is not satisfied, because at every touch there comes some virtue from him. If men bent themselves as much to do good as they press their brains to do evil, they might go to heaven with less trouble than they go to hell. Our idle hours are enough to get wisdom, and knowledge, and faith, until we are like saints among men. If you look only to the stops, and tell all the thorns which lie in the way, you shall go fearfully, wearily, and unwillingly, everything shall turn you aside, and every snail shall step before you, and take your crown from you; but then lift up your eyes from the earth, and look to Christ calling, the Spirit assisting, the Father blessing, the angels comforting, the word directing, the crown inviting, and your fetters shall fall from you, and you shall rise like the sun, and marvel how the thing could seem so hard, and be so easy. When you do well, remember that you change not for the worse, and do as you do then, and you shall continue to the end.

Now I have encouraged you like soldiers, and taken away your fear, I will bring you to the sight of your enemies, and will set them before your face; not to weaken you, for that were want of charity, but to make you wary, which is true love indeed. To number them surely I cannot, they are so many, and exactly to describe them, it is beyond my skill, they are so subtle; however, to give you a little taste, I may say as Elisha said to his servant, and you shall see it, if you have your eyes open, "Fear not, for they that be with us are more than they that be with them;" and he that is on our side is stronger than all. But if you will hear what the holy apostle says touching them, I can tell you; he affirms, and that by the very Spirit of God, "We wrestle not against flesh and blood only, but against principalities, powers, worldly governors, the princes of the darkness of this world, even spiritual wickedness in the high places," (Eph. 6:12). And St. John says, "They are the lusts of the flesh, the lusts of the eyes, and the pride of life," (1 John 2:16). Let other men think of them what they will; they that hear them so described, and have felt the force of them in their own souls, could not choose but confess that they have been many in number, mighty in power, subtle in practice, and what not. Who does not know this, that the more enemies we have the more need we have both of force outwardly, and of care inwardly? As again, the more powerful they are, and the more weak we are, the more we should seek for help elsewhere.

But whom shall we look to herein? Other men are as weak as ourselves, if not worse; for all men, (lay them on a balance, they are altogether lighter than vanity itself," (Psa. 62:9). And if we fear and distrust ourselves, how dare we, or how can we, put confidence in others? Especially since God says, "Cursed is everyone that makes flesh and blood his arm," Jer. 17:5. To look up to the holy and elect angels will do us little good; because they go not but being sent, and always wait for a word and warrant from the Lord's own mouth for all their actions; besides that, their own oil and force is little enough for their own supportation. To God, therefore, that is the God of our strength, we must come, yes, and to him alone, or else we are utterly overthrown and cast away. And if we cannot say, and do too, as David did, "Lord, whom have I in heaven but you? and I have desired none on earth with you," we are in a woeful taking, and utterly lost. For fear without and fire within, Satan's malice also, men's mischief, and our corruption, will carry and hurry us, as it were a violent tempest or whirlwind. To bring all into a sum, I say, let all objected be as true as anything may be, yet all these, and a thousand more such like, are nothing to him that is in Christ. For the apostle says, "There is no condemnation to them that are in Christ Jesus," (Rom. 8:1); and it is he alone that has destroyed death, and "became sin for us, that we in him might be made the righteousness of God." And surely such a one may in some good measure of comfort joyfully say, to the defiance even of death itself, and all other ghostly enemies whatsoever, "O death, where is your sting? O grave, where is your victory? The sting of death is sin, and the strength of sin is the law." Wherefore let us not fear all or any of our adversaries or pull-backs, for "true love expels fear," (1 John 4:18); neither let us be faint-hearted in ourselves, but labor rather to "lift up our hands which hang down, and to strengthen our weak knees," (Heb. 12:12); for "faithful is he that has promised, who will also perform it," (Heb. 10:23). "Be faithful unto death, and I will give you the crown of life," (Rev. 2:10). He that so runs, shall be sure to obtain, and have his portion with the saints in the heavenly inheritance, of a crown that never fades nor falls away. Wherefore, as you love life, and loathe death, *run well*, I beseech you; Yes, even as our text was at the beginning, so say I at the ending, "So run, that you may obtain." Which I do not only propound to you by exhortation, but commend and commit, with supplication to God for myself and you, that everyone of us, and I myself especially, may in feeling and faith say, "I am now ready to be offered, and the time of my departing is at hand; I have fought a good fight, and have finished my course, I have kept the faith. From here is laid up for me the crown of righteousness, which the Lord, the righteous judge, shall give me at that day; and not to me only, but to all them that "love his appearing," (2 Tim. 4:6-8). *Amen.*

THE LAWYER'S QUESTION AND THE LAWGIVER'S ANSWER

"And behold, a certain lawyer stood up and tempted him, saying, "Master, what shall I do to inherit eternal life?" And he said to him, "What is written in the law? How do you read it? etc.""—Luke 10:25-26

It is a weighty question, and has been long discoursed, by what means a man may come to heaven; and who is not desirous to be resolved in it? Here the question is propounded by a lawyer, and answered by the Lawgiver, whose judgment in this case is worth the hearing. He propounds the question as one desirous to learn, when indeed he means nothing less. But as Ahab, when he asked Micaiah, in the first book of Kings and the 22nd chapter, if he should go up to fight against Ramoth in Gilead, meant not to follow the prophet's direction, but only desired to hear his opinion; so the lawyer propounds this question, not with a mind to learn of Christ, but with a mind to tempt Christ, and to try his learning.

Of all kind of cattle these are the worst, because they most hurt where they are least mistrusted. Therefore they are compared in Scripture to the wily fox, for their crafty fetches. And Herod is termed a fox for his dissembling, (Luke 13:32). For as the fox feigns himself dead, that he may catch the birds to devour them, so the flatterer feigns himself to be harmless, and honest, and conscionable, and religious, and holy, that he may "deceive the hearts of the simple," (Rom. 16:18). He is like your shadow, which does imitate the action and gesture of your body, which stands when you stand, and walks when you walk, and sits when you sit, and rises when you rise; so the flatterer does praise when you praise, and finds fault when you find fault, and smiles when you smile, and frowns when you frown, and applauds you in your doings, and soothes you in your sayings, and in all things seeks to please your humour, until he has sounded the depth of your devices, that he may betray you to your greatest enemies. As the sirens sing most sweetly when they intend your destruction, so flatterers speak most fair when they practise most treachery. Therefore every fair look is not to be liked, every smooth tale is not to be believed, and every glozing tongue is not to be trusted; but as we must "try the spirits, whether they are of God or not," (1 John 4:1), so we must try the words, whether they come from the heart or not; and we must try the deeds, whether they are answerable to the words or not.

Now we are come to the question, which is, "By what means may a man inherit eternal life?" A weighty question, worthy to be known, not only of lawyers and learned men, but also of all, both men and women, which be persuaded in their hearts, as with their mouth they do confess, that after death their bodies shall rise again. Therefore, though this lawyer were to be blamed, because he came with so bad a mind, yet is he to be commended, because he moved so good a question. Many now-a-days are very curious in idle and unprofitable questions, as, *What God did before he made the world? How long Adam stood in the state of innocency? Whether Solomon were saved or not?* with many such vain and unnecessary questions. But few there are which will ask, as this lawyer did, what they must do to inherit eternal life. You shall see many people very careful and inquisitive how they may get riches, where they may purchase lands and lordships, how they may come to advancement and honor, and by what means they may procure the prince's favor. But we shall see few or none inquisitive concerning the means of their salvation; you shall seldom hear any ask their pastor what they must do to be saved, or which way they may come. This man was a Pharisee, such a one as Paul was before his conversion, one that expounded the law of God to the people and lived after the straightest law of their religion; in a word such a one as both for his life and learning was admired and honored of the Jews. Though this lawyer was learned, yet it was boldly done of him to tempt the Lord. But what is it that learning dare not attempt, if it is not tempered with the fear of God? Christ Jesus found no greater adversaries than the high priests and scribes and Pharisees, which were all learned men; and the church of Christ at this day is by none so much afflicted as by those that carry of singular learning. For look how many heresies are extant in the church, or how many controversies in religion that have been devised and are maintained by learned men. Let learned men therefore learn to fear the Lord; let them learn to "not know so much as Christ Jesus and him crucified," (1 Cor. 2:2), without which knowledge all knowledge is ignorance, all wisdom is foolishness, all learning is madness, and all religion is error, or hypocrisy, or superstition. Our Savior Christ, in the choice of his apostles, called not one that was learned; yet has he not rejected all that are learned, for from heaven he called his apostle Paul, a learned lawyer, (Acts 22:3), to be the apostle and the preacher of the Gentiles, (Rom. 11:13). And there is no doubt but that in all ages, and even at this day, he calls some in every place, and endows them with excellent learning, that they may serve to "the gathering together of the saints, and to the exercising of the ministry, and to the edifying of the church of God," (Eph. 4:12).

Good Master, what shall I do to inherit eternal life? Mark here the discretion of the lawyer in asking this question. As the man was a lawyer, so there is no doubt but that he had read the law and the prophets. If you look into the law, you shall *not* find, "Cursed is he that continues not in all things that are written in the book of the law, to *know* them." If you peruse the prophets, you shall not find, "Cease from doing evil, and learn to *speak* well." But the law says, "Cursed is he which continues not in all things that are written in the book of the law, to *do* them," (Deut. 27).

What shall I do to inherit eternal life? There is a life which is short and temporal, which Job compares to a wind, that soon blows over, (Job 7:7); James to a vapor, that soon vanishes away, (James 4:14). This lawyer asks not after his temporal life, for this is common to beasts with men; but here he inquires concerning that life which is eternal, and shall never have an end. It is strange to see how every man almost desires to be eternal, and yet how few *use* the means to be eternal. As the fowls by a natural inclination delight to fly, the fish to swim, and the beasts to go, so men are naturally carried with an earnest desire to live forever.

To the obtaining of eternal life two things are necessary. The first is, to believe well; the second is, to live well. By the first we are justified in the sight of God, for he respects our faith; by the second we are justified in the sight of men, for they regard our works. And so are the apostles Paul and James reconciled. For when Paul makes faith the cause of justification, (Rom. 3:28), he means such a faith as "works by love," (Gal. 5:6), whereby we are justified in the sight of God. And when James makes works the cause of justification, (James 2:24), he means such works as proceed from faith, (James 2:18), whereby we are declared to be righteous before men.

The Scripture describes this eternal life by various excellent names, to show the worthiness and excellency of it. It is called "a kingdom," (Luke 12:32), but yet such a kingdom as "cannot be shaken," not like the kingdoms of this world, (Heb. 12:28), for it is "a heavenly kingdom," (Mat 8:11). It is called "paradise," (Luke 23:43), for it is more pleasant than the garden of Eden. And "Abraham's bosom," (Luke 16:22), for it is a place of rest and comfort. It is called "the house of the Father, in which there are many mansions," (John 14:2); "the joy of the Lord," in whichto every faithful servant must enter, (Matt. 25:21); and all to express and declare to us the beauty, excellency, and glory of that life which is eternal. And yet as glorious and excellent as it is, such is the love and favor of God to us, that he has appointed it to be our inheritance, as here the lawyer terms it. Inheritance is a kind of tenure, whereby a man in his own right holds or possesses anything as his own; as when a lawful heir does inherit his father's lands; even so the kingdom of God belongs to us, as our lawful inheritance, because we are the sons of God.

It is a great prerogative to be "the Son of God," (John

1:12). But to be heirs, and heirs with Christ, (Rom. 8:17), of that heavenly inheritance, is a wonderful *privilege*. How are we bound to almighty God, that whereas he might have made us stones, or trees, or beasts, or such insensible and unreasonable creatures, it pleased his divine majesty to make us men, the undoubted heirs of eternal happiness! Behold, dear brother, and consider that heaven is your inheritance, eternal glory is your patrimony; you are born to a kingdom, you have a title to it, and when you depart this life you shall be sure to find it, if before you depart this life you do not lose your right and title by your sinful life.

Now you have heard the question propounded, you shall hear the question answered: "And he said to him, *What is written in the law? how readest thou?*" as if he should have said, *I marvel that you, being a doctor of the law, which should be able to instruct others in matters of religion, are ignorant of that which it behoves every man to know, by what means he may inherit eternal life.* In which have you bestowed your study? in which have you employed your wit? and how have you spent your time? you seem to be a lawyer: tell me, what does the law require of you? you seem to have read the Scriptures: let me see how you have profited by your reading. So our Savior sends this lawyer to the law to learn his duty, and sets him to school, that thought himself too good to learn. He came to tempt Christ by asking the question; but now himself must make the answer, unless he will betray his own ignorance.

It follows, ver. 27, "And he answered and said, you shall love your Lord God with all your heart, and with all your soul, and with all your strength, and with all your thought; and your neighbor as yourself," The lawyer in his answer shows himself a learned lawyer; for whereas the law of God consists of ten precepts, he reduces the same to two.

Here is nothing but love (my brethren) and yet here is the fulfilling of the law. For all the benefits that God had bestowed on the Israelites, his people, he requires nothing but love; and for all favors which he has done to us, he asks no more but love again. He asks love; a kind of service which every man may well afford. He asks not learning, nor strength, nor riches, nor nobility, but he asks love; a thing that the simplest, the weakest, the poorest, the basest may perform, as well as he that is most learned, most strong, most rich, or most nobly born. If God had required this of you, that you should be able to dissolve doubts, like Daniel, and to dispute subtle questions, what should then become of you that are unlearned? If the Lord should accept of none but such as were strong and valiant, what should then become of women, old men, and children, which are weak and feeble? If God should regard none but the rich and wealthy, what should then become of the poor and needy? To conclude, if God should make choice of none but such as were of noble parentage, what should we do that are the common people? But now he requires such a thing of us, as the poorest and simplest may perform as well as the wealthiest or wisest man in all the world; for if we cannot love, we can do nothing; especially if we cannot love God, that has so loved us, we go not so far as the wicked do, for "sinners also love their lovers," Luke 6:32. And therefore blessed be God, that for the performance of so small a work, has proposed such a great reward; and for the obtaining of such a happy state, has imposed such an easy task. "The eye has not seen, the ear has not heard, neither can the heart conceive, what God has prepared for them that love him," (Isa. 64:4, and 1 Cor. 2:9). And for all these unspeakable joys which God has prepared, he requires no more of us but *love*. How is God enamored of our love? And how unkind shall we be to withhold it from him? He has an innumerable company of angels, which are inflamed with his love; and not content therewith, he sues to have the love of men. God has no need of our love, no more than Elisha had need of Naaman's cleansing; but as Elisha bade Naaman to wash, that he might become clean, (2 Kings 5:10), so God presses us to love, that we might be saved. It is for our good altogether that God requires our love in earth, because he means to set his love on us in heaven. If the man of God had willed Naaman to do some great thing, ought he not to have done it? So if God had willed us to do some great thing, ought we not to have done it? How much more when he says to us, Love, and you shall live forever?

Now, if you would know whether you have this love of God in you, examine your actions, whether they are done with delight and comfort *in amore nihil amari, in love there is no mislike*. It is like the waters of the Jordan in which Naaman washed; for as his flesh, which before was leprous, became fair and tender after his washing, so all our actions, and labors, and afflictions, which before were tedious and irksome, become joyous, and pleasant, and comfortable, after we are once bathed in the love of God. It is like the salt that Elisha cast into the noisome waters, to make them wholesome, (2 Kings 2:21), or like the meal that Elisha put into the bitter pottage to make it sweet, as in (2 Kings 4:41). So the love of God being shed in our hearts by the Holy Spirit, does make all anguish, and sickness, and poverty, and labors, and watchings, and losses, and injuries, and famishment, and banishment, and persecutions, and imprisonment, yes, and death itself, to be welcomed to us. Such was the love of that chosen vessel, who, for the love that he bare to God, waded through all these afflictions, 2 Cor. 11:23, *etc.*, and 12:10, and could not for all these, and many more, be separated from the love of God, as he protests, (Rom. 8:38, 39).

Wherefore, beloved, seeing God, that has done so much for us, requires no more but love of us, which everyone may easily afford, let him be our love, our joy, and whole delight, and then our life will seem delightful. As Jacob served seven years for Rachel, (Gen. 29:20), and "they seemed to him but a few days, for the love that he bare to her;" so when we have once set our love on God, our pain will be pleasure, our sorrow will be joy, our mourning will be mirth, our service will be freedom, and all our crosses will be counted so many comforts, for his sake whom we love a great deal more than Jacob loved Rachel, because his love to us is like Jonathan's love to David, "passing the love of women," (2 Sam. 1:26).

So we have heard what it is that the Lord requires of us,

namely, love. Now, let us see what manner of love he requires, "Thou shall love the Lord your God with all your heart, with all your soul, with all your strength, and with all your thought." Here the Lord sets down the measure of that love which he requires of us; that, first, it must be true and unfeigned, as proceeding from the heart and mind; secondly, that it must be sound and perfect, "with all the heart, with all the mind," *etc.*

As we must love God with the heart, that is, sincerely, so we must love him with all the heart, that is, with a perfect love. God is like a jealous husband, loathe to have a partner in his love, (Exod. 20:5). He will not have half the heart, nor a piece of the heart, but all the heart. When the heart is divided, it dies; therefore God will not have the heart divided, lest it die, because he desires a living, and not a dying heart. He is not like the unkind mother, that would have the child divided, (1 Kings 3:26), but like the natural mother, who, rather than it should be divided, would forego the child. So God will have all or none; if he may not have all the heart, and all the soul, and all the strength, and all the thought, he will have none at all. The devil, or the world, or the flesh, will play a small game, as we use to say, before they will sit out. If they cannot get full possession of our hearts, then they are content to have some part of our love, as it were a little room in our hearts; a wicked thought, or else a consent to sin. Like Pharaoh, the king of Egypt, who, when he could not keep the Israelites still in bondage, would keep their wives and children back; and when this would not be granted, then he was content to let them go and do sacrifice; but their sheep and their cattle must stay behind; and when this might not be obtained, then he desired them only to bless him before they went, (Exod. 12:32). But God is of another mind; he that made all the hearts of men, and tries them, and knows them, and renews and mollifies them, and lightens them, and rules them, and turns them which way it pleases him, will have all the heart, because he has best right to all. As we love a ring or a jewel for his sake that gave it, so we must love all things of this life for his sake that gave them, and him for his own sake above all the rest. This perfect love we can bestow but once, and but one can have it, and whoso has it must be our God. If we set our heart on riches, we make riches our god; therefore David says in Psa. 62:10, "If riches increase, set not your heart on them," If our whole delight is in eating and drinking, then we make a god of our belly; and the apostle tells us, (Phil. 3:19), that our end is damnation. If we be given to wantonness and fleshly pleasure, then Venus is our goddess; and Solomon tells us, (Prov. 6:26), that our end will be beggary. But if we have set our love on God, "the eye has not seen, the ear has not heard, neither has it entered into the heart of man, what God has prepared for them that love him," (1 Cor. 2:9).

But let us examine the words, "Thou shall love your neighbor as yourself." Here are four things to be observed: First, what is required, namely, love, secondly, who must love, you, that is, every man; thirdly, whom we must love, namely, our neighbor; and lastly, how and in what manner we must love him, as we love ourselves.

Concerning the first; as in the former precept, so in this also, the Lord requires love, in which he deals as a kind father with his children, who is desirous to have them so to resemble him as by their conditions every man may know whose they are. Therefore our loving Father, desirous to have us like himself, requires us to be kind and loving one to another, as he is kind to the unkind, to the evil, to the just and to the unjust, (Matt. 5:45). He will have us perfect as he is perfect, he will have us holy as he is holy, he will have us merciful as he is merciful, he will have us loving as he is love itself.

But let us come to the second thing, which shows who is bound to love: you shall love. Under this word you, God comprehends every particular man and woman; as if he should say, you yourself, and not any other: for "You shall love your neighbor." The poor man is not exempted from this precept, because he may love as well as the rich. If he say, I have no wealth, and therefore I cannot show my love to my neighbor; though he have no wealth, yet he has a heart, he has a mind, he has an affection; let him have a loving heart, a loving mind, and a loving affection: if he cannot do well, let him wish well to his neighbor; if he cannot gratify him with anything that he has, let him not envy at anything that the rich man has. For as the rich man shows that he loves his neighbor if he relieves his necessity, so the poor man shows that he loves his neighbor if he grieves not at his prosperity. This, therefore, as a general precept, binds the poor as well as the rich; it is a common yoke laid on the neck, and a common burden laid on the back of every Christian; but yet it is "an easy yoke, and a light burden," (Matt. 11:30), because it is love, which makes all things to seem delightsome. As there are some that would be content to love if they might not give, so there are some that would be content to give if they were sure they should not want; therefore, when it comes to giving, they post it over to their heirs, or to their executors, or to their successors, when they are dead; they are never liberal until they die, and then they are liberal of that which is none of theirs. They think to be excused by the liberality of their heirs; but they are bound to be liberal for themselves; therefore they must not lay the burden on them, because "every man must bear his own burden," (Gal. 6:5).

Now follows the measure of that love which we owe to our neighbor, expressed in the last words, as yourself. Here is the rule whereby our love must be squared, and a most exquisite example of singular love found in ourselves for us to imitate. He does not say, *As he loves you*, or *as he is beloved of others*, but as *yourself*.

Who knows not how well he loves himself? And therefore who can excuse himself and say, I do not know how well I should love my neighbor? But how do we love ourselves? Feignedly, or coldly, or for an hour? I do not know; but truly, and zealously, and every hour. So we must love our neighbor with a true, zealous, and a constant love. We must not pass by, as the priest and the Levite; but pour our oil into their wounds, with the Samaritan, to help, to relieve them and comfort them. We must love our neighbor though he is envious, as David loved Saul, requiting good for evil; and as Joseph loved Potiphar, not enticed to sin against him. "Love is the fulfilling of the law." Now we come to the answer of Christ to the lawyer's question. The question was, "What must be done to inherit eternal life?" The answer is, *Do that which you have said, that is, Love God above all, and your neighbor as yourself; and you shall live, you shall inherit eternal life.*

But here some man may object and say, *Is any man able to do this that God requires?* And if he is not, why then does God command us that which we cannot perform? Herein almighty God deals with us as a father deals with his children. If a man has a son of seven years of age, he will furnish him with bow and arrows, and lead him into the fields; set him to shoot at a mark that is twelve score off, promising to give him some goodly thing if he hits the mark; and though the father know the child cannot shoot so far, yet will he have him aim at a mark beyond his reach, thereby to try the strength and forwardness of his child; and though he shoot short, yet the father will encourage him. Even so almighty God has furnished us with judgment and reason, as it were with certain artillery, whereby we are able to distinguish between good and evil, and sent us into the world, as it were into the open fields, and set his law before us as a mark, as David speaks, promising to give us the kingdom of heaven if we hit the same; and albeit he knows that we cannot hit this mark, that is, keep the law which he has set before us, yet, for the exercise of our faith, and for the testifying of our duty and obedience towards him, he will always have us be aiming at it; and though we come short of that duty and obedience which he requires at our hands, yet does he accept and reward our good endeavor; but if we stubbornly refuse to frame ourselves after his will, then he may justly be angry and displeased with us. Therefore, though you cannot perfectly keep the law of God, yet if you endeavor yourself to the utmost of your power to observe the same, the Lord, that "works in us both the will and the work," will accept the will for the work; and that which is wanting in us, he will supply with his own righteousness. *Amen.*

THE SWEET SONG OF OLD FATHER SIMEON

"Lord, now let Your servant depart in peace, according to Your word. For mine eyes have seen your salvation, which You have prepared before the face of all people; a light to be revealed to the Gentiles, and the glory of Your people Israel."—Luke 2:29-32

This is the sweet song of old father Simeon, in which is set forth the joyful and peaceable death of the righteous, after that they have embraced Christ Jesus with heart and mind unfeignedly, as he did, seeing their death is to be the beginning of a better and more joyful and pleasant life than the former.

But before we proceed farther in it, let us hear a little of that which went before. The evangelist says, verse 25, *etc.,* "And, behold, there was a man in Jerusalem, whose name was Simeon; this man was just, and feared God, and waited for the consolation of Israel, and the Holy Spirit was on him. And a revelation," *etc.*

Simeon feared God. Religion may well be called fear, for there is no religion where fear is wanting; for "the fear of the Lord is the beginning of wisdom," (Prov. 1:7). And this privilege God has given to those that fear him, that they need to fear nothing else.

And waited for the consolation of Israel, Simeon also waited for the consolation of Israel, until he had embraced in his arms him whom he so long longed to see and feel. How many waiters are there in the world! yet few wait as Simeon did; but some wait for honor, some for riches, some for pleasures, some for ease, some for rewards, some for money, some for a dear year, and some for a golden day, as they call it; but Simeon waited, and expected with many a long look, until he had seen and embraced Christ Jesus, the light of the Gentiles, the glory of Israel, the salvation of all that with a faithful and zealous affection and love do wait for his coming,

282

to the comfort of the afflicted, and to the terrifying of the wicked and ungodly, which have not already waited, neither embraced him, as Simeon did.

And waited for the consolation of Israel. Faith in all afflictions does lift up her head, waiting in assured hope beyond all hope; and seeing the clouds scattered over her head, yet she is ever comfortable to herself, saying, *Anon* it will be calm; and although all the friends in the world do fail, yet it never fails nor faints, but even keeps that promise by which the truth of the Spirit of God assures it, until her joy is fulfilled.

And when the parents brought in the child Jesus to do for him according to the customs of the law, then he took him in his arms. Happy Simeon embraced Christ; but not happy that he embraced him with his hands; but therefore happy, because he embraced him in heart. "Happy are the eyes and blessed which see the things that you see, and the ears that hear the things that you hear," says Christ, (Matt. 13:16); but cursed are we that hearing and seeing do not repent; for we cannot be blessed by hearing and seeing only, unless we hear and see with profit, so that we in heart embrace Christ. But we will object that we are Israelites, and are circumcised, and have received the sacrament of Christ's blood, that we might be his people, and he our God. But this will not excuse us, nor make us seem anything better in the sight of God, but rather worse, if we have not ceased to embrace the world, to embrace vanities, and have not unfeignedly embraced the word of God, and also the Lord Jesus Christ. For it is said, that Christ "came among his own, and his own received him not," (John 1:11); but therefore accursed are so many of them as reject their own salvation, which being freely offered to them, they will not stretch forth their hands to receive it; that is, will not attend with their ears to hear it, or at least will not enlarge their hearts to embrace it.

Simeon praised God, Simeon was thankful. Here is the example, but where are they that follow it? If nine lepers be cleansed, yet but one returns to give thanks; then one is all. Unthankfulness is the first guest that sits at the table; for some will not stick to say, that they never said grace since they were children; but if they had said, they never had grace since they were children, I would rather believe them. Do you not say, "Give us this day our daily bread?" If you do, for shame say so no more, beg no more at God's hands, until you are more thankful for that which you have received.

Lord, now let you your servant depart, Simeon waiting for the consolation of Israel, longing to see the Savior, was like the dear panting for the water-brooks, until he had beheld his best beloved; but as soon as he had taken him in his arms whom his soul desired to see, he so thirsted for death, that he thenceforth thought of, sought after, besought God for, nothing, but to leave this life, and hence to depart; for he forthwith, singing, prayed, "Now let you your servant depart." But do you, say some, commend him herein? Did he well? May not any man desire death? May not the fastened ship in a strange land desire to be loosed, to hasten to his longed-for port at home? May not a man imprisoned among bitter enemies desire to be set at liberty, to return to his own country, in freedom to live among his sweet friends? Are we not strangers here, and by unpeaceable, most deadly enemies, our own flesh, the world, and the devil, held prisoners in the chains of sin and manifold infirmities? and is not our home heaven, and the saints and angels our most dear friends? No marvel, then, that Simeon here desires to be loosed, or let depart. And Paul professes he desires to be dissolved, (Phil. 1:23), or unloosed, as ships in a strange land fastened, as strangers among cruel enemies imprisoned. They were unnatural if they did not; it were unreasonable to require they should not; for we not only may think it lawful, but must also acknowledge it even a necessary duty, to desire death. For is there, until then, in us any perfect, yes, any pure obedience of God? Does not sin, as long as this life lasts, dwell in our members? Is there any passage to the perfect life but by the first death? The fish which is taken in the net out of the sea struggles to get in again; and Adam, thrust out of paradise, would fain have been within again: how much more should we be desirous to be settled in the new paradise, in assurance never to be put from thence? Therefore also it is not only our duty to desire death, but also as soon as any clearly sees Christ, presently he desires to die. For though his state be never so pleasant, though his life be most delightful, though he excel in riches, and pleasures, and honors, and knowledge, and glory, and far exceed all that ever were; yet at the sight of Christ he even rejoices to forego all; the love of the world falling away like the mantle of Elijah, when he was wrapped into heaven; and so cries with the apostle, "I desire to be dissolved," that he may be with Christ. For Christ is light, and as soon as they see him, they see also themselves, and the world's false happiness; his glory, and their shame and filthiness, which makes them wish for death, that they may cease to sin against God, and perfectly please him, and enjoy true happiness with him; for all sin is blood in their eyes, and all worldly pleasures vanities.

None but the truly righteous, none but they that by faith are assured they are before God righteous, can rightly desire death. For who would desire a change but for the better? But all that are ignorant of God, all the unfaithful, what knowledge soever they have, cannot be in better ease dead than they are now in living, though most miserably pained; *no*, they cannot be without just fear, when they forego this life, to feel forever the second death. But the faithful, having their consciences quiet, and also joyful in Christ, free from the fear of that death they have deserved, and assured by death to pass to that life which God to all the faithful has promised, earnestly wish to die, in all fervent love of God, and zeal of his glory, that they may cease from offending their good God, and never cease magnifying his mercy; showing by this that they are weary of the service and bondage of Satan and sin, and assured after death to enjoy the true life, most fully glorifying God, and most perfectly pleasing him forever; and therefore also they desire death, not shortening their life, but waiting his leisure and calling, thereby glorifying God, as in their lives they have done and sought to do.

For man was not born at his own will, and therefore

may not die at his own pleasure. Therefore they beg it of God, referring themselves ever to his good will, when, where, and how by death they shall glorify him, still desiring it, but never wilfully procuring it.

Have seen, etc., O Lord, he says, I desire now to be dissolved and free from the bondage of sin, which so long has inhabited in my mortal body; for now he has come by whom you have promised to free us and set us at liberty; he has come by whom you have promised to break the serpent's head; and he has come that will heal our infirmities, and give strength against sin and Satan, by faith and peace towards God, through love. And now, he says, I have embraced him, and thankfully do receive him. I believe and am persuaded that this is the same Messiah whom the Father promised, and the prophets foretold, all Israel longed for and expected, who is the light of the Gentiles, the glory of Israel, and the God of the whole world. So they which love the truth of God, and wait with desire to be fulfilled with the knowledge of it, such shall not die until they have their hearts' desire with contemplation of it.

Have seen thy, etc. There are many sights of Christ; all go not up to the mount, as Peter, James and John, (Matt. 17:1): all do not see his face, with Moses, (Exod. 33); all do not sleep in his lap with John, (John 13:23, 21:20); all are not taken up into heaven, like Paul, (2 Cor. 12:2); all do not embrace him in their arms, with Simeon. But as pleases God, so he shows himself to us; and all that love him, both see him and embrace him. To some he shows himself as in a glass, to some generally, to some particularly; some he calls early, and some he calls late; and there is no hour in the day in which he calls not some to go labor in his vineyard, (Matt. 20). To some he shows himself by angels, and to others by visions. Abraham saw three angels, (Gen. 18:2), Lot saw but two, (Gen. 19:1), Manoah's wife saw but one, (Judges 13:3); and yet one was enough. It is said that Abraham saw Christ's days, (John 8:56); but we see him clearer than Abraham, and clearer than John, if we believe in him as we should. Some see Christ, and not his salvation; and some

286

see his salvation, and do not embrace it. We see Christ when we hear his word, and we embrace his salvation when we believe it; they see him that hear him, they embrace him that follow him. But how can they believe the word of God which do not hear it? How can they embrace Christ which do not know him? And they do this all through ignorance, not having the means to see him, because their leaders are either blind guides, sleepy watchmen, or hireling shepherds.

Your salvation. He did not come by angels, or by men, or by any other means, but only from the alone and eternal God. He calls him "your salvation;" for his name was not given him by Joseph, nor by Mary, but by the angel of God, (Luke 1:31), signifying that he had come from heaven. The Father saw him when he was born, the Spirit came on him when he was baptized, the angels ministered to him in the wilderness, his enemies subscribed to him on the cross, the virgin travailed, the star walked, the wise men came out of far countries to worship him. Then is not this Jehovah, the mighty God, whose birth is glorious, whose life is famous, whose death is meritorious?

Your salvation. The only Savior is here called salvation itself; for if he were called a bare Savior only, then you might likely understand by him some other savior; but here he is called *salvation itself*, to show that there is no other. For there are more saviors, but no more salvations; as there are many ways to death, and yet but one death. The brazen serpent was a figure of Christ, (Num. 21, John 3:14, 15), that they which are stung by sin, by fire, and by the serpent which beguiled Eve, may make speed, because there is no remedy but to come to Christ.

Salvation is born; therefore we were all in the state of condemnation before. Light has come; therefore we sat all in darkness before. Glory has come; therefore we were all loaden with shame before. Life has come; to show that we were all dead in sin before. Life has come, and light, and salvation; life to the dead, light to the blind, and salvation to the damned. For Christ is called salvation, to show that without him we are all damned, fire-brands of hell, heirs of condemnation, and forsaken of God. To him that is sick, it is easy to be thankful when he is whole; but when he is whole, it is harder to be thankful than to be sick.

Your salvation. This word *salvation* is a sweet word, yes, the sweetest word in all the Scripture; and yet many despise this worthy jewel, because they do not know what it is worth; like a bird, which would rather have a barley-corn than a pearl or a jewel, because they do not know the value of it.

"O Lord, what is man, that you are so mindful of him?" (Psa. 8:4). O man, what is God, that you are so unmindful of him? If a friend had given us anything, we would have thanked him heartily for it; but to him that has given us all things, we will not give so much as thanks. Now, therefore, let the rock gush out water again, and let our stony hearts pour forth streams of tears in unfeigned repentance. We have all called on you, but none regards us; as though God were as Baal, and as though Dives felt no pain, nor Lazarus joy, but all were forgotten. Many times Christ comes into the temple, and there is scarce a Simeon to embrace him. The babe is here, but where is Simeon?

If God had not loved us better than we loved ourselves, we should have perished long before this; and yet we embrace not Christ, as Simeon, who has saved us from temporal and spiritual punishment. We are invited to a banquet; he who calls us to it is God. What is the banquet? *Salvation.* Who are the guests? The angels and the saints. What is the fare? Joy, peace, righteousness. This is the fare, and we invite you everyone; yet who will come at our bidding? Some for want of faith, some for want of love, some for want of knowledge, have despised his holy banquet; yet to this are you called still, O soul unworthy to be beloved.

Which you have prepared before the face of all people, etc. He speaks this to the end that the eyes of all mankind may be fixed on him, as the eyes of all Israel were fixed on the brazen serpent in the wilderness, (Num. 21); and when they are stung with the sting of that fiery serpent which deceived our forefathers, they may fly to him for help, lest they perish in their sin, and their blood be on their own heads.

Which you have prepared. He was prepared long ago, as it does most plainly appear; for the virgin which bare him, the place of his birth, the poor state in which he was, his miracles, his apostles, his torments, his cross, his death, his resurrection and ascension into heaven, all these were foreshowed and foretold long before they came to pass. Therefore some said, *Who is this that is so often spoken of by the prophets?* Who is this that can do many miracles that the scribes and Pharisees cannot do? that can raise the dead, that can cease the winds, that can calm the waters, at whose suffering the earth quaked, the sun hid his face, darkness came over all, and who, being dead, rose again by his own power, and ascended into heaven in the sight of a great multitude? How can it be then but it must be known "before the face of all people," which was so manifest by dreams, by visions, by oracles, by power, by authority, and everything? For there was nothing which did not have a tongue to speak for God. Everything was prepared for him before he came to be revealed. He came not in the beginning nor in the ending. He did not come in the ending, that we which come after him might long for his second coming. He came not in the beginning, because that such a Prince as he should have many banners and triumphs before him. He did not come in the beginning, because the eyes of faith should not be dazzled in him, and lest they which should live in the latter times should forget him and his coming, which was so long before; even as you forget that which I have said as soon as you are gone from here. He did not come in the beginning, because if he had come before man had sinned, man would have acknowledged no need of a physician; but he came when man had sinned, and had felt the smart of sin. For when they were cast out of paradise, they ran to Christ, as the Israelites did to the serpent. He did not come in the beginning, but in the perfect age of the world, to show that he brought with him perfection, perfect joy, perfect peace, perfect wisdom, perfect righteousness, perfect justice, perfect truth; signifying thereby, that notwithstanding he came in the perfect age of it, yet he found all things imperfect.

If you love joy and gladness, Christ is joy and gladness; if you love comfort, why, Christ is the comfort of all that bear his cross; if you love life, Christ is eternal life; if you love peace, Christ is peace; if you love riches, Christ is full of heavenly riches, and full of liberality, to bestow them on all such as love God. So Christ is all in all to the godly, and they have more joy in Christ always, and in all things, than the richest and most glorious and sumptuous prince in the world, than Solomon himself had in worldly riches, honors, pleasures, joy, ease, or felicity. For the wicked, which put their trust in riches, and make them gods of gold and money, of ease and pleasures, though they do all that they can to fulfill their lusts, and take never so much pleasure, and be never so merry, yet they can have no true joy, nor peace of conscience; for all the peace, the mirth and sport they have is but deceit, all false and undurable, like the grass, green in the morning, and withered during the night. So then we see, that perfect joy can be had in nothing but in God and in Jesus Christ. Wherefore, as by the stream you may be led to the fountain; even so let the joy and peace of this life serve to lead us to God, who is perfect joy and peace; and there let us rest, like the wise men, which were guided by the star to come to the true Son of grace, Jesus Christ, when he was born. And if we rest not in him when we have found him, there is no rest for us; we shall be like the restless dove, which fluttered about, and found no rest any way until she returned to the ark.

To be revealed. You must have an eye to the future tense; that which is not, shall be. As for example, Solomon was wise, but he is foolish; Samson was strong, but he is weak; Judas was a preacher, but he is a traitor; Paul was a persecutor, but he is a preacher; Peter was a denier of Christ, but now he is a bold professor of Christ; Moses was learned in the wisdom of the Egyptians, but now he is learned in the wisdom of God, by which the wisdom of the Egyptians is made but mere foolishness in the sight of God. Others, as heathen philosophers, Plato, Aristotle, Cato, Crates, and such like, were counted very wise men in the sight of the world; yes, they wrote so many books full of wisdom, and also adorned with notable sentences and witty sayings, that one would think all wisdom were buried with them, so famous were they, and so full of earthly understanding, teaching manners, counsels, and policies. Yet, for my part, I have neither seen nor heard of any such being wise in worldly things, and without the wisdom of God, but that they have committed some notorious foolishness in the sight of all men. For if your wisdom consist in eloquence of words, in profundity of wit, to gain craftily and spend warily, to invent laws, to expound riddles, and interpret dreams, to tell fortunes, and prophesy of matters by learning, all your wisdom is but vexation of the spirit; for all these, without the fear of God, do us no more good than their mind did these philosophers, which notwithstanding sat in darkness.

What then is to be done? As Jacob said to his wives and children, *Give me your idols, that I may bury them*, (Gen. 35); so I say to you, *Give me your superstitions, that I may bury them, that they may remain with you or in you no longer, to the dishonor of God, offending of your weak brethren, or to my grief.* For I am jealous over you; and because you are mine, and I am yours, oh that my voice were as the whirlwind, to beat down, root out, and blow away all your superstitions, that they may no longer reign among you! Or rather, oh that Christ, which is our light, were come into us all, and shined so bright, that we were ashamed of all our darkness; of all, not of mind only, but of will also, and of works, that we no longer would walk in darkness. *Amen.*

THE BENEFIT OF CONTENTMENT

"Godliness is great gain, if a man is content with that he has."—1 Tim. 6:6

Because when we preach, we do not know whether we shall preach again, my care is, to choose fit and proper texts, to speak that which I would speak, and that which is necessary for you to hear. Therefore, thinking with myself what doctrine would be most fit for you, I sought for a text which speaks against *covetousness*, which I may call the Londoners' sin. Although God has given you more than others, which should turn covetousness into thankfulness, yet as the ivy grows with the oak, so covetousness has grown with riches; every man wishes the philosopher's stone; and who is within these walls that thinks he has enough, though there are so many that have too much? As the Israelites murmured as much when they had manna, as when they were without it, (Exod. 16:2, Num. 11:4); so they which have riches covet as much as they which are without them; that conferring your minds and your wealth together, I may truly say, this city is rich, if it were not covetous. This is the devil which bewitches you, to think that you have not enough, when you have more than you need. If you cannot choose but covet riches, I will show you riches which you may covet, "Godliness is great riches." In which words, as Jacob craved of his wives and his servants to give him their idols, that he might bury them, (Gen. 35:4); so Paul craves your covetousness, that he might bury it; and that you might be no losers, he offers you the vantage; instead of gain, he proposes great gain. "Godliness is great gain;" as if he should say, will you covet little gain before great? You have found little joy in money, you shall find great joy in the Holy Spirit; you have found little peace in the world, you shall find great peace in conscience. So seeing the world strive for the world, like beggars thrusting at a dole, lawyer against lawyer, brother against brother, neighbor against neighbor, for the golden apple, that poor Naboth cannot hold his own, because so many Ahabs are sick for his vineyard, (1 Kings 21:4); when he had found the disease, like a skillful physician, he goes about to pick out the greedy worm which makes men so hungry, and sets such a glass before them that will make a shilling seem as great as a pound, a cottage seem as fair as a palace, and a plough seem as goodly as a diadem; that he which has but twenty pounds, shall be as merry as he which has an hundred; and he which has an hundred, shall be as jocund as he which has a thousand; and he which has a thousand, shall be as well contented as he which has a million.

He will not only prove godliness to be gain, but great gain; as if he should say, more gainful than your wares, and rents, and fines, and interests, as though he would make the lawyer, and merchant, and mercer, and draper, and patron, and landlord, and all the men of riches believe, that godliness will make them rich sooner than covetousness.

He was not content to call godliness gain, but he calls it *great gain*; as if he would say, gain, and more than gain; riches, and better than riches; a kingdom, and greater than a kingdom. As when the prophets would distinguish between the idol-gods and the living God, they call him the great God; so the gain of godliness is called great gain. The riches of the world are called earthly, transitory, snares, thorns, dung, as though they were not worthy to be counted riches; and therefore, to draw the earnest love of men from them, the Holy Spirit brings them in with these names of disdain, to disgrace them with their loves; but when he comes to godliness, which is the riches of the soul, he calls it great riches, heavenly riches, unsearchable riches, everlasting riches, with all the names of honor, and all the names of pleasure, and all the names of happiness. As a woman trims and decks herself with an hundred ornaments, only to make her amiable, so the Holy Spirit sets out godliness with names of honor, and names of pleasure, and names of happiness, as it were in her jewels, with letters of commendation to make her be beloved. Lest any riches should compare with godliness, he gives it a name above others, and calls it *great* riches, as if he would make a distinction between *riches* and another kind of *riches*, between the gain of covetousness and the gain of godliness, the peace of the world and the peace of conscience, the joy of riches and the joy of the Holy Spirit. The worldly men have a kind of peace, and joy, and riches. But I cannot call it greats because they have not enough, they are not contented as the godly are; therefore only godliness has this honor, to be called great riches. The gain of covetousness is nothing but wealth; but the gain of godliness is wealth, and peace, and joy, and love of God, and the remission of sins, and everlasting life. Therefore only godliness has this honor, to be called great gain. Riches makes bate, but godliness makes peace; riches breeds covetousness, but godliness brings contentment; riches makes men unwilling to die, but godliness makes men ready to die; riches often hurt the owner, but godliness profits the owner and others. Therefore, only godliness has this honor, to be called great riches.

So every labor has an end, but covetousness has none; like a suitor in law, which thinks to have an end this term, and that term, and the lawyer which should procure his peace, prolongs his strife, because he has an action to his purse, as his adversary has to his land; so he which is set on coveting, does drink brine, which makes him thirst more, and cries no haven until he arrive at death; when he has lied, he is ready to lie again; when he has sworn, he is ready to swear again; when he has deceived, he is ready to deceive again; when the day is past, he would it were to begin again; when the term is ended, he wishes it were to come again; and though his house be full, and his shop full, and his coffers full, and his purse full, yet his heart is not full, but lank and empty, like the disease which we call the wolf, that is always eating, and yet keeps the body lean. The ant does eat the food which he finds; the lion does refresh himself with the prey that he takes, but the covetous man lies by his money, as a sick man sits by his meat, and has no power to taste it, but to look on it; like the prince to whom Elisha said, that he should "see the corn with his eyes, but none should come within his mouth," (2 Kings 7:22). So the covetous man makes a fool of himself. He covets to covet; he gathers to gather; he labors to labor; he cares to care; as though his office were to fill a coffer full of angels, and then to die like an ass, which carries treasure on his back all day, and at night they are taken from him, which did him no good but load him. How happy were some, if they did not know gold from lead? "If you be wise," says Solomon, "you shall be wise for yourself," Prov. 9:12. But he which is covetous, is covetous against himself. For what a plague is this, unless one would kill himself, for a man to spend all his life in carking, and pining, and scraping, as though he should do nothing but gather in this world, to spend in the next, unless he is sure that he should come again when he is dead, to eat those scraps which he has gotten with all his stir? Therefore covetousness may well be called misery, and the covetous miserable, for they are miserable indeed

When the law is ended, if the man is not content, he is in trouble still; when his disease is cured, if he is not content, he is sick still; when his want is supplied, if he is not content, he is in want still; when bondage is turned into liberty, if he is not content, he is in bondage still; but though he is in law, and sickness, and poverty, and bondage, yet, if he is content, he is free, and rich, and merry, and quiet, even as Adam was warm though he had no clothes, (Gen. 2:25).

Such a commander is contentment, that wheresoever she sets foot, an hundred blessings wait on her; in every disease she is a physician, in every strife she is a lawyer, in every doubt she is a preacher, in every grief she is a comforter, like a sweet perfume, which takes away the evil scent, and leaves a pleasant scent for it. As the unicorn's horn dipped in the fountain makes the waters which were corrupt and noisome clear and wholesome on the sudden, so, whatsoever estate godliness comes to, it says like the apostles, "Peace be to this house," (Luke 10:5), peace be to this heart, peace be to this man.

I may liken it to the five loaves and two fishes, wherewith Christ fed five thousand persons, and yet there were twelve baskets full of that which was left, which could not fill one basket when it was whole. So their little feast was made a great feast; so the godly, though they have but little for themselves, yet they have something for others, like the widow's mite, (Matt 12:41); that they may say as the disciples said to Christ, they want nothing, though they have nothing, (Luke 22:35). Contentment wants nothing, and a good heart is worth all. For if she wants bread, she can say as Christ said, "I have another bread," (John 4:32); if she wants riches, she can say, I have other riches; if she wants strength, she can say, I have other strength; if she wants friends, she can say, I have other friends. So the godly find all within that they seek without. Therefore, if you see a man contented with what he has, it is a great sign that godliness is entered into him, for the heart of man was made a temple for God, and nothing can fill it but God alone. Therefore Paul says after his conversion, that which he could never say before his conversion, "I have learned to be content," (Phil. 4:12). First he learned godliness, then godliness taught him contentment. Now (says Paul), "I have learned to be content;" as though this were a lesson for every Christian to learn, to be content.

When the churl's barns were full, he advised his soul to take rest, thinking to gain rest by covetousness, that he might say, *Riches gain rest, as well as godliness*; but see what happened: that night when he began to take his rest, riches, and rest, and soul, and all, were taken from him, (Luke 12:16). Did he not gain fair? Would he have taken such pains if he had thought of such rest? Covetousness may gain riches, but it cannot gain rest; you may think like this churl, to rest when your barns, and shops, and coffers are full; but you shall find it true which Isaiah says, "There is no rest to the ungodly," (Isa. 58:22); therefore the wise man, to prevent all hope of rest, or honor, or profit by sin, speaks as though he had tried, "A man cannot be established by iniquity," (Prov. 12:3). Therefore he cannot be quieted, nor satisfied by the gain of deceit, or bribes, or lies, or usury, which is iniquity. Therefore blessed is the man whom godliness does make rich; "for when the blessing of the Lord makes rich," says Solomon, "he does add no sorrow to it;" but, he says, "the revenue of the wicked is trouble," as though his money were care about. Wherefore let patron, and landlord, and lawyer, and all, say now, that Paul has chosen the better riches, "which thief, nor moth, nor canker can corrupt;" these are the riches at last, that we must dwell with, when all the rest which we have lied for, and sworn for, and fretted for, and cozened for, and broken our sleep for, and lost many sermons for, forsake us, like servants which change their masters; then godliness shall seem as great gain to us as it did to Paul; and he which loved the world most, would give all that he has for a dram of faith, that he might be sure to go to heaven, when he is dead, though he went towards hell so long as he lived.

Therefore what counsel shall I give you, but as Christ counseled his disciples, "Is not friends to riches," but "make you friends of riches;" and know this, that if you cannot say as Paul says, "I have learned to be content," (Phil. 4:12), godliness is not yet come to your house; for the companion of godliness is contentment; which, when she comes, will bring you all things. Therefore as Christ says, "If the Son make you free, you shall be free indeed," (John 7:36); so I say, if godliness make you rich, you shall be rich indeed. The Lord Jesus make you doers of that which you have heard. *Amen.*

THE AFFINITY OF THE FAITHFUL

"Then came to him his mother and brethren, and could not come near him for the press. And it was told him by certain which said, "Your mother and brethren stand without and would see you." But he answered and said to them, "My mother and brethren are those which hear the word of God, and do it.""— Luke 8:19-21

Here is Christ preaching, a great press hearing, his mother and his friends interrupting, and Christ again withstanding the interruption, with a comfortable doctrine of his mercies towards them which hear the word of God and do it. When Christ was about a work, and many were gathered together to hear him, the devil thought with himself, as the priests and Sadducees did in the fourth chapter of the Acts: If I let him alone so, all the world will follow him, and I shall be like Rachel, without children; therefore, devising the likeliest policy to frustrate and disgrace but one of his sermons, thereby to make the people unwilling to hear him again, as he set Eve on Adam, (Gen. 3:6), and made Job's wife his instrument, (Job 2:9), when he could not fit it himself; so he sends Christ's mother, and puts in the minds of his kinsmen, to come to him at that instant, when he was in this holy exercise, and call on him while he was preaching, to come away, and go with them. Christ seeing the serpent's dealing, how he made his mother the tempter, that all the auditory might go away empty, and say where they came, *We heard the man which is called Jesus, and he began to preach to us, with such words, as though he would carry us to heaven*; but in the midst of his sermon came his mother and brethren to him, that it might be known what a kinsman they had; and so soon as he heard that they were come, suddenly he broke off his sermon, and slipped away from us, to go and make merry with them. Christ, I say, seeing this train laid by Satan, to disgrace him (as he does all his ministers), did not leave off speaking, as they thought he would; but as if God had appointed all this to credit and renown him, that which was noised here to interrupt his doctrine, he takes for an occasion to teach another doctrine, that there is a nearer conjunction between Christ and the faithful, than between the mother and the son, which are one flesh. Therefore when they say, "Your mother and brethren are come to speak with you," he points to his hearers and says, "These are my mother and brethren which hear the word of God *and do it.*"

Note, that in holy Scripture there are four sorts of brethren: brethren by nature, so Esau and Jacob are called brethren, (Gen. 27:30), because they had one father and one mother; brethren by nation, so all the Jews are called brethren, (Deut. 15:1), because they were of one country; brethren by consanguinity, so all are called brethren which are of one family, and so Abraham called Lot his brother, (Gen. 13:8), and Sarah his sister, (Gen. 12:13), because they were of one line; brethren by profession, so all Christians are called brethren, (Matt. 23), because they are of one religion. These are brethren of the third order, that is, of consanguinity, because they were of one family.

Now, when his mother and his brethren were come to see him, it is said, that they could not come near him for the press. Here were auditors enough. Christ so flowed now with his disciples, that his mother could have no room to hear him; but after a while it was low water again. When the shepherd was struck, the sheep were scattered, (Matt. 26:31); when he preached in the streets, and the temples, and the fields, then many flocked after him; but when he preached on the cross, then they left him which said they would never forsake him; then there was a great press to see him die, as there was here to hear him preach. And many of these which seemed like brethren and sisters, were his betrayers, and accusers, and persecutors, (Matt. 27); so inconstant are we in our zeal, more than in anything else. So much of their coming and calling to Christ Now, to the doctrine which lies in it

Here are two speakers: one says, "Your mother and your brethren are come to speak to you," the other says, "Those are my mother and brethren which hear the word of God and do it." The scope of the evangelist is this: first, *that Christ would not hinder his doctrine for mother, or brethren, or any kinsman*; then, to show that there is a nearer conjunction between Christ and the faithful, than the mother and the son. The first is written for our comfort; touching the first, he which teaches us to honor our father and mother, (Exod. 20), does not teach here to condemn father and mother, because he speaks of another mother, for it is said, that "he was obedient to his parents." This he shows, when, being found in the temple among the doctors, he left it all, to go with his mother, because she sought him; so he honored her, that he left all for her, (Luke 2:46). This he showed again at his death; being on the cross, he was not unmindful of her, for pointing to John, he said, "Mother, behold your son;" and pointing to her, he said, "Behold your mother," (John 19:26).

Three things children receive of their parents, life, maintenance, and instruction. For these three they owe three others; for life, they owe love; for maintenance, they owe obedience; for instruction, they owe reverence. For life, they must be loved as fathers; for maintenance, they must be obeyed as masters; for instruction, they must be reverenced as tutors. But as there is a King of kings, which must be obeyed above kings, so there is a Father of fathers, which must be obeyed above fathers; therefore sometimes you must answer like the son, when he was bid to go into his father's vineyard, "I will go;" and sometimes you must answer as Christ answered, "I must go about my Father's business,"

When two milk cows carried the ark of the Lord to Bethshemesh, their calves were shut up at home, (1 Sam. 6:10), because the cows should not stay, when they heard their calves cry after them; so when you go about the Lord's business, you shall hear a cry of your father, and your mother, and your brethren, and your sisters, and your kindred, to stay you, but then you must think of another Father, as Christ thought of another mother; and so, as those kind went on until the Lord brought them where the ark should rest, so you shall go on until the Lord bring you where you shall have rest. It is better to fly from our friends, as Abraham did, (Gen. 11:3, and 12:11), than to stay with some friends, as Samson did with Delilah, (Judges 16:14), *etc.*

I may say, Beware of kinsmen, as well as our Savior said, *Beware of men*, for this respect of a family relation Eli made his sons priests, (1 Sam. 2); and this respect of familial relation has made many like priests in England. This respect of familial relation has made Samuel's sons Judges, (1 Sam. 8:1); and this respect of familial relation has made many like judges in England. This respect of familial relation brought Tobias into the Levites' chamber, (Neh. 13:4, 5); and this respect of familial relation has brought many gentlemen into preachers' livings, which will not out again. As Christ preferred his *spiritual* kinsmen, so we prefer our earthly kinsmen. Many privileges, many offices, and many benefices, have stooped to this voice, *Your mother calls you*, or, *Your kinsmen would have you.* As this voice came to Christ while he was laboring, so many such voices come to us while we are laboring. One says, *Pleasure would speak with you*; another says, *Profit would speak with you*; another says, *Ease would speak with you*; another says, *A deanery would speak with you*; another says, *A bishopric would speak with you*; another says, *The court would speak with you.*

Here is a genealogy of Christ, which Matthew and Luke never spoke of. As Christ says, "I have another bread which you do not know;" so he says, I have other kinsmen which you do not know.

St. John, writing to a lady which brought up her children in the fear of God, calls her "the elect lady," (2 John 1), showing that the chief honor of ladies, and lords, and princes, is to be elect of God. St. Luke, speaking of certain Bereans, which received the word of God with love, calls them "more noble men than the rest," (Acts 17:11), showing, that God counts none noble but such as are of a noble spirit. As John calls none elect but the virtuous; and Luke calls none noble but the religious; so Christ calls none his kinsmen but the righteous; and of those only he says, "These are my mother and my brethren, which hear the word of God and do it."

Now for this love. Christ calls them by all the names of love; his father, and his brethren, and his sisters. In Rom. 6, they are called his servants; if that is not enough, in John 15, they are called his friends; if that is not enough, in Luke 24, they are called his brethren; if that is not enough, in Mark 1, they are called his children; if that is not enough, here they are called his mother; if that is not enough, in Song of Songs the 5th chapter they are called his spouse, to show that he loves them with all love; the mother's love, the brother's love, the sister's love, the master's love, and the friend's love.

If all these loves could be put together, yet Christ's love exceeds them all; and the mother, and the brother, and the sister, and the child, and the kinsman, and the friend, and the servant, would not do and suffer so much among them all, as Christ has done and suffered for us alone. Such a love we kindle in Christ, when we hear his word, and do it, that we are as dear to him as all his kindred together.

Now as we are his mother, so should we carry him in our hearts, as his mother did in her arms. As we are his brethren, so we should prefer him, as Joseph did Benjamin, (Gen. 43:34). As we are his spouse, so we should embrace him, as Isaac did Rebekah; if you be a kinsman, do like a kinsman.

Now we come to the marks of these kinsmen, which I may call the arms of his house. As Christ says, "By this all men shall know my disciples, if they love one another;" so he says, By this shall all men know my kinsmen, if they "hear the word of God, and do it."

As there is a kindred by the father's side, and a kindred by the mother's side, so there is a kindred of hearers, and a kindred of doers. In Matthew it is said, "He which hears the will of my Father and does it;" here it is said, "He which hears the word of God, and does it;" both are one, for his word is his will, and there-fore it is called his will, (Psa.119).

As he spoke there of doing, so he speaks here of a certain rule, which he calls, the word of God, whereby all men's works must be squared; for if I do all the works that I can to satisfy another's will or mine own will, it avails me nothing with God; because I do it not for God. Therefore he which always before followed his own will, when he was stricken down, and began to repent himself, he presently cried out, "Lord, what will you have me do?" (Acts 9); as if he should say, I will do no more as men would have me, or as the devil would have me, or according as the flesh would have me, but as you would have me. So David prayed, "Teach me, O Lord, to do your will," not my will; for we do not need to be taught to do our own will, no more than a cuckoo to sing cuckoo, her own name. *Every man can go to hell without a guide.*

Here is the rule now; if you live by it, then you are kin to Christ. As other kindreds go by birth and marriage, so this kindred goes by faith and obedience. Hearers are but half kin, as it were in a far degree; but they which hear and do, are called his mother, which is the nearest kindred of all. Therefore if you have the deed, then are you kin indeed; there is no promise made to hearers, nor to speakers, nor to readers; but all promises are made to believers or to doers.

So have I showed you Christ preaching, a great press hearing, his friends and kinsmen interrupting, and Christ again withstanding the interruption; by this you may see what a spite the devil has to hinder one sermon; therefore no marvel though he cause so many to be put to silence; no marvel though he stand so against a learned ministry; no marvel though he raise up such slanders on preachers; no marvel though he write so many books against the Christian government in the church; no marvel though he make so many non-residents; no marvel though he ordain so many dumb priests; for these make him the god of this world; the devil is afraid that one sermon will convert us, and we are not moved with twenty; so the devil thinks better of us than we are.

Again, by this you may learn how to withstand temptations; whether it is your father which tempts, or your mother which tempts, or your brother which tempts, or your sister which tempts, or your kinsman which tempts, or ruler which tempts, or master which tempts, or wife which tempts. As Christ would not know his mother against his Father, so you should not know any father, or mother, or brother, or sister, or friend, or kinsman, or master, or child, or wife, against God.

If the mother's suit may be refused sometime, a nobleman's letter may be refused too; he that can turn his hindrance to a furtherance, as our Savior did here, makes use of everything. Again, by this you may learn how to choose your friends. As Christ counted none his kinsmen, but such as "hear the word of God, and do it;" so we should make none our familiars, but such as Christ counts his kinsmen. Again, you may see the difference between Christ and the world; Christ calls the godly his kinsmen, be they never so poor, and we scorn to call the poor our kinsmen, be they never so honest; so proud is the servant above his Master. Again, by this you see how Christ is to be loved; for when he calls us his mother, he shows us the way to love him as a mother; for indeed he is the mother of his mother, and his brethren too. Again, by this, all vaunting and boasting of kindred is cut off. Glory not in that you have a gentleman to your father, glory not that you have a knight to your brother, but glory that you have a Lord to your brother.

Therefore, now we may conclude. You have heard the word; if you go away and do it, then you are the mother, brethren, and sisters of the heavenly King, to whom, with the Father and the Holy Spirit, be all praise, majesty and dominion, now and evermore. *Amen.*

MARY'S CHOICE

"Now it came to pass, as they went, that he entered into a certain town: and a certain woman, named Martha received him into her house. Now she had a sister called Mary, which also sat at Jesus' feet, and heard his preaching. But Martha was cumbered about much serving, and came to him, and said, "Master, Do you not care that my sister has left me to serve alone? bid her therefore that she help me." And Jesus answered and said to her, "Martha, Martha, you care and are troubled about many things. But one thing is needful; Mary has chosen the good part which shall not be taken away from her."—Luke 10:38-42

Oh happy house, that entertained such a guest! But three times as happy inhabitants, to whom such a guest would vouchsafe to come! When he came to the swinish Gadarenes, they desired him to depart out of their coasts, preferring their swine above their Savior, (Luke 8); but this godly family received him into their houses, preferring their God before their gold, and the health of souls before their worldly wealth. They received him into their house, who had not a house in which to put his head, (Matt. 8:19), in which their hospitality is commended, and shall certainly be rewarded at the dreadful day; for with this and such like works of mercy, the Lord shall answer the sentence of judgment, which is to be denounced against the wicked, that never exercised those works of mercy.

Let us learn by their example to be harborers, and given to hospitality, which is so often commended to us in the Scripture, and shall be so richly rewarded at the last day. Those godly fathers, Abraham and Lot, entertained angels in the habit of strangers, (Gen. 18 and 19); so we may duly entertain Christ Jesus in the habit of a poor man, of a blind man, or of a lame man; and whatsoever is done to any of these that are his members, he accounts and accepts as done to himself.

When Martha had so entertained Christ, as he was

there in her house, Mary began to entertain him, as he was God into her heart; she sat at his feet to hear his preaching; for no sooner was Christ come into the house, but that he took occasion to teach and to instruct the family; and instead of bodily food, which they bestowed on him, he gave them the food of the soul. So he always shows himself a thankful guest, into what house soever he enters; he leaves better things behind him than he finds. He does not love to be in Zacchaeus' debt for his dinner, for instead of it he brings salvation to his house, (Luke 19); neither does he leave his supper unpaid for here, for instead of it he bestows on them an heavenly sermon. This should be the exercise of faithful ministers, when they are invited to great feasts, that as they are called the salt of the earth, (Matt. 5:13), which serves to season the meats, to make them savory, and preserve them from putrefaction, so they should season the table-talk with some godly conference, to minister grace to the hearers, (Eph. 4:29).

These sisters were godly women, and both earnest favorers of Jesus Christ, and yet in the manner of their devotion there is such difference, that the worldly affection of the one may in some sort be misliked, in respect of the godly exercise and practice of the other. Martha is sore encumbered with much serving, where a little service had been sufficient; but Mary is attentive to hear the word of God, which never can be heard sufficiently.

Mary sits to hear the word, as Christ used to sit when he preached the word, (Matt. 5, Luke 4, John 8), to show that the word is to be preached and heard *with a quiet mind.* In a still night every voice is heard, and when the body is quiet, the mind most commonly is quiet also. But Martha is troubled with other affairs, and therefore unfit to hear the word, as the ground that is surcharged with stones, or overgrown with weeds and thorns, is unfit to receive the seed, or yield any fruit to him that tills it. As often therefore as we come to hear the word of God, we must not come with distracted minds, we must not trouble ourselves with the cares of this life, which, as our Savior said, are thorns to choke the word, and to make it unfruitful. For Moses was unfit to talk with God, until he had put off his shoes, (Exod. 3), and the blind man unfit to come to Christ, until he had thrown away his cloak, (Matt. 10); so we must think ourselves unfit to hear the word, and unapt for every heavenly exercise, until we have put off our shoes, that is, our worldly cogitations and affections.

So in Christ we have the patience of a good pastor, and in Mary the pattern of a good hearer. Let ministers learn by his example to take all occasions to preach the word, to be instant in season and out of season, (2 Tim. 4:2); and let Christians learn by her example, first, to seek the kingdom of God and his righteousness, and then to provide for the things of this life, (Matt. 6).

While Mary was careful for the food of the soul, Martha was curious to provide food for the body; her greatest care was to entertain Christ, and to make him good cheer, to testify her thankful mind to him that had done such great things for them: he had raised her brother Lazarus from death to life; therefore he was worthy to be well entertained.

It was well done therefore of Martha to show her thankful mind to Christ, but it was not well done at that time to show herself thankful in that manner; it was then time to hear the word, for at that time Christ preached the word; it was no time for her to spend that time in other affairs, and to neglect the greatest affairs, the means of her own salvation.

It was not unlawful for Martha to labor on, more than it was unlawful for Peter to sleep, (Matt. 25); but when Christ was preaching, it was no time for her to be so busy in serving, no more than it was time for Peter to sleep when Christ willed him so earnestly to watch and pray. When Christ preached out of Simon's ship to the people that stood on the shore, (Luke 5), it was no time for Peter to play the fisherman. But when Christ had left speaking, and commanded him to launch into the deep, then it was time for Peter to let down the net.

There is a time in which we ought to labor in our vocation, and a time in which we ought to hear the word; and as we may not utterly neglect our lawful callings to follow sermons, so must not we bestow the Sabbath, which is consecrated to the service of God, in following the works of our vocation. All things have their appointed time, says the wise man, (Eccles. 3), and everything is seemly in his convenient season; but when things are done preposterously and out of order, there follows confusion.

The repetition of Martha's name argues the vehemency and earnestness of this admonition. The Lord is fain to be very earnest and importunate with us, before he can reclaim us. So when God spoke to Abraham, he called him twice by name; Christ called Peter thrice by name, (John 21), to cause him to make his threefold confession, to make amends for his threefold denial. And when the Lord spoke to Samuel, he called him four several times by name before he answered, for such is the great mercy of God, that he is content to admonish us often of our duty; and such is the dullness and perverseness of our crooked nature, that we cannot be gained by the first admonition; but the Lord must call us often and earnestly, before we will hearken to him.

There are two things in the speech of Christ to be observed: the first is, his *modest reprehension* of Martha's *immoderate* care; the other is, his *friendly defense* of Mary's choice. Though Martha was very careful to entertain Christ in the best manner, yet if he perceive anything in her worthy reprehension, he will not stick to tell her of it; he will not soothe her in her saying, nor smooth her in her own conceit, for all the trouble and cost that she bestows on him. If we be often invited to some man's table, and kindly entertained, it would be unkindly taken if we should find fault with any disorder; but forasmuch as all Christ's actions are the instructions of Christians, therefore every Christian, but especially preachers, whom it more specially concerns, must learn by this example how to behave themselves, when they are invited to great feasts, namely, speak their conscience freely when they see a fault The best requital that we can make for our good cheer, is to give good counsel and wholesome admonitions to them that invite us.

So is Martha reprehended for her curiosity; now let us see how Mary is excused, and commended for her godly care. *One thing is necessary*, says Christ; and what is that one thing? Even *to hear the word preached, which is the power of God to salvation, to everyone that believes*. A man may better want all things than that one needful thing; and yet we desire all other things, and neglect that one thing, which is so needful.

This one thing has Mary chosen, and therefore has chosen the better part. Martha's part is good, because it provides for this present life; but Mary's part is better, because it leads to eternal life. It is good to be occupied about our calling, to get our living; but it is better to be occupied in hearing the word, which is able to save our souls. As the head and the foot are both needful in the body, so Mary and Martha are both needful in a commonwealth; man has two vocations, the one earthly by his labor, the other heavenly by his prayer. There is the active life, which consists in practicing the affairs of this life, in which man shows himself to be like himself; and there is the contemplative life, which consists in the meditation of divine and heavenly things, in which man shows himself to be like the angels; for they which labor in their temporal vocations, do live like men; but they which labor in spiritual matters, live like angels. When they hear the word, God speaks to them; when they pray, they speak to God; so that there is a continual conference between God and them, because they are continually exercised in hearing and praying.

Christ loved Martha for her hospitality, as Isaac loved Esau for his venison. So did he love Mary for diligence in hearing his word, as Rebekah loved Jacob for hearkening to her voice. A nurse which has her breast full of milk, does love the child that sucks it from her; and Christ which has his breast full of heavenly milk, is glad when he has children to suck the same; let us therefore, as the apostle wants us, (1 Pet. 2:12), "laying aside all maliciousness, and all guile, and dissimulation, and envy, and all evil speaking, as new born babes, desire the sincere milk of the word, that we may grow thereby," to be perfect men in Christ Jesus. Let us breathe after the fountain of the living water, which springs up into eternal life; and as the fainty dear desires the water-brook to quench his thirst, (Psa. 52:1). And forasmuch as many things are so troublesome, and one thing is so needful, let us seek that one needful thing, the end of all things, *even to fear God and keep his commandments. Amen.*

THE CHRISTIAN'S SACRIFICE: EPISTLE DEDICATORY

To my late Auditors, the Congregation of Clement

Danes, all the good will which I can wish.

Beloved in Christ Jesus, my first fruits, I have nothing but this mite to leave with you, which is the sum of all my sermons. You have heard it already; and as the apostle calls the Corinthians *his epistle*, (2 Cor. 3:2), so *you* should be *my sermon*; that is, my sermon should be printed in your hearts, as this is printed in paper. If you have not given your hearts to him that sent for them, now think that God has sent for them again, and hear me writing, whom you cannot hear speaking. Take not custom for religion; shun occasion as well as sin; seek the use of everything; desire not to have your kingdom here. And so I leave you all with Christ, whom I have preached, to bring forth the fruit of that seed which is sown, beseeching you for all the love that you have of heaven, that you would not count anything in this world worthy to keep your hearts from God, but think of the day when you shall give account for every sermon which you have heard; and he which has called you in this prison will glorify you in his palace, where you shall see him to whom you have given your hearts, and enjoy that blessing of blessings which makes all the world to worship him. The Father of our Lord Jesus Christ, which has begun to draw you to his kingdom, never leave you until you come to it. *Amen.*

Your late unworthy servant for the Lord,
H.S.

THE CHRISTIAN'S SACRIFICE

"My son, give me your heart."—Prov. 23:26

To bind all the lessons together which you have learned since I came, this sentence came to my mind, "My son, give me your heart," which is the sum of all that you have heard, and shows in what chest you should lay up these treasures in your heart, and then give that heart to God and he will keep all safe.

A supplication has come as it were from God to man, that man would send God his heart. He which always *gave* now *craves*, and he which craves always now gives. Christ stands at the door like a poor man, and asks not bread, nor clothes, nor lodgings, which we should give to his members, but our heart, that is, even the continent of all, and governor of man's house, which sits on the bench like a judge to give the charge, and teaches the tongue to speak, the hand to work, the foot to walk, the ear to attend, the eye to observe, the mind to choose, and the flesh to obey. That we must present to God, like a burnt-sacrifice, in which all is offered together, (Lev. 1:9), a wise tongue, a diligent hand, a wary foot, a watchful eye, an attentive ear, an humble mind, an obedient flesh, put all together, and it is but the heart: "My son," says God, "give me your heart." Here you are a giver, God the petitioner, your heart the gift which he claims by the name of a son.

Mark what God has chosen for himself: not that which any other should lose by, like the demands of them which care for none but themselves, but that which, being given to God, moves us to give to every man his due.

Once God required offerings and sacrifices which men were unwilling to give, because it was a dear service of God, (Mal. 1:13, and 3:13); but now he says that the heart is more than all burnt-offerings and sacrifices, (Mark 12:33). Jacob loved Joseph more than all his brethren, (Gen. 37), so God loves the heart more than all her fellows; this mite God will have for all his benefits, which we may best afford him. Your alms to the poor, your counsel to the simple, your inheritance to your children, your tribute to Caesar, but your heart to God; he which is a Spirit requires a spirit, (John 4:24), and delights to dwell in the hearts of men. Here God plants himself, as in a castle which is always besieged with the world, the flesh, and the devil. If the enemy gets a thought, or a word, or a work, yet he has but razed the walls; but if he take the heart, then the fortress is lost. For that time all our thoughts, words, and works are captive to him: he bids them go, and they go; do, and they do it.

As a man considers what he does when he gives, so God licenses us to consider of that which we do for him, whether he deserves it, whether we owe it, whether he can require it, lest it should come against our will; therefore *give me*, says God, as though he would not strain on us or take from us; but if you will give him your heart, then he accepts it; it must come freely like a gift, as his blessings come to us, and then his demand is granted. Here is no respect of time, how long you may stay it, or how long he will keep it; but give it, is the present time; as though he would have it out of hand while he asks, before you go out of the church; for what can we ask of him, when we deny him but one thing when he asks of us? Therefore consider who is a suitor to you, and let all suitors have their answer, that your heart is married already. As Isaac answered Esau, "Jacob have I blessed, and he shall be blessed," (Gen. 27), so you may say, God has my heart, and he shall have it; and them that crave it hereafter, send them to Christ for it, for it is not yours to give, if you have given it to God already. But take heed your heart do not lie to yourself, and say it is God's when it is the world's; like Jeroboam's wife, which would not seem to be Jeroboam's wife, (1 Kings 14:2). By this you shall know whether you have given it to him or not; if the heart be gone, all will follow. As the sun rises first, and then the beasts arise from their dens, the fowls from their nests, and men from their beds; so when the heart sets forward to God, all the members will follow after it, the tongue will praise him, the foot will follow him, the ear will attend him, the eye will watch him, the hand will serve him, nothing will stay after the heart, but everyone goes, like handmaids after their mistress.

This is the melody which Paul speaks of in Eph. 5:19, "Make melody to the Lord in your hearts;" showing, that there is a concert of all the members when the heart is in tune, and that it sounds like a melody in the ears of God, and makes us rejoice while we serve him. We have example hereof in Christ, which said it was meat and drink to him to do his Father's will, (John 4:34); and in David, which danced to see the ark, (2 Sam. 6:14); and in the Israelites, of whom it is said, that they rejoiced when they offered from their heart to the Lord, (1 Chron. 29:9).

Therefore Solomon, picking out the heart for God, spoke as though he would set out the pleasantest, and fairest, and easiest way to serve him, without any grudging, or toil, or weariness. Touch but the first link, all the rest will follow; so set the heart a-going, and it is like the poise of a clock, which turns all the wheels one way. Such an oil is on the heart, which makes all nimble and current about it; therefore it is almost as easy to speak well, and do well, as to think well. If the heart indite a good matter, no marvel though the tongue be the pen of a ready writer, (Psa. 45:1), but if the heart be dull, all is like a left hand, so unapt and toward, that it cannot turn itself to any good.

As Joseph charged his brethren that they should not come to him for he was not to come unless they brought Benjamin to him, whom they left at home, (Gen. 13:15, Mark 15:8), so God will not have us to speak to him, nor come to him for anything, unless we bring our hearts to him, which we leave behind. The tongue without the heart is a flattering tongue; the eye without the heart is a wicked eye; the ear without the heart is a vain ear; the hand without the heart is a false hand. Do you think that God will accept a flattering tongue, a wicked eye, a vain ear, a false hand, which rejects a sacrifice if it is but lean or bruised? No, says Paul, in his first epistle to the Corinthians, chap. 13 verse 1, "If I give all that I have, and not love," that is, give not my heart, "it avails me nothing," he does not say, that they which give not their heart give nothing, but that they shall have nothing for such offerings. He which brings but a mite, and brings his heart, brings more than he which offers a talent, (Mark 12:42); and he shall go away more justified than he which said, "All these have I kept from my youth upward," (Matt. 19:20); for God is not mocked, (Gal. 6:7), but knows how much is behind, though Ananias seem to bring all, (Acts 5:3). He marks how I speak, and how you hear, and how we pray in this place; and if it does not come from the heart, he repels it as fast as it goes up, like the smoke which climbs towards heaven, but never comes there. Man thinks when he has the gift, he has the heart too; but God, when he has the gift, calls for the heart still, (Psa. 73:1). The Pharisee's prayer, the harlot's vow, the traitor's kiss, the sacrifice of Cain, the feast of Jezebel, the oblations of Ananias, the tears of Esau, are nothing to him, but still he cries, Bring your heart, or bring nothing; like a jealous husband, when he has a wife, yet he is jealous whether he has her heart or not, so, whatsoever you do, yet God is jealous still, and respects not what you dost, but whether you do it from your heart; that is, of mere love toward him. If Pilate had washed his heart when he washed his hands, (Matt. 27:24), he had been cleaner than Naaman when he came out of Jordan, (2 Kings 5:13).

Of all the suitors which come to you, it seems there is none which has any title to claim the heart but God, which challenges it by the name of a son, (Mal. 1:8), as if he should say, you shall give it to your Father which gave it to you: Are you my son? My sons give me their hearts, and by this they know that I am their Father, if I dwell in their hearts, for the heart is the temple of God, (1 Cor. 6:16); therefore, if you be his son, you will give him your heart, because your Father desires it, your Maker desires it, your Redeemer desires it, your Savior desires it; your Lord, and your King, and your Master desires it, which has given his Son for a ransom, his Spirit for a pledge, his word for a guide, the world for a walk, and reserves a kingdom for your inheritance. Can you deny him anything, which has given the heir for the servant, his beloved for his enemy, the best for the worst? (Rom. 8:32). Can you deny him anything, whose goodness created us, whose favor *elected* us, whose mercy *redeemed* us, whose wisdom *converts* us, whose grace *preserved* us, whose glory shall *glorify* us? Oh, if you knew, as Christ said to the woman of Samaria when she was about to give him water, (John 4:10), "If you knew who it is that says to you," give me *your heart*, you would say to him, as Peter did when Christ would wash his feet, (John 13:9), "Lord, not my feet only, but my hands and my head;" not my heart only, but all my body, and my thoughts, and my words, and my works, and my goods, and my life, take all that you have given.

If Abraham gave Lot leave to choose what part he did like, (Gen. 13:8-9), shall we not give God leave to choose that which he likes? If he did not love you, he would not require your heart; for they which love, require the heart. The master requires labor, the landlord requires service, the captain requires fight; but he that requires the heart, requires it for love, for the heart is love. We will give him little, if we will not give him that which he asks for love towards ourselves.

So you have heard what God requires for all that he has given you, and how all your services are lost until you bring it. What shall I wish you now before my departure? I wish you would give all your hearts to God while I speak, that you might have a kingdom for them. Send for your hearts where they are wandering, one from the bank, another from the tavern, another from the shop, another from the theatres; call them home, and give them all to God, and see how he will welcome them, as the father embraces the son, (Luke 15:22). If your hearts were with God, could the devil fetch them? Could those sins come at them? Even as Dinah was deflowered when she strayed from home, (Gen. 34:2), so is the heart when it strays from God. Therefore call your members together, and let them fast, like a quest of twelve men, until they consent on the law, before any more terms pass, to give God his right; and let him take the heart which he *woos*, which he would marry, which he would endow with all his goods, and make it the heir of the crown. When you pray, let your heart pray; when you hear, let your heart hear; when you give, let your heart give; whatsoever you do, set the heart to do it, (Prov. 3:1); and if it is not so perfect as it should or ought to be, yet it shall be accepted for the friend that gives it, (Dan. 10:12).

I have but one day more to teach you all that you must learn of me, therefore I would hold you here until you assent to give all your hearts to God. If you give them not now, where have I cast the seed? And how have you heard all this year? If you will give them now, you shall be adopted this day the sons of God, and I shall leave you in the bosom of Christ, which will give you heaven for your hearts. The Lord Jesus grant that my words are not the savor of death to any soul here, (2 Cor. 2:16), but that you may go in strength of it through prosperity and adversity, until you hear that comfort from heaven, "Come, you blessed, and receive the inheritance prepared for you." *Amen.*

THE LOST SHEEP IS FOUND

"Try the spirits whether they are of God."—1 John 4:1

Neither too bold nor too credulous, John the Baptist sent to Christ a question, "Are you He that should come? Or look we for another?" (Luke 7:19); so I send to him which calls himself Elijah. Are you he which was prophesied? Or is he come already? But will Elijah answer as well for himself, as Christ proved His authority to St. John? "Go your way, and tell John what things you have seen and heard; how that the blind see, the lame walk, the lepers are cleansed, the deaf hear, the dead are raised, to the poor the Gospel is preached," (Luke 7:22). These tokens the Lord used for an answer, because He did not want men endangering their salvation, to believe every man that calls himself Christ, or Elijah, or a prophet, unless he brings the testimony of the Holy Spirit in fullness of power. Therefore He requires this of Himself, "If I do not the works of My Father, believe Me not," (John 10:37). Therefore He says again, "The works that I do bear witness of Me, that the Father has sent Me," (John 5:36); therefore it is written, "All that heard Him were astonished at His understanding and answers," (Luke 2:47); therefore the servants came back, and could not bring Him, but told the Pharisees how their hearts were stricken, "Never man spoke like this man," (John 7:46). Therefore it is written of Stephen, "They were not able to resist the wisdom and the spirit by which he spoke," (Acts 6:10). Therefore the disciples would not receive Paul before Barnabas gave witness of him, (Acts 9:27). Therefore all the Prophets prophesied of Christ's coming, that when He came we should know Him, and receive our salvation, (Acts 3:24). Therefore Christ has foretold us all the tokens of His second coming, and all the signs which shall go before His day of judgment. And as He had left nothing out, He says in a full conclusion, "Take ye heed," (Mark 13:33), "let no man deceive you, I have showed you all things before." But what has Elijah done? Or what has Elijah spoken? Or who cannot dispute with Elijah? Or who gives witness of Elijah? Or who has prophesied of Elijah? Or who has received Elijah? Or who has said, *Of a truth this is the Prophet?* (John 7:40). Oh, how necessary had it been, that Christ, among all other tokens of His coming, should especially have noted to us that Elijah, that great Prophet, that crier, that trumpet, that destroyer, that Noah, that Lot, that soldier of the Lord, that Sun of Righteousness, that man which no man shall accuse of sin, if there had been any such to come! Surely we would have respected more that sign, than all the rest. But so it is that Christ has forewarned us of many false Prophets, (Mark 13:6), but of any one singular Prophet of God He has not in all His tokens once remembered. Alas, Elijah, where were you that the Lord forgot you? Has the Lord revealed all tokens to us, and yet will you be a token above number? He that "comes in without his wedding-garment shall be thrust out," (Matt. 22:13), and shame shall come on him which is without shame.

It is enough for our belief, to say, that an angel called you Elijah; Satan is transformed into an angel of light. "Search the Scriptures, (says Christ), for they testify of Me," (John 5:39). Will it excuse Adam to say, *The woman deceived me? Be not deceived*, (says Christ), if an angel from heaven teach you any other doctrine than this, *believe him not*; he whom God has sent, speaks the words of God. "If you continue in My word, then are you My disciples indeed," (John 8:31). He which has the gift of prophecy, let him have it according to the faith. You say, *We are true in religion*; if you were Elijah, you would let us so continue. Why are *we* in the true religion? Because we truly believe the Scriptures. But the Scriptures so plainly, so often, so vehemently point to us, that Elijah has come already, that now we cannot believe him that calls himself Elijah, unless we falsify the Word of God. You therefore which say we stand in the true faith, and yet would inveigle us from the faith which we truly hold, to believe contrary to His infallible Word, have a secret meaning to call us to one heresy after another, which he may easily do, whosoever can prove the Son of man a liar, and go under the name of Elijah. "It is hard for you to kick against the goads," (Acts 9:5). Read, see, and behold, how the Spirit consents against you. *I say to you that Elijah has come already, and they did not know him, but have done to him whatsoever they desired.* All the Prophets and the Law itself prophesied to John; and if you will believe it, this is Elijah which was to come; if you have ears to hear, *let him hear.* Elijah verily, when he comes, first restores all things; "but I say to you, Elijah has come, and they have done to him what they would," (Matt. 17:11, 12); as it is written of him, John shall go before Him in the spirit and power of Elijah, to turn the hearts of the fathers to the children, (Luke 1:17). What do you say to all these which bear witness against you? Do all the Evangelists speak in parables? Did not Elijah come, because they did not know him? If the Scribes and Pharisees had taken John for Elijah, then you would have said the cause is plain; for all men believe that Elijah has come. But now the Scribes did not know him; though Christ says, *he has come, yet you will not know him:* what is this but to confess the Scribes, and deny Christ? You therefore which do not speak the words of God, are not sent of God; you which do not continue in His saying, are not His disciples; you which prophesy not according to the faith, have not the right gift of prophecy. This is the sentence of truth, under which if Elijah fall, all the false Prophets cannot raise him up again.

Now show your testimony, Elijah; you are of age, answer for yourself, (John 9:23). How many Elijahs will you make? Or of what Elijah did Christ speak? (Matt. 17:1-12). His disciples understood Him of John, for to him the Jews had done what they would; or that Elijah was to be fulfilled? not he that was prophesied? Or what Elijah did the Scribes think should first come, before the Son of Man should rise from the dead? Or to what prophecy did they learn, why they should look for Elijah? Did they not stand on the prophecy of Malachi? (Mal. 4:5-6). Yes, there is no question, for they had no other to trust to do so; but Christ made an answer to His disciples, that Elijah which the Scribes looked for had come already; therefore the Elijah of Malachi had come already; for they did not know of any other but of Malachi; and the Apostles asked Him in

320

their meaning, to give an answer to the Scribes, (Matt. 17:10). If Christ says, *Elijah has come already*, does He not mean that Elijah which was prophesied and expected, has come already, that the Scripture might be found true? No truth can say that He meant other. Then if Elijah which was prophesied has come already, how can you be he which was prophesied? The Apostles said, *The Scribes looked for Elijah*; Christ said *Elijah has come already*; is not this as much as if He had said, *Let them look for him no more, for he that has come shall not come again*; if we were now to look for another, he that comes not in at the door, is not the right shepherd, (John 10:11), and you are as worthy to be welcome, as he which comes before he is bidden; but if you had done wisely, you would have come before Christ, so, He had broached these things to the people; then if you had made this tale, and framed your matters cunningly, perhaps some credulous person would have said, *This may be Elijah*. If Christ had not come when Christ came, then St. Patrick might have been *Christ*. Can you not be content to think as the Apostles did? Sure it is, they did not know that any Elijah should arise in those days, but accounted the prophecy of Malachi fulfilled, when they heard Christ give sentence of it, and they all in one spirit understood Him of John, (Matt. 17:13). Furthermore all the Prophets prophesied to John, (Matt. 11:13), but after John we read of no prophet, but the ministers of the Lord. So that if you will interpret a Prophet as they were in the old law, by this sentence, you cannot be a Prophet; but if you say that place of Matthew is not so to be understood, then you have to construe it this way,—that all the Prophets prophesied to John, that is, that all which any of the Prophets said to Elijah they prophesied in meaning to John, and so Malachi's prophecy is fulfilled in John. So Matthew construes himself in the next verse, saying, "This John to whom the Prophets prophesied, is the Elijah which was to come," (Matt. 11:14).

You grant that John had the spirit, the power, and office of Elijah, and that he did fulfill his duty: stand there, for in this point Luke's words agree with the words of Malachi.

Now I demand of you, whether names be anything with God, and when the Spirit prophesied a Prophet, whether He prophesied the name, or the office and the power? Christ says, "They which do the works of Abraham, are children of Abraham, and none but they," (John 8:39). So when Malachi prophesied, that Elijah should come, he meant not that Elijah which was taken up in a fiery chariot should descend again, but that one should come in the spirit and power of Elijah, as Luke interprets the Prophet, saying, "He shall go before Him in the spirit and power of Elijah," (Luke 1:17). The prophecy is fulfilled, when the thing prophesied has come to pass, and that is done which was spoken. He is not a Prophet that bears the name of a Prophet, but he that has the spirit and power, and does the office of a Prophet. But if your name be Elijah, why were you not so called from your birth. You have as much reason for Elijah as the Jews that thought Christ called for Elijah when He said, *Eli, Eli, lama sabackthani*, if you are Elijah at all, you are Elijah as well at one time as at another. Elizabeth could not choose but called her son John, (Luke 1:60). Mary was warned before she was delivered, to call her fruit *Jesus*, (Luke 1:31). Your angel speaks to none but to yourself. Does God make prophets in such secret? The Holy Spirit lights on Christ in the likeness of a dove, that John might "see and bear witness," (John 1:32); Paul was stricken down to the ground in the "sight of all his companions," (Acts 9:4); a voice came from heaven that the people heard, and Jesus answered, "This voice came not because of Me, but for your sakes," (John 12:30); but of this angel I may say, he which intends evil hates light. But John said, "I am not Elijah," (John 1:21); he said well, for Elijah was taken up into heaven, and nothing was prophesied to come again, but one in the spirit and power of Elijah, (as I have proved before), and this was John; but he would not call himself Elijah, nor say he came in the spirit and power of Elijah, though God had given him both his spirit and power. This was John's modesty, to humble himself, as Christ advanced him; so he said, I am not a Prophet, and yet he was a Prophet, and more than a Prophet. "You, child, (says his father), shall be called a Prophet of the Highest," (Luke 1:76). So little John respected the name of Elijah, or of a Prophet. But are the Prophets of the Old Testament or the Prophets of the New Testament to be fulfilled in our days? I thought the Prophets had determined about Christ, and that Christ had prophesied of us; so St. Paul taught the Hebrews before Elijah came; hold fast Elijah, for if this is true, your kingdom is but short. But I come nearer to you, do you believe, as St. John, as a Prophet, or an Apostle? Then you can show me your faith by your works. These tokens, (says Christ), shall follow them that believe: "In My name they shall cast out devils, they shall speak with new tongues, they shall take up serpents, and if they drink poison, it shall not hurt them; they shall lay hands on the sick, and they shall recover," (Mark 16:17-18). If you cannot do all these, or none of these, then I may believe as well as Elijah; shall he that is full of the Holy Spirit be unable to yield one token of faith? (Luke 1:15): hold fast Elijah. But whether you be a true Prophet or a false, yet you shall have power to cast out devils, for the false Prophets shall come to me (says Christ) and shall say, "We have cast out devils in Your name," (Matt. 7:22). But if you be but a pettifogger, and have no cunning, but set a face on things, then take heed how you adjure these spirits, lest they turn on you again, and say, Jesus I know, and Elijah I know, but who are you?

Truly, Elijah, make account of this, that whomsoever you serve the same shall pay to you your wages. Yet a little nearer to you, you ask your brother, as I read in a piece of a letter, under your name, *If I be a false Prophet, what false doctrine have I taught?* Indeed if you were the Prophet of God, the Holy Spirit should speak within you, and the Spirit of Truth should lead you into all truth, as it is written. And if you had the spirit of John, as John had of Elijah, then you shall be full of the Holy Spirit from your mother's womb. The Prophet of God cannot speak, but that which God puts into his mouth, (1 Kings 22:14); but you err, and that against God, and against His Word, and yet you ask, *What false doctrine have I taught?* First, you call yourself Elijah, to which now I say no more, but set you the ensample of Christ, which you should follow: If I bear witness of Myself, My witness is not true, (John 5:31). You presume further, that Christ descended into hell both in soul and body; which is so *absurd*, that never either Protestant or heretic avouched; the Creed says plainly, *His body was buried*; and if in this Article we do not believe truly, how do you say that we are in the true religion, which are not yet come to the knowledge of our salvation? You avouch stiffly that the Patriarchs before Christ remained in hell, where was no darkness, but light; I stand not to repel *absurdities*, I rather look for your proof, than you to expect my confutation; some have said, in Abraham's bosom, some in *Limbo Patrum*, some in heaven, and some in hell; but show me Scripture, or one doctor, or true professor since the world began, which ever said as Elijah says. Did the angel tell you this? Ask him when you talk with him again, where this delicate hell is, and to what purpose it serves since Christ fetched His Patriarchs forth of it. You say that Christ knew all things saving the day of the resurrection; which will not stand with His humanity, for so He did not know all things; nor with His Deity, for so He knew the day of resurrection, and all things else. In this point you over-shoot yourself for want of learning to distinguish of the two natures in Christ, whereby I perceive there is nothing in you, but that which is of practice, and you know no more than you have learned at school. You pervert the words of Matthew 17. He says, "Elijah shall first come and restore all things," (verse 11): you say, Elijah shall come and destroy all things, and so on a false foundation you ground a busy argument to no purpose; shall this be your proceedings to falsify the truth, to prove a lie? What doctrine is this that shall destroy all things? Antichrist is called the son of perdition, (2 Thes. 2:3), because he destroys others, and shall be destroyed himself. "My power (says Paul) is to edification, not to destruction," (Gal. 1:10). Construe your words wisely, for if the sheep hear his voice, they will think that the wolf comes rather than the true Shepherd. Did John have your office, and did he not destroy? Had John your power, and could he not destroy? In this word all your doctrine is manifest; if Matthew says *Destroy*, then Elijah's doctrine shall stand for truth; but if Matthew says *Restore*, then Elijah shall be content to go for a false Prophet, because you have changed the truth into a lie. You prophesy that your father shall be cast over into ignorance, and all that he has shall perish. Now Elijah expounds how he means to destroy, and first he begins with his father: O miserable child for whom his father is accursed! Was John the Baptist's father cast over into ignorance? Was Mary accursed? Did their cattle perish? No, "thou shall have joy and gladness," says Gabriel to Zacharias, (Luke 1:14); "Elizabeth was filled with the Holy Spirit," says Luke," (verse 41); "Blessed Are you among women," says the angel, (Verse 28). Is it true, Elijah? This will go hard on your side. You would bear men in hand, that never plague, nor dearth, nor earthquake, nor waters shall touch your country, so long as you continue among them. This is more than ever was granted Christ. What shall we think? They promise liberty, (says Peter), and they themselves are bond-servants. "Ah, Lord God! (says Jeremiah), behold, the Prophets say to them, you shall not see the sword, neither shall you have famine; but I will give you assured peace in this place. Then the Lord said to him, *The prophets prophesy lies in My Name. I sent them not, neither have I commanded them, neither spoke to them; they prophesy to you a false vision and divination, and a thing of nothing, and the deceit of their own heart; and by sword and famine shall those prophets be consumed,* (Jer. 14:13, 15). You avouch that religion is most sincerely-professed, and thoroughly purged from ceremonies in England. Now I would that Elijah were not a false Prophet. But here I descry that Elijah the Prophet does not know what is done beyond seas. No, Elijah, Geneva is yet to learn of England. I would all the wisdom of Elijah could move England to learn of her sister Geneva; then should we have more religion, and less ceremonies. You pretend that Calvin was a good man, and yet in your article of Christ's descent, you make him a plain reprobate, for he never believed as Elijah does. You term your three apparitions,—visions; and yet you do what they say were true; in which you will beguile yourself, because you go further than your knowledge, you do not know what a vision means; but read, and you shall find that visions are false. Though Elijah make a mingle-mangle of truths, and seemings together, as though you could dream and be awake; either all must be a vision, or part of a vision, all truth or no truth. You say your soul was taken from your body; indeed St. Paul does not say so, lest any man should think of him above that which he did see him to be, and that he heard of him, (2 Cor. 12:11); but Elijah had need speak for himself, for no man will speak for him. But Christ says, "The words which I speak are not Mine, but the Father's which sent Me," (John 14:10). Mark the strong reasons of our new Prophet: he proves not as we do, by Scripture; but does speak as one that has some authority, *ipse dixit*: for how would you have him prove else that he walked on the clouds, and that the roof opened to let forth his soul? I fear his time is not yet come to prove this by *Scriptum est*. But what says Paul? Say I these things as a man? Or does not say the law the same also? (1 Cor. 9:8). This gear will not hold, Elijah; you did not look well at the knitting, how these things would agree. Paul refrains to glory of himself, because men should not account him above that which they saw in him, (2 Cor. 12:6); Elijah boasts himself of secret visions, because he would that men should account of him above that which they see in him to be; Christ would not be known before His time, Elijah will be a Prophet before he can prophesy. Be followers together of me, (Paul says), and mark them that walk so as you have us for an example, (Phil. 3:17). Therefore fashion yourself to Paul, and we will look on you; for he that commends himself is not allowed, but he whom the Lord commends. Is this man likely to have revelations, which cannot reveal any more to us than we know? God did bear witness to the doctrine of the Apostles, with signs and wonders, divers miracles and gifts of the Holy Spirit, (Heb. 2:4). Is Elijah also among the Apostles? Well, he is the least of the Apostles; we will not look for wonders, we will crave but truth.

"The Prophet which shall presume to speak a word in

My name, which I have not commanded him to speak, even that Prophet shall die; and if you say in your heart, *How shall we know the word which the Lord has not spoken?* If the thing does not follow, or comes to pass, that is the thing which the Lord has not spoken, but the Prophet has spoken it presumptuously," (Deut. 18:20, 22). Is it come to pass that the word of Matthew, *Restore*, is turned to *destroy*? Is it come to pass that England is before Geneva in sincere profession? We see, (alas!) it is not so; therefore we know the Lord has not spoken to this man, but he speaks of himself; therefore you shall not be afraid of him, says God. You were sick as nature inclined, and you say that the angel prophesied you should be a leper; you were bound prentice as others are, and you say the angel prophesied you should be a bond-man; your country has done well, as many more, and you say the angel prophesied it should fare well for your sake. This is to prophesy of the weather, when the time is past. Who cannot have enough of such angels, if men would believe them? Yet Hanno wrought with more credit than this, he taught birds to sing, Hanno is a god; and when they had learned their lesson, he lets them fly in the air, and wheresoever they came they cried, Hanno is a god. This had some miracle in it, but Elijah will face us out with a card of ten.

This is a young devil. You affirm, that at the desire of the proud, Elijah is beheaded; this is prophetical indeed, and it passes my understanding. The Spirit of truth speaks plainly to edify in truth, and gives understanding to the simple; but the spirit of Satan leads men's minds to construe his saying as they list, that under ambiguous words he might sow erroneous opinions and contention among men. These are the wells without water, or those which be deep that men can draw no water out of them. This sentence cannot be verified, unless you make John, Elijah; and so we receive your *submittimus*; see how Satan shall be taken in his own snares. You demand confidently, *If I be a false prophet, what evil have ever I done?* Or where is the person that can accuse me of sin? Christ might very well say so, which had power and reigned over sin; but

Elijah is a man subject to infirmities, as we are, so says James, (James 5:17). But was there any Prophet or Apostle whom man could not accuse of sin? O Solomon, you were not the wisest man, if a child be wiser than you! O David, you were not a man after God's own heart, if your heart was not as pure, and your life as holy, as a simple prentice's! If no man rebuke you of sin, you have no faithful friend; if no man could accuse you before, now I accuse you of sin: you have made yourself wiser than the wisest, and you have said, I am purer than he which is a man after God's own heart. Woe be to that holiness which leads in hypocrisy to damnation! Indeed, I hear well of your conversation towards all men, and I am heartily sorry that such a good name should impart credit to a false doctrine. I lament that the wisdom of the flesh should be readier to godly works, than the wisdom of the spirit. It may pity a good heart that a body so well mortified from sin should not have a spirit fitted to it. But what do you think of these false prophets? Shall they not make a show of godliness? Shall they not set forth a kind of good works (as the Papists do to merit heaven)? Yes, no doubt, else Christ would never have said, "If it were possible, they shall deceive the very elect," (Matt. 24:24). "Satan himself is transformed into an angel of light," (2 Cor. 11:14); therefore it is no great thing if his ministers be transformed into ministers of righteousness. The damsel cried after Paul and Barnabas, "These men are the servants of the most high God, which show to us the way of salvation," (Acts 16:17), and yet she had a foul spirit; Judas kissed, and yet he betrayed; Pilate washed his hands, and yet he was guilty; Satan alleged Scripture, and yet he was but a devil; some preach Christ of envy and strife, and some of good-will (says Paul). If the false prophets rise not in these days, when shall they come? if they confess not many truths, how shall their lies be credited? if they do not make a show of good works, how shall they be seen and held up are true prophets? Whatsoever you are, Elijah, the false prophets shall come daily, they shall come in sheep's clothing, and they shall call themselves great men; and they shall speak strange words; they shall work wonderful things; and they shall seem holy among men, and shall deceive many; but the end shall try them. Judas received thirty pieces, but after he cast them down. You may win glory among some, but when desperation shall see from whence his torments came, then they shall cry, *Woe to that Prophet! Woe to that Prophet!* Cast down those thirty pieces, if you are not a child of perdition as Judas was, cast down your false name, cast down all which you hope to gain by that cursed spirit; Do you not know that he is a liar? What do you look for at his hand? Build again the things that you have destroyed, then Saul shall be called Paul; if it is such a glory to be called a false prophet, why do you call yourself a true Prophet, and detract from your praise? If you have not your reward here, where will you call for it? Is the Dragon become so familiar? Is hell-fire become so tolerable, that any man should look for ease with the devil, and make his pastime to lead a number after him into hell? Truly, Elijah, you cannot seduce the elect, for their names are written in the Book of Life, and the Lord has promised, "No man shall pluck them out of My hands," (John 10:28). Alas, will you lose yourself, to lose those that are the children of perdition already! This is a strong delusion; yet a little nearer to you, and if you can suffer me, even to your heart. You are Elijah, and you must preach; will you teach a new doctrine? *accursed be that man,* (Gal. 1:8). Will you teach the truth? You say we know that already; but yet you will labor with us, and preach together. It is spoken like a friend, why then can you not join yourself with the disciples? Why does not the Spirit put it into their hearts to receive you? If God had sent you to us, no doubt He would have sent us to you, that as many as he elected might believe; for so did the Jews when Peter came; and so did the Gentiles where Paul preached; and as the angel warned Peter to come, so he warned Cornelius to send. Surely the Lord will do nothing, but He reveals His secrets to His servants the Prophets, (Amos 3:7). Among the people some said He is Elijah, some John the Baptist, some a Prophet; but the disciples had Him straight before He told them, you are the Son of the living God, (Matt. 16:16). "For the spirits of the Prophets are subject to the

Prophets," (1 Cor. 14:32); so says Paul, which had the Spirit of God. "My sheep know My voice," (says Christ), but a stranger they will not follow, (John 10:4, 5). What Prophet is he that the Spirit does not tolerate, and the elect do not believe? It is I, says Elijah, and none else; God grant that never false prophet find no more credit.

But you pretend your time is not yet come, *etc.* No, Elijah, your time is past; you were filled with the Holy Spirit from your mother's womb; and do you not believe, or is not your time yet come, in which men shall believe you? Why then do you speak for credit before your time? Or why do you bid us believe you? I am weary of these tales, and have been too long in reproving that spirit, which I trust no brother will believe. Mark therefore, you shall hear, in a word, all which I have spoken; you which bear witness of yourself, which have done nothing wonderful, which speak like other men, which cannot answer in disputation, of whom no disciple bears witness, of whom no Prophet has prophesied, whom no brother has received, which are not in the number of all the tokens; which come without your wedding garment, which prophesy not according to the faith, which lead us from our belief, which make the Son of Man a liar, which construe the simplicity of the Apostle, in parables and figures, which confess the Scribes and deny Christ, which presume Christ did not respect the prophecy, which come before you are bidden, which come in at the wrong door, which come to prophesy when the Prophets are gone, which think not as the Apostles did, which understand not Christ as His disciples, which make the Spirit prophesy names, which were not called Elijah from your birth, whose angel speaks to none but yourself, which claim your calling from the prophecy of the Old Testament fulfilled before Christ, which have not the tokens which follow them that believe, which come to destroy, whose father is accursed, which privilege your country above all the promises that were granted to Christ, which teach false doctrine, which pervert the text of the Scripture, which prophesy of things when they are past, which speak darkly to divers senses, which cast

330

yourselves in your own sayings, which proclaim, *Who can accuse me of sin?* which glory of yourself above that which all men see in you, which will be wiser than the wisest, and more righteous than he which is a chosen man after God's own heart, which rise in these suspicious days, which make a show of holiness, which confess truths to infer lies, which cannot join yourself to the disciples; what are you, a true Prophet or a false? If these are the marks of a true Prophet, how shall we try spirits of Satan? Our religion takes these for the marks of a false prophet. Elijah says, *We believe the truth*; therefore he which takes Elijah with all these marks for a true Prophet, by Elijah's own sentence is in a wrong belief. "Let us hold fast the profession of our faith without wavering; for He is faithful that promised," (Heb. 10:23). "Do not be shaken in your mind, or be troubled, neither by spirit, nor by word, nor by letter, as from us," (2 Thes. 2:2). "If there arise among you a Prophet or a dreamer of dreams, and gives you a sign or wonder, and the sign or the wonder come to pass, whereof he spoke to you, saying, Let us go after other gods; you shall not hearken to his words; for the Lord proves you, to know whether you will love Him with all your heart and with all your soul," (Deut. 13:1, 3). The Prophet at whom Jeroboam stretched out his hand, was charged by word from heaven, neither to eat, nor to drink, nor turn again in the same way he came; but when he was gone, a man of Bethel overtook him, and said, "I am a Prophet also as you are, and an angel spoke to me by the word of the Lord, saying, "Bring him again with you to your house, that he may eat bread and drink water."" But he lied to him. So he went back with him, and did eat bread. But as they sat at the table, the word of the Lord came to the Prophet that brought him back, "Forasmuch as you have not done as the Lord commanded you, but earn back, and have eaten bread and drunk water, your carcass shall not come into the sepulcher of your fathers. And when he was gone, a lion met him by the way, and slew him," (1 Kings 13:18, 24). God spoke once to Balaam, but Balaam sought out God to speak to him again, and so the foolish Prophet was rebuked of his ass, because he tempted God to alter His commandment. How long will we look after deceitful signs? How long will we halt between two opinions? If the Apostles speak the truth, believe them; if Elijah speaks the truth, hear him: a prentice in Mansfield calls himself Elijah; but Thomas will not believe, how shall Thomas be made to believe? "Put to your hand, Thomas, and feel My wound," (John 20:27). So show me your testimony, Elijah; let me feel your heart, let me see your works, let me hear your faith, your wisdom, your knowledge, and what you can foretell to come. If you will not come to this reckoning, then I say no more, but warn all men to beware. If I had not known the truth, I would have *thought* this man had spoken truth.

God is my witness, I have suffered the Spirit to speak to you, because I seek your conversion; but if you will not return, while mercy is ready, I bring you sorrowful tidings, when Satan shall not help you, the rack must prove this doctrine. Will you heap God, and the devil, and man on you all at once?

O wretched creature, and miserable Prophet! "Who is able to sustain? My son, (says Solomon), if your heart be wise, my heart shall rejoice, even mine," (Prov. 23:15); so I, which, have gone so far to bring you to Christ, if your portion is among the righteous, and you have an hour yet in which you shall be called, if you can go with me, and it may please the Divine Providence to call you at my voice, I will sing praises, I will give thanks, I will say to my soul in all her troubles, *Rejoice, my soul*; remember since you prayed for Elijah, and the Lord heard you out of His holy sanctuary; and your conversion shall not be hid from Israel. Pity yourself before the day of payment, and always remember the sentence of Gamaliel, which was never false, (Acts 5:38, 39). If you are not of God, you shall come to nothing, and your end shall be worse than your beginning. The word that I have spoken, the same word shall judge you in the last day, (John 12:48).

THE CONFESSIONS OF ROBERT DICKONS

[The previous sermon is in relation to this confession and difficulty with a parishioner that Smith was dealing with as a result of these "visions."]

The Declaration of Henry Smith to the Lord Judges, how he found, and how he left, Robert Dickons.

When I came first to Mansfield with your Honors' precept, I found this Robert Dickons in these and like opinions, which he presumed he would hold to death:—

He said he had seen three visions by an angel, which showed him strange things, promised him rare gifts, and power to come.

He said that the angel called him Elijah, whereon he affirmed that the Prophecy of Malachi remains to be fulfilled in him.

He said that the angel told him, that he should be a leper two years, and a bondman eight years.

He avouched that his father should be cast over into ignorance, and that all he had should perish.

He avouched that there should be neither battle nor dearth in his country for eight years, which is the time of his service.

He pretended that after two years his time should come to preach, and that no man should be able to confound him.

But before I left him (as the Word of God does always exercise his natural power) he pronounced before us all, *Now I am converted by Scripture*; whereon he requested me to set down his recantation, which he uttered in these words:—

The Confession of Robert Dickons on the first day's Examination.

I did believe my visions to be true before I heard the

Scriptures prove the contrary, and now I esteem them but a delusion of Satan. Therefore I desire to be set to learning for my own salvation, and for the edifying of my brethren.

Witnesses:

William Dabridgecourt, Esq.
Henry Smith
Edward Immims
William Whaly
Hugh Peace, his master, and a number more.

Robert Dickons

This (I trust) he spoke unfeignedly; and for so much as his desire to learn is commendable, and his gifts not common to men of his degree, as your wisdom shall better see if you talk with him alone; I leave this motion to your Honors' good consideration, which can best judge how to quench, or how to kindle, such sparks.

Robert Dickons' *Confession* on my second examination, in which he declares that he had no visions at all, but that he coined them, and to what end.

The matter of the first Vision.

I did see, on Valentine's Day was eight years, green leaves, which was strange in winter, for which cause I brought them home, and the leaves of the same oak in summer became red; it chanced at the same time to thunder and lightening; after this I was visited, as pleased God, for two years.

The matter of the second Vision.

Four years after I dreamed much like to the matter of the first vision, and the same night it chanced to lightening, (Yet of this I take God to be my Judge) I found a leaf printed in my chamber next morning, with those six sentences, saving only the first line; which leaf, unless it was lost out of my fellows' books, I do not know how it came.

The matter of the third Vision.

  This time twelve months I saw light in the shop alone, whereat I was astonished, and imagining with myself what it should mean, it came into my head to tell my fellows, which came in and found me afraid, that I had seen an angel in a flame of fire, which called me Elijah, and bade me write all that I had seen and heard; hereon I, remembering my former sights and dreams, thought to make me strange to men, and so turned all that which I had seen, as if God had showed me visions. Here is all the matter and sum of my supposed visions. To this confession I take God for my Judge, as I shall be saved in the latter day; but to the other I never swore, though I was never so often examined.

Robert Dickons.

  On this he yielded up his books into my hands, which I have and keep; and now he has nothing to show for that false title.

Henry Smith.

N.B.—*The sermon on* Trying the Spirits, *has special reference to the foregoing Confessions.*—*Editor's Note.*

QUESTIONS GATHERED OUT OF HIS OWN CONFESSION, BY HENRY SMITH, WHICH ARE YET UNANSWERED.

Whether you are sure you shall live these three years, because you say after three years you must preach?

Whether may a man expect visions from God, because you say for these three years you are to look for more visions?

Whether shall you be able at any time to interpret the truth of the Scripture in all places, without error, better than all the doctors?

One of your sentences says you shall live chaste in wedlock; when must you take a wife? and why should you not rather continue single?

Whether there has been neither pestilence, nor dearth, nor war, nor earthquake in your country these five years, nor shall be any time of your continuance there, because the angel so promised? Is this more than ever was granted to Christ?

What Bible, or Translation, mean you, when you say this Bible is truly translated?

Whether it is necessary to salvation to believe all the Articles of the Creed?

Whether any man, since the Apostles, did stand so right in the whole doctrine of the Scripture, that he did hold and believe the true interpretation of all the words and sayings through all the Prophets and Apostles in all the Bible?

Whether predestination, election, *etc.*, are to be preached to laymen? What free-will had Adam? And what free-will

336

remains to us?

What Scriptures are canonical, and which are not canonical?

Whether a man may marry his child with a Papist, or other heretic, hoping to convert him?

Whether ministers should have livings or stipends?

Whether, in some cases, a minister may not be non-resident?

Whether heretics, living to themselves, without corrupting others, are to be punished with death?

Whether Satan knows the inward thoughts, further than by the outward habit of the body? and whether he can read and say, *Verbum caro factum est*?

Whether Christ was, or is, or shall be, known, and preached to all nations of the world?

Where is hell? And what shall be the manner of punishment there to the reprobate?

What think you of the Antipodes, and those monstrous people which live in Asia, and of monsters in general?

What think you of that saying of Christ, "This day shall you be with Me in paradise?" (Luke 23:43); what kind of place is this, and where, and to what purpose now it serves?

And whether it was a material apple Adam did eat?

How esteem you of astronomy, physiognomy, palmistry, casting of a figure, of music in the church, *etc.*?

What think you of our Common Prayer Book and Litany?

What esteem you of fairies, hobgoblins, *etc.*? Whether their money is true, and how they have it?

Whether should one meaning to be a preacher first study the arts, or else study nothing but divinity, as you have done?

Whether the font, surplice, caps, tippets, bells, holy-days, fasting-days, and such like ceremonies, are better observed, or omitted?

Whether they which are called Protestants, or those whom we call Puritans, be of the purest religion, and most reformed to the Primitive Church?

What is meant by the prison in Peter, where Christ descended in spirit?

Whether our joys in heaven shall be to all equal, and the torments in hell to everyone alike? and whether we shall see and know one another?

Where was the soul of Lazarus, while his body was in the grave?

Whether Elisha, cursing the little children, did not sin?

At what age and stature shall all rise in the resurrection? and whether the wounds and scars shall remain in our bodies glorified?

What think you of the Scribes in the third chapter of Mark that said, *Christ had an unclean spirit, and casted out devils by Beelzebub*; did they sin against the Holy Spirit?

Whether images are in no respect tolerable, and whether a man remembering Christ by seeing, the cross, does sin?

Which is the greatest sin that reigns this day in England?

How is the soul created in man, and when it comes, and how, or in what part it is placed in the body?

In what estate shall the sun, and moon, the heavens, and elements be after the last day, when there shall be no creature on earth?

What think you of plays, and representing divine matters, as in pageants?

Whether all things among the faithful Christians ought to be common? (Acts 4:32).

What do you think concerning the bishoping of children?

What city is described of John in the seventh chapter of his Revelation?

Whether did the Apostles know sufficiently their salvation, before Christ died and rose again?

Answered to every point, or yield.

Henry Smith, of Husbands Boreswell, at the commandment of the right worshipful his Uncle, Master Brian Cave, High-Sheriff of Leicestershire.

GODLY PRAYERS FOR THE MORNING AND EVENING

PRAYERS FOR THE MORNING

O eternal God and merciful Father, which are the Light; that no man can attain to, and by Your marvelous lightness drives away the darkness of the night and shadow of death, and by Your grace enlightens all those that being in darkness come to You; I, Your unworthy servant, do bless and praise Your most holy name for all the mercies and gracious benefits that from time to time I have received from You, and most humbly thank You that You have vouchsafed me this favor,—to pass this night in so quiet and comfortable rest, and have brought me again to see and enjoy the light of the morning. And now I beseech You, O Lord, of your infinite goodness and mercy, by the merits of my blessed Savior, that Your merciful compassion may this day be extended to me, that being enlightened with Your grace, I may not be carried away by the power of darkness, to spend this day after the lusts and pleasures of my own corrupt mind; but that I may, with all care and conscience, follow Your fatherly will, which you have revealed to me in Your Holy Word. Increase in me, O Lord, all spiritual gifts and graces, and beat down in me all carnal and corrupt affections. Enable me by Your blessed Spirit, in some measure, both to withstand that which is evil, and to perform what is good and pleasing to You: and that neither by my own negligence, nor the power of any temptation which either the world, the flesh, or the devil shall present to me, I be driven away from a true faith; but may lay hold of those gracious promises that you have made to me in Jesus Christ my Savior. Dispel, O Lord, the thick mist and clouds of my sins, which corrupt my soul, and darken my understanding, and wash them away, I most humbly beseech You, in the precious blood of Your Son's passion; that so I may be acknowledged for one of your elect, when I shall appear before Your judgment seat.

340

Give me a will carefully to follow my vocation, and let Your blessing be on me in the same. Bless me in my body, in my soul, and in whatsoever belongs to me: lighten my mind, and inflame my heart with a love of those things that are good. And as my body (by Your power) is risen from sleep, so let my soul daily be raised from the slumber of sin and the darkness of this world: that so both together may enjoy that everlasting light which you have provided for Your saints, and purchased with the blood of Your dear Son our Savior Jesus Christ; to whom with You, O Father, and the blessed Spirit, be all honor and glory forevermore. *Amen.*

O LORD, PREPARE OUR HEARTS TO PRAYER

O Lord God our heavenly Father, we Your poor and wretched creatures give You most humble and hearty thanks for our quiet and safe sleep, and for raising us up from the same. We beseech You, for Jesus Christ's sake, to prosper us this day in our labor and travel, that it may be to the discharging of our duty in our vocations, principally to Your glory; next, to the profit of this Church and Commonwealth; and, last of all, to the benefit and content of our masters. Grant, dear Father, that we may cheerfully and conscionably do our business and labors, not as men-pleasers, but as serving You our God, knowing You to be the chief Master of us, and that you see and behold us with Your fatherly eyes, who have promised reward to them that faithfully and truly walk in their vocation, and threatened everlasting death and damnation to them that deceitfully and wickedly do their works and labors. We beseech You, O heavenly Father, to give us the strength of Your Spirit, that godly and gladly we may overcome our labors, and that the tediousness of that irksome labor which Thou for our sins have poured on all mankind may seem to us more delectable and sweet. Fulfill now, O Lord, these our requests, for Your Son our Savior's sake, in whose name we pray, as He Himself has taught us, Our Father, which are in heaven, *etc.*

ANOTHER PRAYER FOR THE EVENING

O almighty and everlasting God, the Father of mercy and God of all consolation, that by Your merciful Providence defends all those that walk before You and put their trust in You: I, poor and miserable sinner, unworthy of the least of Your favors, do yet presume, in the name and mediation of Jesus Christ, to present myself before You, and to offer up this poor sacrifice of praise and thanksgiving to You, that you have nourished and preserved me by Your power, and have guided and governed me by Your Word and Spirit: and, as for all other Your blessings, so for that mercy that has this day accompanied me, whereby I have both been preserved from many sins that the wickedness of my nature was inclined to, and also delivered from many punishments that the sins that I have committed have deserved. I most humbly beseech You, in the merits of Christ Jesus, to pardon and forgive me all my sins, which either in thought, word, or deed, I have this day, or any time heretofore, committed against You: whether they are the sins of my youth or of my age, sins of omission or commission, whether wittingly or ignorantly committed: good Lord, pardon them to me, and let them not cause You this night (as justly you may do) to take vengeance on me; but be merciful to me, O Lord, in forgiving the evil I have committed, in supplying the good that I have omitted, in restoring me to that which I have lost, in healing my sores, in lighting my blindness, in cleansing my filthiness, and in altering the whole course of my corrupt mind, that I may be diverted from that which is evil, and enabled to perform that which is agreeable to Your blessed will and Word. And, Lord, as you have this day preserved and kept me in safety; so I most humbly beseech You to protect me this night from all danger, both bodily and ghostly, and to give me such quiet and comfortable rest, as may enable me to walk on in that vocation in which you have placed me, and that I may both be delivered from the darkness of this present night, and may also escape that everlasting darkness which you have provided for those that without repentance continue in their sins: from which, good Lord, deliver me, and all those that belong to You: and that for the merits of the death and passion of my blessed Savior Jesus Christ, in whose name I continue my prayers for myself and Your whole Church, saying as He has taught us, Our Father, which are in heaven, *etc. Amen.*

A GODLY PRAYER TO BE SAID AT ALL TIMES

Because I have sinned, O Lord, and done wickedly in Your sight, and provoked You to anger by my abominable wickedness, making my body, which you have ordained as a vessel for your honor, an instrument of most detestable filthiness; O Lord, be merciful to me, and pardon me this great wickedness. Look not on me, good Father, with the eyes of justice, neither do you draw against me the sword of judgment; for then how shall I that am but dust stand in Your presence, when Your wrathful indignation comes forth as a whirlwind, and Your heavy displeasure as a mighty tempest, seeing the earth trembles, the depths are discovered, and the very heavens are shaken, when you are angry? Exercise not therefore Your fury against me, that am but chaff before the wind, and as stubble against a flaming fire; though I have sinned grievously in Your sight, preferring my wicked desire before Your holy commandments; esteeming the pleasure of a moment before eternal and everlasting joys: no, which is worse, making more account of vileness and vanity, and extreme folly and madness, than of the glory and majesty of the most excellent, wonderful, and blessed God, nothing dreading His displeasure, whose wrath makes the devils to quake, and burns unquenchable to the bottomless pit of hell; whose might is so great, that by the breath of His nostrils He can in the twinkling of an eye destroy a thousand worlds. Yet am I bold, prostrating myself before the throne of Your Majesty, heartily to beseech, and humbly to entreat You, that you will not deal with me according to my merits, for I have deserved, that you should rain down fire and brimstone from out of heaven on me to devour me, or to open the earth under me, to swallow me up quick into hell: but you are gracious and full of compassion, and rich in mercies, therefore do men put their trust under the shadow of Your wings. I have none in heaven to fly to but You, nor in earth, of whom I may receive any comfort, but at Your favorable hands, which are stretched out day and night, to receive all that by earnest repentance turn to You, being ready to ease all those

345

that are laden with the burden of their sin, and to refresh their distressed consciences. In the multitude of Your mercies I approach to You, O Lord, desiring You to look down from the height of Your sanctuary, on me poor and wretched sinner, and to wipe away mine offences, and to blot out my misdeeds; especially this my ungracious, unclean, and ungodly act, that it may not come up in remembrance with You, nor be imputed to me forever, for Your Son's sake, O Lord, in whom you are well pleased, in whom you wast fully satisfied on the cross for my sins; grant me free pardon and remission of that I have so foolishly, by my exceeding frailty, committed against You in this shameful deed. But, O you my unclean and unthankful soul, my ungodly and rebellious heart, what did I, sinful wretch and execrable caitiff, so blindly and desperately attempt? How are you become quite senseless that you were so ready to anger your most loving God, and to provoke your most mighty Judge, that you might satisfy your flesh, suborned both by your and God's most malicious adversary, to grieve and vex the Spirit of the Lord, and so damn yourself forever! Has not God, of His singular favor, made the heavens of old, and placed the sun and moon in them, two glorious lights, with innumerable stars, a wonderful workmanship for Your use and benefit? Has He not lifted up the clouds by His strong arm, and heaped treasures of rain, hail, and snow, to do you service? Has He not in the midst of the world laid the foundations of the earth, that you might have a stable habitation, and might from thence behold, every way you look, the walls of this beautiful place? Has He not gathered the waters into one place, and made the dry land appear, and drawn forth by His power a pure substance of air between heaven and earth, that fishes might multiply in the seas, fowls in great abundance fly in the open face of the firmament, tender plants, herbs, flowers, trees in all variety grow and fructify on the ground; Yes, creeping things, cattle and beasts, increase in infinite number, in pastures, fields, gardens, orchards, and groves, and all these to do you pleasure? Has He not further given you springs and rivers, gold and silver, pearls and jewels, even plenty of streams, stones, and metal, to further you with whatsoever for profit you needest, or for pleasure desirest? Has He not made you lord and ruler over all His creatures, even over all the huge elephants, the whale, the strong lion, and unicorn, and horse of war? Over the savage tigers, bears, and wolves? over the mighty eagle, griffin, vulture, ostrich, and hawk? Are you not clad and defended, fed and enriched, cheered and renowned by these His creatures, and that all the parts of the body, and senses of the mind, might be partakers of His goodness, and with His sweetness refreshed, comforted, and delighted in great measure? Yes, above all this, has He not breathed into your body an immortal soul, that you might remain with Him in glory forever? Did He not at the first frame you like to Himself, that He might therefore love you as His Son? Did He not cast into your spirit the beams of His wisdom, that you through your understanding might behold Him and His glory, and stir up sparks of goodness in your heart, that you might by your affection embrace Him and His bounty, and be made perfectly blessed by His infinite happiness, who, when Adam your ungrateful father by distrusting Him that has faithfully promised, was thoroughly able to fulfill His will, and resolutely determined exceedingly to advance him, having given him this whole world in testimony of it, by discontenting his mind with the excellent estate he was placed in of unspeakable love, unless he might be as good as God Himself, proudly desiring to make dust the fellow of Him who was from everlasting, infinitely full of wisdom, power, grace, and majesty; and had done all this at the persuasion of the most traitorous rebel of his right gracious King, and spiteful enemy of his most bountiful Master; even then when this most villainous conspiring with God's notorious adversary had deserved immortal hatred against him, and all that pertained to him: Yes, they are yet unborn, but contained in him, whose whole mass, by this impious disobedience, became by just judgment a temple of cursed estate forever and ever; you also yourself bringing forth fruit of contempt of His law, which is most holy, merciful and mighty;

yet even then, I say, of unspeakable pity and compassion intended, *no,* promised, *no,* labored to deliver him and you from that dreadful vengeance which you have purchased by your wicked and ungracious demerits, and to reconcile you, base abjects and vile castaways, and yet stubborn and spiteful haters of the great God Jehovah, who when there was no means to be found in heaven, nor seas, nor in the earth, nor under the earth, but that He should damn His only begotten Son, the very brightness of His glory, who never offended Him, but was an eternal delight to His soul, and rejoicing to His Spirit, that you might be saved, a gross lump of slime and clay, still vexing Him by your wickedness! yet delivered His Son into the full power of Satan, to put Him to a most shameful death, by the hands of most detestable persons, and did cast Him far away out of His favor, and threw Him down into the bottomless pit of His unsupportable wrath and indignation, that you might be placed between His own arms in the kingdom of heaven, in all royalty and glory, as His dear and entirely beloved son! Why therefore were you, O my unholy and unthankful nature! so ready and prone, so violent and headstrong to commit things highly displeasant in His sight, who in a manner, and as far as was possible, slew Himself for your safety, when He had no creature so disobedient as you?

O you my inward soul, and spirit of my mind, awake and stand up to defend yourself, for you are besieged with mighty enemies, the prince of darkness, the rulers of the air, the spiritual craftiness and policies of hell! Why do you not arise, you sluggard? Your foes in great number are prepared with many ambushments, having a huge army, all maliciously bent with venomous darts to pierce through your heart; they are entered your holds at all five gates of your outward sense, yes, they have broken down your door, and have left you but one window towards heaven to escape by, even by your prayers, whereto the Spirit of God waits your speedy coming: make haste, O you heavy with sleep, or you are taken by your cruel enemies, whose hands are of iron, and their teeth of steel, to grind your very bones to powder! Hearken no longer to that stinking harlot, your wicked appetite, which, lying in your bosom, desires nothing but your utter destruction; she persuades you that you are in no present danger, that she may rejoice at your miserable end. It may be you are fed to the slaughter, that though you go on a little way in your pleasant path, you may return back when you will, and your little wandering will not greatly be regarded. O you unwise and sottish heart! when will you understand? Has the Son of God endured such pain for the smallest of your sins, and makes you so light account of so grievous crimes? Does the law thunder curses, and plagues, and everlasting torments against your least inordinate motions, and did you not dread to perform so shameless a practice? Do you not know that the eyes of God and His angels behold you doing that you would be ashamed to do in the presence of ungodly men, or unclean beasts; or do you consider how you did grieve the Spirit of God, who has vouchsafed of His infinite mercy to dwell in your body to this end, chiefly that He might mortify your carnal lusts? Why did you then defile this temple which He has sanctified to be a house for Himself to dwell in? Take heed you drive not One so worthy a guest by such swinish and fleshly behavior, who if He once depart, then shall you be a hold for devils, and legions of damned spirits, that they may stuff you full of all manner of iniquity, and then at length become pitch and brimstone to maintain the fire of God's scorching wrath in your sinews, spirit, and inward bowels, drinking out in full measure the dregs of the wine of His rage and fury. And can you be blind and reckless, that for the vain pleasure of sin for a little while, you will constrain God to torment you everlastingly, who it may be, even at this instant, if you will still try His patience and long-sufferance, will suddenly take your spirit from you, or come in judgment to recompense to all sinners by His final sentence in the burning of the whole world, the stipend of horror, shame, confusion, and utter reprobation; and weigh with yourself, that to approach to God, is the chief joy of His chosen, to behold His glorious countenance in the face of His Son, whereas your sins do separate you from Him, and make you afraid to speak to Him by prayers, which is your chief and greatest solace in this mortal life; how much more will your ungodliness make you wish delay of the last judgment, the speedy and present coming whereof is a chief prop of our faith; and remember how the devil, that roaring lion, labors by his impure act to make you most loathsome in the sight of God, and rejoices to see your gracious Father, merciful Savior, and comfortable Sanctifier, so abused and withstood and angered by you, whom He has wonderfully made, carefully preserved, and dearly redeemed, and tenderly loved, that if it may be, you should by utter apostasy dishonor Him in the face of the world, who has advanced you in the presence of all His angels; and though you be so sure in faith that you cannot utterly fall (the consideration whereof should make you more dutiful, and not encourage you in a sinful course) yet may you little by little, and by often falling, bring yourself into a better liking, both of the wicked and of wickedness itself, whom you ought to hate with a perfect hatred, and then God by just judgment cast you into a sure sleep, that your filthiness maybe seen of men, and you condemned, to the grief of the righteous, and scorned to the shame of the ungodly, and in the mean season, by provoking God's judgment, be spoiled of your goodly ornaments, of your godly desires, of religious thoughts, of zealous affections, of Christian communication, of holy endeavors, of assured persuasions of faith, of steadfast waitings through hope, of constant suffering by patience, and hearty rejoicings from love. In the perfect consummation of which things be, use all happiness consists, beware, you careless wretch! lest suddenly by your abominable filthiness, you either for a time wholly deprive yourself of comfortable feeling of these things, or much diminish your present graces and blessings received of the Holy Spirit, to the glory of God the Father. But why do I utter my voice, or strive to make a dead carcass move? O quicken me, that are the Fountain of life, and call you out of heaven Your dwelling-place, that my wandering soul may hear the voice of her Shepherd, and follow You wherever you lead; *no,* of Your tender compassion take me up on Your shoulders, and carry me gently into Your fold again; for thieves have stolen me away, and have bound my feet, so that I cannot go; and they watch for me until you are gone, that they may carry me away quick from Your pastures I O do you therefore presently deliver me, and give me Your helping hand. O cast down by Your Spirit my raging lust, and by Your grace subdue my untamed affections.

I am weak, O Lord, and unable to resist the force of my mighty adversary; send Your help from above, and save me out of the jaws of this cruel lion. You have delivered me out of the mouth of hell; O let not the gates of it any more prevail against me; let me not any longer be occupied in ungodliness, lest my enemy triumph over me, saying in his malicious heart, There, there, so would I have it. Let this sin be far from me, O Lord, lest I should defile myself any more with this notorious wickedness: work therefore in my heart an utter detestation of it, that I may ever hereafter keep myself pure and unspotted for Your kingdom. You that are able to make of stones children to Abraham, mollify, I pray you, my stony heart, that all manner of son-like affections may be imprinted in that; pluck up, O good Father, these roots of bitterness, that no unsavory fruit may come of the tree, which you by your own hand have planted. I desire, I look, I call, I cry for Your assistance, that I may conquer this unruly motion. O blessed Savior, that have granted so many petitions on earth to them that were careful for the body, fulfill, I pray You, this my desire, not for health, nor strength, nor riches, nor honor, nor for food, nor apparel, but for Your heavenly grace and inspiration; Yes, let me lose all those rather than be left in my sinful flesh, that I should be ruled any longer thereby. Mortify, good Father, in me the old body of sin, and give to me a new body, purged from these dead works, to serve the living God; renew my spirit daily, that I may cast away these works of darkness; let it be enough, O merciful Father, that my weakness in falling heretofore, has been made known to me, lest I should be too proud. Now let Your strength appear in putting this mine enemy under my feet, that thereby I may be bold to put my confidence in You.

Why should my body made by your hand, and my soul framed according to Your image, be given over as a prey into the hands of Satan? Deliver me, O Lord, from the snares of the hunter, and preserve me from the hand of mine enemy, who lies in wait for my spiritual life, and labors my everlasting destruction; so shall I praise You for Your great goodness, and magnify Your name for giving me conquest over my adversary that is too strong for me. To You I fly for succor until this tempest is overpast; hide me I pray You under Your shield and buckler, that none of the fiery darts of Satan take hold on me. Good Lord, for the love you bear to mankind, for Your Son's sake, who has taken our nature on Him, grant that I may not be tempted above my strength, and that in all temptations I may fly to You as the horn of my salvation, yielding You most humble and hearty thanks for that which you have given me a desire to withstand my sinful flesh, which Your work I beseech You for Your name's sake to perfect, and fully accomplish.

Watch and pray, that you enter not into temptation: the spirit indeed is willing, but the flesh is weak, (Matt. 26:41).

A ZEALOUS PRAYER

Eternal God, almighty and most merciful, we Your unworthy servants, prostrate before Your throne of grace, do yield ourselves body and soul to You for all Your benefits, which you from our birth have heaped on us, as though we had always done Your will, although we were occupied about vain things, never marked, never loved, never served, never thanked You so heartily for them, as we esteem a mortal friend for the least courtesy. Therefore we come with shame and sorrow to confess our sins, not small but grievous, not a few but infinite, not past but present, not secret but presumptuous, against Your express word and will; against our own conscience, knowledge, and liking, if any had done them, but ourselves: O Lord, if you should require but the least of them at our hands, Satan would challenge us for his, and we should never see Your face again, nor the heavens, nor the earth, nor all the goodness which you have prepared for man. What shall we do then, but appeal to Your mercy, and humbly desire Your fatherly goodness, to extend that compassion towards us, which Your beloved Son, our loving Savior, has purchased, so mightily, so graciously, and so dearly for us? We believe and know that one drop of His blood is sufficient to heal our infirmities, pardon our iniquities, and supply our necessities; but without Your grace, our sighs, our strength, our guide, we are able to do nothing but sin, as woeful experience has taught us too long, and the example of them which are void of it, whose life is nothing else but the service of the world, the flesh, and the devil. Therefore, good Father, as you in special favor have appointed us to serve You, like as you have ordained all other creatures to serve us, so may it please You to send down Your heavenly Spirit into our hearts, change our affections, subdue our reason, regenerate our wills, and purify our nature to this duty; so shall not Your benefits, nor Your chastisements, nor Your word return void, but accomplish that for which they were sent, until we be renewed to the image of Your Son. Good Lord, we beseech You, look down, in the multitude of Your compassions, on your militant Church, this sinful realm, Your gracious servant, our dread Sovereign, her honorable council, the civil magistrates, the painful ministers, the two universities, the people that sit in darkness, and all that bear Your cross. Gather us into one communion of Your truth, and give to every man a spirit to his calling, that we being mindful of the account, and that we are called Christians, may firmly resolve, speedily begin, and continually persevere in doing and suffering Your holy will. Good Lord, bless and sanctify our meeting, that no temptation hinder me in speaking, nor them in hearing, but that Your word may be heard and spoken as the Word of God, which is able to save our souls in that day. There is no cause, O God most just, why you should hear sinners, which are displeased with sin, but for His sake which suffered for sin, and sinned not; in whose name we lift up our hearts, hands, and voices to You, praying as He has taught us, Our Father, which are in heaven, *etc. Amen.*

THREE PRAYERS

ONE FOR THE MORNING
ANOTHER FOR THE EVENING
AND THE THIRD FOR A SICK MAN

WHERETO IS ANNEXED A COMFORTABLE SPEECH OF A PREACHER ON HIS DEATH-BED, AND A GODLY LETTER TO A SICK FRIEND.

A PRAYER FOR THE MORNING

O Lord, prepare our hearts to prayer. Eternal God, Giver to them which want, Comforter to them which suffer, and Forgiver to them which repent; we have nothing to render You but your own. If we could give You our bodies and souls, they should be saved by it, but you were sever the richer for them. All is our duty, and all of us cannot perform it; therefore Your Son died, and Your Spirit descended, and Your angels guide, and Your ministers teach, to help the weakness of men. All things call on us to call on You; and we are prostrate before You before we know how to worship You: ever since we rose we have tasted many of Your blessings; and you have begun to serve us before we begin to serve You. Why should you bestow Your health, wealth, rest, and liberty on us more than others? We can give no reason for it, but that you are merciful. And if you should draw all back again, we have nothing to say, but that you are just. Our sins are so grievous and infinite, that we are fain to say with Judas, we have sinned, and there stop, because we cannot reckon them. All things else serve You as they did at first: only men are the sinners in this world. Our heart is a root of corruption, our eyes are the eyes of vanity, our ears are the ears of folly, our mouths are the mouths of deceit, our hands are the hands of iniquity, and every part does dishonor You, which would be glorified of You. The understanding, which was given us to learn virtue, is apt now to apprehend nothing but sin; the will, which was given us to

355

affect righteousness, is apt now to love nothing but wickedness; the memory, which was given us to remember good things, is apt now to keep nothing but evil things. There is no difference between us and the wicked. We have done more against You this week than we have done for You since we were born; and yet we have not resolved to amend; but this is the course of our whole life; first we sin, and then we pray You to forgive it, and then to our sins again, as though we came to You for leave to offend You. And that which should get pardon at Your hands for all the rest (that is, our prayer) is so full of toys and fancies, for want of faith and reverence, that when we have prayed, we had need to pray again, that you would forgive our prayers, because we think least of You when we pray to You. What father but you could suffer this contempt, and be condemned still? Yet when we think on Your Son, all our fear is turned into joy, because His righteousness for us is more than our wickedness against ourselves. Settle our faith in Your Beloved, and it suffices for all our iniquities, necessities, and infirmities. Now, Lord, we go forth to fight against the world, the flesh, and the devil; and the weakest of our enemies is stronger than we. Therefore we come to You, for Your Holy Spirit to take our part; that is, to change our minds, and wills, and affections, which we have corrupted; to remove all the hindrances which prevent us to serve You; and to direct all our thoughts, speeches, and actions to Your glory, as you have directed Your glory to our salvation. Although we are sinners, O Lord, yet we are Thine; and therefore we beseech You to separate our sins from us, which would separate us from You, that we may be ready to every good, as we are to evil. Teach us to remember our sins, that you may forget them; and let our sorrow here prevent the sorrow to come. We were made like You; let not flesh and blood turn the image of God to the image of Satan. Our foes are Your foes; let not your enemies prevail against You, to take us from You: but make Your Word to us like the star which led to Christ; make Your benefits like the pillar which brought to the land of promise; make Your cross like the messenger which compelled guests to the banquet; that we may walk before like examples, and always look on Your Son how He would speak and do, before we speak or do anything. Keep us in that fear of Your majesty, that we may be conscience of all that we do, and that we may count no sin small, but leave our lying, and swearing, and surfeiting, and coveting, and boasting, and flaunting, and inordinate gaming, and wanton sporting, because they draw us to other sins, and are forbidden as straightly as others. Let not our hearts at any time be so dazzled, but that in all temptations we may discern between good and evil, between right and wrong, between truth and error; and that we may judge of all things as they are, and not as they seem to be. Let our minds be always so occupied, that we may learn something of everything, and use all those creatures as means and helps prepared for us to serve You. Let our affections grow so toward one another, that we may love You as well for the prosperity of others as if it were our own. Let our faith and love and prayer be always so ready to go to You for our help, that in sickness we may find patience, in prison we may find joy, in poverty we may find contentment, and in all troubles we may find hope. Turn all our joys to the joy of the Holy Spirit, and all our peace to the peace of conscience, and all our fears to the fear of sin; that we may love righteousness with as great good will as ever we loved wickedness, and go before others in thankfulness towards You as far as you go in mercy towards us before them, taking all that you send as a gift, and leaving our pleasures before they leave us; that our time to come may be a repentance of the time past, thinking always of the joys of heaven, the pains of hell, our own death, and the death of Your Son for us. Yet, Lord, let us speak once again; like Abraham, one thing more we will beg at Your hands: our resolutions are variable, and we cannot perform our promises to You; therefore settle us in a constant form of obedience, that we may serve You from this hour with those duties which the world, the devil, and the flesh would have us defer until the point of death. Lord, we are unworthy to ask any thing for ourselves: yet Your favor has preferred us to be petitioners for others; therefore we beseech

You to hear us for them, and them for us, and Your Son for all. Bless the universal Church with truth, with peace, and Your holy discipline. Strengthen all them which suffer for Your cause, and let them see Your Spirit of comfort coming towards them, as the angels came to Your Son when He was hungry. Be merciful to all those which lie in anguish of conscience for remorse of their sins: as you have made them examples, so teach us to take example by them; that we may look on Your Gospel to keep us from despair, and on Your law to keep us from presumption. Prosper the armies which fight Your battles, and show a difference between Your servants and Your enemies, as you didst between the Israelites and the Egyptians; that they which serve You not may come to Your service, seeing that no God does bless besides You. Make us thankful for our peace, whom you have set at liberty; while you have laid our dangers on others, which might have laid their dangers on us. And teach us to build Your Church, in our rest, as Solomon built Your temple in his peace. Have mercy on this sinful land, which is sick of long prosperity; let not Your blessings rise up against us; but endue us with grace as you have with riches, that we may go before other nations in religion, as we go before them in plenty. Give us such hearts as Your servants should have, that Your will may be our will, that Your law may be our law, and that we may seek our kingdom in Your kingdom. Give to our prince a princely heart, to our counsellors the spirit of counsel, to our judges the spirit of judgment, to our ministers the spirit of doctrine, to our people the spirit of obedience; that we may all retain that communion here, that we may enjoy the communion of saints hereafter. Bless this family with Your grace and peace, that the rulers of it may govern according to Your Word, that the servants may obey like the servants of God, and that we may all be loved of You. Now, Lord, we have commenced our suit, our understanding is weak, and our memory short, and we unworthy to pray to You, more unworthy to receive the things which we pray for; therefore we commend our prayers and ourselves to Your mercy, in the name of Your beloved Son, our loving Savior, whose righteousness pleads for our unrighteousness. Our Father, which are in heaven, *etc. Amen.*

A PRAYER FOR THE EVENING

O Lord God, what shall we render to You for all Your benefits, which have given Your Son for a ransom, Your Holy Spirit for a pledge, Your Word for a guide, and reserves a kingdom for our perpetual inheritance; of whose goodness we are created, of whose justice we are corrected, of whose mercy we are saved? Our sins strive with Your benefits, which are more: let us count all creatures, and there are not so many of any kind as Your gifts, except our offences which we return to You for them, you might have said before we were formed, let them be monsters, or let them be infidels, or let them be beggars, or cripples, or bond-slaves, so long as they live: but you have made us to the best likeness, and nursed us in the best religion, and placed us in the best land; that thousands would think themselves happy, if they had but a piece of our happiness. Therefore why should any serve You more than we, which want nothing but thankfulness? you have given us so many things, that we have scarce anything left to pray for, but that you would continue those benefits which you have bestowed already; yet we covet as though we had nothing, and live as though we knew nothing. When we were children, we deferred until we were men; now we are men, we defer until we are old men; and when we be old men, we will defer until death. So we steal Your gifts, and do nothing for them: yet we look for as much at Your hands as they which serve You all their lives. The least of Your blessings is greater than all the courtesies of men: and yet we are not so thankful to You for all that we have, as we are to a friend for one good turn. We are ashamed of many sins in others, and yet we are not ashamed to commit the same sins ourselves, and worse than they: Yes, we have sinned so long almost, that we can do nothing else but sin, and occasion others to sin too, which would not sin but for us. If we do any evil, we do it cheerfully, and quickly, and easily; but if we do any good, we do it faintly, and rudely, and slackly. When did we talk without vanity? when did we give without hypocrisy? when did we bargain without deceit?

when did we reprove without envy? when did we hear without weariness? when did we pray without tediousness? Such is our corruption, as though we were made to sin in deed, or in word, or in thought. We have broken all commandments, that we might see what good is in evil, which have felt nothing but guilt, and shame, and expectation of judgment, while we might have had peace of conscience, joy of heart, and all the graces which come with Your Holy Spirit. Some have been won by the Word; but we would not suffer it to change us: some have been reformed by the cross; but we would not suffer it to purge us: some have been moved by Your benefits; but we would not suffer them to persuade us; *no*, we have given consent to the devil, that we will abuse all Your gifts so fast as they come: and therefore Your blessings make us proud, Your riches covetous, Your peace wanton, Your means intemperate, Your mercy secure; and all Your benefits are weapons to rebel against You; that if you look to our hearts, you may say our religion is hypocrisy, our zeal envy, our wisdom policy, our peace security, our life rebellion; our devotion ends with our prayers, and we live as though we had no souls to save. What shall we answer for that which our conscience condemns? We are one day nearer to death since we rose, when we shall give account how every day has been spent, and how we have got those things which others shall consume when we be gone. And if you should ask us now what lust assuaged, what affection qualified, what passion expelled, what sin repented, what good performed, since we began to receive Your benefits this day, we must confess against ourselves, that all our works, words, and thoughts have been the service of the world, the flesh, and the devil. We have offended You, and condemned You all the day, and at night we pray to You. Father, forgive us all our sins, which have dishonored You, while you did serve us; run from You while you did call us; and forgotten You while you did feed us: so you spare us, so we sleep, and tomorrow we sin again. This is the course of all our pilgrimage, to leave that which you command, and to do that which you forbid. Therefore you might justly forsake us, as we forsake You; and condemn us, whose conscience condemns ourselves: but who can measure Your goodness, which gives all, and forgives all? Though we are sinful, yet you love us: though we knock not, yet you open: though we ask not, yet you give. What should we have if we did serve You, which have done all these things for your enemies! Therefore you which have given us all things for our service, O Lord, give us a heart to serve You, and let this be the hour of our conversion. Let not evil overcome good; let not your enemy have his will; but give us strength to resist, patience to endure, and constancy to persevere to the end. Instruct us by Your Word, guide us by Your Spirit, mollify us by Your grace, humble us by Your corrections, win us by Your benefits, reconcile our nature to Your will, and teach us to make profit of everything; that we may see You in all things, and all things in You. And because, O most merciful Father, we walk between Your mercy and justice, through many temptations, govern our steps with such discretion, that the hope of mercy may prevent despair, and the fear of justice may keep us from presumption; that in mirth we are not vain, in knowledge we are not proud, in zeal we are not bitter: but as the tree brings forth first leaves, then blossoms, and then fruit, so first we may bring forth good thoughts, then good speeches, and after a good life, to the honor of Your name, the good of Your children, and the salvation of our souls; remembering the time when we shall sleep in the grave, and the day when we shall awake to judgment. Now the time has come, O Lord, which you have appointed for rest, and without You we can neither wake nor sleep, which have made the day and night, and rules both: therefore into Your hands we commend our souls and bodies that you have bought, that they may serve You: restore them, O Lord, to their first image, and keep them to Your service; and resign us not to ourselves again, but finish Your work; that we may every day come nearer and nearer to Your kingdom, until we hate the way to hell as much as hell itself, and let every cogitation, and speech, and action, be so many steps to heaven. For Your name's sake, for Your promises' sake, for Your Son's sake, O Lord, we lift up our hearts, hands, and voices to You in His name, which suffered for sin, and sinned not. Our Father, which are in heaven, *etc. Amen.*

A PRAYER FOR A SICK MAN

Almighty God and all-merciful Father, which are the Physician of our bodies and souls, in Your hands are life and death; you bring to the grave, and pull back again: we came into this world on condition to forsake it whensoever you would call us; and now the sumners are come, Your fetters hold me, and none can loose me but He which bound me. I am sick in body and soul: but He has stricken me which in judgment shows mercy. I deserved to die so soon as I came to life; but you have preserved me until now; and shall this mercy be in vain, as though we were preserved for nothing? Who can praise You in the grave? I have done You no service since I was born, but my goodness is to come; and shall I die before I begin to live? But, Lord, you know what is best of all; and if you convert me, I shall be converted in an hour: and as you accept the will of David, as well as the act of Solomon, so you will accept my desire to serve You, as well as if I did live to glorify You. The spirit is willing, but the flesh is frail; and as I did live sinfully, whensoever Your Spirit was from me, so I shall die unwillingly, unless Your Spirit prepare me. Therefore, dear Father, give me that mind which a sick man should have, and increase my patience with my pain, and call to my remembrance all which I have heard, or read, or felt, or meditated, to strengthen me in this hour of my trial; that I, which never taught any good while I lived, may now teach others how to die, and to bear their sickness patiently. Apply to me all the mercies and merits of Your beloved Son, as if He had died for me alone. Do not be far from me when the enemy comes; but when the tempter is busiest, let Your Spirit be busiest too. And if it please You to loose me out of this prison, when I shall leave my earth to earth, let your angels carry up my soul to heaven, as they did Lazarus, and place me in one of those mansions which Your Son is gone to prepare for me. This is my Mediator which has reconciled me and You, when you did abhor me for my sins; and you did send Him from heaven to us, to show that you are bound to hear Him for us. Therefore in

Him I come to You. In Him I call on You. O my Redeemer, my Preserver, and my Savior, to You be all praise, with Your Father and the Holy Spirit, forever. *Amen. What shall stay me from my Father, my Brother, and my Comforter?*

A COMFORTABLE SPEECH, TAKEN FROM A GODLY PREACHER, LYING ON HIS DEATH-BED; WRITTEN FOR THE SICK

I owe to God a death as His Son died for me. Ever since I was born I have been failing to this haven, and gathering patience to comfort this hour: therefore shall I be one of those guests now that would not come to the banquet when they were invited? What hurt is in going to Paradise? I shall lose nothing but the sense of evil, and *anon* I shall have greater joys than I feel pains: for my Head is in heaven already, to assure me that my soul and body shall follow after. O death where is your sting? Why should I fear that which I would not escape, because my chief happiness is behind, and I cannot have it unless I go to it? I would go through hell to heaven; and therefore if I march but through death, I suffer less than I would suffer for God. My pains do not dismay me, because I travail to bring forth eternal life: my sins do not frighten me, because I have Christ my Redeemer: the Judge does not astonish me, because the Judge's Son is my Advocate: the devil amazes me not, because the angels pitch about me: the grave grieves me not, because it was my Lord's bed. Oh that God's mercy to me might move others to love Him! for the less I can express it, the more it is. The Prophets and Apostles are my forerunners: every man is gone before me, or else he will follow after me. If it pleases God to receive me into heaven before them which have served Him better, I owe more thankfulness to Him. And because I have deferred my repentance until this hour, whereby my salvation is cut off, if I should die suddenly; lo! how my God in His merciful providence, to prevent my destruction, calls me by a lingering sickness, which stays until I be ready, and prepares me to my end like a preacher, and makes me, by wholesome pains, weary of this beloved world, lest I should depart unwillingly, like them whose death is their

366

damnation. So He loves me while He beats me, that His stripes are plasters to salve me: therefore who shall love Him, if I despise Him? This is my whole office now, to strengthen my body with my heart, and to be content as God has appointed, until I can glorify Him, or until He glorify me. If I live, I live to sacrifice; and if I die, I die a sacrifice; for His mercy is above my iniquity. Therefore if I should fear death, it were a sign that I had not faith nor hope, as I professed; but that I doubted of God's truth in His promise, whether He will forgive His penitent sinner or not. It is my Father, let Him do what seems good in His sight. Come, Lord Jesus, for Your servant comes: I am willing, help my unwillingness.

So the faithful depart in another sort, with such peace and joy round about them, that all which see them wish that their souls may follow theirs. *Amen.*

A LETTER TO A FRIEND

A LETTER WRITTEN TO ONE'S FRIEND IN HIS SICKNESS

Beloved, I marvel not that you have pain, for you are sick: but I marvel that you cover it not for offence, because the wisdom of man is to bite in his grief, and always to show more comfort in God than pain in suffering. Now God calls to repetitions, to see whether you have learned more constancy than others. If sickness be sharp, make it not sharper with frowardness: but know this is a great favor to us, when we die by sickness, which makes us ready for Him that calls us. Now you have nothing to think on but God, and you cannot think on Him without joy: your grief passes, but your joy will never pass. Tell me (patient) *how many stripes is heaven worth*? Is my friend only sick in the world, or his faith weaker than others? You have always prayed *Your will be done*; and are you now offended that God's will is done? How has the faithful man forgotten that all things (even death) turn to the best to them that love God! Teach the happy (O Lord) to see his happiness through troubles. Every pain is a prevention of the pains of hell; and every ease in pain is a foretaste of the ease and peace and joys in heaven. Therefore remember your own comforts to others as before; and do not be impatient when there is most need of patience: but as you have ever taught us to live, so now give us an example to die, and deceive Satan, as Job did.